W9-BMU-587

More Praise for *Creative Destruction*

"In the tradition of *Beat the Market* and *A Random Walk Down Wall Street*, *Creative Destruction* blows holes in the conventional wisdom about management, corporate cultures, and the underpinnings of a successful corporation. It argues a whole new paradigm for survival and growth which hopefully will have a far-reaching effect on the actions of boards, management, and investors going forward. Foster and Kaplan are on to something profound."

—Frank Biondi, Senior Managing Director, Waterview Advisors, Former Chairman and CEO of Universal Studios, and President and CEO of Viacom

"A provocative wake-up call for leaders."

—Mike Masin, Vice Chairman and President, Verizon

"As this book with its long-term analysis makes clear: A successful past is but an opportunity to build the future. The only true winners are those that relentlessly drive innovation and change and continually challenge organizational practices and culture."

—Linda Robinson, Vice Chairman, Young and Rubicam

"A compelling road map for management to strike a necessary balance between operational excellence and creative destruction. Those who do not heed its advice to challenge conventional mind-sets aggressively do so at their peril."

—John Hagel, co-author of *Net Worth* and *Net Gain: Expanding Markets Through Virtual Communities*

"Offers a clear blueprint for how corporations can modify their thinking in order to remain competitive."

—Pamela Thomas-Graham, Executive Vice President, NBC, President and CEO, CNBC.com

"I felt the scales fall from my eyes as I read through *Creative Destruction.* I see things differently now, as if taking off the bandages after a cataract operation."

—Robert McKinney, former U.S. Ambassador to Switzerland

"I spend a good deal of every week listening to business leaders and economists from around the world discuss their writings and experiences. This is the single most informative account of the eternal battle between managers and markets, and it explains with intellectual force and hard research why managers must prune their corporations in order to survive the remorselessness of the market. "

—Leslie H. Gelb, President, Council on Foreign Relations

CREATIVE DESTRUCTION

CREATIVE DESTRUCTION

Why Companies That Are Built to Last
Underperform the Market—and
How to Successfully Transform Them

RICHARD N. FOSTER
AND
SARAH KAPLAN

CURRENCY

NEW YORK   LONDON   TORONTO   SYDNEY   AUCKLAND

A CURRENCY BOOK
PUBLISHED BY DOUBLEDAY
a division of Random House, Inc.
1540 Broadway, New York, New York, 10036

CURRENCY and DOUBLEDAY are
trademarks of Doubleday, a division of Random House, Inc.

Copyright © 2001 by McKinsey & Company, Inc. United States
All Rights Reserved
Printed in the United States of America

Library of Congress Cataloging-in-Publication Data
Foster, Richard N.
Creative destruction : why companies that are built to last
underperform the market, and how to successfully transform them /
Richard Foster and Sarah Kaplan.—1st ed.
p. cm.
Includes bibliographical references and index.
ISBN 0-385-50133-1
1. Organizational change. 2. Strategic planning. 3. Technological
innovations—Management.   I. Kaplan, Sarah, 1964–   . II. Title.
HD58.8 .F687 2001
658.4'06—dc21
00-065887

Book design by Tina Thompson

First Edition: April 2001

Currency Books are available at special discounts for bulk purchases for sales promotions or premiums. Special editions, including personalized covers, excerpts of
existing books, and corporate imprints, can be created in large quantities for special
needs. For more information, write to Special Markets, Currency Books, 280 Park
Avenue, 11th floor, New York, NY 10017, or email
specialmarkets@randomhouse.com

10   9   8   7   6   5   4

To my youngest son, Thomas William Foster, for his energy, inquis-itiveness, sparkle, and infinite patience; to my wife Catherine for her unending, unshakeable and enthusiastic support, confidence and patience; to my older sons: Doug for his market insight and practical understanding, and Lucien for his wisdom and counsel.

RNF

To my parents who set me on my path and to my sisters who have traveled with me along the way.

SK

Contents

Introduction: The Game of Creative Destruction   1

CHAPTER 1: Survival and Performance in
   the Era of Discontinuity   7
CHAPTER 2: How Creative Destruction Works:
   The Fate of the East River Savings Bank   25
CHAPTER 3: Cultural Lock-In   61
CHAPTER 4: Operating vs. Creating:
   The Case of Storage Technology Corporation   90
CHAPTER 5: The Gales of Destruction   125
CHAPTER 6: Balancing Destruction and Creation   143
CHAPTER 7: Designed to Change   161
CHAPTER 8: Leading Creative Destruction   181
CHAPTER 9: Increasing Creation by Tenfold   209
CHAPTER 10: Control, Permission, and Risk   236
CHAPTER 11: Setting the Pace and Scale of Change   261
CHAPTER 12: The Ubiquity of Creative Destruction   288

Appendix A: List of Companies   297
Appendix B: Managerial Approach of Principal Investors   311
Appendix C: Dynamic Performance Analysis (DPA)   312
Notes   339
Selected Sources   350
Index   353

Acknowledgments

"Creative Destruction" is the result of over a decade of research, sponsored by our colleagues at McKinsey & Co. and our clients. First and foremost, we would like to thank all of them for their support and counsel during this period.

While many colleagues have contributed time and thought to the arguments put forth in this book, some deserve special mention. First on the list is Peter Walker, the Managing Director of our New York Office. Pete has been a steady supporter of the effort since it earliest days. His path remained steady, even when it was not clear that we were still on the scent. Without his long-term support, this enterprise would not have succeeded.

As the work has moved along, others have played key roles in keeping the effort alive and the standards high. They include Rajat Gupta, Herb Henzler, Ian Davis, Bill Meehan, David Meen, John Bookout, Steve Coley, Mike Nevens, Bruce Roberson, Ron Hulme, Tim Koller, Bill Fallon, Ron Farmer, Peter Freedman, Anton von Rossum, Andreas Beroutsos, Eric Lamarre, Michael Silber, Jessica Hopfield, Endre Holen, Hugh Courtney, Kathleen Hogan, Bill Pade, Peter Bisson, Larry Kanarek, Suzanne Nimocks, and Kevin Coyne.

Several of our friends in academia have made strong and steady contributions to our thinking over the years. They include Tim Reufli from the University of Texas, David Campbell from the University of Illinois, Martin Shubik, Will Goetzmann, and Stan Garstka from Yale, Ronel Elul from Brown, Joe Bower, Clay Christensen and Teresa Amabile from Harvard Business School, Ron Heifetz from Harvard's Kennedy School of Government and Mihalyi Csikszentmihalyi formerly of the University of Chicago (now at Claremont Graduate University).

Early readers and advisors included Brian Arthur and Eric Beinhocker, both of whom took enormous time to think through and comment on the strengths and weaknesses of our ideas.

Early McKinsey contributors to the effort included Karen Barth, Vince DePalma, Carl Hanson, Anna Slomovic, Bro Uttal, and Lily Zaidman. They helped in taking the earliest ideas and turning them into something tangible. Chip Hughes and Kenneth Bonheure conducted early explorations into the practical implications of our work as they turned our abstract ideas into useful tools for day-to-day life.

On the operating level, Shishir Shroff began working on the Performance Database that forms a critical part of our analysis while a graduate student at NYU Stern School of Business in the early '90s. Little did he suspect that the task might turn into a career, but it has. To this day, there is no one who understands more about the database and its construction than Shishir, who now is a Practice Specialist with our Corporate Finance and Strategy practice in our New York Office. In the early days Shishir worked under the guiding hands of Michael Allison and Mike Ghenta. Robin Tsai, one of the best statistical analysts that either of us ever have known, provided expert advice on what was knowable and what was not, along with insightful early statistical analyses. Later we had sustained contributions from Larry DiCapua, Tom Ball, and Ravi Chanmugam.

Ajay Shroff, now at Harvard Business School, undertook the job of rebuilding and updating the McKinsey Performance Database after the first efforts clearly showed that it would be valuable. Ajay brought enormous clarity to the effort. After the data were clearly portrayed, Christopher Baldwin and Robert Reffkin came on to write the key case studies which put a human face on the data. Their deep digging, unimpeachable standards for completeness, and strong writing skills will be seen in many chapters which follow. In the early days Anne Biondi provided expert bibliographic summaries and catalogs. Cara Davis provided continual facts for all phases of the book's preparation, gave us expert literary advice, and found accurate answers and arcane facts to address our endless questions. Without Cara there would be no book.

As we worked out the details, many colleagues have made substantial contributions. Steven Abernethy, now chairman of Transecure, and Qiang (John) Feng did yeoman's work interpreting the early results of the database four years ago. Paul Brown-Kenyon, Jurgen Kaljuvee, Rajini Sundar, and Antony Blanc did early case studies. After the initial data showed some surprises, Christian Weber and Stephan Leitner from our German offices provided intellectual leadership in interpreting why the anomalies occurred. Their early work found clues to future interpretations that proved reliable. Subsequently, Toshi Moghi and Nick Robinson did strong work in developing automated ways of displaying the data so that mere mortals could understand almost four decades of data for over one thousand companies. Somu Subramaniam was a constant guide to when we were on the right and wrong tracks.

Our work to understand the long-term record of company performance grew out of our practical experience with our clients. One client in particular stands out as the foremost source of our insights, Johnson & Johnson. We would like therefore to recognize our debt to our clients and friends, Ralph Larsen, Robert Wilson, Roger Fine, Bill Weldon, Jim Lenehan, Russ Deyo, Bob Darretta, Christian Koffmann, JoAnn Heisen, Brian Perkins, Bill Nielsen, Jim Utaski, and Bernie Walsh for all their guidance to us over the years.

As the analytic work came together, Stephen Fenichell helped to turn our initial thinking into the first draft of *Creative Destruction*. This draft showed us how far we had come, and how far we had to go. Amanda Urban from International Creative Management gave us much needed encouragement and expert guidance so we continued on. Erik Calonius, a skilled writer for *Fortune* and the *Wall Street Journal* then came on to guide the final draft. At the point the draft was ready for other eyes, Roger Scholl, president of the Currency Books Division of Doubleday, took pen in hand and led us to the final product that follows. Roger's experience and judgement have made the book both more readable and to the point. Our assistants throughout this process, Heidi Smith, Lin Sierzenga, and Loreta Kelly, have unfailingly delivered the goods on time and to very high-quality standards, despite the press of daily business. Of these, the job has fallen to Heidi to complete the task. She has delivered with enormous energy, patience, wit, and style in the last two years of preparation.

The Fosters' good friends Kelly and Robert Day also provided critical shelter, quiet, and unending friendship when book writing overlapped house refurbishment. Carole and Arthur Broadus have been faithful and encouraging friends throughout the exercise. Many others have quietly supported this effort as the authors labored away including Parker Merrow, Sarah and Bill Manson, Jude and Eric Boass, Patricia Henry, and Ulda Calderon

Throughout this effort, one is constantly reminded of old, yet fresh lessons in life: these kinds of enterprises are impossible without family support. Richard Foster has received more support from his wife Catherine than any one should be able to expect. Through years of "just one more chapter to go" stories, she tirelessly and enthusiastically supported the effort no matter the personal cost to her. Foster's six-year-old son Thomas has his mother's understanding for his father's long absences. He is mature beyond his years. If Dad needed to do it, it was OK with Thomas. His understanding is quite remarkable for any age. Foster's older sons, Douglas and Lucien, have continued to be both great companions and helpful readers and advisors on this project, as well.

Sarah Kaplan extends a debt of gratitude to her parents, Meredith McGovney Kaplan and Hesh Kaplan; to her sisters, Esther, Sharon, and Rachel,; and to her close friends and supporters, David Ashen, Laurie Blitzer, Joe Haviv, Chip Hughes, Sylvia Mathews, Noah Walley, Kristina Wollschlaeger, and the late Joe Merolla, for their unfailing encouragement through all of the peaks and valleys that come with such endeavors.

It is standard, but necessary, to say that all those mentioned above have made their efforts to help us. To the extent they have succeeded, the success is theirs, to the extent they have not, the responsibility is ours.

New York, NY
January 2001

CREATIVE DESTRUCTION

To our amazement, we found that it was not easy to gather this data. No one, it seemed, had assembled a data set comprehensive enough to determine which companies really were the strongest performers over the long term.

Undaunted, we set out to gather the missing data on corporate performance and its determinants. We selected more than sixty variables to examine, including sales growth, margins, return on invested capital, debt and debt ratings, R&D spending, and total return to shareholders (defined as the increase in stock price per year plus any dividends or special payments made). We wanted to look back far enough to ensure that we had included the major events that had occurred in companies, industries, and the economy as a whole over the past thirty-eight years. We wanted to be able to see what role discontinuities played in the economy, in individual industries, and within companies. We wanted to see the patterns of the economy, to determine what was regular and routine, and what was irregular or periodic (for example, major technological shifts or major changes in federal regulations, or changes in industry structure owing to entry and exit of competitors). We wanted to be able to measure the pace and the extent of these changes.

In particular, we wanted to objectively measure "good" and "poor" performance as it appeared in the economy at different times (for example, during the expansionist period of the 1960s and the inflationary period of the 1970s). We wanted to use these standards to recognize "normal" performance when we saw it, as well as *exceptional* performance—whether exceptionally good or exceptionally bad. We wanted to look over a long enough period of time, and across a wide enough range of industries, that we could tease out the forces at work—to see the contextual changes and their causes. We wanted to be able to test the conventional wisdom of the day: "it's all about technology," or "it's all about macroeconomics," or "high multiples presage low returns," or "it's all about growth," or "it's all about profitability," or "it's all idiosyncratic" or "excellence is . . ."

After more than a decade of effort, and with the assistance of more than fifty of our McKinsey colleagues, we had successfully built a database of the performance of more than 1,000 companies in fifteen industries over almost four decades in order to model capital markets in the U.S. economy. We will refer to this database from here on as "The McKinsey Corporate Performance Database."

Our McKinsey Corporate Performance Database is built entirely of U.S. companies. It includes longtime competitors like Exxon and Chevron, and New Economy companies like Cisco and Dell. It includes such slow-

Introduction
The Game of Creative Destruction

In 1986, Richard Foster published a best-selling book titled *Innovation: The Attacker's Advantage,* which explained the limitations of long-term corporate performance, based on the inevitability of profound changes in the way business is conducted (which we call "discontinuities"). The conclusion reached in the book was that during technological discontinuities, attackers, rather than defenders, have the economic advantage. Although they often lack the scale associated with low costs, neither do they have the psychological and economic conflicts that slow, or prevent, them from capturing new opportunities.

Foster drew these conclusions from a study of about a dozen companies. But as the years passed, he found them to be true of hundreds of other companies as well. Yet the attacker's advantage did not seem to last. Once a company attacked, it began to act suspiciously like a defender, with all the associated weaknesses. In fact, as the '80s passed and we made our way through the '90s , both of us observed that almost as soon as any company had been praised in the popular management literature as excellent or somehow super-durable, it began to deteriorate. Searching for excellent companies was like trying to catch light beams: They were so easy to imagine, but so hard to grasp.

Was this just a peculiarity of the companies we knew, or was something more fundamental taking place? Keeping in mind an admonition attributed to Winston Churchill, "The farther backward you look, the farther forward you can see," we began to examine the long-term record of some of the country's leading companies and their competitors to gain a better understanding of long-term performance.

moving industries as electric utilities and such "hot" industries as software and semiconductors. It includes such low-tech industries as paper and trucking and such technologically sophisticated industries as medical and pharmaceutical products. It includes such regulated industries as airlines and such unregulated industries as specialty chemicals. It includes the oil industry with its ups and downs, and the defense industry with its steady dependence on the U.S. government.

The McKinsey Corporate Performance Database differs from the real economy only in that it does not include all the industries or companies represented in the real economy—although it does offer a detailed history of 1,008 companies, which as far as we know is the largest study of its kind. These companies represented, at the end of 1998, $2.1 trillion in sales and $5.2 trillion in market cap.

All the companies in the McKinsey Corporate Performance Database are more or less "pure" plays—that is, more than half of their sales come from the industry of which they are a part. The database does not track "complex" companies, like General Electric or Johnson & Johnson, that compete in many different industries. Nor does it track industries with a small number of players (e.g., automobiles or razor blades), because without a larger number of competitors we have no standard for "normalcy." (Nonetheless, we have used the McKinsey Corporate Performance Database to "synthesize" what a "model" J&J would look like, and then compared this model to the real thing. Assembling the components of our database economy in the same way, say, as J&J assembles its business, yields a pattern of return that very closely matches the actual observed patterns.)

We allowed new companies to "form" (i.e., enter the database) when they were large enough to be part of the largest 80% of U.S. companies, as measured by market capitalization (a number that the University of Chicago Center for Research on Security Prices provided for us). These companies are referred to later in this book as "new entrants." The year of "entry" refers to the year these companies qualified to enter the database, not the year they were formed.

We also allowed companies to die when they were acquired (most "dying" companies are acquired) or went bankrupt (which only a few do). These companies are referred to later in this book as "departures." When a company leaves or "departs" the database, all prior data relating to that company is retained in the database. We also captured companies in the database that both entered and left during the period covered by the data-

A DEFINITION OF MARKETS AND CORPORATIONS

Let us be more specific about what we mean when we say "market" and "cognitive structure." To us markets, including capital markets, are "informal aggregations of buyers, sellers, their owners, and other intermediaries who come together for the purpose of economic exchange." The "capital markets" are markets where capital is exchanged—for example, money for equities and debt. The buyers and sellers are usually corporations, and they may or may not list their shares in an equity market for the purpose of establishing a current value of the enterprise.

These informal aggregations, and the processes they employ, set the balance between continuity and change in the economy. The rules of the capital markets govern entrance, conduct, and exit (including bankruptcy) of the players in the markets. In our economy, it is the consumer who makes the individual decision about whether to continue with the present products and services or to change to new ones. The capital markets provide the cash to serve up the options for the customer, but the consumer sets the rate of change.

Clearly, capital markets are very different from corporations. Corporations have a "cognitive superstructure." They have a chairman and a board of directors. They plan and they control. Their people take their responsibilities very seriously, as the law requires them to. Their executives have trained their entire life for their positions, and they have gone through exceptionally rigorous selection processes. They are not administered by distant committees, as the capital markets are.

A major purpose of corporate planning and control is to eliminate surprise or risk:

> *Control, which essentially means "keeping things on track," ranks as one of the critical functions of management. Good control means that an informed person can be reasonably confident that no major, unpleasant surprises will occur.*

As Robert Simons, the Charles M. Williams Professor of Business Administration at Harvard Business School, says, "Measurement focuses on errors of commission (mistakes) and shortfalls (negative variances) against goals. Control systems are negative feedback systems. Control reports are used primarily as confirmation that everything is 'on track.' Surprise is the enemy."

Capital markets, because they are designed to provide for admission of new competitors and the elimination of weak ones, perhaps increase the chances of surprise. While capital markets do "control," they control process and adherence to standards, not results. Nor do capital markets establish "goals." The Federal Reserve comes as close as any institution to attempting to "control" the economy through some sort of target setting and adjustment policy, but this is not at all similar to a corporate control process.

With the exception of the Fed, capital markets do not "think" about improving their overall levels of performance. Administrators think about how well the markets are functioning, but they do not influence their performance levels. While capital markets are controlled by regulators, judges, police, court systems, and the Federal Reserve Bank, no one would confuse any of these with the management tasks of a corporation.

Because of this lack of managerial control, the capital markets, when properly performing, introduce new options and adaptations more quickly than do corporations. Efficient capital markets eliminate the old without reflection or remorse—or the delay that remorse brings about—and when government policy contravenes these simple objectives, such as in state-owned companies, the positive effects of capital markets often are lost.

base, such as Rolm. Finally, of course, there are a few companies that were captured in the first year of the database (1962), and remained until the final year of the database (1998). We refer to these companies as "long-term survivors." Only 160 of the 1,008 companies we tracked fell into this category. Our database is like a videotape (taken with a hidden camera) that followed individuals around as they awakened, bathed, ate, worked, returned home, relaxed, and slept. But rather than track individuals, we tracked companies. The McKinsey Corporate Performance Database allows us to trace to specific industries such macro effects as the great decline in stock prices in 1974 and 1975 (almost all declined, with the exception of oil and computer hardware stocks), as well as trace the effects to specific companies (Champion International and International Flavors and Fragrances, for example, were clobbered). Our database allows us to ask questions about cause and effect—and get the answers quickly—without the need to build a new database for each new question. It gives us the range and scope to understand both the core and the periphery of the economy simultaneously, and in a way that relates to the overall performance of the economy (since our database faithfully tracks the macromeasures of the economy that others have put together—for example, the S&P 500 total return to shareholders indices).

Our research shows us that the McKinsey Corporate Performance Database mimics the real economy with exceptional fidelity. If an event took place in the real economy—for example, the stock market crash of 1974 and 1975—it shows in our database. We can track both the event and the nation's recovery from the event. In the 1970s, the economy was enriched by the computer hardware and oil industries, and our database reflects that. Defense and pharmaceuticals gained leverage in the '80s, and our database shows that, too. The exhibit below compares the annual returns to investors, as measured by our databases, with the returns to investors, as measured by the S&P 500. As one can see, it is nearly a perfect match. One can quite easily see the cycles of performance in the U.S. economy.

How Total Return to Shareholders (TRS) in the McKinsey Database Compares with Total Return to Shareholders in the S&P 500

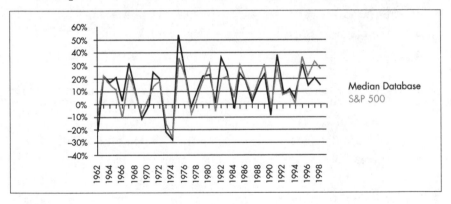

Again, the data that underlies our analysis of creative destruction is based on our analysis of the McKinsey Corporate Performance Database, which has been built from the real experiences of 1,008 U.S. companies. Our findings and analysis have been bolstered by our personal relationships, as well, with some of the largest and most successful companies in the United States. As advisers, we have worked to uncover what works and what does not. We hope our findings will allow other companies to improve their performance—more quickly, and with more assurance, than they might have had otherwise.

October 16, 2000

CHAPTER 1

Survival and Performance in the Era of Discontinuity

This company will be going strong one hundred and even five hundred years from now.

C. JAY PARKINSON, PRESIDENT OF ANACONDA MINES
statement made three years in advance of Anaconda's bankruptcy

In 1917, shortly before the end of World War I, Bertie Charles (or B.C., as he was known) Forbes formed his first list of the one hundred largest American companies. The firms were ranked by assets, since sales data were not accurately compiled in those days. In 1987, *Forbes* republished its original "Forbes 100" list and compared it to its 1987 list of top companies. Of the original group, 61 had ceased to exist.

Of the remaining thirty-nine, eighteen had managed to stay in the top one hundred. These eighteen companies—which included Kodak, DuPont, General Electric, Ford, General Motors, Procter & Gamble, and a dozen other corporations—had clearly earned the nation's respect. Skilled in the arts of survival, these enterprises had weathered the Great Depression, the Second World War, the Korean conflict, the roaring '60s, the oil and inflation shocks of the '70s, and unprecedented technological change in the chemicals, pharmaceuticals, computers, software, radio and television, and global telecommunications industries.

They survived. But they did not perform. As a group these great companies earned a long-term return for their investors during the 1917–

Long-Term Survivor Performance

Source: *Forbes*, July 1987

1987 period 20% less than that of the overall market. Only two of them, General Electric and Eastman Kodak, performed better than the averages, and Kodak has since fallen on harder times.

One reaches the same conclusion from an examination of the S&P 500. Of the five hundred companies originally making up the S&P 500 in 1957, only seventy-four remained on the list through 1997. And of these seventy-four, only twelve outperformed the S&P 500 index itself over the 1957–1998 period. Moreover, the list included companies from two industries, pharmaceuticals and food, that were strong performers during this period. If today's S&P 500 today were made up of only those companies that were on the list when it was formed in 1957, the overall performance of the S&P 500 would have been about 20% less *per year* than it actually has been.

For the last several decades we have celebrated the big corporate survivors, praising their "excellence" and their longevity, their ability to last. These, we have assumed, are the bedrock companies of the American economy. These are the companies that "patient" investors pour their money into—investments that would certainly reward richly at the end of a lifetime. But our findings—based on the thirty-eight years of data compiled in the McKinsey Corporate Performance Database, discussed in the Introduction—have shown that they do not perform as we might suspect. An investor following the logic of patiently investing money in these survivors will do substantially less well than an investor who merely invests in market index funds.

McKinsey's long-term studies of corporate birth, survival, and death in America clearly show that the corporate equivalent of El Dorado, the golden company that continually performs better than the markets, *has never existed.* It is a myth. Managing for survival, even among the best and most revered corporations, does not guarantee strong long-term performance for shareholders. In fact, just the opposite is true. In the long run, markets always win.

THE ASSUMPTION OF CONTINUITY

How could this be? How could a stock market index such as the Dow Jones Industrial average or the S&P 500 average—which, unlike companies, lack skilled managers, boards of experienced directors, carefully crafted organizational structures, the most advanced management methods, privileged assets, and special relationships with anyone of their choosing—perform better, over the long haul, than all but two of *Forbes*'s strongest survivors, General Electric and Eastman Kodak? Are the capital markets, as represented by the stock market averages, "wiser" than managers who think about performance all the time?

The answer is that the capital markets, and the indices that reflect them, encourage the creation of corporations, permit their efficient operations (as long as they remain competitive), and then rapidly—and remorselessly—remove them when they lose their ability to perform. Corporations, which operate with management philosophies based on the assumption of continuity, are not able to change at the pace and scale of the markets. As a result, in the long term, they do not create value at the pace and scale of the markets.

It is among the relatively new entrants to the economy—for example, Intel, Amgen, and Cisco—where one finds superior performance, at least for a time. The structure and mechanisms of the capital markets enable these companies to produce results superior to even the best surviving corporations. Moreover, it is the corporations that have lost their ability to meet investor expectations (no matter how unreasonable these expectations might be) that consume the wealth of the economy. The capital markets remove these weaker performers at a greater rate than even the best-performing companies. Joseph Alois Schumpeter, the great Austrian-American economist of the 1930s and '40s, called this process of creation and removal "the

gales of creative destruction." So great is the challenge of running the operations of a corporation today that few corporate leaders have the energy or
time to manage the processes of creative destruction, especially at the pace
and scale necessary to compete with the market. Yet that is precisely what is
required to sustain market levels of long-term performance.

The essential difference between corporations and capital markets is in
the way they enable, manage, and control the processes of creative
destruction. Corporations are built on the assumption of continuity; their
focus is on operations. Capital markets are built on the assumption of *discontinuity;* their focus is on creation and destruction. The market encourages rapid and extensive creation, and hence greater wealth-building. It is
less tolerant than the corporation is of long-term underperformance. Outstanding corporations do win the right to survive, but not the ability to
earn above-average or even average shareholder returns over the long term.
Why? Because their control processes—the very processes that help them
to survive over the long haul—deaden them to the need for change.

THE REALITY OF DISCONTINUITY

This distinction between the way corporations and markets approach the
processes of creative destruction is not an artifact of our times or an outgrowth of the "dot.com" generation. It has been smoldering for decades,
like a fire in a wall, ready to erupt at any moment. The market turmoil we
see today is a logical extension of trends that began decades ago.

The origins of modern managerial philosophy can be traced to the eigh-
teenth century, when Adam Smith argued for specialization of tasks and
division of labor in order to cut waste. By the late nineteenth century these
ideas had culminated in an age of American trusts, European holding companies, and Japanese zaibatsus. These complex giants were designed to convert natural resources into food, energy, clothing, and shelter in the most
asset-efficient way—to maximize output and to minimize waste.

By the 1920s, Smith's simple idea had enabled huge enterprises, exploiting the potential of mass production, to flourish. Peter Drucker wrote the
seminal guidebook for these corporations in 1946, *The Concept of the Corporation.* The book laid out the precepts of the then-modern corporation,
based on the specialization of labor, mass production, and the efficient use
of physical assets.

This approach was in deep harmony with the times. Change came slowly in the '20s, when the first Standard and Poor's index of ninety important U.S. companies was formed. In the '20s and '30s the turnover rate in the S&P 90 averaged about 1.5% per year. A new member of the S&P 90 at that time could expect to remain on the list, on average, for more than sixty-five years. The corporations of these times were built on the assumption of continuity—perpetual continuity, the essence of which Drucker explored in his book. Change was a minor factor. Companies were in business to transform raw materials into final products, to avoid the high costs of interaction between independent companies in the marketplace. This required them to operate at great scale and to control their costs carefully. These vertically integrated configurations were protected from all but incremental change.

We argue that this period of corporate development, lasting for more than seventy years, has come to an end. In 1998, the turnover rate in the S&P 500 was close to 10%, implying an average lifetime on the list of ten years, not sixty-five! Drucker predicted the turning point with his 1969 book *The Age of Discontinuity*, but his persuasive arguments could not overcome the zeitgeist of the '70s. The '70s were, for many managers, the modern equivalent of the 1930s. Inflation raged, interest rates were at the highest levels since before World War II, and the stock market was languishing. Few entrants dared risk capital or career on the founding of a new company based on Drucker's insights. It was a fallow time for corporate start-ups. As the long-term demands of survival took over, Drucker's advice fell on deaf years.

The pace of change has been accelerating continuously since the '20s. There have been three great waves. The timing and extent of these waves match the rise and fall of the generative and absorptive capabilities of the nation. The first wave came shortly after World War II, when the nation's military buildup gave way to the need to rebuild the consumer infrastructure. Many new companies entered the economy at this time, then rose to economic prominence during the 1940s and 1950s, among them Owens-Corning, Textron, and Seagram.

The second wave began in the 1960s. The rate of turnover in the S&P 90 began to accelerate as the federal defense and aerospace programs once again stimulated the economy, providing funds for the development of logic and memory chips, and later the microprocessor. They were heady days—"bubble days," in the eyes of some. The hot stocks were called

Change in the S&P 500
7-Year Moving Average

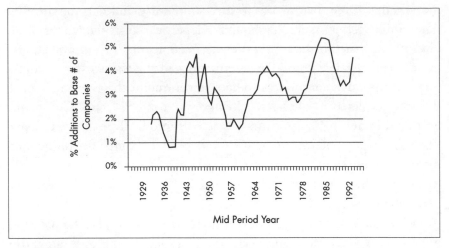

"one-decision" stocks: Buy them once and never sell them, and your future fortune was assured.

The bubble burst in 1968. The New York Stock Exchange, which had risen to almost 1000, did not return to that level again until the early 1980s. During this absorptive, or slack, period, when the country was beset with rising oil prices and inflation, and when bonds earned returns substantially greater than equities, few new companies joined—or left— the S&P 500. Interestingly enough, though, despite the worst economic conditions the nation had endured since the Depression, the minimum rate of corporate turnover did not drop to the low rate of turnover seen in the 1950s. The base rate of change in the economy had permanently risen.

Paul Volcker, chairman of the Federal Reserve Bank, finally led the charge that broke the back of inflation, and the number of new companies climbing onto the S&P 500 accelerated. In the 1980s, once again the S&P began substituting new high-growth and high-market-cap companies for the slower-growing and even shrinking-market-cap older companies. The change in the S&P index mix also reflected changes in the economic mix of business in the United States. When the markets collapsed in the late '80s and a short-lived recession hit the American economy in the early '90s, the rate of substitution in the S&P 500 fell off. But again, even at its lowest point, the rate of turnover was higher than it was during the 1970s decline. The minimum level of change in the economy had been quietly building, and was increasing again. This was even more evident as the technology-charged 1990s kicked into gear, accelerating the rate of the S&P Index turnover to levels never seen before. By the end of the 1990s, we were well into what Peter Drucker calls the "Age of Discontinuity." Extrapolating from past patterns, we calculate that by the end of the year 2020, the average lifetime of a corporation on the S&P will have been shortened to about ten years, as fewer and fewer companies fall into the category of "survivors."

Average Lifetime of S&P 500 Companies

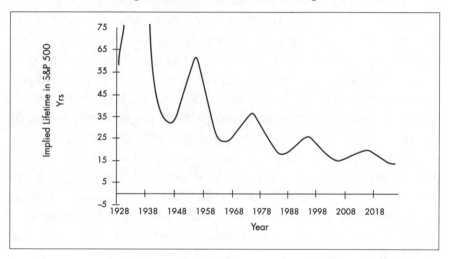

THE GALES OF DISCONTINUITY

The Age of Discontinuity did not arrive in the 1990s by happenstance. It arose from fundamental economic forces. Among these are:

- The increasing efficiency of business, due to dramatic declines in capital costs. As industry shifted from goods to services, there was a concurrent decline in interaction and transaction costs. These costs declined because of the advent of information technology and the steady rise in labor productivity due to advances in technology and management methods.
- The increasing efficiency of capital markets, due to the increasing accuracy (and transparency) of corporate performance data.

- The rise in national liquidity, due to the improved profitability of U.S. corporations, and a favorable bias, unparalleled anywhere else in the world, toward U.S. equities.
- Strengthened fiscal management by the federal government, including an effective Federal Reserve, and reduced corporate taxes.

These forces have helped to create the likes of Microsoft, with a market capitalization greater than all but the top ten nations of the world (Microsoft's real assets make up about 1% of its market value). Computer maker Dell has virtually no assets at all. Internet start-up companies begin with almost no capital. For these companies, returns on capital are unimaginably large by previous standards. Productivity is soaring. The pipeline of new technology is robust. There are more than 10,000 Internet business proposals alone waiting for evaluation at venture capital firms, even after the Nasdaq collapse in March and April of 2000. By all reports, the number (if not the quality) of these proposals is increasing all the time. Information technology is not nearing its limits. The effectiveness of software programming continues to grow; communications technology is just beginning. The global GDP will double in the next twenty years, creating approximately $20–$40 trillion in new sales. If, through the productivity improvements the Internet enables, the world can save 2% of the $25 trillion now produced, the market value of those savings will run into the trillions.

Incumbent companies have an unprecedented opportunity to take advantage of these times. But if history is a guide, no more than a third of today's major corporations will survive in an economically important way over the next twenty-five years. Those that do not survive will die a Hindu death of transformation, as they are acquired or merged with part of a larger, stronger organization, rather than a Judeo-Christian death, but it will be death nonetheless. And the demise of these companies will come from a lack of competitive adaptiveness. To be blunt, most of these companies will die or be bought out and absorbed because they are too damn slow to keep pace with change in the market. By 2020, more than three quarters of the S&P 500 will consist of companies we don't know today— new companies drawn into the maelstrom of economic activity from the periphery, springing from insights unrecognized today.

The assumption of continuity, on which most of our leading corporations have been based for years, no longer holds. Discontinuity dominates. The one hundred or so companies in the current S&P 500 that survive into the 2020s will be unlike the corporate survivors today. They will have to be masters of creative destruction—built for discontinuity, remade like the market. Schumpeter anticipated this transformation over a half century ago when he observed: "The problem that is usually being visualized is how capitalism *administers* existing structures, whereas the relevant problem is how it *creates* and *destroys* them."

THE NEED TO ABANDON THE ASSUMPTION OF CONTINUITY

How can corporations make themselves more like the market? The general prescription is to increase the rate of creative destruction to the level of the market itself, without losing control of present operations. As sensible as this recommendation is, it has proven difficult to implement.

Hundreds of managers from scores of U.S. and European countries have told us that while they are satisfied with their operating prowess, they are dissatisfied with their ability to implement change. "How do the excellent innovators do it?" they ask, presuming that excellent innovators exist. "What drives an innovation breakthrough?" Others question how one grows a company beyond its core business. And most fundamentally of all: "How do we find new ideas?"

The difficulties behind these questions arise from the inherent conflict between the need for corporations to control existing operations and the need to create the kind of environment that will permit new ideas to flourish—and old ones to die a timely death. This may require trading out traditional assets, challenging existing channels of distribution, or making dilutive acquisitions. But whatever the challenges, we believe that most corporations will find it impossible to match or outperform the market without abandoning the assumption of continuity. Author James Reston, in his book *The Last Apocalypse*, observed Europe's fear that the first millennium would end in a fiery conclusion:

When the millennium arrived the apocalypse did take place; a world did end, and a new world arose from the ruins. But the last apocalypse was a process rather than a cataclysm. It had the suddenness of forty years.

The current apocalypse—the transition from a state of continuity to a state of discontinuity—has the same kind of suddenness. Never again will American business be as it once was. The rules have changed forever. Some companies have made the crossing. Under Jack Welch, General Electric has negotiated the apocalypse and has seen its performance benefit as a result. Johnson & Johnson is moving across the divide quickly, as we will see later. Enron has made strong progress by transforming itself from a natural gas pipeline company to a trading company. Corning has been successful in shedding its dependence on consumer durables and becoming a leader in high-tech optical fiber. In France, L'Oréal seems to be on the right track, having found a new way to organize itself and transfer beauty concepts from one economy to another. But these are the exceptions. Few have attempted the journey. Fewer still have made it to the other side successfully.

CULTURAL LOCK-IN

For half a century, Bayer aspirin drove the growth of Sterling Drug until Johnson & Johnson introduced Tylenol. Out of fear of cannibalizing its Bayer aspirin leadership, Sterling Drug refused to introduce its leading European non-aspirin pain reliever (Panadol) to the United States. Instead, it tried to expand its Bayer line overseas. This failure ultimately led to its acquisition by Kodak. Sterling Drug had become effectively immobilized, unable to change its half-century-old behavior out of fear. Its strong culture—its rules of thumb for decision making, its control processes, the information it used for decision making—blocked its progress and ultimately sealed its fate. It had locked itself into an ineffective approach to the marketplace despite clear signs that it needed to act in a new way.

"Cultural lock-in"—the inability to change the corporate culture even in the face of clear market threats—explains why corporations find it difficult to respond to the messages of the marketplace. Cultural lock-in results from the gradual stiffening of the invisible architecture of the corporation, and the ossification of its decision-making abilities, control systems, and mental models. It dampens a company's ability to innovate or to shed operations with a less-exciting future. Moreover, it signals the corporation's inexorable decline into inferior performance. Often, as in the case of Sterling Drug, cultural lock-in manifests itself in three general fears—the fear of cannibalization of an important product line, the fear of channel conflict with important customers, and the fear of earnings dilution that might result from a strategic acquisition. As reasonable as all these fears seem to be to established companies, they are not fears that are felt in the market. And so the market moves where the corporation dares not.

Cultural lock-in is the last in a series of "emotional" phases in a corporation's life, a series that mirrors remarkably that of human beings. In the early years of a corporation, just after its founding, the dominant emotion is passion—the sheer energy to make things happen. When passion rules, information and analysis are ignored in the name of vision: "We know the right answer; we do not need analysis."

As the corporation ages, the bureaucracy begins to settle in. Passions cool and are replaced by "rational decision making," often simply the codification of what has worked in the past. Data is gathered, analysis is performed, alternatives are postulated, and scenarios are developed. Attempts are made to avoid the game of information sculpting. Only when "rational" decision making is in vogue does all the relevant information flow to the right decision maker, at the right time, and in the right form to be easily analyzed and interpreted. Rational decision making is triumphant, at least for a while. This stage is often pictured as the normal state of the corporation, although in our experience, particularly as the pace of change increases, rarely does this ideal state accurately describe how the company actually operates.

Eventually, rational decision making reveals that the future potential for the business is limited. Often at this point, threatened by the prospects for a bleak future, the corporation falls back on defensive routines to protect the organization from its fate, just as defensive emotions emerge in our lives when we sense impending trauma. Management now sees the future filled more with trouble than with promise. Decisions are made to protect existing businesses. The fear of discarding the old for the new (product cannibalization), the fear of customer conflict, and the fear of earnings dilution through acquisition paralyze acts of creative destruction, and often effectively shield the corporation from the perception of future trouble—as well as the need to act—for a long time. Cultural lock-in is established, thwarting the emergence of a leader or team that might save the day.

THE CAUSES OF CULTURAL LOCK-IN

Why does cultural lock-in occur? The heart of the problem is the formation of hidden sets of rules, or mental models, that once formed are
extremely difficult to change. Mental models are the core concepts of the
corporation, the beliefs and assumptions, the cause-and-effect relationships, the guidelines for interpreting language and signals, the stories
repeated within the corporate walls. Charlie Munger, a longtime friend of
and co-investor with Warren Buffet, and vice chairman of Berkshire Hathaway, calls mental models the "theoretical frameworks that help investors
better understand the world."

Mental models are invisible in the corporation. They are neither explicit
nor examined, but they are pervasive. When well crafted, mental models
allow management to anticipate the future and solve problems. But once
constructed, mental models become self-reinforcing, self-sustaining, and
self-limiting. And when mental models are out of sync with reality, they
cause management to make forecasting errors and poor decisions. The
assumption of continuity, in fact, is precisely the kind of disconnect with
reality that leads corporations into flawed forecasting and poor decisions.

Mental models manifest themselves in corporate control systems. These
systems are designed to ensure predictable goal achievement, whether it be
cost control, the control of capital expenditures, or the control of the deployment of key personnel. Effective control means that an informed manager
can be reasonably confident that unpleasant surprises will not occur.

Unfortunately, control systems can also create "defensive routines" in
organizations, including the failure to challenge the status quo, the failure
to encourage a diversity of opinions, failure to disagree with superiors
(thereby displeasing them), communicating in ambiguous and inconsistent ways, and making these failures, even when known, "undiscussable."
Change becomes impossible.

Corporate control systems also undermine the ability of the organization
to innovate at the pace and scale of the market. Under the assumption of
continuity, for example, the arguments for building a new business can be
turned back, since its probable success cannot be proven in advance. Under
these circumstances, it is more likely that ideas based on the incremental
growth of current capabilities and mental models will be encouraged.

Corporate control systems limit creativity through their dependence on *convergent thinking*. Convergent thinking focuses on clear problems and provides well-known solutions quickly. It thrives on focus. Order, simplicity, routine, clear responsibilities, unambiguous measurement systems, and predictability are the bedrock of convergent thinking. Convergent thinking is tailor-made for the assumption of continuity. Convergent thinking can be effective at handling small, incremental changes and differences, but transformational changes completely flummox the system.

Discontinuity, on the other hand, thrives on a different kind of thinking, *divergent thinking*. Divergent thinking focuses on broadening—diverging—the context of decision making. It is initially more concerned with questions than getting to the answer in the fastest possible way. Divergent thinking places enormous value on getting the questions right, then relinquishes control to conventional convergent thinking processes.

Divergent thinking thrives as much on the broad search as on the focused search. It focuses as much on careful observation of the facts as on interpretation of the facts. It focuses as much on the skills of reflection (which requires time away from the problem) as on the skills of swift decision making (which seek to avoid delay). We refer to these three skills—conversation, observation, and reflection—as the COR skills of divergent thinking. Unfortunately, conventional corporate control systems, built on the assumption of continuity, stifle the COR skills of divergent thinking, or kill it outright.

When mental models are out of sync with reality, corporations lose their early-warning system. Leaders with genuine vision are suppressed. As Ron Heifetz, director of the Program on Leadership at the Kennedy School of Government at Harvard, observed: "People who lead frequently bear scars from their efforts to bring about adaptive change. Often they are silenced. On occasion, they are killed."

Abbott Laboratories, for example, flush with the success of their strategy to build strong positions in the medical diagnostic and test equipment business, was anxious to avoid the shocks to the pharmaceutical industry posed by the emergence of Medicare and Medicaid in the early to mid 1970s. Yet it found itself with an incumbent CEO who squelched three potential successors seeking to change strategy.

Once cultural lock-in guides a company's decisions, in the absence of some great external shock, the corporation's fate is sealed.

HOW THE MARKETS ENABLE CHANGE

Markets, on the other hand, lacking culture, leadership, and emotion, do not experience the bursts of desperation, depression, denial, and hope that corporations face. The market has no lingering memories or remorse. It has no mental models. The market does not fear cannibalization, customer channel conflict, or dilution. It simply waits for the forces at play to work out—for new companies to be created and for acquisitions to clear the field. The markets silently allow weaker companies to be put up for sale and leaves it to the new owners to shape them up or shut them down. Actions are taken quickly on early signs of weakness. Only when governments are brought in, as with a bailout, does the market mimic a probable corporate response. Most of the time, the market simply removes the weak players, and in removing them, improves overall returns.

Lacking production-oriented control systems, markets create more surprise and innovation than do corporations. They operate on the assumption of discontinuity, and accommodate continuity. Corporations, on the other hand, assume continuity and attempt to accommodate discontinuity. The difference is profound.

REDESIGNING THE CORPORATION BASED ON DISCONTINUITY

The right of any corporation to exist is not perpetual but has to be continuously earned.

ROBERT SIMONS

The market has pointed the way to a solution. In response to the tension that builds between the potential for improved performance and the actual performance of large businesses, in an era of increasing pace of change in the economy, there are certain kinds of firms—particularly private equity firms, as we discuss in Chapter 7—that have demonstrated the ability to change at the pace and scale of the market, and they have earned sustained superior returns for doing so. The two kinds of private equity firms—principal investing firms and venture capitalists—are quite different from each other, but each looks somewhat like the holding companies of the late nineteenth century. It is possible to imagine that they will form the seeds of the industrial giants of the twenty-first century.

These newly important firms have been able to outperform the markets for the last two to three decades, longer than any other company we know of. The difference between these partnerships and the conventional corporation is in their approach to organizational design. These financial partnerships have discovered how to operate at high levels of efficiency and scale while engaging in creative destruction at the pace of the market, exactly as Joseph Schumpeter envisioned. Created around the assumption of discontinuity, they have then determined how best to incorporate or fold in the requirements of continuity.

These firms never buy any company to hold forever. Rather, they focus on intermediate (four- to seven-year) value creation. Corporations, in contrast, concentrate on the very short term (less than eighteen months) for operations and the very long term (greater than eight years) for research.

Private equity firms make as much money by expanding the future potential of their properties as they do from increasing the properties' operating incomes. When a private equity firm invests in a company, or buys all of the equity, it buys it with a "take-out" strategy in mind: Management knows what it must do in the next four to seven years to build the property so that it has long-term value for the next buyer.

Finally, private equity companies think of their business as a revolving portfolio of companies in various stages of development. They realize they will sell some of their properties each year and buy others. They keep the pipeline full of new properties at the front end and supplied with buyers at the back end, cultivating both simultaneously (a skill at which they excel).

These firms differ from conventional corporations not only in their divergent thinking, but also in the depth and speed of their research activities. Moreover, private equity firms allow each of the companies they buy to retain their own control systems. This allows the private equity firm to concentrate on creation and destruction to a far greater extent than do traditional corporations, and even to a greater extent than their own wholly or partially owned subsidiaries do.

THE ROAD AHEAD

Long-term corporate performance has not matched the performance of the overall markets because corporations do not adapt as fast as the markets do. This is due to the way they evolve, not because of the way they accomplish their day-to-day work. For historical reasons, as we have discussed above, corporations have been designed to operate—to produce goods and services—rather than to evolve. In order to evolve at the pace of the markets, they have to get better at creation and destruction—the two key elements of evolution that are missing.

Redesigning the corporation to evolve quickly rather than simply operate well requires more than simple adjustments; the fundamental concepts of operational excellence are inappropriate for a corporation seeking to evolve at the pace and scale of the markets. One cannot just "add on" creation and destruction; one has to design them in. And only if the corporation is redesigned to evolve at the pace and scale of the market will long-term performance improve. Markets perform better than corporations because markets allow new companies to enter more freely, and they force the elimination of those companies without competitive prospects more ruthlessly than corporations do. Moreover, markets do these things faster and on a larger scale than do corporations.

We believe that corporations must be redesigned from top to bottom based on the assumption of discontinuity. Management must stimulate the rate of creative destruction through the generation or acquisition of new firms and the elimination of marginal performers—without losing control of operations. If operations are healthy, the rate of creative destruction within the corporation will determine the continued long-term competitiveness and performance of the company. Today's financial partnerships give us confidence that this realignment can work. They also suggest a way to do it.

To create new businesses at a faster rate, corporations also need to ponder the details of divergent thinking. Divergent thinking is a prelude to creativity. Many divergent thinkers possess apparently opposing traits: They may be passionate and objective, or proud and humble; they may be both extroverted and introverted; in negotiations they may be flexible and unyielding, attentive and wandering. They possess what Mihalyi Czikszentmihalyi, one of today's leading thinkers on creativity and the author of *Flow,* has called "a sunny pessimism." F. Scott Fitzgerald described it in this way:

> *The test of a first-rate intelligence is the ability to hold two opposed ideas in the mind at the same time, and still retain the ability to function.*

One should, for example, be able to see that things are hopeless and yet be determined to make them otherwise.

Managing for divergent thinking—that is, managing to ensure that the proper questions are addressed early enough to allow them to be handled in an astute way—requires establishing a "rich context" of information as a stimulus to posing the right questions. It requires control through the selection and motivation of employees rather than through control of people's actions; ample resources, including time, to achieve results; knowing what to measure and when to measure it; and genuine respect for others' capabilities and potential. It also requires the willingness to remove people from responsibility when it becomes clear they cannot perform up to standard. In the end, both divergent and convergent thinking must successfully coexist.

Next, to improve long-term performance, the overall planning and control processes of the corporation need to be rethought. The conventional strategic planning process has failed most corporations. As practiced, it stifles the very dialogue it is meant to stimulate. New ways of conducting a dialogue and conversation among the leaders of the corporation and their inheritors are needed.

Finally, corporate control systems must be built that can manage both to control operations and increase the rate of creative destruction. Control what you must, not what you can; control when you must, not when you can. If a control procedure is not essential, eliminate it. Measure less; shorten the time and number of intermediaries between measurement and action, and increase the speed with which you receive feedback.

The point is to let the market control wherever possible. Be suspicious of control mechanisms—they stifle more than they control. Let those who run a business determine the best mix of controls for their business (they know the system best) and shift the burden of integration to the corporate level, rather than designing uniform systems that have to be implemented throughout a corporation independent of the business. When such changes are implemented, the focus of the corporation will shift from minimizing risk, and thereby inadvertently stifling creativity, to facilitating creativity—and that is what is needed to strengthen long-term performance.

To implement these ideas, the role of leadership must be rethought. Ron Heifetz of Harvard says:

The adaptive demands of our societies require leadership that takes responsibility without waiting for revelation or request. One may lead perhaps with not more than a question in hand. A leader has to engage people in facing the challenge, adjusting their values, changing perspectives, and developing new habits of behavior.

If these steps are taken effectively, they will help prevent the emergence of cultural lock-in.

This book offers a clear storm warning to dot.com companies: You have been born at a special time—one where all the elements of the ideal creative environment exist simultaneously. By focusing on "getting the product out" and "building the website," you are following in the footsteps of millions of companies since the time of Adam Smith. You are blessed to exist at a time of rapid change, which gives you the opportunity to peer into the future and design your corporation accordingly. But after the early heady days of growth, your challenges will be the same as those of other companies of the past: to grow and avoid being trapped by cultural lock-in.

A NEW BEGINNING

The agenda outlined above is substantial. Not all companies will be willing to take it on. The first step is to recognize the description of the business world as an increasingly *discontinuous* place. In the following pages, we will lay out in more detail why we see the world as a place of discontinuity, and outline the specific problems—and solutions—corporations must address if they are to break the paradigm of underperformance over the long term and truly act as companies built on excellence. Building a company to last—managing to survive—is no longer enough in an age of discontinuity. The chapters that follow will help point the way.

CHAPTER 2

How Creative Destruction Works: The Fate of the East River Savings Bank

Some things are hurrying into existence, and others are hurrying out of it. And of that which is coming into existence, part is already extinguished. Motions and changes are continually renewing the world . . .

ROMAN EMPEROR MARCUS AURELIUS
Meditations (A.D. *fourth century*)

Driving up West Ninety-sixth Street from the Henry Hudson Drive on the way to Central Park, one approaches a venerable-looking bank at the corner of Amsterdam and West Ninety-sixth. The building is not large, but it is impressive. It has been built to last.

Monumental in design, it is one huge story tall (with double-height windows), built solidly of limestone, and about half a block long. It has five very permanent Ionic columns guarding its main entrance. The dates "1849–1926" are etched in the stone of the frieze. Aphorisms about the virtues of saving, authored by Thomas Jefferson and Abraham Lincoln, grace the frieze on each side of the dates. As one approaches the building, the thought occurs: "I would like to have my money in that bank. It will be there forever."

But as you cross Amsterdam you realize that this bank is not a bank at all. Today it is a CVS pharmacy. The bank's history serves as a reminder that what seems strong and permanent in this world can easily be swept

The East River Savings Bank as a drugstore in 2000

aside. And the more venerable an institution appears, the more vulnerable it is likely to be.

The East River Savings Institution was founded in 1848 and prospered quietly as the city of New York grew. Darwin R. James, the eighth president of the bank, often said that the savings bank atmosphere seemed to him to be quiet—that it required little energy or activity on the part of the president.

This pattern was not to last, however. In 1925, James changed the bank's name to East River Savings Bank and set off on a series of innovations: advertising its services to the public and sponsoring legislation to permit local savings banks to open branch offices.

Located in the limestone and marble monument at Amsterdam Avenue and Ninety-sixth Street, the first branch of the East River Savings Bank opened its doors in 1927. It was designed by the well-known architectural firm Walker & Gillette, which had created many of New York's fashionable town houses, as well as the New York Historical Society, the Greenwich Country Club, and the entire town of Venice, Florida. "Since savings banks relied on the small deposits of large numbers of patrons, their buildings were often impressive structures that would attract the attention of local residents, and draw them into the spacious and richly appointed interiors," explains Andrew Dolkart of Landmark West! "Here, they could open an account with the assurance that in such a grand building their money would be safe."

As the Great Depression took hold across the nation, banks everywhere failed. But the East River Savings Bank continued to prosper. In 1932, it acquired both the Maiden Lane Savings Bank, a bank established for German immigrants working mainly in the jewelry industry, and the Italian Savings Bank of the City of New York. These banks, though not built with the structural elegance of the East River Savings Bank, for the next three decades provided the bank with the savings of New York's immigrants.

But the 1970s proved perilous for the East River Savings Bank. Interest rates soared; and home and multifamily loans fell precipitously as a result. In a bid to diversify, East River acquired two upstate New York S&Ls. It also took advantage of new laws that permitted S&Ls to invest 5% of their assets in real estate. That move, however, attracted a real estate developer, who bought East River and changed its name to the River Bank of America. The new name reflected the "nationwide real-estate, corporate lending and capital markets activities of the company."

But the River Bank began going downstream fast. Management invested in advertising and new consumer products, but bad loans overcame them. In 1991, the Federal Deposit Insurance Corp. ordered River Bank to "cease and desist." By 1992, nonperforming assets had risen to $575 million, or 29% of all assets. In 1995, the branches of River Bank were sold to Marine Midland.

In 1997, Marine Midland Bank (before it itself was acquired by the Hongkong and Shanghai Banking Corporation) decided to sell the bank branch. Local residents were alarmed. "The Marine Midland Bank on the northeast corner of Amsterdam Avenue and Ninety-sixth Street is the sort of solid, stately presence that nearby residents have come *to assume is permanent,*" *The New York Times* opined. But despite the reservations of local residents, Essex Capital Partners, a real estate firm specializing in urban retail space, bought the branch office in early 1998. Six months later, residents learned that Essex would lease the bank to CVS, a nationwide pharmacy chain with thirty-six stores in New York.

And so the bank became a drugstore. It is the way creative destruction works.

THE ACCELERATION OF
CREATIVE DESTRUCTION

The demise of institutions like the East River Saving Bank branch at West Ninety-sixth Street may be unfortunate, but it's not unusual. The turnover in our institutional giants is not a consequence of the Internet or of the New Economy. Rather, it is a phenomenon that has been building slowly since the 1920s, long before the beginning of the end for the East River Savings Bank.

Today, the rates of change can be seen in the rapidity with which powerful new companies climb onto the S&P list, and the equal pace with which older, venerable companies tumble off. This turnover, which would have been unimaginable in the 1920s, was almost as surprising just twenty-five years ago. Yet in light of the number of new companies admitted to the S&P list, it has been accelerating for the past seventy years.

This accelerating rate is important, because these new companies generate higher levels of total return to shareholders than do the older survivors. Without them, the overall performance of the markets, and arguably, the economy, would have been far less than it is. For example, if the S&P 500 were today made up of only those companies that were on the list when it was formed in 1957, the overall performance would have been significantly less as seen in the following chart.

Total Return to Shareholder of S&P 500
Long-Term Survivors vs. Median for the S&P 500

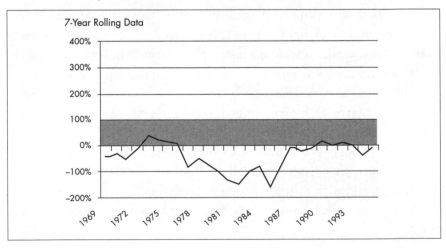

The McKinsey Corporate Performance Database, which tracks data over the last thirty-eight years, reflects these changes as the first chart below demonstrates. More insight into the nature of the changes shows that many of the companies that played a significant role in the U.S. economy have ceased to exist, and many others have come into the economy.

Change in S&P 500 vs. Net New Companies Index

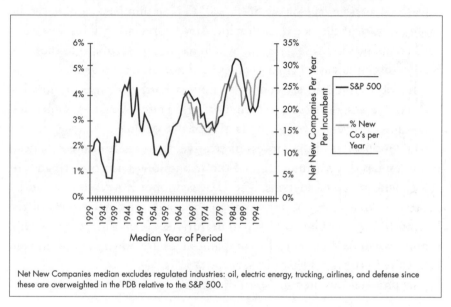

Net New Companies median excludes regulated industries: oil, electric energy, trucking, airlines, and defense since these are overweighted in the PDB relative to the S&P 500.

Percent of Companies by Category

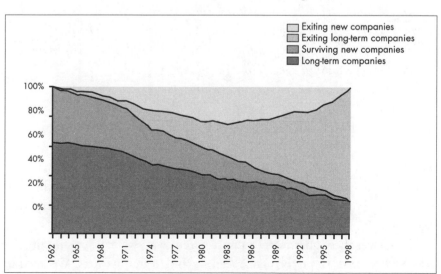

The new entrants to the database over time represent an increasing proportion of the total number of companies included, while the survivors represent a decreasing proportion. Unlike the S&P 500, the number of companies in the McKinsey database is not fixed. And in fact, the number has grown from 249 in 1962 to 696 in 1998, and the rate of growth of such new companies into the database has accelerated from 1.6% per year in the '60s to 4.6% today. The acceleration has occurred in waves, as has been true of the S&P 500. (These numbers would even be more dramatic if the electric utility industry, representing about one hundred companies in the sample, and which has not been subject to the same market disciplines as other companies, had not been included.)

Individual industries, such as computer hardware, telecommunications, or medical devices show even more rapid rates of change, sometimes exceeding the overall averages by factors of two or three.

The robustness of the process of creative destruction in the American economy has directly underpinned the strong long-term performance of the American capital markets. The U.S. economy is now dominated by companies that were not large enough to qualify in the top 80% of the U.S. in 1962. It is quite possible that in thirty-six year's time, the new U.S. economy will be dominated by companies that are now not large enough to qualify in the top 80% of U.S. corporations.

Schumpeter captured the spirit of this change in 1938 when he noted:

> . . . the . . . process of industrial mutation . . . incessantly revolutionizes the economic structure from within, incessantly destroying the old one, incessantly creating a new one. This process of Creative Destruction is the essential fact about capitalism. It is what capitalism consists in and what every capitalist concern has got to live in.

PORTRAITS OF CONTINUITY

The S&P Index clearly tells the story of the acceleration of change and the growth of discontinuity in the overall economy. But what of individual industries? How do they track over time? How does creative destruction really work?

To answer these questions in a transparent way, we have to simplify the complex patterns of performance seen in the capital markets. We need to be able to understand what proportion of the changes we see can be attributed to the overall economy, to individual industries, and to individual companies.

To accomplish this purpose we have developed the performance chart. The performance chart allows us to visualize the past patterns of creative destruction—to determine when it began and when it stopped; to determine how normal or abnormal it appears; to compare an industry to the economy, and to compare one industry with another.

The performance chart is a portrait of long-term performance. It transforms the complexities of annual changes in total return to shareholders into a simple, yet accurate, picture that abstracts the essential details of industry or company performance from the noise of annual variation.

There are two kinds of performance charts: one that compares the performance of an industry, say pharmaceuticals, to the performance of the overall economy (the collection of all the industries in the McKinsey Performance Database) and one that compares the performance of a company, say Merck, to its industry.

The core of each industry chart is the "normal" range of the economy; the core of the company charts is the "normal" range of performance of each industry. In each chart, the top of the normal range is represented by 100% and the bottom by 0%. The exact position of the industry or company line relative to the normal range depends on the industry or company's performance in a given year relative to the performance of the overall stock market in that same year. To make the charts even more transparent, rather than plot individual years, we have plotted seven-year rolling averages. This process "filters" the annual "noise" from the data, and leaves only the telltale underlying traces of true performance levels and changes. If the industry has exactly the same performance as the economy, it will lie halfway between the top and bottom, at 50%. As long as the industry or company performance is within the "normal range," that is between 0% and 100%, its performance is statistically indistinguishable from the performance of the economy or industry. When the results are either greater or less than the normal range, then creative destruction may be at work and an explanation for the exceptional (either positive or negative) performance is required.

Many industries—specialty chemicals, for example—perform within the "normal" range of U.S. markets. The performance chart for the specialty chemicals industry follows.

Specialty Chemicals
7-Year Rolling Total Return to Shareholders (TRS) vs. Economy

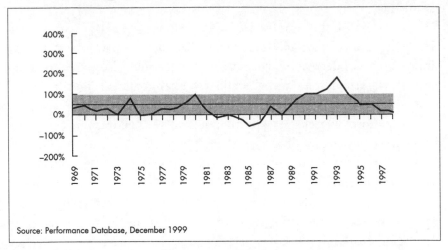

Source: Performance Database, December 1999

Other than a brief period in the late '80s, which, it might be argued, offset a weak period in the late '70s, there has never been a period of exceptional performance in the specialty chemical industry. The market has priced it "fairly" in all periods. In each period this industry has tracked the U.S. economy. In fact, for most of the periods we have examined, the specialty chemical industry was below the median, although the difference is not statistically significant. Individual companies within the specialty chemical industry offer a different story, as we will examine later. The same conclusions can be reached for five other industries: commodity chemicals, paper, electric utilities, toiletries, and, with the exception of a brief time in the early '60s, the trucking industry. These industries account for about one third of the sales in the McKinsey Database and represent the forces of continuity. It is an important force, but, according to our database, not a dominant force in the U.S. economy.

A similar pattern holds for individual companies, particularly long-term survivors. As a general rule, companies that have survived over the long term do not outperform their industries. In medical products, for example, Becton-Dickinson has been an enduring and important company. While Becton-Dickinson has had some very good years in an absolute sense, it did not outperform its industry, as the following chart demonstrates.

Medical Supplies
Becton Dickinson & Co.

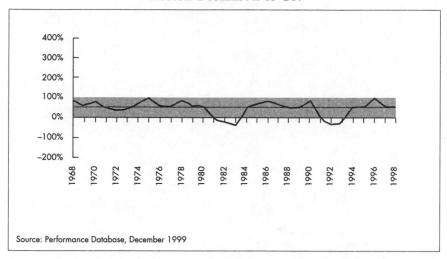

Source: Performance Database, December 1999

Becton-Dickinson's fate was interlocked with the fate of the medical products industry as a whole.

Rohm and Haas, for example, has risen above and fallen below the mean of its industry, but while one can find periods when Rohm and Haas has done better than the industry, there are an equal number of periods when it has done worse. Other companies, such as Raytheon and International Flavors and Fragrances, follow this same basic pattern. These companies arguably have more real risk than close competitors that stay within the range of their industry. It is one thing to expect a down cycle to be met with an up cycle in a year or two. It is quite another to have to wait a decade or two for a reversal.

This is true of other companies in other fields, as well: Rockwell and General Dynamics in defense; Westvaco and Mead in paper; American Home Products and Bristol-Myers Squibb in pharmaceuticals; Texas Instruments in electronics; AMR, the parent company of American Airlines, in air transport.

Some companies, like Delta Air Lines, have had great performances in the past, but for the most recent two or three decades have stayed within the "normal" range of performance for their industry. Other such companies include Air Products and Chemicals, Dow Chemical, Ethyl Corporation, and Baxter International.

Paper
Champion International Corp.

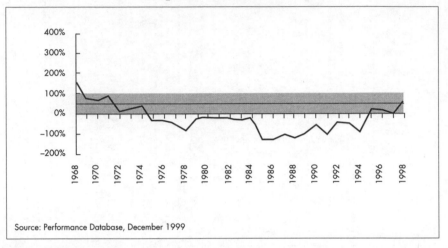

Source: Performance Database, December 1999

Not all long-term survivors necessarily performed at the median of their industry, however. A small group of companies consistently under-performed their industries year after year. An example is Champion Inter-national, although it recently came back into the normal performance range just before being acquired by International Paper. Gates Learjet is another example, as is NL Industries. Compared to their peers they have sustained substandard performance.

There is a small, select group of companies that have been able to sustain their long-term performance above the average level of their industry—even if it has not exceeded the normal range. Among them are Hewlett-Packard, Medtronic, Abbott, Merck—and for the last ten years or so—Warner-Lambert. It is interesting that all the companies in this group participate in industries where there is a great deal of change in the normal course of events. Their results may be the best results possible for companies that don't move into new industries (which, as we will see shortly, will have higher levels of total return to shareholders because of the performance of the industries in which they participate). The companies that succeed in these industries do so because they are able to continually outpace the expectations of analysts. This is a tall order.

There is also a small, select group of companies that have been on a long-term march to superior performance in their industry. Among this group are Kimberly-Clark and Sherwin-Williams. Kimberly-Clark was in the com-

Computer Hardware
Hewlett-Packard Co.

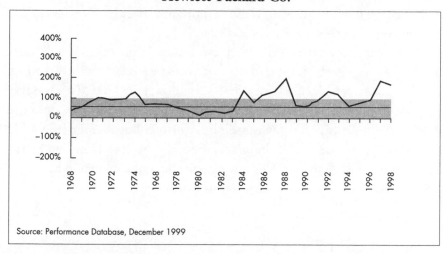

Source: Performance Database, December 1999

modity paper industry until the early '70s, when it decided to move into the consumer paper business, which had stronger long-term performance than the commodity paper business. It chose to compete with Procter & Gamble in the paper diapers business and successfully created the Huggies brand, which, while producing results that were normal for the consumer paper business, were superior to the results in the commodity paper business. Unable to break the pattern of the commodity paper industry, the company moved into an adjacent and more rewarding field. As a result, Kimberly-Clark began an era of greater performance for its shareholders.

Paper: Kimberly-Clark Corp.
7-Year Rolling TRS Relative to Industry

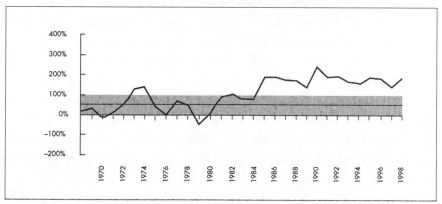

Sherwin-Williams offers a similar story. It switched its focus from making paints to multi-channel paint distribution, and it opened more than 2,000 stores during the '80s. These important moves have rewarded the shareholders of these companies.

In general, however, companies rarely escape the gravity of their industries. They play by the rules, and their performance is determined more or less by those rules. They achieve what the industry achieves. This too was the fate of the East River Savings Bank. The industry was dying and the bank could not escape its downward pull. The building, despite its marble columns and ornate plinth, built to reflect the bank's permanence, was closed up—and reborn as a drugstore, just as Schumpeter would have predicted. It is the way creative destruction works.

PORTRAITS OF DISCONTINUITY

Continuity is not the only story in the capital markets. In fact, discontinuity plays a far more crucial role when industries and companies outperform the market.

WITHIN INDUSTRIES

In some industries, performance differs from that of the general economy for sustained periods of time. For example, the computer hardware industry, from its early days in the '60s until the beginning of the 1980s, steadily outperformed the general market.

The '60s and '70s were a time of substantial innovation. IBM dominated the industry, and there was plenty of technological headroom. By the early '80s those conditions did not hold any longer. Apple and DEC were challenging IBM. Meanwhile, software companies like Microsoft were beginning to emerge; computer hardware underperformed the overall market, vanquished by a pair of powerful technological discontinuities, the personal computer and software. Only recently has the computer hardware industry recovered, but with an entirely restructured industry focused on personal computers and client servers, not the large mainframe hardware that generated the strong returns in the '60s and '70s. The computer industry was more difficult for the analysts to price consistently. There were periods where they underestimated what the price should be and were

Computer Hardware
7-Year Rolling TRS vs. Economy

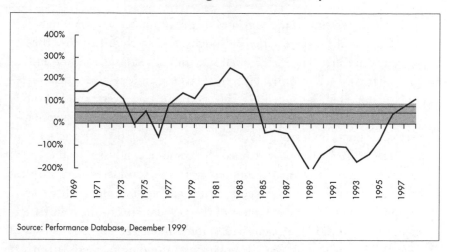

Source: Performance Database, December 1999

pleasantly surprised, driving returns up. And there were other periods where they overestimated what the price would be, and were unpleasantly surprised, driving returns down. A more detailed description of the evolution of the computer hardware industry begins on the next page.

The same is true in other industries. For example, the semiconductor industry had superior performance for investors in the '70s, reflecting not

Semiconductors
7-Year Rolling TRS vs. Economy

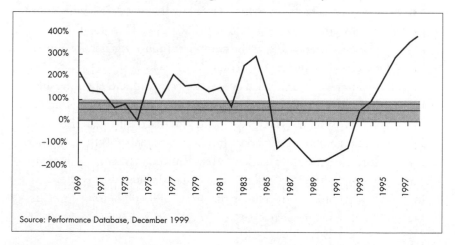

Source: Performance Database, December 1999

COMPUTER HARDWARE INDUSTRY EVOLUTION

In 1962, there were eight companies in the computer hardware industry: IBM and the seven dwarfs (Burroughs, Sperry, etc.). In 1967, IBM accounted for more than 55% of all sales in the sector. It was not until 1988 that IBM fell to below 50% market share in McKinsey's database for that sector, and even in 1995 IBM accounted for over a third of the total sales. Even more significantly, IBM earned 80% of all net operating profits within the industry in 1967; by 1995, that number was near 40%.

Because IBM practically defined the computer industry in the late '60's and early '70s, (when computers were still considered part of the office equipment industry—along with adding machines, dictating equipment, and typewriters), most of the new entrants to the field were competing against IBM in some part of the market. The early successes of Digital Equipment and Wang Laboratories in finding market segments for their computers brought more computer makers into the market. Storage Technology, for example, was created in 1972 with the simple plan of making tape and disk drives that were interchangeable with IBM's offerings and selling them for 10% less.

Storage Technology and similar companies with an "as good as IBM, for less" strategy discovered an underserved market, and were rewarded with rapid sales growth and large returns to shareholders. Generally, these small companies were able to compete on price, and so began to erode IBM's market share. Strong demand coupled with improvements in production technology allowed profit margins and earnings to rise appreciably. While a number of new companies were entering the market, their entry rate was actually slower than the rate of sales growth, allowing companies to enjoy growing sales and growing margins. This situation was a positive one for shareholders, as the computer industry generally outperformed the economy during the decade.

But the impressive returns led even more companies to enter the market. A flush of mainframe and workstation companies like Amdahl, Floating Point Systems, Intergraph, and Stratus challenged IBM and Digital Equipment in the market for larger systems. With computer manufacturers entering the market faster than the market grew, margins started to drop by 1982, a trend that continued through the decade, causing many shareholders to reevaluate the profitability of their investments, pushing total return to shareholders, or TRS, in a downward direction through the '80s. Hardware ended the decade well below the rest of the economy.

The high rate of entry into the hardware market in the late '70s and early '80s is an indication of how easy it had become to join the party. Any computer scientist with a garage could build a low-cost system that was comparable to many products on the market. New companies like Apple, Compaq, and (later) Dell, along with component makers like Seagate, Western Digital, and Quantum, went after the desktop market, which had grown up from home hobby computers sold by Tandy and Commodore.

IBM legitimized and ultimately standardized the desktop computer with its PC. Simultaneously, the number of companies in the market grew dramatically. Interpreting these potentially conflicting trends, Standard and Poor's speculated in 1985 that it was unlikely that anyone would even bother to try to "clone" IBM's latest personal computer, the AT, based on Intel's 286 processor and sporting 256k of RAM and no hard drive, presumably since IBM had such a commanding lead. Clearly, young Michael Dell missed the report.

In fact, many of the entries into the market continued to grow at the expense of IBM. Although its market share declined from its peak in 1970, it was still able to hold on to its profit margin until 1982, when it finally recognized the difficulties that it faced from competition. At that time, IBM announced that it expected the industry's sales to grow at a rate of 15%, and that IBM intended to grow faster than the industry. In reality, the industry's growth actually slowed from 15% in 1984 to 7–10% over the '90s. IBM's expectations of its own growth proved even less accurate. To drive its growth, it ramped up spending on R&D to $4.2 billion (9% of sales) in 1984. Unfortunately for IBM, its investments were not sufficient to fuel growth.

IBM's business was built around large, proprietary systems that left them vulnerable to the new entrants in the field. IBM did not adapt to the development of standardized computer components, and only a few years after the introduction of the IBM personal computer, it began losing the battle for the burgeoning market.

By the mid-'80s, the hardware industry was suffering, and yet new companies continued to be formed. With margins falling and hardware companies underperforming the market in 1983, there seemed little incentive for new companies to join the fray. Yet the number of companies continued to grow through the rest of the '80s.

only the growth of computer hardware but also the growth of telecommunications, particularly the Internet. Like the computer hardware industry, the semiconductor industry has gone through major technological discontinuities. The economic implications of these discontinuities were apparently difficult to forecast, as shown by the long periods of over and under performance of the semiconductor industry. In this case the discontinuity was the result of the switch from memory chips to microprocessors, but the effects for shareholders were the same as they were during the transition in computer hardware from "big iron" to personal computers and software. It was difficult for the analyst and investor community to properly price the equities of semiconductor companies in the face of the technological risk and the aggressive actions of Japanese manufacturers to expand their share in the United States.

Software, the wunderkind of the late '80s and early '90s, has had two major periods of outperformance since it came into existence. The ability of the software industry to develop and deliver products that apparently "surprise and delight" its customers on a continuing basis for two decades now has exceeded anyone's expectations. In many ways the patterns in software appear to be similar to the early patterns in computer hardware and semiconductors. The future will tell whether this industry is able to sustain its above-average performance. The box titled "Software Industry Evolution" on page 42 provides a more complete description of the changes in the software industry.

Software
7-Year Rolling TRS vs. Economy

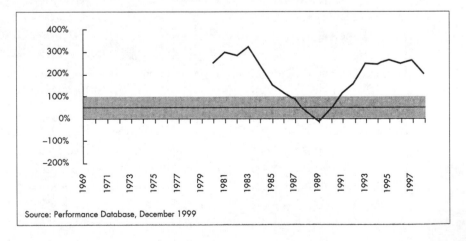

Source: Performance Database, December 1999

The oil industry has, quite by chance, shown a pattern that is similar to that of the computer industry, but for quite different reasons. It proved difficult to accurately forecast, due to the difficulty in predicting the price of oil. The late '70s afforded the industry a period of outperformance, since all the surprises were positive. But, like computers, it eventually substantially underperformed the economy. These changes directly reflect the formation and subsequent demise of OPEC and its control of the world's oil supply and pricing.

Oil
7-Year Rolling TRS vs. Economy

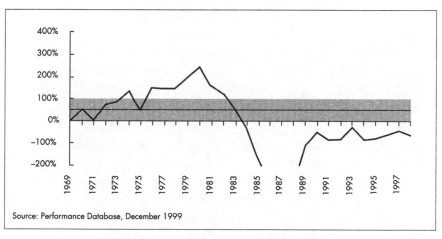

Source: Performance Database, December 1999

The pharmaceutical industry provides another example of forecasting difficulties (see graph, page 42). Pharmaceuticals performed well in the '60s and early '70s, then hit a bump as Medicare and Medicaid legislation threatened to pop the balloon. This industry has come back, however. It benefits from exceptionally strong drug discovery and marketing skills, and strong patent protection of what it discovers. It is still delighting analysts and investors alike.

The medical products industry faced similar issues, but has rebounded, benefiting from the rapid advance in technology (see graph, page 44).

The defense industry, controlled entirely by the strategic needs of the nation rather than raw market forces, shows a pattern different from that of either the computer hardware or semiconductor industries, but is nevertheless as difficult to forecast as was the flowering of *glasnost* and the demise of the Soviet Union (see graph, page 44).

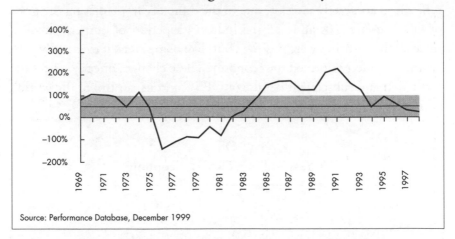

Pharmaceuticals
7-Year Rolling TRS vs. Economy

Source: Performance Database, December 1999

SOFTWARE INDUSTRY EVOLUTION

The computer industry first began to separate into the hardware and the software industries in 1970, when IBM made the decision to charge separately for the software that ran on its mainframes. Although companies like Ross Perot's Electronic Data Systems had been around since the '60s, selling specialized data processing software for mainframe systems, the move by IBM created an opportunity for companies to build generic, "packaged" software applications that could compete with some of IBM's offerings. The industry's fate didn't truly begin to diverge from that of the hardware industry until the arrival of the personal computer in the early '80s. At the end of 1981, the software industry remained small. Software is primarily purchased for an installed base of computers, rather than for computers that have just been released, so the transition from mainframes to PCs that occurred in the mid-'80s wasn't fully reflected in the software industry until six years later. In fact, in 1990, the top two software companies in the world were IBM and Unisys. IBM's software sales reached nearly $10 billion, about as much as the remaining top ten companies combined.

The potential of the PC, however, brought companies into the industry at an incredible rate, with each year between 1982 and 1986 finding as many new entrants in the industry as existed in the industry at the beginning of the year. Earlier in the decade, while software sales were growing rapidly, an influx of new entrants reduced the average size of software companies, increased competition, and lowered expected profitability. As a result, the median return to shareholders fell, bottoming out in 1986. Since then, however, total return to shareholders in the software industry has improved substantially, and has remained significantly better than that of the economy as a whole.

In 1987, the prospects for software companies brightened with the buildup of an installed PC base. Improvements in PC hardware (the introduction of the Intel 286 chip and a broader adoption of hard disk drives) allowed software companies to offer more complex and useful tools to PC users. Spreadsheet and word processing packages became ubiquitous (if antiquated by today's standards). Improvements in PC operating systems, first with Apple's Macintosh and later with Microsoft Windows, enabled users to interact with computers through a standardized graphical interface, giving them access to complex features without needing to memorize a host of new keystrokes.

As computer usage increased, so did users' need to share files with others. This helped drive consolidation around particular applications. In 1985, for instance, five of the top fifteen business applications were word processors (including Wordstar, Microsoft Word, and WordPerfect). By 1990, the number was down to two, and by the mid-'90s, Microsoft Word was the only dominant player.

In many ways, software companies have reaped the rewards of innovation in the hardware industry, even when hardware companies have not been able to benefit themselves. A faster hard drive with greater capacity has little utility to consumers unless it enables them to actually do something better or faster—and that requires software. Since personal computer components (except, perhaps, computer processing units, or CPUs) are interchangeable with the products of other hardware manufacturers, companies in that industry have had to rely on price to gain market share, whereas software companies have not. In fact, competition in the hardware industry enables more customers to purchase greater computing for less, leaving more resources to spend on new and improved software to utilize the excess capacity.

Medical Supplies
7-Year Rolling TRS vs. Economy

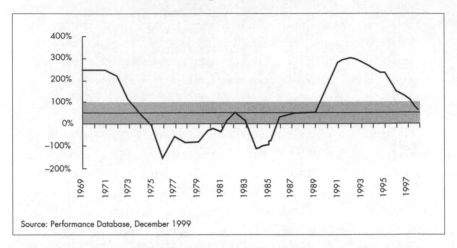

Source: Performance Database, December 1999

Defense
7-Year Rolling TRS vs. Economy

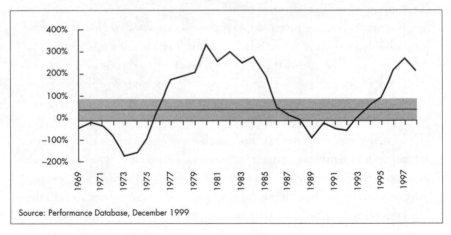

Source: Performance Database, December 1999

Investors in the defense industry benefited from both the intensification of the cold war and in its demise. The period of outperformance was substantial, but like all other periods of outperformance, it had a beginning and an end.

There also have been industries that have more or less continuously *underperformed* the markets, proving to be continually disappointing to investors and analysts alike. The airlines industry stands out in this regard.

Underperformance in that industry can be blamed on any number of things—regulation or deregulation, increasing or decreasing fuel prices, the power of airframe manufacturers or engine manufactures, or just blind, and unfulfilled, optimism on the part of investors. It shows, however, that it is possible to underperform the economy for sustained periods of time.

Airlines
7-Year Rolling TRS vs. Economy

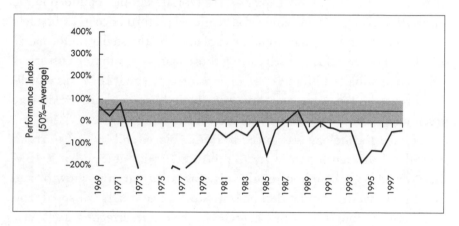

The sources of discontinuity vary greatly, as we have seen. Some are due to technological change, as is true of computer hardware and software; some are due to international competitive changes, as in the oil industry; others are due to the changing attitudes and policies of government, as we have seen with the defense industry or in telecommunications. And in some industries there are several causes. In pharmaceuticals, for example, both technological change and changing government policy play a part. In all cases they are very difficult to forecast accurately, and thus open the window to "abnormal" returns. Try as we might, we have not found a single example of an industry that has continuously outperformed the overall market over this period of time. What the data shows is that outperforming the market is possible at the industry level, but it is almost always temporary.

WITHIN COMPANIES

With regard to individual companies, we did not find any long-term survivors that had significant sustained outperformance. Nonetheless, we did find many (though certainly not all) new entrants that had stronger performance than that of their peers. The period of exceptional performance for these entrants varies, just as the period of exceptional performance for a newer industry varies, but ultimately it always comes to an end.

Storage Technology, a maker of computer storage devices (which we describe in more detail in Chapter 4), is a typical example. Founded in the early 1970s, the company enjoyed exceptional performance in its first few years—better, in fact, than could be explained by the stellar performance of the computer industry itself during those years—by offering customers IBM-compatible mainframe components for a price that IBM was unwilling to match. Ten years later, however, the industry had eroded Storage Technology's lead, as the following exhibit shows.

Storage Technology was forced to think "bigger and bigger" to try to stay ahead. It even began to try to produce a mainframe to battle IBM head-on. After a couple of costly missteps, sales, earnings growth, and return on invested capital declined, its stock price finally collapsed, and the company found itself in Chapter 11—before resurrecting itself once again by returning to its core business.

Storage Technology—Initial Year: 1972
7-Year TRS Performance Chart

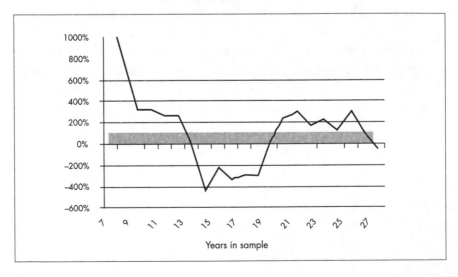

What does this indicate? As Richard Foster pointed out in *Innovation: The Attacker's Advantage,* new entrants into an industry have the upper hand in competing with older companies. To be sure, some, like Exabite, International Rectifier, and Unitrode, underperform the industry and there are circumstances in which new entrants fare worse than long-term survivors do (particularly in monopolies such as defense or electric utilities, or in industries such as pharmaceutical and medical products where research and product licensing discourages entrepreneurial efforts). But in most industries, new entrants, or "attackers," have the advantage. That is not to say that all attackers are winners. That is certainly not the case. But it is the case that most winners are attackers.

In fact, if one looks at companies in all the industries we examined in the way described above, the results, while less dramatic, are quite similar. As the following chart shows, it is the new entrant that performs in a superior way.

Eventually, its performance deteriorates to the industry average, and then below. There are three reasons for this pattern, which we will elaborate on in later chapters. First, the original innovation that the entrant brings is imitated or bested in the market, often by even newer entrants, leaving little excess profitability or growth available for the original innovator. Second, the market learns how to properly value the company, and returns accordingly approach the cost of equity for the industry. Third,

Eventually the edge wears off . . .

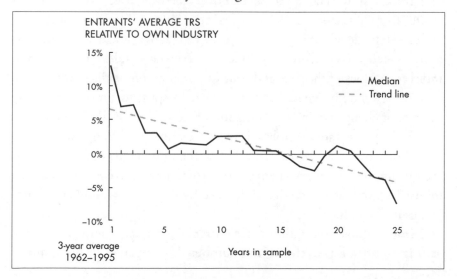

the new entrant falls prey to cultural lock-in and can no longer create innovation on the scale that brought its original success.

Companies that outperform the market are temporary members of a permanent class. Many of these companies are in pioneering industries, or are pioneers in their own industry. During their period of outperformance they bring something new to the economy, either as an entire industry or as an individual company. Their "excellence" is a result of their newness and utilitarian novelty rather than their enduring managerial skills. We have found that very few companies attempt to change at the pace and scale of the market. Yet only this kind of broad-based change can assure such corporations that their long-term survival will not result in long-term underperformance of the market. Excellence as such has been transitory rather than permanent; it has been episodic. Corporate "excellence," like the exceptional performance of an industry, does not last forever. It is always crushed by the forces of creative destruction.

DISCONTINUITY AND CREATIVE DESTRUCTION

The relationship between "newness" and performance within companies and industries is vital. Newness within an industry is represented by the net rate of companies' entry and exit from the industry. The "newer" an industry is, the "fresher" it is. Turnover in industries is similar to turnover in a grocery store. The faster the turnover, the fresher the food. Newness is a measure of the pace and scale of creative destruction in an industry.

To see the details of how the processes of creative destruction work, we have created a New Company Index, or Newness Index. The Newness Index is an index of the pace and scale of net new companies entering into an industry. The Newness Index is similar in spirit to simply measuring the rate of change among the companies listed in the S&P 500 index.

The Newness Index simply subtracts the number of companies leaving an industry over a seven-year period from the number of companies entering during those same seven years. To better allow us to compare between industries, we then divide that difference by the starting number of companies in the industry.

In our sample, the ratio of net entrants (entering companies minus exiting companies) relative to the number of companies in the industry has been increasing over the past thirty-six years, from about two net new companies for every ten companies in the economy in the early '60s, to about three in 1998. These rates of change can be thought of as the base rate of change for the economy. They are the rates of change that we will use later to judge corporate rates of change.

Just as market indexes are bolstered by new entrants, so are industries. New entrants are drawn into areas of opportunity by the potential for strong returns. Not all the new entrants succeed, of course. But the more successful among them are able to find a way to conduct their business with much higher rates of return than that of the incumbent survivors.

A few industry examples may help make the point more clearly. During the '70s, the medical products industry had a rate of net entry lower than that of the economy overall. While the economy was adding two companies for every ten companies in existence over a seven-year span, the medical products industry was actually losing companies through consolidation and contraction. At the end of the '70s, however, this period of contraction reversed itself. The fear of adverse effects from Medicare and Medicaid had abated, and spurred by the potential of new technology, new companies began to enter into the medical products field. By the early '90s, the medical products industry was adding more than five companies for every ten that existed over a seven-year period. That is an enormous rate of change.

Net Rate of New Economy Entry: Medical

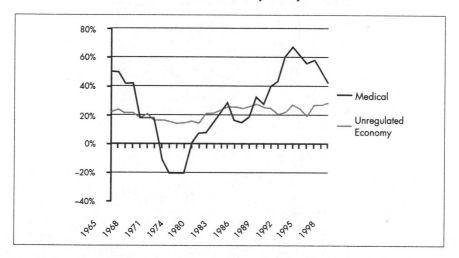

Medical Supplies
TRS vs. Net Rate of New Company Entry

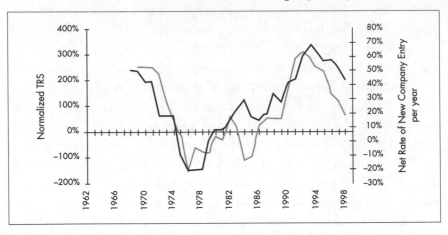

The rates of change are closely related to the returns investors received, as the above graph shows.

The same pattern is observed in other industries, as well. In the oil industry, during the price boom of the '70s, the net rate of entry increased.

So, too, did the return to shareholders.

Moreover, the return to shareholders was highest during the period of rapid entry. During periods of price collapse and economic pressure, the industry contracted, as can be clearly seen in the charts.

Net Rate of New Company Entry: Oil

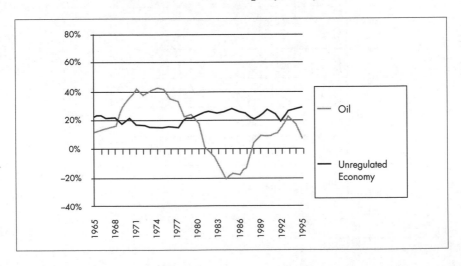

Oil
TRS vs. Net Rate of New Company Entry

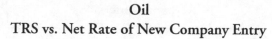

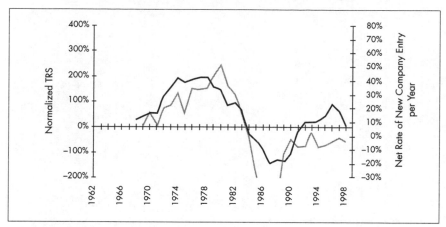

In the telecommunications industry, with the breakup of AT&T in the early '80s, new spin-offs were formed, and the industry took on a dynamic character.

With the breakup, new customer services were founded, and new opportunities for cost and asset reduction were identified. Industry performance blossomed.

While it might not be surprising that these relationships exist, it is surprising that they are so strong. Many factors affect industry profitability

Net Rate of New Company Entry: Telecommunications

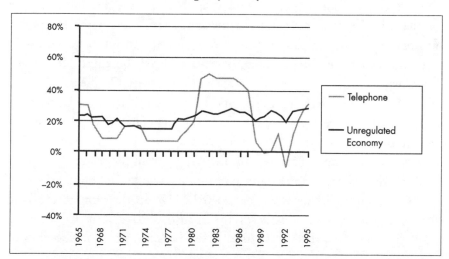

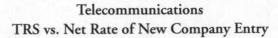

Telecommunications
TRS vs. Net Rate of New Company Entry

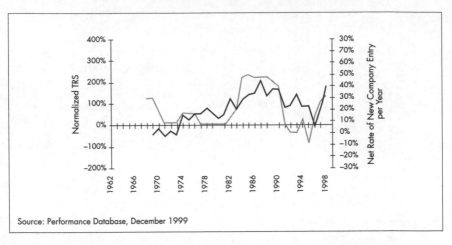

Source: Performance Database, December 1999

and growth, as well as investor expectations about profitability and growth in the future. Such a strong correlation between total return to shareholders and the Newness Index of change suggests that these relationships are among the strongest in these industries.

WHY "NEWNESS" WORKS

Why does "newness" correlate with shareholder returns? The missing link so far in our discussion of companies and newness is the role and influence of the investor. It is, after all, the investors' views about the long-term future value of the company's equity that count. It is investors who must be convinced that the value is there, or they will sell the equity. If enough investors sell, price pressure will drive the stock down. On the other hand, if enough investors feel that the prospects for the company are better than implied in the current price of the stock, they will buy it. If more investors seek to buy the stock than sell it, the price will go up until the demand of buyers is once again in balance with the supply from the sellers.

How does the investor, or group of investors large enough to affect the price of a stock, decide what it's worth? How do they know what the future will be? As we saw earlier, some industries have been characterized more by continuity than by change. The forces at work kept the rates of entry and exit rather low. The game changes only slowly. To the astute observer, rather regular patterns of variation became clear. Under these circumstances, over time "rules of thumb" can be developed. As long as the industry continues to operate within the limits that existed when the rules were established, the rules work.

Forecasts of the future are often made, as a practical matter, by analogy with the past. If continuity provides the general economic context, history will be an adequate guide to the future. In this case, one would expect the prices of stocks to be reasonably "fairly" set, increasing only by the amount required to cover the cost of equity, as prescribed by well-known financial theory.

However, the markets are made up not only of industries characterized by continuity but of industries characterized by change, such as the computer hardware and software industries; the oil industry in the '70s; pharmaceuticals and medical products during the age of managed care; and now industries affected by the Internet. How does one's forecast change? The answer, it appears, is only with great difficulty.

In the presence of discontinuities, the old rules of thumb do not work. Surprise events throw off traditional forecasting, such as the unfolding of the Medicare and Medicaid plans by the government in the early '70s; or the increase and then decrease in oil prices due to the formation of OPEC in the early '70s; or the oversupply of DRAMs in the semiconductor market in the early '80s followed by the proliferation of microprocessors; or the technological transformation of the computer industry in the '80s; or the breakup of AT&T and the gradual deregulation of the telecommunications industry in the '80s; or the emergence of the Internet in the '90s.

G. K. Chesterton, the late-nineteenth-century British novelist, social commentator, and the man who inspired Ghandi to work to bring nationalism to India, captured the conundrum of valuation during creative destruction when he said,

> *The real trouble with this world of ours is not that it is an unreasonable world, or even that it is a reasonable one. The commonest kind of trouble is that it is nearly reasonable, but not quite. Life is not an illogicality; yet it is a trap for logicians. It looks just a little more mathematical and regular than it is; its exactitude is obvious, but its inexactitude is hidden; its wildness lies in wait.*

It is not hard to understand why, when markets are rapidly changing, they are difficult to forecast and their "wildness lies in wait." As a practical matter, one can't decipher the structure, determine how it works, and "run it forward" to see the future as the East River Savings Bank discovered. The conventional model works in limited cases, but these cases will be less frequent in the future.

If one could foresee these discontinuous events, proper price adjustments could be made, but this appears to be a difficult task in practice. Moreover, discontinuities, and periods of rapid change, can trigger a major shift upward or downward. Outperformance occurs because an industry or company is able to surprise the investment community.

Nonetheless, the initial surprise cannot by itself explain the periods of exceptional performance, either on the high side or the low side, that extend far longer than the duration of the discontinuity. How can this be? We think the reason for the extended period of outperformance is the failure of analysts and investors to reset future expectations of the industry or company rapidly enough. Because analysts are anchored to the past, they are unable to weigh the anchor and accurately reset their scenarios for the future at a sufficient pace.

There is a great deal of evidence that suggests that when people—for example, investors and managers—are taken out of a familiar environment—an environment of continuity—their ability to deal with the future deteriorates rapidly. John Sterman, J. Spencer Standish professor of management and director of the System Dynamics Group of MIT, who has studied the ability of managers to learn over long periods of time, says that in complex environments, the more experience people have the more poorly they perform. Here is a distillation of Sterman's findings:

- "Even in perfectly functioning markets, modest levels of complexity cause large and systematic deviations from rational behavior."
- "There is little evidence of adaptation of one's 'rules' as the complexity of the task increases." When the environment is complex, people seem to revert to simple rules that ignore time delays and feedback, leading to lowered performance.
- Individuals "forecast by averaging past values and extrapolating past trends. [They] actually spend less time making their decisions in the complex markets than in the simple ones."
- The lowered performance people exhibit as a result of greater com-

plexity does not improve with experience. People become "less responsive to critical variables and more vulnerable to forecasting errors—their learning hurts their ability to perform well in the complex conditions."

- Most individuals do not learn how to improve their performance in complex conditions. In relatively simple conditions—without time delays or feedback—people "dramatically outperform the 'do nothing' rule, but in complex situations many people are bested by the 'do nothing' rule." Attempts individuals make to control the system are counterproductive.

Markets that are undergoing rapid or discontinuous change are extremely complex. Economic systems are highly networked and involve substantial feedback. Given Professor Sterman's findings, it is not surprising that forecasting deteriorates in the face of rapid change.

THE DIFFICULTY OF FORECASTING DISCONTINUITY

We believe investors deal with the complexity of the future by adopting a skeptic's bias in the face of good prospects—and an optimist's bias about poor prospects. It would not be unreasonable to attribute the deep cause of this "bias" to risk aversion. However, there is another—and more compelling—reason for this bias: the use of forecasting algorithms that are anchored in the short-term (e.g., two-year) past of the industry or company, rather than analogies and patterns of industry evolution drawn from other sectors of the economy.

The McKinsey Corporate Performance Database shows that after a discontinuity, industries and the products and services that constitute them evolve slowly at first until they are established in the eyes of their customers. Then they evolve more quickly, until they have reached nearly all the customers they can, at which point the evolution slows down again. The pattern can be seen in the chart on the top of page 56.

We refer to this common pattern as an S-curve. While this pattern may vary somewhat for sales or earnings—for example, near the top of the S-curve it is not uncommon for sales to go into a cyclical period, or turn down rather than stay constant—it is a reasonable approximation in all

Typical Evolution of Industry Earnings

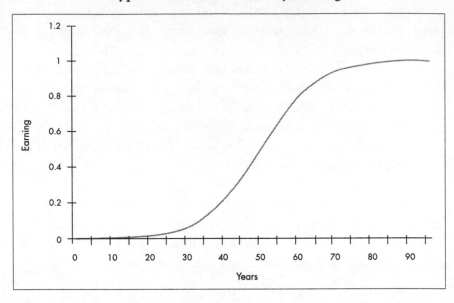

industries we have studied. For example, in the commodity chemical industry, which is probably in its mature state, the evolution of sales has followed the pattern shown below. Often these patterns are difficult to detect for those in management or in the investment community focused only on the last few—and the next few—years, since the patterns are revealed only by a long view. The implications of the S-curve evolution of industries on traditional forecasts based on reasonable extensions of the past are significant.

Sales Evolution

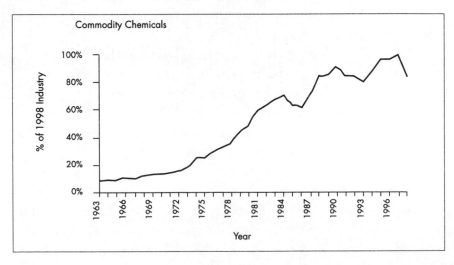

First, early forecasts of long-term sales or earnings of a given company will be too low—too conservative—and will have to be continually adjusted upward as new data is accumulated. As these upward revisions are made, the stock price will rise and returns to shareholders will increase. In addition, later-stage forecasts will be too high, as analysts' predictions, based on previous quarters' growth, eventually outstrip actual performance as the growth curve begins to flatten. Eventually analysts find themselves continually adjusting their predictions lower, reducing returns to shareholders. In this way, discontinuities give rise to periods of a company's stock outperforming and underperforming the market.

This is exactly what happens in fast-moving industries like computer hardware. During the period from 1962 to the mid-1970s, both the total return to shareholders and the price-to-earnings ratio of the computer industry were above the corresponding levels in the U.S. economy as a whole. This proved to be a nightmare for value investors who shunned this industry waiting for a better time to invest. When the "better time" came, the companies were underperforming the market, and both TRS and price-to-earnings ratios fell below the level of the economy—until a new group of leaders took over in the market and drove performance up again by riding the new S-curve of personal computers and eventually the Internet. Of course, this flies in the face of a model of the capital markets that assumes high price-to-earnings ratios are associated with the probability of low returns.

Forecast Errors

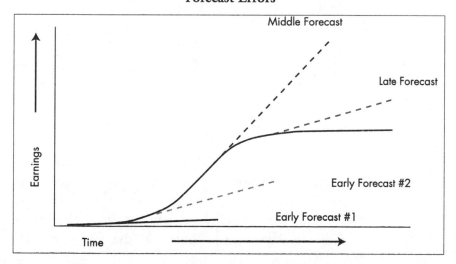

Consequences of Forecast Errors for P/E and TRS

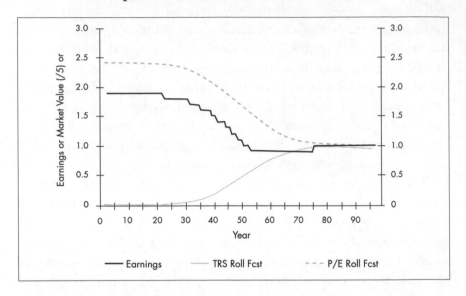

Moreover, analysts and investors tend to be skeptical that companies can sustain high levels of growth for low levels of investment for long periods of time. When managers confound these expectations—as Microsoft, Cisco, and Dell were able to do throughout the 1990s—they are richly rewarded as we pointed out earlier. Some companies have shown that they can confound the markets for a decade or more if they are skilled at the arts of creative destruction.

HOW CREATIVE DESTRUCTION WILL WORK IN THE FUTURE

One implication of this understanding of how the processes of creative destruction work is that as the speed of change accelerates, the relative misforecasting can be expected to increase. Readers who have been following the "dot.com revolution" know this can be the case. As the speed of change hits very high levels, there will be times when the estimated short-term value of the company will be several times (e.g., five times) in excess of any sustainable long-term model. As the forecasting errors are realized, market capitalizations come crashing down, as do price-to-earnings multiples and returns. A sad consequence of this phenomenon, which is nothing more than the application of the errors we have described above, is that total returns to shareholders can become substantially negative and can remain there for years, waiting for reality to catch up with forecasts. The inadequacy of forecasts is to blame for the "bubbles" one sees in the market. And while the bubble begins at just about the midway point of the earnings evolution, it reaches its peak before the earnings growth slows. This is generally far earlier than most analysts expect.

There are several implications for management:

- The opportunity for investments are more attractive in earlier years than one may have thought. Companies should take these effects into account when considering acquisitions.
- The risks of substantial reductions in price and total return to shareholders (albeit from very high levels) will increase as the pace of industry and company evolution increases.
- As the pace of industry and company evolution increases, there will be less connection between the quarter-to-quarter performance of the company and its stock price.
- Market volatility is likely to increase as the speed of industry and company evolution increases.

THE IMPORTANCE OF FOSTERING CREATIVE DESTRUCTION

Creative destruction underlies the realities of performance to this day—perhaps more than ever, as the Schumpeter quotation earlier in the chapter noted.

No company has demonstrated an ability to outperform its industry for long periods of time. The markets are simply too competitive to let one company get ahead and stay ahead. And analysts are too quick to try to match a company's share price to its rate of change and growth. Despite strong companies like Hewlett-Packard, GE, J&J, and comeback stories such as Kimberly-Clark, Colgate-Palmolive, DuPont, and Sherwin-Williams, in general the only companies to achieve and maintain above-industry-average returns are new, emerging companies. And even they earn their returns for a limited period, often less than a decade. They do well for a period of time because they are able to grow for longer periods of time at higher levels of profit than analysts expected. This combination of results surprises the analysts and results in strong total return to shareholders. The conventional notion of excellence—the company that lasts forever and performs in a superior way, rewarding its investors continually over time at above-average rates—is a myth. The assumptions on which it is based simply don't hold up.

But perhaps the markets that excel at the arts of creative destruction suggest a model for stronger long-term performance: mastering continual change. It is the markets that set the standard for pace and scale of change. As we've seen, specific industries can sustain significantly higher levels of performance than that of the economy as a whole, and it is the industries that have faced and managed change the most that have had the best sustained levels of performance. The message is clear: Only companies that change at the pace of the market can hope to match or exceed the overall market's performance. Unless companies change at the pace and scale of the market, their performance will almost inevitably slide into mediocrity.

The key for corporations is to mimic the pace and scale of change in the markets—without losing control of the operations they oversee. The markets, of course, do not have to worry about operations. Corporations do. Blending the creative destruction of the markets with operating excellence is an extremely tall order. Nonetheless, it is essential, for the pace of creative destruction in the economy is increasing. Over the past seventy years, hidden from general view, there has been a relentless acceleration in the introduction of "newness," to the U.S. economy.

Our studies suggest that the pace of creative destruction will probably continue to accelerate in the decades ahead, albeit in cycles, putting substantially increased strains on corporations, many of which today continue to operate under the assumption of continuity. The reasons for a corporation's lack of willingness to change are deep, as we will explore in the next chapter, and the problems are exceptionally difficult to address. But they *can* be addressed—if strong leadership can be found. New systems of management will have to be developed to capitalize on the "wildness" of creative destruction, despite the difficulty of this task. For those who do not learn the lessons of discontinuity and creative destruction, the fate of the East River Saving Bank may well be their own future.

CHAPTER 3

Cultural Lock-In

Things should be must be made as simple as possible, but not simpler.
ALBERT EINSTEIN

For many years, IBM was everyone's favorite company. It represented technological virtue: innovation; an aggressive American spirit; the essence of American competitiveness. Yet, under John Akers, the company fell hard in the 1980s, and for a time its very survival seemed in question. As *The Economist* noted in 1993:

> When John Akers took over as chairman of IBM in 1985, it looked as if he had won the best job in American business. Still only 50, Mr. Akers had had a meteoric rise through the ranks. He seemed set for a secure tenure at the top of a great company whose technological and managerial prowess was both admired and feared throughout the world. Mr. Akers himself thought that IBM was poised for explosive growth. So did most other people. Instead, it has plunged into huge losses, and a chorus of critics is demanding his head.

When IBM failed, it failed in a major, dramatic, and public way rather than the slow, Alzheimer's-like way that many imagine to be the fate of large companies. It did not, like MacArthur's old soldier, simply fade away. It went with a crash, taking John Akers and many of his top managers with it.

What happened to this "excellent" company? Could it have avoided its fate? How did so many intelligent executives misread the company's situation so completely? Why did they fail to take corrective action for so long? How could a dynamic leader like John Akers not see what was coming? Did IBM simply become too big? Did it become too bureaucratic? Did its technology lose its edge? Did its marketing become anemic? Did it lose touch with its customers?

In our view, none of these things, in and of themselves, were responsible. Rather, the company's collapse was a collective failure of the mental processes, or the "mind," of the corporation. IBM's failure was the failure to see the present for what it is, a failure to see the rich mosaic of possibilities for the future. It was a failure of hubris—thinking that one company, no matter how powerful, is more powerful than the collective forces of the market. It was a failure to understand the context for decision making in the corporation. It was a failure of dialogue among the most senior managers, who preferred to review programs and make decisions within the context of the view that IBM, and only IBM, was in charge of the pace of change of the computer industry. It was a failure to recognize that continuity—business as usual—is a fallacy.

In the 1980s, IBM was not facing business "as usual." IBM, in fact, was in the midst of a *market discontinuity* as personal computers came of age. Market discontinuities change and contort almost every aspect of managerial perception, rendering old ways of seeing and describing the world obsolete. Discontinuities challenge the most basic assumptions of continuity that companies create for themselves. In IBM's case, the company's thinking was based on the assumption that "we should continue to invest in mainframe computers, where there is much more room for productivity improvement." This may have been true, but it missed questioning whether even greater productivity improvements could be achieved with investments in personal computers. (Perhaps this second question was not asked with force within the company because of an implicit fear of cannibalizing its mainframe business.) Discontinuities of this sort present management with an almost unending stream of enigmas, dilemmas, paradoxes, puzzles, riddles, and mysteries, which remain unsolved until the mental context of the viewer changes. They present management with a maelstrom of disorder.

For many CEOs, being caught in a discontinuity is like falling into an Alice in Wonderland–like nightmare, where familiar people play vastly different roles, where the weak become strong and the strong are made weak. Would John Akers have guessed in 1983 that his successor at IBM would have virtually no knowledge of the computer businesses, and be drawn from the managerial ranks of tobacco and cookie companies? Would he have imagined a CEO with a background in credit cards and consulting who would one day be recognized as the savior of the corporation? Would John Akers have imagined that a little start-up software company that had been an insignificant contractor to IBM would one day have a market capitalization several times as large as IBM's? Clearly not.

The reason IBM stumbled was that something was wrong with John Akers's view of the world—with his mental model. Akers believed in continuity in gradual, incremental change. But the world had become discontinuous. The world Akers and IBM knew was shifting under their feet as the dominance of the mainframe computer faded. Discontinuities present management with an almost hallucinogenic trip through territory that they think they know but are suddenly incapable of navigating.

John Akers was not alone. The seismic shock that ran through the computer industry at the time was merely representative of shifts in other markets. The drug industry collapsed in the mid-'70s; defense rocketed up and then down; semiconductors went on a roller-coaster ride; airlines never escaped the gravitational pull of their markets, and sometimes dived to the bottom of the financial Marianas Trench. Discontinuities bring fundamental shifts in the way competition interacts in the marketplace (resulting in changes in companies' underlying performance) and the way in which investors infer possible future patterns, and therefore demand changes in mental models. As we shall see, mental models are often useful and necessary constructs. The world would be too complex to comprehend without them. Unfortunately, however, more often they feed the assumption of continuity than of discontinuity, for reasons we will describe later in this chapter.

MENTAL MODELS

The originator of the concept of the mental model was Kenneth Craik, a Scottish psychologist who in 1943 proposed that mental models are the manipulation of a vast variety of internal representations of the external world:

If the organism carries a "small-scale model" of external reality and of its own possible actions within its head, it is able to try out various alternatives, conclude which is the best of them, react to future situations before they arise, utilize the knowledge of the past events in dealing with the present and future, and in every way to react in a much fuller, safer, and more competent manner to the emergencies which face it.

We form mental models of just about everything—cars, airplanes, corporations, ballet, opera, markets and their evolution, competition, operations, customer loyalty, consumer marketing, innovation, operational excellence, knowledge development and management, and so on. Forecasting, in particular, is an exercise in applied mental modeling. Some of these models may be static, while others—frequently the most useful ones—are dynamic. Some are quite real; many are symbolic. Some may be visionary. Some may have multiple legitimate interpretations, which depend on the perspective and context of the viewer.

Few business strategies are elaborated today without recourse to mental models, which depict the corporation and its role in the market, the economy, the competitive landscape, and the world as a whole. More often they are implicit and inarticulate, and often hidden or invisible. But they are there nonetheless. We cannot function without them. They are essential to reasoning. Anton Pavlovich Chekhov, the Russian playwright and poet who wrote hauntingly about the inability of people to communicate with one another, maintained that one must "snatch at small details, grouping them in such a manner that after reading them one can obtain the picture on closing one's eyes." Mental models are the mechanism by which we "snatch the small details" and group them. As Albert Einstein observed, "Man seeks for himself a simplified and lucid image of the world."

Philip N. Johnson-Laird, a cognitive psychologist at Princeton University, notes, "Small scale models of reality need neither be wholly accurate nor correspond completely with what they model in order to be useful." In other words, there is some give and take. The painter, the poet, the speculative philosopher, and the natural scientist, each in his own way, make mental models of the world they intend to represent to others. So, too, with great investors or great managers, like Charlie Munger. John Akers, we could safely say, needed to apply more effort to the creation and use of mental models.

There are many examples of how models simplify the world without ignoring useful information. In the physical world, the science of data compression is focused precisely on this task. Data compression is an essential art in the computer and telecommunication industries. The mechanism for the compression is the removal of all nonessential data. What is nonessential information? Nonessential information is defined as all the information between two points that does not change—the white spaces on a page, for example. If all the white spaces—the areas where there is no information—are removed, while an accurate, but short, note is made of which white spaces were excised, where they began and where they terminated, one would have a shorter but accurate "model" of the page. In this way, the message is simplified without losing its exact character. This is essentially the way mental models work.

Virginia Woolf once said, "If there is one gift more essential to a novelist than another, it is the ability to develop single vision." The concept of "vision" is clearly a mental model of the future order of things. In business, visions are simplified representations of what the corporation stands for, where it is going, and which actions are acceptable and unacceptable. Members of the organization need to understand management's vision in order to assess whether their rewards are sufficient to justify their participation in it.

Of course, corporations have more than one mental model. There are, indeed, many mental models within a corporation. The mental model at a traditional manufacturing company, for example, may be built on the image of the company as a manufacturing process, with billing, receivables, and payables. A computer company may see itself as a network of interconnected nodes.

Whatever the specific representation, the mental models formed at the highest levels of the organization filter down to the divisional level. Lower-level models may be smaller versions of the corporation's larger mental model, or they may be different. But in either case, they must fit compatibly with the overarching model of the corporation if the corporation is to function smoothly.

THE POWER OF MENTAL MODELS

Craik would agree with Charlie Munger that mental models help investors and managers better understand the world, since they simplify an incomprehensibly complicated world. The need to simplify arises from our limited cognitive capacities. Our mental capacities, cognitive psychologists tell us, are quite limited compared to the complexities of life. We have limitations in our attention span, memory, recall, and information processing. The human mind's solution to the overwhelming complexity of today's world is to form mental models.

Johnson-Laird elaborated on the usefulness of this in his 1983 book *Mental Models*:

> *Mental models play a central and unifying role in representing objects, states of affairs, sequences of events, the way the world is, and the social and psychological actions of daily life. They enable individuals to make inferences and predictions, to understand phenomena, to decide what action to take and to control its execution, and above all, to experience events by proxy; they allow language to be used to create representations comparable to those deriving from direct acquaintance with the world; and they relate words to the world by way of conception and perception.*

Mental models are useful to the extent that they edit the world around us down to what we perceive as the essentials. "A tight analogy or model permits us to know more about the world with less work," notes Dean Keith Simonton, cognitive psychologist, historiographer, and noted researcher on the process of creativity at the University of California–Davis. As such, mental models can facilitate success or, if inaccurately shaped, bring failure. They help us determine how to take advantage of opportunities and how to hedge risks. They help us spot problems and work out solutions. Mental models and the rules of conduct generated from them—whether explicit or implicit—are at the core of most managers' reasoning processes.

Mental models aid managers in problem solving, as well, particularly the complex problems that corporate decision makers face. Without recourse to mental models, our cognitive systems would be too overloaded with data to function successfully. The great virtue of mental models is their ability to simplify complex situations and distribute decision making so that thousands of people in a company can make decisions day in and day out without having to coordinate each of them with everyone else in the organization. However, there is great risk as well, since inaccurate mental modeling can leverage a myriad of decisions.

Mental models also facilitate dialogue and discussion. They allow us to interpret the language and acts of others. Language is essential to the construction of mental models. As James March, a professor of political science and sociology at Stanford University, noted, "Language is used to create new meaning out of old, to make metaphorical leaps, to discover what a person might come to understand."

John Akers had a mental model of IBM, but it was wrong. Bill Gates, too, had a mental model, which was right for a while, until he recognized it had to be changed. George Soros, Warren Buffet, and Charlie Munger all had mental models that worked very well for a while and now are under stress. As Brian Arthur, a professor at the Santa Fe Institute and, in the eyes of many the "chief economist" of the New Economy, has noted, competition is competition within an "ecology of mental models."

THE LIMITS OF MENTAL MODELS

As useful as mental models are for a while, they clearly have a dark side, as John Akers discovered. When faced with discontinuous conditions, the mental factors that people generally favor, based on experience, expertise, knowledge, and learning, become liabilities. The very mental models that are at the heart of managerial strength are also at the heart of managerial weakness in an age of discontinuity. This is precisely the environment that has been increasingly prevalent in today's market, one that will become even more common in the future.

When accurate, of course, mental models can help predict the future, and offer a distinct competitive advantage. But as appealing as they are, managers must remain vigilant, because mental models can be fraught with uncertainty, ambiguity, and errors. Inaccurate mental models can propagate errors in judgment and system design, result in errors of action, and, finally, result in poor performance. Shifting mental models requires real work. Because so many of our mental models lie hidden beneath the fabric of corporate life, shifting course can be difficult.

There are four general problems associated with mental models and their use: First, they can be wrong because they are limited by the simplifications that made them useful. Second, they can be improperly used. Third, they can lead to wrong answers if fed by incorrect information. And fourth, their effectiveness is rarely assessed. We will cover each of these points in turn.

They Can Be Wrong

The effectiveness of mental models can be limited by the very simplifications that underlie them. Oversimplification can lead to systematic errors of judgment, logic, and forecasting. For example, an online marketer who assumes that consumers are going to continue to provide data about their habits, practices, and desires for free is making an assumption that could easily turn out to be incorrect. Already, some marketers are beginning to see that for relatively small fees they can circumvent major potential privacy liability.

Professor Kurt Gödel (1906–1978) of the Institute for Advanced Study at Princeton proved in the 1930s that no system can be both complete and consistent and that the errors inherent in mental models are inevitable. That is why those using mental models must be aware of their potential limitations and find ways to reduce the consequences of those limitations.

They Can Be Improperly Used

When the environment becomes truly complex, decision makers fail to respond appropriately by constructing new mental models. Instead they seem to revert to older, simpler models, as John Sterman suggested. Sterman observed that decision makers, for example, often forecast by averaging past values and extrapolating past trends rather than rethinking the forces at work in the industry and imaging how they might play out. Yet such complex relationships are increasingly common in the wired world of the Internet.

To the extent that mental models are inaccurate, they lead directly to risk (although it is often hidden risk, since the model does not alert the modeler to it). For example, in the last chapter we discussed the disastrous collapse of semiconductor returns in the early '80s. The surprise in this was that no one anticipated it, even though it was well known that the Japanese were building new semiconductor plants at a large enough scale to swamp the industry with chips and cause prices to collapse. This is exactly what happened. But the mental models American semiconductor companies used led them to believe that prices could not decline as much as they did. The collapse took several companies with it, including Mostek, one of the leading players at the time. Mostek completely missed the impending collapse—and paid for that flawed mental model with its corporate life.

Require Correct and Timely Information

Mental models are only as strong as the information they are based on. That information can be wrong, late, incomplete, distorted through emotion, ambiguous, or irrelevant, or it can be the result of inept measurement due to selection or other cognitive biases. Such imperfect information will inevitably misrepresent reality. If one does not have accurate and timely input, one will never get an accurate or timely output.

Require Assessment

The construction and use of mental models, as Piaget pointed out, is often a process generally hidden from view, rather than a managerial process that is open to debate and challenge. Yet, as we've seen, the fact that mental models exist does not mean they are correct.

Rarely are "quality control" processes used to check and test the validity of a mental model before it is put into use, or when it is in use to see if it is still accurate. Among the testing used to verify the effectiveness of other products, such as pharmaceuticals, are the use of "double-blind" procedures to ensure that the absence of negative effects is not confused with the confirmation of a positive effect; actively seeking contradictory evidence, rather than seeking only evidence that confirms effectiveness; and searching for and considering alternatives to help ensure that the best alternative is selected rather than simply selecting an alternative that works. Without such quality control, the modeling process is open to error. Yet rarely are any of these procedures used, or even considered.

The need for new mental models can be obscured by contradictory data and incremental fixes to existing models. Changes in context should trigger reexamination of one's mental model, but often they do not. Since the mental models decision makers use specify the information they require, decision makers frequently reject information that challenges the relevance of the model itself. As the context changes, there is a strong preference for a leader to retain the existing model—for example, as the case of John Akers's insistence on relying on "big iron."

Loyalty to a flawed model can be costly. If a mental model becomes outmoded—in the sense that it no longer provides an accurate simplification or rendering of reality—then any conclusions or predictions derived from it will be distorted as well. There is a reluctance on the part of managers to change models because there is no guarantee that the new models will be more effective than the ones they are replacing. Consequently, if the existing models seem to be working, managers are reluctant to abandon them. Moreover, the leaders who created the existing mental models often have a vested interest in protecting them. They are unlikely to abandon them unless a change in leadership of the organization ushers in a new, more appropriate mental model. Studies show that decision makers seek data that confirms existing mental models, rather than data that contradicts such models. There is a natural human bias toward confirmation.

James March offers a telling illustration of the difficulties in changing mental models in his report about the accidental discovery of the hole in the Antarctic ozone layer:

> *The NASA scientists' belief that low ozone readings must be erroneous (because they knew the ozone layer existed) led them to design a measurement system that made it impossible to detect low readings that might have invalidated their models. Fortunately, NASA had saved the original, unfiltered data and later confirmed that total ozone had indeed been falling since the launch of Nimbus 7. Because NASA created a measurement system immune to disconfirmation, the discovery of the ozone hole and the resulting global agreements to cease CFC production were delayed by as much as seven years.*

Richard Foster had a similar experience in 1987 in China, while visiting a preeminent hospital there. When he asked the head of the hospital's diagnostics lab about the incidence of AIDS in China, the hospital administrator replied, "We have no AIDS in China." Amazed, Foster pressed further. "In all your blood testing in China, you have never found a single case of AIDS?" he asked. "Oh, no," the administrator replied, "we know we don't have AIDS in China, so we don't test for it." As James March observed, "Experience is edited to remove contradictions."

Dean Keith Simonton offers a possible reason for this potentially dysfunctional cognitive behavior:

To give up one's intellectual framework willy-nilly simply to accommo-
date the confusion of random events is to risk expanding psychological
disorder, with a corresponding loss in behavioral adaptiveness.

The ability to dismiss disconfirming data is an ancient art. One way
that people do it is through "issue avoidance," by simply avoiding threatening or negative data. Chris Argyris, the James Bryant Conant Professor
of Education and Organizational Behavior at Harvard, calls this form of
avoidance a "defensive routine." Defensive routines may result in avoiding
alternatives, or denial. "You're wrong. We *are* innovating, changing, and
keeping up with the markets, perhaps now more than ever," an executive
might argue when, in fact, all the innovation is incremental.

In a more contemporary example, when former McDonald's chairman
Mike Quinlan was asked by *Business Week* whether, in view of McDonald's
flagging performance, they needed to change their approach, Quinlan
replied, "Do we have to change? No, we don't have to change. We have the
most successful brand in the world." His admission was apparently so
starkly wrongheaded in the eyes of the company's board that they fired
Quinlan and found a new CEO.

The evidence is overwhelming that mental models, built to assist in decision making, once constructed often become the single most important
barrier to change. We believe this problem will become increasingly pervasive as discontinuous shifts occur in industry after industry. The move
to the Internet is just the first in a long series of what are likely to be confusing changes in context that will face most business leaders.

In this era of rapid change and increasing complexity, mental models
represent a tool of tremendous promise—but also of tremendous risk. *To*
the extent they are built on the assumption of continuity, they are more of a
liability to the user than a benefit. We cannot avoid using mental models,
however. It is the way we are wired. Our only choice lies in deciding which
one to use, and how to use it. This means recognizing the need to change
mental models, and finding a way to change them that is less costly than
holding on to mental models that do not work. The executives at Mostek
could compellingly discuss the costs of remaining with an inaccurate mental model.

CREATING AND CHANGING
MENTAL MODELS

Piaget's research showed that we unconsciously create mental models from our earliest days. As we age we learn, from both formal and informal processes. Learning is one way of characterizing the process of changing mental models. "The most powerful learning comes from direct experience," says Peter Senge, author of *The Fifth Discipline*. We use our experience to change our mental models.

Jay Forrester, well-known inventor of magnetic-core memory storage, a precursor to today's RAM technology, and father of "system dynamics," a systematic method of modeling complex structures, commented in 1971 on the simplicity of the mechanisms for changing our mental models:

> *A mental model changes with time and even during the flow of a single conversation. The human mind assembles a few relationships to fit the context of a discussion. As the subject shifts so does the model. Each participant in a conversation employs a different mental model to interpret the subject. Fundamental assumptions differ but are never brought into the open.*

James March agrees. Mental models are often changed through the extended and informal process of corporate dialogue. This happens through "myths, symbols, rituals, and stories. They are the ligaments of social life, establishing links among individuals and groups across generations and geographic distances." March says elsewhere: "They give context for understanding history and for locating oneself in it."

During the dialogue process, mental models are adjusted to reflect local context. These adjustments are then fed back into the mental models of top management. In this way, the mental models change. As March noted about "visions"—mental models in the process of formation "cannot be established in an organization by edict, or by the exercise of power or coercion. It is more an act of persuasion, of creating an enthusiastic and dedicated commitment . . . because it is right for the times, right for the organization, and right for the people who are working in it. By focusing attention on a vision [mental model], the leader operates on the emotional and spiritual resources of the organization, on its values, commitment, and aspirations."

Sterman also attests to the power of informal processes to change mental models:

Active modeling occurs well before sensory information reaches the areas of the brain responsible for conscious thought. Powerful evolutionary pressures are responsible: our survival depends so completely on the ability to rapidly interpret reality that we long ago evolved structures to build these models automatically.

Forrester's, March's, and Sterman's comments on the importance of conversation as a tool for aligning different mental models offer an important insight into how corporations can change mental models in a visible way, which we will explore in more detail in Chapter 11.

But more than conversation and dialogue is required to change a company's mental models. "The constructive process is guided by contextual cues and implicit inferences based on general knowledge," says Johnson-Laird. Contextual clues provide the puzzle edges that let us know where we are going—but only if we can interpret them (i.e., the context) correctly. Often the culture of the organization sets the context. Language, visual imagery, beliefs and behavior are the primary carriers of the culture and thus set the context.

Johnson & Johnson's response to the Tylenol crisis in the mid-'80s provides an example of the power of context for establishing new mental models, in this case a mental model of the right approach for dealing with the crisis. The crisis presented a complex problem for J&J because the causes were not clear, the consequences of not dealing with it were enormous (seven people in the Chicago area died after taking the pills), and the cost of stopping and fixing the problem was very large—large enough to jeopardize the market value of the corporation.

But one of the beliefs underlying Johnson & Johnson is its Credo, crafted by Robert Wood Johnson, which is still used as a guide to decision making and behavior today. The Credo establishes the hierarchy of values at J&J: mothers first, employees second, community third, and investors fourth (the assumption is that if the first three are done well, the fourth will follow). The clarity of the Credo, and the dedication of the management and staff of J&J to the Credo, allowed Jim Burke to easily and rapidly decide what to do and how to act. His immediate decision was to recall Tylenol from drugstore shelves across the nation when there was a threat that the widely used pills were tainted. The incident cost J&J a reported $100 million that year, but the decision was made in hours when the threat to consumers became clear. In other corporations, recalls are not handled as quickly, and perhaps not as effectively, as they are at J&J because they do not have J&J's Credo. The Credo is a key element of J&J's culture, which plays a strong role in establishing the company's mental models when it faces a new situation, or in deciding when old ones are in need of repair.

Rarely do companies say they are "setting out to build a new mental model." But they do say they will "develop a strategy to capitalize on the new opportunities in electronic commerce," or that they will "reexamine the principles on which our organizational structure is based to compete more effectively in the future." These are examples of statements of intent to create new mental models. Once built, mental models are enormously powerful in determining how the corporation responds to opportunities and challenges.

HOW MENTAL MODELS AFFECT CORPORATE BEHAVIOR

Mental models have an impact on four primary areas of conventional "corporate architecture": information systems, decision-making processes, executional capabilities, and control systems.

INFORMATION SYSTEMS

The amount, type, quality, form, and frequency of data are effectively determined by senior management's mental model, whether that model is explicit or implicit. For example, many corporations believe that their performance is more dependent on sales margins than on capital employed. In these companies, the monthly profit-and-loss statements therefore capture information on sales and cost of goods sold (so that margins can be calculated), but do not reflect the capital employed in the business at all, despite the fact that investors are very much concerned with how much capital a corporation will need in the future.

DECISION-MAKING PROCESSES

The major decision-making processes of the corporation—planning systems, calendar management, agenda setting, decision criteria, and all the rest—are designed to be compatible with the mental models of the corporation. Needless to say, these decision-making systems are fed by, and therefore have to be compatible with, the information systems of the corporation. If the corporation feels that it is driven by the product-development cycle, as semiconductor manufacturers like Intel and Texas Instruments are, then this cycle drives the key decision-making processes (e.g., the decision to start the design of a new chip, or the decision to begin considering construction of a new plant, or the decision to switch suppliers for the next product offering), the executive calendar, the agendas of the major management meetings, and the strategic planning process. For a consumer retailer like Saks Fifth Avenue or the Gap, the calendar is driven by the major seasonal merchandising decisions, as well as very close monitoring—often day by day—of store sales to determine when a holiday sale (that is, selling their merchandising at lower prices to reduce inventories of already purchased products) should be started, stopped, or have its terms changed.

EXECUTIONAL CAPABILITY

Third, the mental model must be compatible with the executional capability of the organization. The human resources processes, staffing, evaluation procedures, and so on are determined within the context of the mental models of the corporation. For chemical companies like DuPont, international experience may be seen as key, since they see themselves very much as global players; indirect experience of, say, the business practices in China will not be sufficient. Direct line experience is preferred. For airline companies such as AMR, the parent of American Airlines, customer experience may be considered key, and those who have had frontline experience are seen as the most valuable.

CONTROL PROCESSES

Last, the control processes—whether they be the operational control processes, the compensation systems, or the capital allocation processes of the corporation—all are determined by the mental models of the corporation. A company that has slim margins, such as an electric utility like Con Edison, will value those people most who know how to control costs on a day-to-day basis. A pharmaceutical company like Merck, Pfizer or Johnson & Johnson, which values the transformational innovation required for the discovery of new drugs, will not look at cost control as the most important control process, but will focus much more on finding the right scientists and giving them the freedom of time and resources necessary to maximize the chances that they will discover the new chemical entities that will be the key to more effective treatment of disease.

These four elements, as well as the mental models that determine how they interact, constitute what we call the architecture of the corporation. We call this corporate architecture "MIDAS"—Models, Information, Decisions, Actions, and Systems of Control—to make it easier to remember. The elements of the corporate architecture change as the corporation matures and the mental models change. And it is the evolution of corporate architecture—with the mental models steering the direction—that determines the competitiveness of the corporation. Thus the process of building mental models—whether these processes are explicit and examined or implicit and unexamined—is the core managerial process of the corporation.

THE NATURAL EVOLUTION OF CORPORATE ARCHITECTURE

As companies grow and mature, the five core elements of the corporate architecture, or MIDAS, and the relationships between those elements evolve in response to changing resources (including talent), competitive pressures, the culture of the organization, and prospects for the future.

We believe it is the nature of the evolution of the corporate architecture that accounts for the declining innovativeness of the typical corporation, leaving it more vulnerable to attack from smaller companies. Unlike older companies, newer companies, steered by different mental models, use different information sets, decision-making approaches, and systems of measurement and control. When those mental models are more accurate than older models, newer companies gain a huge competitive advantage.

Consider Transecure and General Motors, to take two extreme examples. Transecure is a very small Internet start-up focused initially on the resolution of legal conflicts that arise on the internet. Transecure has experienced some early success and is rapidly building its business. Its mental model has evolved several times since Steve Abernethy and Ahmed Khaishgi founded the company in mid-1999. Early on in the process of starting the company, it was called WebLaw. WebLaw intended to offer legal services over the Web. As time went on, this notion was transformed into the present focus on dispute resolution, and the name was changed to Transecure. Having clarified its focus, at least for a time, it began to market the concept to other Internet companies that could build an inventory of disputes to resolve. There was no information system in place other than a list of people Abernethy and Khaishgi knew—or could get to know at Internet portals and auction sites. Decision-making systems were simple and aimed at getting the right people on their board to establish credibility and to find initial customers. The control processes were put into place by angel investors, who put up the initial funds to allow Abernethy and Khaishgi to eat while building Transecure. Most of this control stems from the right of investors to take over Transecure if things do not go as they should. There are very few other control systems in place: There are no "strategic planning" systems, although there are frequent meetings to determine where to go next. There are no elaborate employee evaluation and feedback systems. That is more or less done on the fly—but with care. Abernethy and Khaishgi were fueled by the pure passion to create something new; to change the world for the better with something they themselves had built. They were willing to risk everything to make it happen, and they were highly energized by the challenge and the risks involved. Transecure is not based on the assumption of continuity—quite the opposite. Transecure is based on the assumption of discontinuity. Abernethy and Khaishgi intend to create discontinuity, and they are comfortable with the assumption that Transecure itself will undergo several discontinuous transformations in its own development.

Contrast this architecture with that of a large established company, like General Motors. General Motors is clear about what it intends to do— and has been doing it for a long time. The key elements of its mental models were established by Alfred Sloan in the '20s. To make decisions and communicate among its thousands of employees around the world, and among its many different kinds of transportation businesses, it has well-developed information systems based on huge investments in computers and communications. GM's decision-making systems have been honed for decades; many are now routine. Planning and control processes, including human resource processes, have been in place for decades, and are well fed by the information systems, which are tailored to the needs of these decision-making and control systems. Major investments have been made in enterprise resource management systems (ERPs) to help evolve the control systems in the most cost-effective way, and to integrate them as seamlessly as possible into the purchasing and supply chain systems, as well as the marketing and sales departments. It would be hard to say that General Motors is fueled by passion. The senior management group is a very experienced and competitively oriented group dedicated to doing the best they can for General Motors, its customers, its employees, and its investors. But passion is not the hallmark of that system.

At one time General Motors was the size of Transecure, and it probably was ruled by passion then; but that was long ago. The architecture of General Motors today has as little similarity with the architecture of Transecure as it does with its own original architecture. The architecture of General Motors has changed over time—often with great purpose and forethought, but sometimes with consequences that were difficult to see in advance, including the emergence of the assumption of continuity, and the narrowing of the range of possible decisions, at least at the intermediate levels of the corporation.

The comparison between Transecure and General Motors illustrates the differences between the early architecture and the mature architecture of corporations. It is the assumption of continuity, when discontinuity rules the marketplace, that shapes the mental models of long-term corporations, and these mental models affect the rate of adaptation of the corporate architecture. It was the inadvertent—and unmanaged—evolution of IBM's corporate architecture that resulted in John Akers's difficulties. Akers was not able to see the need to transform his mental model of the computer hardware business; he was more comfortable operating with the model that had brought him and his colleagues success within IBM. With this understanding, there was no need to change information systems (say, to more closely track the progress of smaller competitors that were selling different products to IBM's clients, products that these customers in some cases liked very much), decision-making systems, implementation approaches, or control systems. In fact, there was no need, in Akers's mind, to change much other than the effectiveness of the sales force. They should just get out and sell more, and the "problem" (i.e., the enormous earnings decline) would be solved.

It was the wrong analysis, and it led to the wrong answer. It also led to Akers's removal. While Akers's model was based on the assumption of continuity, the industry was going through one of the most significant discontinuities in its history. It was a discontinuity that was effectively hidden from the view of IBM's management committee at the time, as incredible as it seems. They could not see it because their mental models would not allow them to accept the validity of the information they were receiving. Defensive routines had silently crept into the corporation, unannounced and unnoticed.

Unmanaged, the evolution of the corporate architecture proceeds in a predictable way, which inevitably leads to cultural lock-in—a state in which the corporation is effectively frozen in place by three fears: the fear of cannibalization of the existing product line, the fear of moving into businesses that will conflict with its customers', and the fear of acquiring companies that will result in the short-term dilution of the company's earnings and therefore a potential decline in stock price. Unable to act in the face of these three fears, the corporation sets the context for its own underperformance, just as IBM was doing until its board of directors acted by replacing John Akers with Lou Gerstner. There are four key stages in the evolution of an industry. We present a light sketch of each to give the reader some sense of how cultural lock-in occurs within intelligent, thoughtful corporations despite the best efforts of managers.

STAGE 1—FOUNDATION (ATTACK)

In any new industry, many new companies are drawn to capitalize on the opportunities. We saw in Chapter 2 how this had routinely happened in computer hardware, computer software, medical products, and several other industries. Many of these companies are very much like Transecure, created and led by a few people in their twenties or thirties who are fueled by their passion to change the world. They are willing to work all day and all night. Their mental models are still fluid. Decision making is ad hoc, or at best, guided by the structure imposed by investors and board members. As Robert Simons says,

In the start-up phase, there is little demand for formal control systems. Because employees are in constant face-to-face communication with each other, it is possible to control key aspects of the business without formal reporting structures. Internal accounting controls to ensure that assets are secure and accounting information is reliable are the only formal control systems needed.

During this phase, success either happens or it does not. There is little reflection about why. The day-to-day work is all-consuming.

Outsiders might consider these companies creative, but, in fact, the creative stage, the stage where the idea is first laid out, is largely finished. Abernethy and Khaishgi did not formulate the original idea for WebLaw when they were at Transecure. In fact, they developed it while they were at McKinsey working as hard as they could for their clients during the day, and at night working as hard as they could to figure out how to start WebLaw. This is often the way it is, whether the new entrepreneurs are at McKinsey, a university, or another corporation. The creative ideas are often revealed during the off hours of the day. Once the business starts, there is little time left for anything other than making it work.

At this stage, many of the competitors in the sector are not able to survive. Frequently they are purchased by other larger companies in their field. Some go bankrupt. A few, however, survive, and advance to the next stage.

STAGE 2—GROWTH

The second stage in the evolution of a new industry is characterized by rapid growth. Frequently this is at the lower knee of the S-curve, as we explained in Chapter 2. Many Internet companies are in this stage now, as are a number of biotech companies. Having passed the first test of survival, with a few hundred people to manage (which is a typical number at this stage), some of these companies begin to reflect on the causes of their success. Often, they will attribute their success to their "unique" blend of market insight, technological strength, and managerial methods and culture. In fact, their success may have been due to good fortune rather than good management, although it can be difficult to sort out. They believe they have done well— that is, grown from a few people to several hundred people—because of their intelligence and the actions they have taken, the quality of the people they have hired, and the managerial systems they have built.

In this stage the company tends to operate in many locations and in multiple markets. Formal training systems have been implemented in an effort to make sure that new employees are told about the corporate culture, why it is successful, and how it works, regardless of where they work or whom they work for. Mission statements are created and distributed. Managers have been told that certain activities are taboo. Decision making is increasingly delegated to lower levels. Measurable goals are established. Diagnostic control systems are implemented to meet the information and control needs of senior managers. Performance incentives are tied to the achievement of measurable targets. Once in place, these formal systems and additions to the invisible corporate architecture become difficult to change. The original passion has given way to the superiority of rational decision making. There wasn't time for it in Stage 1; there was too much to do.

The growth prospects of such companies are typically as strong as, or stronger than, ever. There are many opportunities to pursue extensions of their existing strategy, and these still make money and do not require changes in the skill base. Management is aware that the markets and competition are constantly changing, so they look outside for evidence of competitive threats to determine the need to do something more radical, but often they don't find anyone doing "just what we are doing." There is no crisis looming. The present course can be stayed without risk, although today companies in this stage are perhaps more sober about their success and prospects than they were a year ago.

At the end of Stage 2, a few more of these companies are acquired by competitors, although often at a premium price. In communications, for example, Cisco is a likely acquirer today, as is Lucent. Despite the premium they have to pay, they see these companies as attractive complements to their current product lines, and a valuable resource for the future.

STAGE 3—DOMINATE

Those companies that survive to Stage 3 have come of age. A few have risen to dominate their industries and become models of managerial acumen. They have scale, resources, talent, and insight. It seems as if they will last for a long time. Ariba, Commerce One, Broadcom, and others are examples of such companies today. They have become the "excellent" companies that reporters, academics, consultants, and executives drop by to see. When asked how they did it, they often respond with details about their corporate architecture—the systems, their information, their ability to execute, and their control processes.

The frequent implicit objective at this stage is to refine and extend their successful system of management, often by acquiring other companies and indoctrinating them into the parent's successful culture. Everything and everyone runs like clockwork. Robert Simons describes this stage as follows:

> *In mature firms, senior managers learn to rely on the opportunity seeking behavior of subordinates for innovation and new strategic initiatives. At this stage, they begin to use selected control systems interactively. Belief systems, strategic boundaries, diagnostic control systems, and interactive control systems now work together to control the formation and implementation of strategy. Finally, businesses' conduct boundaries are imposed any time that a crisis demonstrates the costs of errant employee actions.*

The company has become a real machine. There is little surprise—as long as continuity prevails.

But surprise is often lurking at this stage, out of view of the newly large and successful company. Stage 3 companies often have difficulty identifying threatening Stage 1 companies because these companies exist on the periphery of an industry and often look different than what Stage 3 companies are used to. Perhaps they base their oblique attack on insights from a dissatisfied group of customers, or a potentially risky or potent new technology, or just on the slow reaction speed of the Stage 3 company. If a credible attack forms, it will be aimed precisely at the weakest spots of the current market leaders. Nothing else will have a chance of success, due to the scale and market power of the leaders. It is generally virtually impossible to predict which of the would-be attackers will be successful, but it is easier to assess whether the attack itself will be successful. The outcome is a matter of economics and timing, and more attacks fail than succeed. Nevertheless, some do succeed, and these reach prominence in the market outside the vision of the successful Stage 3 company. These attackers are the carriers of discontinuity.

Amazon.com is an example of the impact a Stage 1 company can have on a mature company, in this case Barnes & Noble. How could Amazon, a start-up company with few resources, compete with established super-store chain Barnes & Noble? As everyone knows, Amazon had a new idea—that literate people would be great users of the Internet, and that they would buy more books that way than in the store. Amazon took this simple idea and executed it well. Within two years, people were asking, "How can Barnes & Noble compete with Amazon?"

Barnes & Noble didn't take Amazon seriously at first because it was so locked into the assumption of continuity (as well as the traditional myths about advantages of scale, market power, consumer knowledge, and financial resources). It could not imagine that discontinuity could so rapidly alter the bookstore landscape. Barnes & Noble has since gotten the message, but it allowed Amazon to gain an enormous online advantage because it was so focused on the assumption of continuity.

Not surprisingly, many new companies fail. Most end up being bought by another company, or end up in bankruptcy court. The markets are simply not big enough to hold all the companies that want to capitalize on the opportunity they see. Unsuccessful competitors either entered the market too early or too late, or could not implement their ideas successfully, or didn't offer enough of a competitive advantage over existing companies. A few new companies survive, however. The handful of new entrants that survive will have found some weakness to exploit in the existing order. The market will reward them by boosting their stock at every surprising advance.

Finally, there comes a time when a younger attacker goes for the jugular. It has gained the upper hand. The attack almost always comes as a "surprise" to the incumbent. Was Time Warner prepared to be acquired by AOL in 2000? Was IBM prepared for the strength of Ariba and Commerce One—or, earlier, the strength of the younger Microsoft Corporation?

STAGE 4—CULTURAL LOCK-IN: THE EMERGENCE OF THE THREE FEARS

In this final stage, the formerly dominant company finds itself in a fight for its very survival. Often, the only real defense a company has at this point is to cut prices. There are many ways to do this that do not appear to be price cutting, such as increasing the value of the product offered. But in the end, most companies resort to price cutting. If the prices can be cut far enough, and fast enough, the attack may be postponed, at least for a while. But the problem is unlikely to end there. One or two attackers may be turned back, but new competitors will continue to come if they perceive a business opportunity. Eventually one will break through.

In such fights, emotions sway both combatants. The attacker will use passion, conviction, and other "hot" emotions. Incumbents often slip into dark denial, first denying that the attack is imminent, then that it is under way or that it is having a significant impact. The battle constitutes an assault on the mental models of the corporation, the foundation beliefs upon which decision making is based. Just as the human mind recoils, first in denial and then in anger, from the suggestion that its assumptions are wrong, so, too, does the corporation.

Psychologist Elisabeth Kübler-Ross has discovered that the human mind shuffles through five distinct phases as it deals with trauma and other negative information: denial, anger, bargaining, depression, and, finally, acceptance. Each stage is interwoven with bouts of hope, followed by despair. These are normal and natural progressions in corporations as well as individuals, as the mind attempts to shield itself. But each step in this natural process slows or blocks incoming information. Accordingly, the need to change mental models is blocked, and disaster is courted; defensive routines appear. At IBM in 1989, for instance, John Akers boldly announced: "I don't think there were fundamental changes in the market conditions."

In 1991, as everything came crashing down around him, Akers angrily sent out what he thought was an internal memo denouncing the sales force—which immediately found its way to *The New York Times*: "Everyone is too damned complacent, and it makes me goddamned mad."

Where you see anger among top management, look for the signs of denial.

As psychologist Priscilla Vail notes, in discussing how children learn,

We know from common sense, experience, and now neuro-psychological research that positive emotional stances enhance a child's capacity for learning, just as negative ones—some of which become habitual—deplete intellectual energies.

The same is true of corporations.

The cycle of denial and disconfirmation in a corporation manifests itself in the fear of cannibalization, the fear of customer conflict, and the fear of dilution.

CANNIBALIZATION

In the business world, cannibalization is the act of introducing products or services that compete with the company's existing product line, as Richard Foster explained in *Innovation: The Attacker's Advantage* and as Clayton Christensen elaborated on in *The Innovator's Dilemma*. When companies decline to cannibalize their own products, they are operating under the delusion that if they don't introduce the new product, no one else will either. Thus, they reason, prices will remain firm, and profits will be protected. Companies further support this rationale by pointing to their strong market share, and the high costs that consumers would suffer if they switched to a competing product.

The fallacy in this thinking is that new competitors *do* enter markets (unless a company has a monopoly, which is rare). Furthermore, the value of the incumbent's market share is actually minimal, since the new product, if it is a serious contender, by definition offers substantial new benefits. Customers, taking the long view, may decide to switch to the new product, despite the near-term costs of switching.

The decision not to cannibalize, then, can lead to a loss of share and deteriorating performance. In some cases it can lead to permanent market losses. IBM's decade-long inattention to the software market is a case in point. Had Lou Gerstner not taken over as chairman, IBM might not have survived.

COMPETING WITH YOUR CUSTOMERS

The second fear, competing with your customer, can be as fatal as the failure to cannibalize. Companies resist doing anything to jeopardize their relationships with customers, particularly when the company has a small number of important customers. Unfortunately, the customers realize this, and use that leverage to keep the company from expanding its distribution channels.

As with cannibalization, the error is in assuming that a new set of companies will not emerge to compete for a share of the market, skipping wholesale channels and selling directly to end customers. Dell, for example, does not deal with Wal-Mart. They went directly to the customer. Other companies, such as Compaq, could have gone the same route, but they were afraid of alienating their existing customers. This was the market opening that Dell charged into with such astounding success. Cisco, the supplier of routers and hubs, has shown the same courage in its distribution system, but not without some conflicts. The Internet and e-commerce have accelerated this trend. (CEO John Chambers cemented customer loyalty by introducing the Internet as a direct distribution channel.) Cisco's dedication to customer satisfaction subsequently has been exemplified by this use of the Internet to lower customer costs through efficient transactions and provide comprehensive customer support. This decision ultimately resulted in huge savings ($535 million in 1998) and deepened relationships with customers. Shipments were accurate and on time 98% of the time, and 60% to 80% of questions were handled online. In 1998, Cisco reported dramatic on-line growth: almost 1 million log-ins per month, with a 25% increase in customer satisfaction.

EARNINGS DILUTION

The third fear is the fear of dilution. The fear of dilution makes it very difficult, if not impossible, for incumbents to purchase companies on the periphery—those that are pursuing a potentially superior business strategy, or that have access to unique talent or other assets. The argument (based on traditional financial analysis) is that if one dilutes one's earnings per share, the market will simply apply the same multiple to the new combined company that it used before the acquisition. Stock prices will decline and value will be destroyed.

Today, dilution is the argument many incumbents use to explain why they have not acquired Internet start-ups. Unfortunately, this argument also blocks them from entering vigorous new markets. In the end, it could destroy more value than what is risked in the acquisition. Moreover, this analysis assumes that the market cannot be convinced that the acquisition will improve the long-term prospects of the incumbent. Dilution analysis also assumes that the growth of the acquired company will not more than offset the dilutive effect of the purchase in a reasonable period of time. In the early days of biotech, most of the major pharmaceutical companies could have bought Amgen but did not, for fear of dilution. Now Amgen earns more per quarter than the entire acquisition price would have been a decade ago (regardless of the multiple at the time). Clearly, conventional economic thinking led to the wrong conclusions. The right way to look at this problem is to develop a point of view on what the future value of the company will be, as we showed in Chapter 2, and then decide if it is worth it to pay that price.

• • •

These three fears of corporations—which amount to the fear of making contrarian strategic decisions—determine whether or not a corporation has the courage to position itself well for the future. The market, we have seen, has no fear. The market will cannibalize; it will compete with customers, and it will encourage the growth of high-multiple companies. The market does not suffer from denial. *To achieve the success of the market, corporations have to change their mental models at the pace and scale of the market. They will have to overcome the disconfirmation biases and the defensive routines that sustain it.* Unless the corporation can learn to overcome the natural bias for denial, it will, in the long term, fail, or at best underperform. Such fears culturally lock corporations into inaction. Survival may be assured, but so is a company's underperformance. The assumption of continuity hurts or inhibits a corporation's future. In the fifteenth century, Machievelli advised leaders to ignore discontinuities:

> *When a problem arises either from within a republic or outside it, one brought about either by internal or external reasons, one that has become so great that it begins to make everyone afraid, the safest policy is to delay dealing with it rather than to do away with it, because those who try to do away with it almost always increase its strength and accelerate the harm which they feared might come from it.*

Such advice may have worked in fifteenth century Italy, but it will not work in the twenty-first century global economy. The solution, today, is to recognize and embrace the prospect of discontinuity.

THE MIND OF THE CORPORATION; THE MIND OF THE MARKET

We began this chapter with a story about IBM and the difficulties John Akers faced. The question that we raised was Why do the indices of the capital markets over the long run outperform all but a handful of even the best individual companies—despite the fact that markets have no intelligent executive committees, boards of directors, CEOs or CFOs to lead them? The capital markets are not "managed" in the conventional sense of the word. They are merely "administered." Moreover, the markets have no performance objectives. No one at the SEC is "controlling" the total return to shareholders of the New York Stock Exchange. We administer markets, we don't manage them. Attempts at the opposite approach have failed, as any Russian can attest.

The question, then, is Why should an unmanaged system achieve a level of long-term performance that is matched only by a few companies in the managed system? Why does a system lacking a centralized cognitive superstructure consistently prevail over a system richly equipped with one?

The answer, as we outlined in Chapter 1, is that the capital markets are naturally more robust and adaptable than our corporations. Adam Smith noted in *The Wealth of Nations:*

> *Every individual is continually exerting himself to find out the most advantageous employment for whatever capital he can command . . . [and] is led by an invisible hand to promote an end which was no part of his intention.*

Smith's invocation of the invisible hand was the first attempt to explain the superior performance of the unmanaged system against a conscientiously managed one. The much-sought-for "sustainable competitive advantage" is an unattainable ideal. It does not exist. It is continually and inexorably carved away by the relentless winds and tides of the capital markets. Many managers and executives have a deep, presumptive belief in the success of rational thinking. It is a belief psychologists are increasingly challenging.

Markets effectively "reason" through social process; corporations use "rules of inference." Daniel Kahneman, a psychologist at Princeton, and Amos Tversky, a psychologist at Stanford until his death in 1996, who had extensively studied the psychology of decision making, questioned the assumption that "only rational behavior can survive in a competitive environment, and the fear that any treatment that abandons rationality will be chaotic and intractable." The effectiveness of orderliness in a discontinuous world must be questioned.

One would not say that the markets are necessarily orderly, although the rules they live by are orderly and rational. The rules of the market do not prevent discontinuity; rather, they encourage it. Our inadvertent reliance on stable, often invisible, mental models may have worked in previous decades, when the future was more or less like the past. But it does not work today, with the markets' current rate of change, nor will it work in the future, as the rate of change continues to accelerate, in line with long-term historical trends.

The fact is that capital markets embrace creative destruction more effectively than corporations do. Moreover, markets engage in creative destruction at a greater pace than ever before. Operational excellence will continue to be essential for competitiveness. But it simply will not be enough. The assumption of continuity and its intimate link to operational excellence must give way to the more complex assumption of discontinuity and its intimate link with creative destruction. That is the challenge to management in the coming decades.

In the following chapters, we will lay out the nature of these changes and describe what is required for the corporation to act more like the market.

CHAPTER 4

Operating vs. Creating: The Case of Storage Technology Corporation

The data storage company Storage Technology was founded in 1969 by four IBM engineers who believed they could build disk and tape drive systems for IBM computers at a lower price than their former employer did. Storage Technology was one of the first companies to spin off from IBM with the explicit idea of challenging IBM. After reporting its first profit in 1972, Storage Technology grew dramatically, exceeding $1 billion per year in sales in 1982.

Jesse Aweida, founder of Storage Technology and CEO until 1984, was convinced that a high level of operational management and "just enough" innovation would keep the company ahead of IBM. Transformational innovation, he decided, was not necessary. "To compete with IBM," Aweida said, "a small company has to focus down and concentrate on a very narrow market, such as tape drives. In that market, you have to commit to technological innovation."

Aweida implemented this strategy by investing in highly focused R&D

that minimized manufacturing costs and yet enabled Storage Technology to match new IBM products within six months of their arrival in the market. This became the company's strategy for accommodating operational effectiveness *and* innovation. Aweida knew that he could not take on IBM directly, so he limited innovations to a specialized area, attempting to keep the company ahead through manufacturing cost reductions. Aweida's objective was to operate and manage the process of creative destruction in parallel. Implicitly, he was attempting to overcome the assumption of continuity.

Initially, Aweida's strategy worked. Throughout the 1970s, it sold its products at a 15% discount to IBM's products. Storage Technology's market share rose, and it won a reputation for providing components of equal or better quality than IBM's. Sales surged at well above industry average growth rates.

The stock market responded to Storage Technology's success, giving the company a high multiple and rewarding its long-term shareholders with higher returns than were being earned in the computer industry in general (which itself was above the capital markets averages).

Innovation played its part in the company's success. Storage Technology's first tape drive not only matched IBM's newest release but even surpassed it, since it could read tapes of an earlier IBM format (a feature the new IBM devices did not offer). Moreover, when IBM developed disk drives with nonremovable disks in the 1970s (called hard drives

Storage Technology 1972–1981
Sales Growth vs. Industry

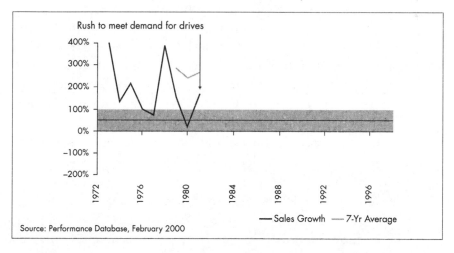

Source: Performance Database, February 2000

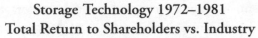

Storage Technology 1972–1981
Total Return to Shareholders vs. Industry

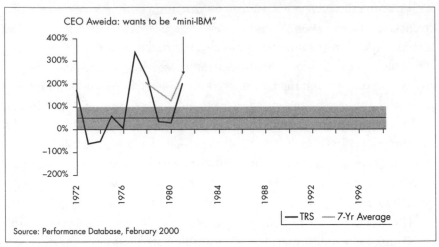

Source: Performance Database, February 2000

today), customers were no longer able to create data backups simply by inserting a second disk. This was manna for Storage Technology, which had been looking for a way to expand into disk drives. By 1981, Storage Technology had made the transition from a Stage 1 company to a Stage 2 company. It was an early survivor, and the shareholders were greatly rewarded for it.

As Storage Technology continued to grow, however, the delicate balance between operational excellence and innovation began to destabilize. Seeking more growth, Aweida shifted his vision for the company. His new goal was to make Storage Technology a "mini-IBM."

The first step of this journey was to expand Storage Technology's original narrow vision (focused on dominating hard drives) to a grander vision to compete with IBM in mainframes. Discovering that it would be difficult to match IBM with only its own research, Storage Technology pursued the acquisitions of Amdahl Corporation (headed by former IBM chief engineer Eugene Amdahl) and Magnuson Computer—small companies trying to produce IBM-compatible mainframes and minicomputers. Ultimately, Storage Technology spent $120 million in collaboration with limited partners to develop its own mainframe. Aweida's second step was to spend heavily on the development of optical storage drives. Storage Technology believed that optical storage drives would leave magnetic media in the dust. The vision was pure creative destruction. But in trying to develop optical storage drives, operations at Storage Technology had taken second place. The balance was about to become unbalanced.

Because IBM experienced delays in its new 3380 line of disk drives and had none to sell, Storage Technology had an opportunity to sell all the drives it could produce. But Storage Technology tripped on its own operational shoelaces. "We said to ourselves, 'Boy, here is an opportunity to really double up the market,' so we tripled production. That was a big mistake," Aweida later reflected.

In order to triple production, Storage Technology accepted component parts from suppliers that did not meet specs. Within a year, 10% of the drives the company produced were faulty. Storage Technology's excellent reputation was tarnished. With Storage Technology preoccupied in fixing its operations fiasco, IBM finally introduced its new drives, recapturing the market and leaving Storage Technology with a suspect reputation and excess capacity. IBM had out-operated and out-innovated Storage Technology.

With Storage Technology reeling, IBM decided to compete with the company on price. Initially, IBM had resisted reducing its margins because it was being challenged in court by the Justice Department. But in 1982, after the Justice Department dropped its decade-old charges against IBM, IBM cut the price of its latest disk drive by 15%.

The repercussions were felt in 1983, when Storage Technology's disk drive sales fell by $200 million, leading to a $40 million loss. Storage Technology reacted in early 1984 by canceling plans to produce its mainframe and by beginning to cut costs; nonetheless, by October 1984, Storage Technology had announced that it would report a quarterly loss of over $20 million. The loss violated loan agreements that the company had made with ten banks for a $125 million credit line. In a last-ditch effort to avoid bankruptcy, Storage Technology announced the layoff of 10% of its workforce and a 10% pay cut for management.

On October 31, 1984, Storage Technology filed for Chapter 11 bankruptcy. By this time, the estimated quarterly loss had tripled to $60 million. Compounding its troubles, Storage Technology's 70% market share in the tape drive business was eroding rapidly, as customers began to fear Storage Technology's demise. After failing to obtain an additional line of credit to continue operations, CEO Jesse Aweida resigned. The balance between creative destruction and operational excellence had completely collapsed. Stage 3 proved to be much more difficult than Stage 2. As Aweida said later, "Maybe that [growth in sales in the late '70s] made us a little cocky." Aweida discovered that the balance between operational excellence and substantial innovation is not easy to maintain.

By January of 1985, the board had found a successor to Aweida, former IBM engineer Ryal R. Poppa, who stepped down as CEO of BMC Industries in Minneapolis to take over running Storage Technology. Poppa had made his name as a turnaround guru by tripling sales at BMC during his three years there. His goals for Storage Technology were less visionary than they were driven by the bottom line: "I want to bring the same profitability to Storage Technology creditors and shareholders that Lee [Iacocca] brought to Chrysler."

Poppa flew around the country to convince customers that the company would cut costs dramatically, refocus itself on its core business—and survive bankruptcy. He cut the workforce by another 30%, killed the optical storage research (which was still years from producing a marketable product), and even sold the $6 million corporate jet. He also sold off chip fabrication and circuit board assembly units that had been purchased to fulfill Aweida's dream of producing his own computers. Creative destruction had taken a backseat. Operational excellence was given top priority. The assumption of continuity was all that mattered.

Poppa's approach didn't facilitate his relationship with some in the company (his nickname, "the Ayatollah," followed him from BMC; as if to underscore this, his decision to kill the optical device unit was announced on Christmas Eve). Still, his approach was quick to generate results. By January 1986, Storage Technology had recorded its first profitable quarter since 1983. The market responded by more than doubling the stock price.

With costs now under control and sales starting to grow again, Storage Technology was able to reach agreements with its creditors, handing over more than 85% of the company's equity to settle most of its $800 million in liabilities. By 1987, Storage Technology had emerged from bankruptcy.

Staying in business, however, would require more than settling claims against its assets. It required maintaining operational excellence—and taking up innovation again. The computer industry was in full bloom. The pace and scale of innovation in computer hardware was stunning (especially measured by the rate at which new companies were crossing the "small company threshold"). But to play the game, a company had to innovate. Creative destruction had to be reinstalled. Fortunately, Poppa had maintained research in magnetic media because it did not challenge the basic business model he was pursuing. By 1986, Storage Technology had caught up with IBM in disk drive technology, matching a new technique developed by IBM that could provide twice the storage capacity of earlier products.

Moreover, Poppa thought he could attack the old-line tape business, which, while mature, was still large ($10 billion). IBM had regained the upper hand in technology and market share after the Justice Department's decade-long antitrust case against it had ended. But Storage Technology thought it had the skills and resources it needed to challenge IBM in this segment and win.

Storage Technology did come up with a new innovation in the tape drive market. Prior to 1986, tape storage systems consisted of reel-to-reel machines that required considerable manual effort to switch from one tape to another. Both IBM and Storage Technology offered their own versions of tape drives that used hand-size cassettes that could store substantially more data in a more convenient format.

Storage Technology went one step further, however, bundling the cassettes into a library system. The library could hold up to six thousand cassettes, which were shelved circularly around a robotic arm that could grab a selected tape and insert it into the tape drive. This allowed the entire data system to be accessible within eleven seconds. While this was quite slow by disk drive standards (which could do the same job in milliseconds), disk drives cost about thirty-five times more per megabyte than tape storage. Compared to manual retrieval, which would take several minutes, tape storage was a dramatic innovation. In fact, the robotic tape library system allowed Storage Technology to become the market leader for mainframe tape storage.

Poppa also focused his attention on the rapidly growing mainframe disk storage market, where IBM had regained market dominance (90% share in 1987) during Storage Technology's troubles. To innovate, Storage Technology (along with several other smaller companies) began to develop a new type of disk drive system. The new concept was to replace the hard disks that were being sold for mainframes with a group of smaller hard disks that would act in unison to provide a single, large storage space. The system was referred to as a RAID system (for redundant array of inexpensive devices). Not only did it allow small and relatively inexpensive hard disks (originally designed for personal computers) to replace the costly mainframe disks, but it allowed data to be replicated over the array, so that any given disk could fail without a complete loss of data. RAID systems promised far larger disk storage at appreciably lower prices than those of the traditional hard disks.

By 1990 Storage Technology had begun discussing its new RAID product, called Iceberg, with its customers. By January 1992, CEO Poppa had secured $150 million in orders and was ready to start discussing the project publicly (even though it was still far from completion). Poppa was so impressed with Iceberg that he even claimed it could make Storage Technology the "IBM of the 90s." The market was suitably impressed. But Poppa's words were eerily reminiscent of Aweida's announcement—exactly a decade earlier—that Storage Technology would become a "mini-IBM."

Storage Technology's first shipment of test units had been delayed by bugs in the computer code. Meanwhile, another small disk supplier, EMC, had entered the market with a RAID product two years earlier. Still, Poppa remained enthusiastic about Iceberg: "I told Dick Egan [EMC's chairman and founder], 'You've got a tricycle compared to our Cadillac,'" he said.

Despite Poppa's sunny pronouncements (classic Stage 4 denial behavior), the balance between operational excellence and innovation at Storage Technology had once again been broken. Delays continued, pushing Iceberg's delivery dates back. And that was just the tip of Iceberg's problems. The capital markets, sensing problems, became jittery. Their nervousness was reinforced in May 1992, when Poppa and fourteen other Storage Technology executives sold more than ninety thousand shares of company stock following Iceberg's announcement. The resulting sell-off cut Storage Technology share value by half in just four months; shares finished the year 76% below their high. By mid-1993, Iceberg was still more than six months from shipment. The conflicts between innovating and operating had dealt a second death blow to Storage Technology.

By the time Iceberg reached the market in 1994, the computer industry was once again in the midst of a dramatic market shift. With the proliferation of personal computers in the '80s, computing power no longer needed to be centralized in a mainframe system. New approaches were proliferating; new companies were racing into the market, sensing the opportunity in the Internet and truly distributed computing. Companies were turning to enterprisewide networks that used servers to share data and files between individual client computers.

While this transformation was a potential boon for data storage device makers, it meant that Storage Technology needed to refocus, readapting its products from being purely IBM mainframe compatible to being compatible with such open systems as UNIX. This change of focus led to a merger with Network Systems.

As Storage Technology worked to extend its product line to open systems and build market share with Iceberg, the company's growth remained flat. In 1995, after pressure from the board of directors, Poppa agreed to retire at the end of 1996. David Weiss, who had spent twenty-three years at IBM before joining Storage Technology in 1991, was named president and COO (and in May 1996 assumed the position of CEO). Storage Technology had given up trying to be an outperformer for investors, and was now operating at average levels, in what we have seen in previous chapters as the classic slow downward spiral.

Weiss realized that Storage Technology did not have the infrastructure necessary to adequately market Iceberg. He needed a partner. He also realized that IBM was no longer the dominant player in the disk storage market. Rather, EMC, with its "tricycle" of a RAID product, had captured the mainframe disk storage market that Storage Technology had planned for Iceberg.

So Weiss negotiated with IBM. In June of 1996, IBM not only agreed to stop making disk storage subsystems but to resell Storage Technology RAID systems to its customers through 2000. Weiss extended his partnering efforts with NCR, which agreed to resell Storage Technology tape drive products. Partnering helped Storage Technology gain market share for mainframe disk sales. Unfortunately, the real game was in the open systems of the Internet, an area dominated by EMC and other competitors.

Storage Technology tried to get into open systems with some of its mainframe storage innovations, such as instantaneous virtual backup software. In August 1999, their efforts appeared to be paying off: Sun Microsystems, a top supplier of Internet servers, agreed to resell Storage Technology tape libraries. That good news was countered, however, when IBM announced that it would reenter the data storage market in 2000 with new products that would compete head-to-head with Storage Technology.

As sales growth continued to stagnate, and with little obvious forward progress, shareholders again became frustrated. In February 2000, Weiss announced that he would step down as CEO as soon as a successor was found.

After starting as a high-technology, fast-growing company, Storage

Storage Technology
Sales Growth vs. Industry

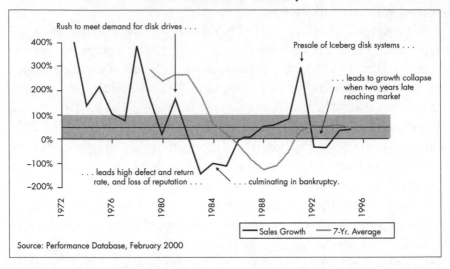

Source: Performance Database, February 2000

Storage Technology
Total Return to Shareholders vs. Industry

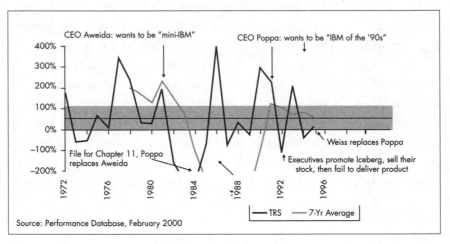

Source: Performance Database, February 2000

Technology, unable to master the art of balancing operational excellence and creative destruction, now finds itself the main player in a stagnant market (tape storage for mainframes). Today, it continues to seek ways to expand into the open systems market and find new routes to expand shareholder value. It has fallen far short of its goals and aspirations.

THE INCOMPATIBILITY OF OPERATIONS AND CREATIVE DESTRUCTION

There are hundreds of cases like Storage Technology's. The facts differ, but the patterns are the same. From the days of Adam Smith's pin factory, the central purpose of the corporation has been production, logistics, selling, and billing. Aided by the elements of the corporate architecture—systems of information, decision making, and measurement and control—the company is expected to run smoothly, anticipate problems, and avoid risks. These are the activities that allow corporations to create wealth and deliver on its promises to its customers. It is an operational system based on the presumption of rational thought, and it is implicitly deterministic. The presumption is that "if these things are done, the results will be as expected." Doing these things constitutes the daily life of most corporate employees.

In reality, of course, the system does not always run as it is supposed to run. Despite its rational expectations, the system stumbles all the time. This is what operational excellence seeks to avoid, and it is in *operations* that every business, large or small, must succeed before it can even begin to think about the future.

In a recent series of meetings, we talked with more than fifty managers from large and small companies in the United States and Europe. They ran the gamut from high-tech to daily consumer-staples firms. We asked them to characterize what it took to be successful in their particular business. Their answers were remarkably uniform, given the vast differences in their corporate purposes, size, and nationality.

Of all the attributes that business leaders saw leading to success, operational excellence was highest on their list. Operational excellence included best-in-class design, manufacturing excellence, logistics and sales skills, adept execution, personal drive, and an obsession with the customer. In addition they felt that strong systematic planning, effective operational controls, ability to leverage their assets over wide geographic areas, and the ability to maintain low overhead were all required to be competitive these days. That is a full boat.

Whether European or American, whether in packaged goods or high tech, these executives and managers felt that operational excellence was the price of admission today. It is "operational excellence that lets you reap the synergies of all the other elements of your business," they routinely explained.

But many of these executives felt the standard they had set for themselves was difficult to achieve. Difficulties in execution were on the top of this list, starting with the failure to execute at all. Some companies, for example, were not able to integrate acquisitions, largely because of enormous cultural differences between the companies. Others failed to integrate functional skills or transition to a new skill base.

The failure to execute effectively was more common than the failure to execute at all. The executives we talked with cited cases where execution was excessively costly, or where a company failed to get products to market on time or misjudged the level of investment required.

Finally, more than a few of the executives we surveyed said they had trouble focusing execution. They were not tough enough in determining at an early stage what would make a difference in the overall performance level of the enterprise—or what projects needed to be cut out of development to avoid starving the remaining projects or bankrupting the company. There were many variants of operational failure. The decision processes of these corporations were simply not up to the tasks before them.

As a consequence, these senior executives wanted to know what the best techniques for ensuring execution were; what practical advice there was to help individuals stay focused; what the best performance measures and control processes were—ideas that would keep everything moving along smoothly—and how to cope with these challenges as the size and complexity of the corporation grow.

Yet there was an irony in their questions. As concerned as they seemed to be with operational effectiveness, they were actually more concerned with creative destruction (although they did not call it creative destruction). They were adamant about discussing the difficulties they had with innovation and the tendency of their companies to stay too long in old product lines. The executives we talked to did not equate innovation and R&D, or even innovation and technology change; they saw innovation as a broader topic—doing new things whatever their origin or doing old things in new ways. Their concerns included R&D, of course, but they were broader than that topic alone.

We are sympathetic to that view. We see innovation as the development of new products and services that meet customer needs cheaper, faster, and better than current alternatives do. Innovation to us also means retooling business processes to develop new products and services. In this sense, innovation can refer to changing approaches to sales and services, or to the structure of large transactions, or to the migration paths customers follow to move from one computer system to another, or to skills for diversification, or to the development of technologies that enable the sales of other products, or to the development of new business models themselves.

Despite the importance of innovation to them, the executives said they had difficulty pulling it off. They cited the inability to grow beyond the core, the lack of ideas compelling enough to change customer behavior, slow product development, and the failure to establish an "innovative culture" (although none could really define what that meant). They are many of the same problems that Storage Technology faced and failed to resolve.

Regarding the elimination of product lines that no longer had potential or fit within the concept of the corporations, many cited their tendency to "ride the wave too long"; even the best of the innovators had a problem with this, and were willing to admit it. Again, their problems are not dissimilar to the experience of Storage Technology.

When asked what stands in the way of better change management in their companies, these executives cited several barriers. The most common complaint referred to problems that stemmed from "rational" analysis— the kind of analysis that markets collectively do not perform. The top reasons cited for lack of change in the corporation was that they had become too financially focused; that the kind of analyses used to justify projects killed them; the inability to move into new areas with sufficient force; the refusal to stand up to unpleasant realities—"If they did not like the characteristics of new technologies, they ignored them." Several told us, "Whenever you find a division of a company that failed because it could not change, look to the parent. That is where the problems are." It was a point that this group of executives generally agreed upon. Parental control, they feel, is the kiss of death for competitiveness. For each of these blockages, our executives would like to have answers.

These executives had three kinds of questions about innovation. The first centered on their confessed inability to develop innovative strategies:

"How do the excellent innovators do it?"—which presumes, of course, that excellent innovators exist
"What drives breakthrough innovative ideas?"
"How should we determine an innovation strategy—meaning, particularly, how do we set the balance between evolutionary and revolutionary innovation?"

"How can we avoid riding the curve too long?"
"How can we develop more compelling ideas to change customer behavior?"

The second kind of question centered on managing the flow of innovations into the corporation:

"How do we grow beyond the core business?"
"How do we bring products to market faster—including prototyping, scaling up, engineering, and launch?" (One executive asked, "How do we handle the bottlenecks caused by four divisional CEOs who have to be involved in most innovation decisions in order to review product line overlapping, brand overlapping, and geographic overlapping?")
"How do we create a culture within the organization that supports innovation?" (Specifically, "How do companies keep the innovative spirit alive as they grow larger and more complex?")
"How do we ensure that innovators are listened to—despite the pressure of the day-to-day business and the resource constraints that come with it?"
"How do we deal with the cultural differences between units working on incremental and those working on transformational innovation?"
"How do deal with risk?"
"How do we evolve skills?"
"How do we prioritize between different great ideas that the organization develops?"

The third, and perhaps most basic, kind of question was centered on how to discover and manage new ideas:

"How do we find ideas?"
"How do we transform ideas into businesses?" ("How do great innovators think about 'easier, faster, better'?")
"How can we better leverage what we have done?" ("How do we overcome the 'not-invented-here' syndrome in some of our third country markets?")
"How do we get companies that are totally integrated around centralized computer systems to become more innovative? The computer systems are strangling us!"

Everyone pointed out that as size and complexity increase, changes become harder. As one executive said, "The question is then how do we create favorable environment in a big organization?" Another executive asked, "How sustainable is this process which has tremendously increased the number of SKUs?" And another turned the question inside out: "How do you manage product complexity that is generated by intense flow of innovation?" These executives could not figure out how to run their corporations in such a way that they could achieve operational excellence *and* creative destruction at the pace and scale of the market. Failing to find a way to address this issue, they simply placed most of their attention on operational excellence. This can work for a while, as we saw with Storage Technology. But not forever. The system of operational excellence is consistent, but it is not complete.

LIMITATIONS OF THE OPERATING ORGANIZATION

What are the origins of this dilemma? First, organizations based on the assumption of continuity do not work well when faced with discontinuity. Three factors, all part of the architecture of the organization, or MIDAS, stand in their way: decision-making systems, managerial control systems, and information.

DECISION-MAKING SYSTEMS

Decision-making systems that support the day-to-day life in many corporations work well only when:

1. History is a good guide to the future, and uncertainty and its risk are at a minimum.
2. The context is simple and unambiguous rather than complex and ambiguous.
3. The decision-making process is balanced and calm, rather than erratic and subject to stress.
4. The competitive, technological, and regulatory environment is stable, rather than in a period of rapid change.
5. Information is standard, unambiguous, and complete, rather than uncertain or difficult to interpret.
6. Decisions can be handled in a hierarchical fashion, with little information distortion.

7. There is a consistency of preferences, such as a common set of beliefs, among decision makers.
8. Mental models match anticipated conditions (when systems are self-referential, analysis of future risks is quite difficult).

Needless to say, these conditions are rarely met.

MEASUREMENT AND CONTROL SYSTEMS

Measurement and control systems, which are intended to keep the organization on course once decisions are made, suffer from similar weaknesses. The purpose of control systems is to help achieve an organization's objectives. They do this by identifying key control variables, determining standards against which results can be compared, measuring the results, diagnosing deviations from the standards, correcting deviations from standards, and adjusting the standards as appropriate. As we mentioned in the Introduction, Robert Simons says, "Measurement focuses on errors of commission (mistakes) and shortfalls (negative variances) against goals. In fact, control systems are negative feedback systems. Control reports are used primarily as confirmation that everything is 'on track.' Surprise is the enemy."

Measurement and control systems, like decision-making systems, perform most effectively in routine functions and processes. Used inappropriately they can thwart the recognition of key, nonstandard issues and even undermine management's intent. When designing control systems, for example, the designers select only a few variables, from the many possibilities, to control. Once the variables are selected, disproportionate attention is placed on them, drawing attention away from potentially important new concerns or problems. In this way, control systems filter out warnings of "disruptive environmental change," as Simons terms it.

INFORMATION SYSTEMS

Finally, information systems suffer from a variety of limitations. These include the high cost of changing them, limited access, and erroneous, irrelevant, or missing information (and the assumption that it will be used by decision makers if it is available). These assumptions are violated frequently. Among the most common errors:

1. Decision makers gravitate to familiar information. They know how to use such information and how to assess its quality; they know the tricks buried in such data. Decision makers are more likely to seek the confirmation of existing information than to look for disconfirming information.
2. When faced with inconsistent data, decision makers tend to rely on the first cue that captures their attention—and exclude all others from consideration.
3. Decision makers prefer certain kinds of information delivered in a certain form. For example, decision makers prefer *vivid* information to *pallid* information; that is, they prefer stories to systematic information, and they prefer information about specific cases to information about abstract statistics. Most decision makers would prefer to see a chart than a table, or a real product rather than a description of a product, or to see a person who represents a particular class of people—say, those with colds—than read statistics about colds.

Psychologists have found that decision makers are like everyone else: They tend to pay more attention to dramatic events (though they may be low in real significance) than they do to routine events that have a high probability of affecting their lives and that of the corporation. Such information may be perfectly delivered, but it is less than perfectly perceived!

These elements of the operating organization are "sticky." That is, they are usually designed to support a single competitive environment and conform to a single model of competition. They are based on the assumption of continuity. They do not function well in discontinuous times. When the assumption of continuity is undermined, they cannot help to create an effective response. In fact, they hinder it.

REQUIREMENTS OF THE INNOVATING ORGANIZATION

The second reason that one cannot easily answer the executives' questions, and deal with the kinds of problems Storage Technology faced, is more

complex. It deals with the fundamental difference between the corporation that operates on the assumption of continuity and one that is built on
the assumption of discontinuity. Innovation is at the heart of the concept
of discontinuity.

Industries are more innovative than the companies in them, since by
definition the market consists of all innovations and a single company can
lay claim only to their own. For example, in cellular telephony, Motorola
has been a leader. It introduced a wide range of products, from the transformational MicroTAC® handheld cellular phone to the incremental
VibraCall® ringing technology. Nevertheless, even a company as innovative as Motorola contributes only a portion of the overall innovation of
the entire industry. There are many other competitors in this industry,
including Nokia and Ericsson, that have also introduced important innovations. In addition to innovation in phones, there was also innovation in
cellular services. AT&T's 1999 announcement of the combined handset
and One Rate Plan, which allowed a customer to pay a flat rate of ten
cents a minute whether using a landline, a cell phone, or a calling card,
changed the model of industry pricing.

As innovative as individual companies have been, none of them can
claim to have dominated innovation in cellular technology. The industry
has a life of its own. Over time, the *industry,* rather than any individual
company, sets the standard for innovation. The continuous cycle of learning, developing insights, selecting ideas, and developing concepts happens
faster and more comprehensively in the market than in any one company.
In the market, many competitors are simultaneously working on new
ideas that could result in growth businesses—large companies, small companies, and entrepreneurs. Conflicting ideas are being pursued simultaneously. Many will not succeed. The competitive standard, therefore, more
than any single company, is the market.

TYPES OF INNOVATION

As the cellular telephone industry illustrates, there are many kinds of
innovation. Innovation can be thought of as occurring at three levels. First
is *transformational* innovation, which matches Schumpeter's concept of a
"historic and irreversible change in the way of doing things." The second
level is *substantial* innovation, which offers less surprise and scope than
Schumpeter's concept but still significantly upsets the conventional order.

Often substantial innovations follow transformational innovations, as aftershocks follow the main earthquake. The third level is *incremental* innovation, which is the everyday engine of change of most corporations.

Organizations rarely distinguish between the kinds of innovation, and that leads directly to trouble. At Storage Technology, for example, founder Aweida made two mistakes because he failed to understand the differences between what he had demonstrated he could do (incremental innovation) and what he wanted to do (substantial and transformational innovation). His first mistake was to attempt to develop a new mainframe (a substantial innovation) to compete head-on with IBM. Basing his estimates on what it would take to compete with IBM on his experience with incremental innovation, he underestimated greatly the magnitude of the challenge of developing a new mainframe. Storage Technology fell far short of market requirements. Moreover, his timing was terrible, since at the same time he chose to compete with IBM in mainframes, the computer industry was beginning a transformational shift away from mainframes and to personal computers. Aweida's second mistake was to attempt to develop optical storage systems years before the underlying technology was ready. Again, Aweida's experience in incremental innovation was not an accurate guide to the requirement of transformational innovation.

Later, President Poppa's success with incremental innovation led him to believe he was capable of beating EMC in RAID storage systems by developing Iceberg, a substantial innovation. Poppa tried to use the same processes that had succeeded in delivering incremental innovations to support transformational innovation, but they were inadequate to meet the tougher technical development standards of Iceberg.

By failing to distinguish between the kinds of innovation and managerial requirements, Aweida and Poppa failed to foresee the demands and challenges in front of them. Their gut instincts, based on their experience with incremental innovation, was an insufficient guide to the rigors and timing requirements of substantial and transformational innovation. Consequently, they mismanaged three major projects and derailed Storage Technology. These errors directly led to their removal.

Two factors determine the level of innovation: how new the innovation is and how much wealth it generates. Incremental innovations are not very new to either the customer or the producer and generally have slight impact; substantial innovations are quite new to either the customer or the producer and can have greater economic impact. And transformational innovations—which can invoke entirely new designs, or manufacturing processes, or uses—have the greatest impact of all. Turned around, if an innovation is very new and creates an enormous amount of wealth, we call it transformational because it transforms the industry. If the innovation is not very new and does not create a lot of wealth, then we think of it as incremental. Substantial innovation falls between the two. You'll never forget a transformational change, while incremental changes go unnoticed all the time.

We believe that the scale of innovation is logarithmic rather than arithmetic. Substantial innovation is often ten times greater than the change that results from incremental innovation, and offers ten times the rewards (and invokes ten times the uncertainties). Moreover, substantial innovation is often generative: Once established, the innovation leads to other innovation (sometimes called *positive returns*).

Transformational innovation is ten times greater than substantial innovation. Transformational innovations tear at the social fabric (and that of the economic markets) far more than incremental innovations do. Based on our experience and the analysis of the innovation portfolios of several large companies, the frequency of innovations is logarithmic, as well. There are perhaps ten substantial innovations for every hundred incremental innovations, and perhaps one transformational innovation for every ten substantial innovations.

The "newness" and wealth creation of an innovation can be drawn on a graph like the Richter scale:

Types of Innovation
Richter Scale of Innovation

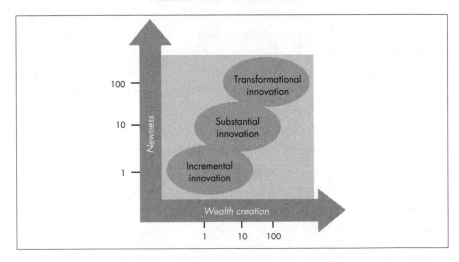

Many businesses, of course, are built on an idea that is not very new—and they can still do very well. At Storage Technology this included the line of tape drives that Poppa had developed. Other examples range from Palm Pilot imitators like Handspring, to new frozen yogurt versions of popular ice cream flavors, to the next generation of Microsoft Word. These are not transformational innovations, but examples of operational excellence—the continued pursuit of ordinary business. Innovations that are very new (remember the Apple Newton, or Snapple beverages?) but do not create wealth are not transformational, in our opinion. Such products are better termed *inventions*.

Each level of innovation—incremental, substantial, and transformational—requires a different managerial process and is managed by a different level of the corporation. Incremental change can be handled by frontline people. Transformational change can be enacted only by senior management. Each presents a different challenge, as well: Incremental change challenges current strategy without challenging the firm's traditional controls; transformational change challenges the corporation's strategy and controls. Managing innovation is impossible without understanding which layer of innovation one is dealing with. Both Aweida and Poppa at Storage Technology did not understand the differences; it cost them the leadership of the company, not to mention shareholders' returns.

Incremental Innovation

Incremental innovation is characterized more by what has *not* changed than what *has* changed. While incremental innovations are not very new and they do not create much wealth, they must be pursued in order to maintain one's competitive position.

Incremental innovations are attractive because not much has to change to assure their implementation. They offer more or less the same value to the customer as does pre-innovation value. They use more or less the same manufacturing equipment. They are sold through more or less the same channels, with the same sales terms, as the pre-innovation product or service. They are improvements over what has preceded them—but not vast improvements.

Incremental innovations are the red blood cells of the economy. Without them, existing corporations could not survive. They are the product of countless total quality management and reengineering programs. They can be accomplished by the rank and file. They are well understood. They do not challenge the existing business model or strategic plan. Senior management participation is not required.

One way to understand incremental innovation is by looking to the past, to the evolution of sailing ships. In the 1880s, clipper ships like the *Glenavlon* were often seen on the horizon (see below). These swift-sailing

The *Glenavlon*

vessels carried cargo between the major ports of England and the United States. They were the FedEx carriers of their time, having been perfected through hundreds of years of incremental improvement. (In fact, FedEx CEO Fred Smith has an extensive collection of clipper ship models, which he displays in glass cases at FedEx headquarters.)

But by 1870, ships powered by steam that had been around for nearly seventy years were challenging the leadership of the clippers. In the beginning, steamships were not at all effective (since the steam engine itself was not terribly efficient in 1820). Most of the cargo-carrying capacity of the steamship was consumed by fuel storage. By 1890, however, steam engines had improved to the point where they could overtake the cost advantage of clippers. The handsome clipper ships began losing market share to the steamships (or, more often in the early days, to a steam-and-sail hybrid).

But the owners of the sailing vessels, and the naval architects who supported them, were not ready to relinquish control of the seas. They fought back by incrementally improving their ships. The following drawing, of the *France II,* shows one of those ships:

The *France II*

This was a much-improved vessel. It had one more mast than the *Glenavlon,* and was also longer at the waterline. It was a faster ship. It also carried more cargo, and thus was cheaper to operate per ton-mile than the *Glenavlon.*

Thus continued a skirmish of technologies, steam versus sail. The *Preussen* was the next improvement in sail. It was again an incremental improvement, with more sail, more length at the waterline, and a cheaper ton-per-mile operating cost.

Did the *Preussen* stop the progress of the steamships? Absolutely not. The steamships kept on attacking.

Undaunted, the naval architects struggled for further improvement, this time with a gaff-rigged design. The *Thomas W. Lawson* was the result. The ship had even more sail and waterline, which resulted in even more speed. But at this point, the incremental change in technology was reaching its natural limit. On Friday, December 13, 1907, nearing the Scilly Islands in England, Captain Turner found he could not control the

The *Preussen*

The *Thomas W. Lawson*

Thomas W. Lawson. With the winds blowing at sixty knots, the sailing vessel ran into the rocks. Miraculously, Captain Turner survived. But the rest of the crew was lost—and so was the age of sail. Incremental innovation had run its course.

Captain Turner and Presidents Poppa and Aweida of Storage Technology had something in common. They all were unwitting victims of the end of incremental innovation. Captain Turner lost his ship and crew; Poppa and Aweida lost their company.

Alas, incremental innovation is *not* the signature of the marketplace. It is the signature of continuity, of companies clinging to incumbency. Incremental innovation is more a part of operational excellence than it is creative destruction.

Transformational Innovation

Transformational innovation can create new markets, turn the tides of commerce, make billionaires, vanquish competitors, and inspire the next generation. While incremental innovation rarely challenges the establishment, transformational innovation *frequently* upsets the conventional concepts of the corporation and its operational systems. Transformational innovations do not spring from "product quality" programs. They come from intensely creative people bent on destroying the established order.

Transformational innovations tend to be "competency destroying." In other words, the competition must destroy the incumbent products in order to compete. Transformational innovations are often conceived of by senior management, and led by them as well. Often the transformational innovation is the very reason for a new company's existence. Frequently the product, the tooling, the distribution methods, the media campaigns, and the value propositions are new as well. The synthesis of these elements can work surprisingly well, even explosively well, stunning Wall Street analysts. Stock prices can explode, enriching lucky or insightful investors.

Existing companies generally do not create transformational innovations. Markets do by enabling the assembly of an entirely new corporation—people, capital, and technology.

Substantial Innovation

Substantial innovations are often the second generation of transformational innovations. These are products or systems that follow the pioneering innovation. One example is the Windows operating system, which supplanted the old DOS system. Huggies to Pampers. Sam's to Wal-Mart. The 747 to the 707. FedEx's SameDay® Service to its Standard Overnight® Service. These are bold new products, but not nearly so bold as the original transformational innovations. What separates these innovations from incremental change is both the extent of the change and the impact of the changes. Windows was not a simple extension of DOS. It was a total rewrite that in the end had a very different look and feel from DOS, incorporating optical interfaces, or "windows," which made it easier for consumers to use. (Those who know the two systems will immediately recall the differences.) Windows was meant to compete with the Macintosh operating system. One could "click" one's way though the various options rather than remembering a seemingly endless series of typed, coded commands.

Substantial innovations offer secure competitive advantage for a time. They tend to build on, and reinforce, the competencies that were required to make the transformational innovation—but they build new core skills as well, differentiating them in an important way from incremental innovations. Substantial innovations stretch the limits of the information and skills of the organization, often requiring outside expertise to pull them off. They are often competency-destroying for the defenders of the old order. They often involve senior management, but mostly in an advisory role.

Substantial innovations generally do not emerge from an accretion of incremental innovations. The intent of these designs is to follow on the heels of the transformation. To stay on the attack. To gain advantage. They tend to be boldly conceived and meticulously assembled. Those companies that think they can achieve substantial innovation by merely stepping up incremental efforts will be sadly disappointed—whether they are an enterprise resources planning system (or ERP, as it has become to be known) designer dreaming of crossing over to the Internet, or a drug maker hoping to evolve its studies of small molecules into genetics. These innovations do not come from the random accretion of small advances. They come from a lofty ambition to do much better in the market coupled with an innovative approach that is different from what has come before (e.g., a new concept for an Internet-based ERP). While the final product will, of course, be assembled from existing subcomponents, lofty goals and a novel approach separate such advances from incremental change.

In failing to recognize the differences between these three different types of innovation—and many managers manage them as one—managers fail to meet the needs of any.

THE CREATIVE FOUNDATIONS OF TRANSFORMATIONAL INNOVATION

The underlying element in all innovation is creativity. Only by understanding creativity can one grapple with what is needed for sustained performance.

CREATIVITY

Most words used in management today have their origins in the fourteenth century. But the word *creativity* is more recent, first cited by Webster in 1875. In the 1880s, William James used the word to support his philosophy of pragmatism. James described the nature of the creative process in this way:

> *Instead of thoughts of concrete things patiently following one another in a beaten track of habitual suggestion, we have the most abrupt cross-cuts and transitions from one idea to another, the most rarefied abstractions and discriminations, the most unheard of combination of elements, the subtlest associations of analogy; in a word, we seem suddenly introduced into a seething caldron of ideas, where everything is fizzling and bobbling about in a state of bewildering activity, where partnerships can be joined or loosened in an instant, treadmill routine is unknown, and the unexpected seems the only law.*

This hardly sounds like the orderliness of the ideal operating organization. It seems more like a state of confusion and disorder, one perhaps waiting for order to arrive.

James believed in the "great man" theory of creativity, which implied that creativity seethed within the person, but he believed that the environment was also crucial. Modern thinkers stress the environment to an even greater degree. Mihalyi Csikszentmihalyi noted:

> *To say that Thomas Edison invented electricity or that Albert Einstein discovered relativity is a convenient simplification. It satisfies our ancient predilection for stories that are easy to comprehend and involve superhuman heroes. But Edison's or Einstein's discoveries would be inconceivable without the prior knowledge, without the intellectual*

and social network that stimulated their thinking, and without the social mechanisms that recognized and spread their innovations.

What is the process of discovery and what are the "intellectual and social networks and mechanisms" that "recognize and spread" those discoveries? How do those processes compare to the processes required to run the operating organization?

THE PROCESS OF DISCOVERY

The process of discovery takes two paths, which in practice are quite recursive. One is divergent thinking—a matter of opening up. The other is convergent thinking—focusing down. It is the latter kind of thinking that is conventionally practiced in the operating organization, where it has been raised to a high art. Divergent thinking is rarely practiced in the operating organization, and in fact appears at cross-purposes with its intent.

Divergent Thinking

The purpose of divergent thinking is to cast the broadest possible net in searching for solutions, as well as in searching for the proper questions that need to be addressed. The tool of intuitive genius, divergent thinking can readily change the definition of the problem to be solved, or the context in which the problem is solved. It involves the ability to switch from one perspective to another fluently, as well as an ability to pick up on or make unusual associations. Chess masters call this "zoom-out" thinking— the process of putting all the known information into context, both within the strategic context of the game being played, as well as in the context of other general knowledge the chess player has about his or her opponent and what other great players in the past have done in similar situations.

Zoom-out thinkers are "wide categorizers." They exhibit a strong interest in disciplines outside their own specialty area. They are trained in diverse disciplines, and they are often aggressive in acquiring new skills. They tend to surround themselves with diverse stimuli, and they change those stimuli regularly. Renowned Harvard professor emeritus E. O. Wilson, for example, typically works on several projects at once. This is a common pattern among creative individuals; it keeps them from getting bored or stymied, and it produces an unexpected cross-fertilization of ideas.

As Dean Keith Simonton notes, "It is evident that a person is more likely to see congruence between hitherto isolated elements if that person has broad interests, is versatile, enjoys intellectual fluency and flexibility, and can connect disparate elements via unusual associations and wide categories that force a substantial overlap of ideas."

Divergent thinking is made up of three highly interlinked, overlapping, and recursive phases—search, incubation, and collision. Collectively, they constitute the unique hub of the discovery process.

Search

During the search phase, individuals seek to define inconsistencies between current theory and new data. "These anomalies provide the raw material on which the subconscious can work," Csikszentmihalyi notes.

> *The creative process starts with a sense that there is a puzzle somewhere, or a task to be accomplished. Perhaps something is not right, somewhere there is a conflict, a tension, a need to be satisfied. The problematic issue can be triggered by a personal experience, by a lack of fit in the symbolic system, by the stimulation of colleagues, or by public needs. Without such a felt tension to attract the psychic energy of the person, the creative process is unlikely to start.*

Anomalies—things that don't fit the established order—can serve as precursors to opportunities or problems. A stock may be undervalued, a customer need unrecognized, a new technology not fully used.

Anomalies do not necessarily jump out at management. It takes someone with what Pasteur called a "prepared mind" to see them. Csikszentmihalyi says:

> *Fleming was not the first bacteriologist to see a petri dish spoiled by a mold contamination, yet he was apparently the first to notice the far-reaching implications of the clear ring around the little fuzzy spot on the gel. Similarly, Archimedes was not the first to have seen a bathtub overflow, Newton the falling of an apple, or Watt the steam escaping from a tea pot, but these three did notice the broader implications of these trivial, almost everyday occurrences.*

"Seeing the broader implications" often requires the observer to "suspend disbelief"—and to use substantial diligence until a new pattern appears. These skills are seldom nurtured in operating organizations. Yet they are essential for transformational innovation. As Kuhn observed in 1962, "The accumulation of anomalies—findings that cannot be assimilated into any framework or tradition—prepares the way for revolution."

There is a fine line to walk here. Lingering too long on a bit of data may lead to wasted work, or it could be the prelude to discovery. Who can make that call? Even those who have been right previously are not necessarily infallible the next time around. In fact, one could argue that as one gathers expertise, he or she becomes less accepting of new data. This, in fact, is a classic characteristic of mature organizations. They fail to innovate because they fail to recognize the fact that they have been rejecting data that does not support the company's mental models. One can't search for anomalies through reading and study alone, although reading and study can trigger creativity. In business one often learns from being mentored, from apprenticeships, through meetings with customers, or from visits to "world-class" corporations, manufacturing sites, distribution centers, or laboratories.

Incubation

The incubation stage is the most mysterious of the three stages of divergent thinking. Sometimes it appears as if the problem-solving process has stopped altogether.

Incubation is the absolute opposite of the normal business processes of the operating organization. It is often totally unpredictable. But since it is also the heart of the creative process, it creates a dilemma for the business executive who wants to support innovation but has little patience for unfocused activity. In the incubation period, observations stew on the edge of consciousness until something clarifies. As Newton observed, "I keep the subject constantly before me, and wait until the first dawnings open slowly, little by little, into the full and clear light."

There is no way to plan "enough" incubation time. What, then, can one do to improve the productivity of this period of incubation? One useful tool is what psychologists call "suspending disbelief"—suspending judgment on data or observations that seem to make no sense. It allows time for the rearrangement of data, allowing one time to find new images that explain or illustrate how things might work. Suspending disbelief is essential to avoiding premature closure on an issue, or entrenchment in existing ideas and approaches. Suspending disbelief helps to improve one's chances of finding a fresh view of the universe. It is an unnatural act for an operating organization, but an essential trait for an innovative organization.

A second useful tool is to deconstruct the problem so that you can recombine elements of it and gain fresh insight. Sir James Black, Nobel Prize winner for the discovery of histamine antagonists, suggests that one "turn the question around." Dr. Black prefers an "oblique attack" to a problem rather than a direct one.

One way to change context, Csikszentmihalyi observes, is to position yourself at the intersection of different cultures or disciplines: "where beliefs, lifestyles, and knowledge mingle and allow individuals to see new combinations of ideas with greater ease. In cultures that are uniform and rigid it takes a greater investment of attention to achieve new ways of thinking. In other words, creativity is more likely in places where new ideas require less effort to be perceived."

Collision

The end of the incubation stage is achieved when a good idea is recognized, a process we call *collision*. Collisions of different information or perspectives often emerge instantly, but the process can drag on as problem definition evolves and solutions emerge. There is often a dialectic between the "irrational and the rational aspects; between passion and discipline." The resolution usually can't be predicted in advance. In the passage that follows, Csikszentmihalyi illustrates this point with a description of the creative writing process:

> *What is so difficult about the process is that one must keep the mind focused on two contradictory goals: not to miss the message whispered by the unconscious and at the same time force it into a suitable form. The first requires openness, the second critical judgment. If these two processes are not kept in a constantly shifting balance, the flow of writing dries up. After a few hours the tremendous concentration required for this balancing act becomes so exhausting that the writer has to change gears and focus on something else, something mundane. But while it lasts, creative writing is the next best thing to having a world of one's own in which what's wrong with the "real" world can be set straight.*

These three phases—search, incubation, and collision—define the divergent-thinking process. Divergent thinking is the headwater of the creative process. Unfortunately, these skills are rarely well developed even in the well-run and well-operating organization. As a result, it is often starved for substantial and transformational opportunities, at least compared to the general market.

Convergent Thinking

The second part of the creative process is convergent thinking. Convergent thinking, the key to analytical genius, is the thinking measured by IQ tests. It involves solving well-defined, rational problems that have a single correct answer. Chess masters call this thinking "zoom-in" thinking. Zooming in is the act of understanding the microdetails of the present situation—where all the players are situated, what the most recent moves have been, and so on. Zooming in is similar to deductive thinking.

Convergent thinkers do their work by focusing in on the essential details, screening ideas for relevance, and exercising their knack for simplifying problems just enough to capture their essence—but without excluding the significant details. Screening is an essential skill, one where the practitioner, according to Teresa M. Amabile, the Edsel Bryant Ford Professor of Business Administration at Harvard Business School, combines a "constricted scan that screens out all but essential information, a narrow focus on bits of information, and a compulsiveness that permits slow mastication, digestion and storage of large amounts of information."

Whereas divergent thinking requires breaking down a problem into smaller bits, convergent thinking depends on "reassembly" and reduction. It is a two-step process involving decision and trial. Most corporations have mastered convergent thinking. It is the *divergent* processes that are strange to the focused corporation.

Observing the creative process in corporations as a whole, one notices that it involves a very complex web of problem definition and solution, during which new information is being generated, analyzed, and interpreted. These processes are so complex, and operate at such different speeds—sometimes almost instantaneously (as in the case of insight), and sometimes ponderously slowly (as ideas incubate)—that it is often difficult to calibrate where one is in the process, and whether the process will have a productive end. This is the risk, the tension, and the energy of the creative process. It is not at all like a normal operating process. It is far messier. We can represent the process simply, as a crudely interrupted circle, as shown below:

The Act of Creation

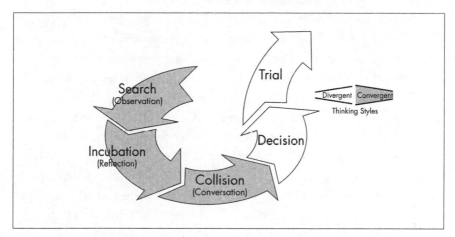

The fact is, the path toward insight is rarely straight. As David Perkins, a professor and codirector of Project Zero at Harvard's Graduate School of Education, said, "In many creative endeavors, the goals, and hence end states, evolve along with the problem. The goals may shift as the search proceeds."

Unlike the "small motor skills" required to control operations, controlling creativity and discovery requires "large motor skills" (see Chapter 9)—changing the people, changing the context, and changing the pace. And it may require unforecastable time. One cannot expect to gain immediate results, but one should not be too surprised if they occur. It is very different from controlling operations. The creative process is also deeply human. It can take enormous personal courage to pursue a creative idea.

What makes the creative process difficult for management is that it has no recognizable parallels in the operating disciplines of decision making, measurement, and control found at the heart of today's corporations. We are dealing with entirely different processes. The role and meaning of information is different. The role and meaning of decision making is different. And the role and meaning of measurement and control are entirely different.

CREATIVE PEOPLE

Arthur Rock, one of the most successful venture capitalists of the twentieth century, and the founder of Arthur Rock & Co., said that "an idea is simply an excuse for getting a team together to make something happen." Yet, as we've seen, the skills required to excel in the creative process are different from the skills required to excel in operations.

What are creative people—those who do excel in the creative processes—like? They tend to have high aspirations. They are impatient. They are open to new experiences, emotion, and risk taking—to the point of being risk seekers. They are willing to risk a great deal because of the happiness and deep satisfaction the creative experience brings to them. As Csikszentmihalyi said, creative people come equipped with a "sunny pessimism," or the ability to have an optimistic sense while looking into the teeth of a negative outlook.

Creative people are willing to face short-term risk to win long-term rewards. Teresa Amabile says, "While many would be dissuaded by the risk of failure, the creative individual does not see the possibility of failure so much as the possibility of success." Moreover, the risk of failure may actually motivate the creative person. Economist George Steiger noted, "In innovation, you have to play less of a safe game if it's going to be interesting. It's not predictable that it'll go well."

Indeed, there are those who actually seek the risk. In a study of lab directors done by Dr. Kevin Dunbar, professor of psychology at McGill University, the directors reported that they liked high-risk projects because they had a long time horizon, which provided the freedom to make some substantial or transformational advances.

In short, creative people are different from traditional operating people. They are comfortable with ambiguity, and they are open to new experiences and thoughts.

THE COR SKILLS OF CREATIVITY

The creative process, particularly divergent thinking, depends on three essential skills that are not often required in the operating organization:

Conversational skills: To successfully pass along your ideas to others, you must converse well.
Observational skills: You must be able to look broadly across industries

and cultures to absorb relevant information—even when its relevance may not be visible to others.

Reflective skills: During the incubation process, you must be able to reflect on the various data and information you have absorbed, and allow these floating pieces to come together into a meaningful pattern or purpose.

We refer to these three skills as the COR skills of the creative process. We discuss them in more depth in Chapter 9.

No amount of experience in the operating environment can prepare one to perform well in the creative environment, and vice versa. The skills, for the most part, are in opposition to one another. To blend them requires exceptional ability.

This ability is required for the leaders of today's corporations if they are to master the dual demands of operations and innovation. Unfortunately, these creative skills are usually dulled by the architecture of the organization (information systems, decision-making systems, executional focus, and the incentives and control systems). As a result, it is nearly impossible for corporations to move from the assumption of continuity to the assumption of discontinuity. Creativity, and its accompanying transformational and substantial innovation, challenges the basic precepts of the corporation focused on operational excellence alone. This is why corporations struggle when they try to embrace creative destruction while remaining operationally excellent.

THE DEFINITION OF INNOVATION

The word *innovation* first appeared, according to Webster's online dictionary, in the fifteenth century. It was derived from the Latin word *novus*, or new. In modern business terms, newness can refer to anything that affects customers, manufacturing, sales, or service. The extent of "newness" can, of course, vary from incremental improvements to wholesale change. Innovation can encompass:

- a new product enabling a pioneering approach to surgery, as Johnson & Johnson accomplished in the '80s with "keyhole" surgery, or laparoscopy
- a new process for making steel, as Nucor launched in the 1970s
- a new service for the customer, as MCI created with their Friends and Family service
- a new way of doing business, as Enron came up with when they created the natural gas trading market.

Innovations are clearly based on more than just technological change.

While innovation is based on creativity and invention, it is much broader. An invention implies the "conversion of a creative idea to some communicable and verifiable form, generally to fulfill some need or perform some task." Innovation is invention that has produced economic value. Without economic value there can be no innovation. Invention *precedes* innovation. It does not presume economic worth. Innovation implies that there is at least an expectation of wealth creation. By such a definition, innovation that does not create value is not really innovation at all. Not every invention is an innovation, because not every invention can be exploited, much less emerge successful in the market.

CHAPTER 5

The Gales of Destruction

Cheyenne Software could not have had a better start in life. It was founded in 1983 by Barry Rubenstein, who had previously started Safeguard Scientifics, where he structured the initial financing of PC networking pioneer Novell. Following Safeguard, Rubenstein realized that the PC networks that were proliferating would need antivirus and backup programs to protect the integrity of their data. In the classic style of a start-up, Rubenstein decided to breathe life into his idea.

The first step was raising money. After contacting three dozen private investors, Rubenstein quickly raised $2.7 million. Next, Rubenstein recruited mainframe veteran Eli Oxenhorn, who was director of computer operations at Warner Communications, to serve as CEO, and ReiJane Huai, a former Bell Labs computer engineer, to lead software development. Although Rubenstein held the position of chairman, Oxenhorn managed the company.

The company initially marketed itself as a custom provider of software for LANs (local area networks), which interconnect PCs. For developing and maintaining its clients' software integration applications, Cheyenne received fees and long-term recurring royalties for its services. Securing clients like Chemical Bank and Fisher Business Systems enabled Cheyenne to go public in 1985.

Soon Rubenstein realized that there was an even bigger market for Cheyenne's custom applications. Most LANs held thousands of gigabytes of critical corporate information, and protecting them was increasingly complex. Responding to that opportunity, Cheyenne introduced ARCserve, a data storage manager for Novell networks that had a much higher level of data management and protection services than any other product.

As Novell boomed, so did ARCserve, which was the only server-based backup product that worked on all Novell platforms. By 1991, Cheyenne's ARCserve software supported more than 90% of the installed base of backup hardware.

By 1993, the company had decided to leverage the widespread implementation of ARCserve by linking ARCserve to InocuLAN, Cheyenne's antivirus software. ARCserve was also linked with Cheyenne's automated server-based facsimile software, FAXserve, which allowed users to send vital reports generated by ARCserve to destinations of their choice.

Despite these additions to the product line, Cheyenne had not been able to expand beyond its dependency on ARCserve sales. In early 1994, Cheyenne stumbled: The latest version of ARCserve shipped late, which led to a failure to meet earnings expectations. The company's stock fell. Fortunately, in April, the new version of ARCserve was released, relieving pent-up demand and allowing Cheyenne to beat estimates. The company also announced that its president, ReiJane Huai, would replace Eli Oxenhorn as CEO. This news reassured wary investors, sending the stock up 13% in a single day.

But the good news didn't last. That June, the SEC announced an investigation of the company based on an allegation that senior executives allegedly had sold shares prior to the missed earnings report. A class-action lawsuit by shareholders followed. Cheyenne's stock price fell by more than 70%. Meanwhile, bugs were being reported in the new version of ARCserve, and some system administrators charged that the company had released its product six months before it was ready. Despite this, Cheyenne bounced back. The bugs were fixed, the suits settled, and profits in 1995 soared.

Cheyenne was still saddled with the need to grow, however. Unfortunately, ARCserve's innovations were not enough. With a highly successful LAN product, but little in the pipeline to expand the business further, Cheyenne became vulnerable to acquisition because it could not both operate effectively and innovate at the pace and scale required by the market to remain competitive. In April 1996, McAfee Associates, a company focused on the market for antivirus software, made an offer of $1 billion in stock for Cheyenne. McAfee CEO Bill Larson was confident that Cheyenne would accept the offer. "This deal will get done," he said. He simply needed to "lay out our options, and enlist the shareholder community to communicate [to Cheyenne's management] that this is a marriage made in heaven."

But Huai was adamantly opposed, calling the offer "absolutely inadequate from a valuation point of view, from the point of view of a strategic business." Huai went on the offensive, questioning McAfee's viability as an antivirus provider. "The long-term prospects [for antiviral products] are really questionable," he said.

Cheyenne fought the McAfee offer, implementing a poison pill strategy and filing suit against McAfee and Larson for making "false and misleading public statements concerning Cheyenne." For his part, Larson suggested that Cheyenne should fire Huai. Though Cheyenne reported a 33% drop in quarterly profits, Larson was not able to apply sufficient pressure. On May 1, McAfee dropped their offer. The McAfee bid, however, had signaled the opening of a "shopping season," and it wasn't long before a suitor more agreeable to Huai and Cheyenne stepped forward: Computer Associates International.

CAI, which was rumored to be interested in Cheyenne before the bid by McAfee, made an offer of $1.2 billion in cash. "Sanjay [Kumar, president of Computer Associates] called and said, 'It seems like a good idea for us to pool our companies together,'" Huai said. Huai accepted the offer. While the deal was a 20% premium on McAfee's offer, the rise in McAfee's stock since its failed bid was announced would have raised its offer value to $1.8 billion, an indication that Cheyenne had paid dearly for its "white knight."

Cheyenne was soon acquired by Computer Associates and downsized to generate more profits. By 1996, the flame that burned so brightly in 1983 had been extinguished. Cheyenne had lost its economic purpose and the market responded as Schumpeter had indicated it would. This is the way destruction happens in the marketplace.

Sometimes the destruction process can take decades. The Studebaker was one of the classic cars of the 1950s. Where is the company that made it now? Studebaker's decline began in the Great Depression, after more than seventy years of almost continuous growth and prosperity. Although sales declined to about 36,000 units in 1933 (from more than 84,000 in 1928), Studebaker's management stubbornly refused to trim its common stock dividend and cut other costs. As a result, the company only slowly recovered from the Depression. In World War II, Studebaker got a substantial cash infusion from the government. In 1954, it acquired Packard Motor Car Co. But Packard itself was weak; Studebaker killed off the Packard line four years later. By the late 1960s, Studebaker stopped making cars altogether. The company "reinvented itself" as a component manufacturer but never regained its star status. In 1979, it "merged" with Worthington of Canada to form Studebaker-Worthington, which was then acquired by a company called McGraw-Edison.

Anaconda Copper is another fallen star. By 1929, the company had amassed a worldwide natural resource empire encompassing copper mines in Chile, Mexico, and the United States; iron ore in Ontario; and vast nickel reserves in Australia. As late as 1968, as we noted at the beginning of Chapter 1, Anaconda president C. Jay Parkinson confidently predicted, "This company will be going strong a hundred and even five hundred years from now." Shortly afterward, in 1971, the Chilean mines were nationalized by the short-lived government of Salvador Allende. Weakened to the breaking point, Anaconda sold the remaining assets to Atlantic Richfield, which subsequently sold them on the open market in 1985, and like that, Anaconda was gone.

Another example, American Locomotive, comes from the railway industry, the industry that in its own time came closest to the booming telecommunications market of today. American Locomotive was incorporated in 1901 and quickly turned to "voracious acquisitions" to take advantage of the explosive growth in railways. In the early years of the century, American became the largest rail equipment manufacturer in the country. However, with the building of a national system of superhighways in the 1950s and the steady progress of the diesel engine, trucking eventually took over much of the railways' market. AL tried and failed to diversify into areas outside their core competencies—heat-transfer equipment and automobiles—but became successively weaker and weaker. In the early 1980s, its remaining fragments were quietly subsumed into Cooper Industries.

As we go through the early years of the Internet transformation, stories like these are certain to continue.

THE EMOTIONAL DIFFICULTY OF DESTRUCTION: THE CASE OF INTEL

There are few things more emotionally upsetting to most people than the thought of killing off a company or a division, or firing a large group of people. Little wonder that within many companies one can find useless businesses, protected by complex accounting systems that "subsidize" one business through another. Very often, divisions continue to operate even after they have outlived their economic purpose, at least as measured by the returns to investors.

The tension that a decision to close such a business division evokes is evident even in the best of companies. Few companies have been able to ride the turbulent waves created by "gales of creative destruction" better than Intel. Yet Intel, too, has experienced the emotional Sturm und Drang of destruction.

In mid-1985, Andy Grove, then president of Intel, paid a visit to Intel's last remaining DRAM (dynamic random access memory) manufacturing facility in Hillsboro, Oregon. His message to the staff: Intel would stop manufacturing DRAMs. It was a momentous decision for Intel, which was once the world leader in the DRAM business. DRAMs were its "heritage" product, the product that got the company going in 1968. But by 1983, the market had become oversupplied. Japanese manufacturers, driven by the determination to dominate world commerce in these vital parts of the information revolution, had virtually destroyed the industry. Had Intel stuck with DRAMs, it would have gone bankrupt. The situation was obvious, but making the obvious decision was agonizing.

At the time of Intel's founding in 1968, semiconductor memory products were overtaking the core memory products of other companies. Semiconductor memories were the new "gale" of the industry. By 1972, Intel's 1-kilobit 1103 DRAM chip had become the largest-selling integrated circuit in the world and accounted for more than 90% of Intel's $23.4 million in revenue. As first mover, Intel commanded nearly 100% share of the memory chip market. By the end of the '70s, Andy Grove was able to say, "Intel still stood for memories; conversely, memories meant Intel."

But in the early '80s, the large Japanese DRAM producers (e.g., Fujitsu, Toshiba, NEC, Hitachi) entered the U.S. market with high-volume, high-quality, low-cost products. Moreover, since the technology was still maturing, Intel was forced to spend ever more heavily on R&D to keep a step ahead of its rivals. As the DRAM approached commodity status, prices collapsed, and with that came a collapse in return to shareholders. It was a pure and simple case of oversupply. In a single three-month period over the summer of 1984, the price of DRAMs fell by 40%, dragging down industry performance with it. Intel slipped further than the industry as a whole because of its dependence on DRAMs—and this was reflected in Intel's total return to shareholders (TRS).

Semiconductors
Return on Invested Capital vs. Economy

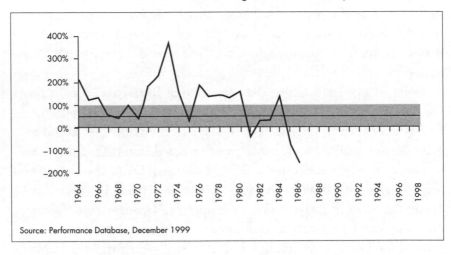

Source: Performance Database, December 1999

Intel's Total Return to Shareholders, 1972–1984

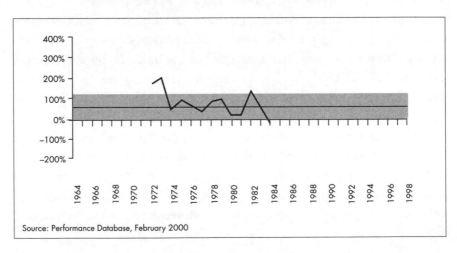

Source: Performance Database, February 2000

One Monday in January of 1983 (subsequently called "Black Monday" at Intel), Karl "Casey" Powell, Scott Gibson, and fifteen coworkers who had worked as a team to find new applications for the newly developed micro-processor resigned en masse from Intel. They left because Intel was still obsessed with developing and producing DRAMs, and would not provide the resources that Powell and Gibson felt they needed to develop a wholly new concept in computer applications: parallel processing. The defecting Intel employees formed a company called Sequent Computer Systems.

By the fall of 1984, Intel was losing money on its declining DRAM business. Intel's CEO, Gordon Moore, and president, Andrew Grove, presided over a series of "meetings and more meetings, bickerings and arguments, resulting in nothing but conflicting proposals" over the future of Intel's fast-fading DRAM business. As Grove would later recall, making an apparently simple strategic decision—exiting from the random-access memory business—was powerfully blocked by the emotional ties the founders and senior executives had for memory chips, the silicon wafers that had "made Intel Intel."

As Grove recalled:

> *As the debates raged, we just went on losing more and more money. It was a grim and frustrating year. During that time, we worked hard without a clear notion of how things were ever going to get better. We had lost our bearings. We were wandering in the valley of death.*

Halfway through that "grim and frustrating year," CEO Moore and President Grove were standing in Grove's office in Santa Clara, California, gazing dolefully down at the Ferris wheel of the Great American amuse-ment park revolving off in the distance. Grove turned to Moore and asked him point-blank: "If we got kicked out and the board brought in a new CEO, what do you think he would do?" To which Moore unhesitatingly replied: "He would get us out of memories." After a few moments of silence, Grove asked Moore: "Why shouldn't you and I walk out that door, come back in, and do it ourselves?"

That rhetorical question started Intel's two leaders on a long, painful course of action that eventually eliminated Intel's core business. As Grove later recalled, even after determining the correct strategic direction, imple-mentation proved next to impossible, so deeply ingrained in the mental models of key employees was the role of DRAMs. As Grove said later,

Intel equaled memories in all of our minds. How could we give up our identity? How could we exist as a company that was not in the memory business? Saying it to Gordon was one thing; talking to other people and implementing it was another.

It was a classic case of cultural lock-in (and what Andrew Grove would later dub a "strategic inflection point"). The "defensive routines" of data disconfirmation, emotional resistance, and elaborate rationalizations were taking their invisible toll. Not only was Grove "far too tentative," by his own account, in attempting to marshal the depth of conviction required to exit expeditiously from the memory business, but he found himself "talking to people who didn't want to hear what [he] had to say."

As Grove observed:

The company had a couple of beliefs that were as strong as religious dogmas. Both of them had to do with the importance of memories as the backbone of our manufacturing and sales activities. One was that memories were our "technology drivers," which meant that we always developed and refined our technologies on our memory products first because they were easier to test. The other belief was the "full-product-line" dogma. According to this [belief], our salesmen needed a full product line to do a good job in front of our customers; if they didn't have a full product line, the customer would prefer to do business with our competitors who did.

Grove and Moore would need to eliminate not merely the memory business itself, but the "twin dogmas" that had protected Intel for so long and insulated it from reality. In practice, eliminating the prevailing mental model of the corporation, and the emotional superstructure that reinforced it, proved at least as difficult as eliminating the DRAM business itself.

To kill the DRAM business, Intel's VP of finance instituted a capital-allocation system. This caused capital investment in Intel's memory business to "gradually and incrementally decline." By late 1984, DRAM production was reduced to a single fabrication site in Oregon. (R&D investment in DRAM continued to absorb about one-third of Intel's total R&D investment, despite the fact that senior management had already arrived at a decision to cease production of DRAM chips.)

That message, unfortunately, would take a while to sink down to the middle-management level. Grove would later credit a group of aggressive middle managers with gradually starving the DRAM business out of existence—even as more senior managers wavered, hesitated, and publicly and privately anguished over the difficulty of achieving an exit. He would later credit these middle managers with pointing the way for the senior managers, and attributed their ability to act to their being "closer to the market" and less prone to sentiment than the senior team.

Other middle managers, with a more personal stake in keeping the DRAM business alive, were not about to give up without a fight. One proposal that the DRAM unit managers desperately advanced was a breakup of the company into two separate entities, one providing a commodity product (DRAMs) and the other a "specialty" business (microprocessors). Although this proposal was never accepted, the company spent time and money on its evaluation.

The conflict continued. At one point Grove replaced the manager in charge of the doomed DRAM unit with another, to whom he clarified his strategic objective: "Get us out of memories!" Yet the new manager found himself unable to offer anything better than a compromise—he would undertake no R&D on *new* memory products, but would continue to do R&D on products "already in the works."

As Grove would later recall, he reluctantly agreed to this request, on the grounds that exiting the DRAM business had to be pursued incrementally. "I rationalized to myself that such a major change had to be accomplished in a number of small steps," he recalled. Indeed, as late as mid-1985, Intel was entertaining a request by the general manager of the Components Group (to whom Memory Components reported) that it acquire advanced DRAM "fabrication facilities in Japan in order to keep Intel abreast of the latest Japanese equipment advances in DRAM manufacture." Needless to say, the market itself would never have embarked on such equivocation and delay. There would have been no one to make it.

Finally, Grove "took charge of the implementation of the exit decision." First, he visited Intel's last remaining DRAM manufacturing facility, in Oregon, and told the staff they would not be making DRAMs there any longer. Once this difficult and momentous decision had at last been made—publicly—there was no turning back. Intel told its sales force to notify the company's memory customers that Intel would no longer be making DRAMs. The key uncertainties at the time were "What will our customers say? Will they abandon us? Will they lose loyalty to our brand?" As Grove recalled, he and his team were pleasantly surprised by their customers' reactions—or rather, lack of one. "Their reaction was, for all practical purposes, benign," said Grove.

Indeed, the image of the market held by Intel's senior managers had become severely distorted by cultural lock-in. They feared taking action. Ironically, key customers had long since accepted the fact that Intel was no longer a major factor in the DRAM market. They had already found other suppliers. "Well, it sure took you a long time," one customer commented.

As Grove would later philosophically observe: "People who have no emotional stake in a decision can see what needs to be done a lot sooner." And this, of course, is the key advantage that markets have over companies.

While significant managerial energy was consumed by the decision to leave its heritage business, Intel also aggressively pursued a transformational innovation—the microprocessor, which was designed to power the original IBM PC. Soon sales of microprocessors outpaced Intel's highest sales levels of DRAMs.

As Grove himself cheerfully concluded: "By 1992, mostly owing to our success with microprocessors, we became the largest semiconductor company in the world, larger even than the Japanese companies that had beaten us in memories. By now, our identification with microprocessors is so strong that it's difficult for us to get noticed for our nonmicroprocessor products."

So powerful was the influence of the microprocessor that the health of the entire semiconductor industry, in fact, improved. (See the top chart on page 135.) Financial success, and reward for patient shareholders, followed. Intel's total return to shareholders soon climbed above the industry average, as the bottom chart on page 135 demonstrates.

Less than half a decade after the microprocessor victory, Intel faced potential cultural lock-in once again. This time it came in the form of the discontinuity that has been shaped by the Internet. In 1996, in response to this challenge, Intel added a fourth strategic objective to what had been a tripartite program: "Encapsulating all the things that are necessary to mobilize our efforts in connection with the Internet." Intel has structured that effort as a venture capital firm would, building several funds that invested some $1 billion in new non-Intel start-ups. Recently (the first quarter of 2000), sales of these investments has added materially to Intel's reported results. The future will tell whether the junior executives at Intel,

Semiconductors
Return on Invested Capital vs. Economy

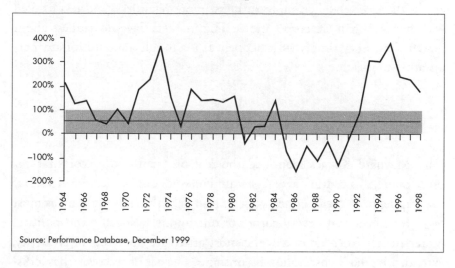

Source: Performance Database, December 1999

Intel's TRS, 1972–1998

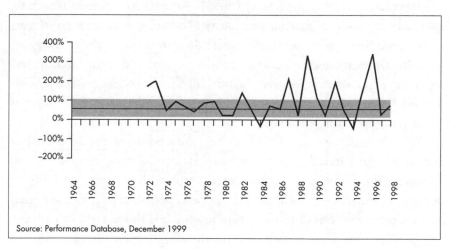

Source: Performance Database, December 1999

those who aggressively fixed the DRAM dilemma, will be able to muster the courage to overcome the cultural lock-in regarding the personal computer industry that now sits at the edge of the campfire.

As Intel's history demonstrates, the time it takes to overcome cultural lock-in—to make the destroy decision—can be agonizingly long. The Intel story, however, is typical. There are hundreds of others like it.

How different Intel and other companies are from the market as a whole, which is stripped down to just buyers and sellers, without emotion, and is therefore tougher, more ruthless, more relentless, and less bridled with remorse than are corporations. The markets have no sadness about destruction. They simply let it happen. It is a tough standard for any corporation to match.

ESCAPING FROM OLD IDEAS

John Maynard Keynes identified the real problem within corporations more than half a century ago: "The difficulty lies not in the new ideas, but in escaping from the old ones, which ramify, for those brought up as most of us have been, into every corner of our minds." Novelist and political writer Arthur Koestler, one of the most articulate observers of creativity, extended Keynes's observation by noting, "The act of discovery has a disruptive and a constructive aspect. It must disrupt rigid patterns of mental organization to achieve the new synthesis." As markets, competitive strategies, and regulations change, previously accurate mental models of customers and their needs, competitors and their strategies, rules of the game and the games themselves, change in incremental and most often unrecognized, or undiscussed, ways. As our McKinsey colleague, Peter Winsemius in Holland, summarizes, "Our organizations tend to be good at what was important yesterday."

Why is this the case? There are several schools of thought. Arthur Koestler claims it is because "we learn by assimilating experience and grouping them into ordered schemata, into stable patterns of unity in variety. The matrices which pattern our perceptions, thoughts and activities are condensations of learning into habit." It is this pattern of converting learning into habit, as well as the unthinking application of habit, that undermines the effectiveness of our past practices. The situation changes, but we do not recognize the changes.

The second school of thought is one that was first described by Elisabeth Kübler-Ross as she studied the reaction of people to life crises (specifically, the reaction of individuals at the moment they learned they were terminally ill). We briefly describe Kübler-Ross's sequence of denial, anger, bargaining, depression, and acceptance in Chapter 3. We believe the Kübler-Ross analysis is a metaphor for the corporate reaction to crisis, and drives to the heart of cultural lock-in. In patients facing a terminal illness the mood swings associated with the Kübler-Ross cycle can be wild and the period of adjustment long—and sometimes unresolved before death. The same happens in business, as senior managers face the potential corporate trauma of separating or terminating a business that has made long contributions to the well-being of the corporation. In life, the Kübler-Ross reaction is a "normal, healthy one." But in business, it delays the sense of urgency surrounding the crises, supports the status quo, and makes the afflicted company easy prey for aggressors. The problem, in other words, is not with objective reality but with the distortion of reality.

THE CONCEPT OF DESTRUCTION

Joseph Schumpeter observed in his studies of the pattern of development of markets and economies that destruction and creation were often paired. This is an ancient meld. Egyptian and Greek history are filled with stories of the mythical Arabian Phoenix bird, foster father of Achilles, which destroyed itself in a pyre and then was reborn every three hundred years or so, marking the turning points in Egyptian history. The Phoenix was an early symbol of the cycle of birth, life, death, and resurrection, leading to immortality. In business, that sense of immortality is known as continuity. The Phoenix, in other words, combined both creation and destruction.

The Buddhists have their Phoenix equivalent in the Garuda, a bird, their religious stories say, that was fond of the daily killing and eating of a snake, until a Buddhist prince taught him the value of abstinence. The penitent Garuda then brought back to life the many generations of serpents he had fed upon.

In Chinese culture the Feng, a bird with the head of a pheasant and the tail of a peacock—a structure not unlike the Phoenix or the Garuda— plays a similar role. Hindus have perhaps the most complex theory of creation and destruction: the Hindu trinity of Brahma (the creator), Shiva (sometimes a destroyer), and Vishnu (the arbitrator), which focuses directly on the balance of destruction and creation.

While the origins of creative destruction probably are lost in religious and cultural history, it is clear that Schumpeter was far from the first to focus on the close bond between creation and destruction, birth and death, continuity and change. In fact, he was one of a long line of thinkers who, to this day, strongly affect our ideas. But Schumpeter did apply the lessons of creation and destruction to the economy in a very persuasive way. Destruction is a mechanism that allows the market to maintain freshness by eliminating those elements that are no longer needed. As such, it is an essential feature of capitalism.

Destruction, of course, is a negative and frightening word, conjuring up images of chaos and disorder. Perhaps without Schumpeter's guidance we would have tried to find a different word to describe the process. But we would have had to have found some word like it—because it *is* what happens in the market. Companies are born and they die or are subsumed. Unlike *creation,* which brings images to mind of a bright future, limitless possibilities, and perhaps personal growth, *destruction* triggers fear and foreboding. One thinks of Al "Chainsaw" Dunlop, the former CEO of Scott Paper whose alleged callousness was synonymous with destruction.

When Schumpeter coined his phrase "gales of creative destruction," he had in mind the fate of collections of companies, old companies being replaced by new ones. The Russian revolutionary Mikhail Bakunin, considered by many to be the most radical of all anarchists, once said, "The urge to destroy is also a creative urge."

But this is not what Schumpeter had in mind. His idea was rather the opposite, that the efficiency of the new corporation placed such economic pressure on the old corporation, which did not change its ways quickly enough, that it eventually could not compete, and over time outlived its economic usefulness. Undoubtedly Schumpeter anticipated that even companies in new industries that had lost their edge would over time be eliminated. Schumpeter would not have been surprised by the fate of Cheyenne Software.

Schumpeter was not talking about processes that occur inside a company itself, although he easily could have addressed this issue. He left it up to us to apply what we mean by "destruction" to individual companies. In Schumpter's sense destruction is "the end of the economically useful life," whether a part of a corporation or of a company. This does not necessarily mean that this part of the corporation will die, however, or otherwise cease to exist. It simply indicates that the economic rationale for having it as part of the company has ended or is about to end. That could be because the potential of the business has played out, or because the basic economic rationale for the corporation has changed. Thus a division that might be appropriate for destruction at Intel does not necessarily warrant destruction at Fujitsu, which may have different objectives and resources.

In other words, *destruction* does not mean "death" in the Judeo-Christian tradition, but rather "transformation" in the Hindu tradition. In this sense, *destroy* really means something much closer to "trade" than to obliterate. In some instances, *destruction* may, of course, refer to the end of economic life altogether, but that would be a special case of the more general principle. In either case, however, whether in the company or in the economy, the new will drive out the old.

There are various "acts of destruction" or "trading." In a corporate setting the most dramatic acts, as we just mentioned, are the decisions to sell or shut down a group. A milder form might be to spin off groups that could make better use of debt capital if their parent retained only a minority (nonconsolidated) share. The point of destruction in these cases is, as Schumpeter implied, to make way for creation, to allow for an increase in the "freshness" of the corporation.

We do not normally think of restructuring as an act of destruction or trading. Restructuring is a normal part of the operational responsibilities of the corporation. One can restructure for growth or for returns, but the intent is to continue to actively manage the enterprise, rather than spin it out to increase the capacity for creation.

The notion of destruction raises some challenging questions for management. First, how can a company be run as a "destroyer"? We actually don't know of any companies that are run specifically that way, other than the occasional asset stripper (few of whom exist, and even fewer of which survive). A good many companies are traders, however, and as we discuss in Chapter 7, many of them are private equity investing firms.

There are, of course, aging companies that generate significant cash flow and yet do not grow. Some of these companies have lost their ability to trade as they have matured. As these companies have aged, so have their employees. Such companies are perfectly comfortable places, but they are not places for one to begin a career and grow. The reality is that recruiting new people is quite difficult for these companies. Over time, despite their strong returns and good dividends, their market capitalization tends to shrink relative to the growth of the economy, because they are not growing. The companies gradually lose relative economic power and simply fade away, as Cheyenne, Studebaker, and Anaconda did. If, along the path, their economic performance deteriorates, they may be bought out or go under even more quickly. But as we pointed out above, such companies can last for quite a long time in this state of "suspended animation." It would not be fair to categorize these companies as "destroyers." They are not intent on destroying anything; they are intent on merely staying alive. But they eventually expire.

How can managers and executives respond to destruction or trading that occurs at the pace and scale of the markets? Are people emotionally equipped to handle this kind of stress? The answer must certainly be "no" regarding destruction. People are not emotionally equipped to live a life of destruction. But then again, neither are many called upon to do that. In most aging companies, the decline is both gradual and relative to the overall market. People gradually move away from the center of the nation's economic activity. The costs to individuals come more in the form of lost opportunity than real losses. With regard to trading, there are firms that have learned to trade at the pace and scale of the markets, as we describe in Chapter 7.

People who are caught up in overt destruction—for example, bankruptcy or a premature ending like Cheyenne—certainly need to find new jobs. And there will be more of this in the future, if our forecasts are correct. There are at least three broad strategies that such individuals can pursue. The first is to ponder the risk in advance, assess the consequences, and prepare an "evacuation plan," just as one would if one lived on the coast and faced an approaching hurricane. Second, people can broaden their skills so that they have more options if their fears about their company or division materialize. Being dependent on a single skill set has always been risky, but it will become more risky in the future. Third, one can live in a place where there are ample opportunities if their current job is eliminated. In Silicon Valley or Silicon Alley, or Austin, Boston, or Raleigh-Durham, people are forever changing positions. When one job ends, another opens up. People become loyal to areas rather than companies. More of this will likely take place in the future. These are not foolproof solutions, nor are they necessarily pleasant. But the reality of destruction is a fact of economic life.

Interestingly, American laws make it more difficult to declare bankruptcy in the United States than in the United Kingdom and many other countries. While this is a plus for creditors and employees, it comes with an economic cost for the nation as it slows the rate at which we can redeploy our resources and thus our rate of progress. Despite this, we have not heard a single voice in favor of making bankruptcy easier in order to increase our rate of progress. If there are voices for policy changes in bankruptcy, it is for more stringency, not less.

Nonetheless, destruction is a reality of the market. It signals the end of economic utility for a division or company or industry. It can be postponed but not avoided. It is an inherent part of capitalism. The danger is that if it is not recognized as a normal part of corporate management, progress and performance can be slowed, and change will strike the company unawares. We have seen many examples of this, as Cheyenne, Studebaker, and Anaconda have demonstrated. To ignore destruction is to invite disaster. The issue, then, is how to deal with it. The way to handle it is to recognize destruction for what it is and make an explicit decision to deal with it, to trade dying assets before they have to be destroyed.

LEVELS OF DESTRUCTION

Destruction, like innovation, can be incremental, substantial, or transformational. In the case of innovation, we characterize the processes by the newness of each innovation and the amount of wealth created. In the case of destruction, the level of change depends on the extent of destruction and the amount of wealth at risk if destruction is not carried out.

Virtually all companies go through some form of *incremental* internal destruction each year. Procedures are changed, individual posts or branch offices closed, and so on. This kind of destruction does not challenge the basic mental model of the corporation; indeed, it is essential for the improvement of the operating routine of the corporation. Such change is essential to the concept of continuity. This kind of incremental destruction can be successfully carried out by the front line of the organization, just as incremental innovation is; it goes on day in and day out in a thousand, often unnoticed, ways.

Substantial destruction—the decision to lay off 10% or more of the workforce, terminate a joint venture, kill an area of research or the development of a new product line—is not a decision that can be taken by the front line alone. Senior management must be involved. They are usually unpleasant to contemplate, plan, and implement. Nonetheless, such decisions are vital to the long-term competitiveness of most organizations. Substantial destruction is warranted when major systems (e.g., corporate planning) get old and encrusted, and need to be replaced by more modern equivalents. Such replacements from time to time can trigger a fundamental change in the mental model of the corporation. Substantial destruction is a process fundamentally different from incremental destruction.

Transformational destruction irreversibly changes the course of the corporation. Closing down a heritage product line—as Intel did with its DRAM business—putting the company into play, and declaring bankruptcy are all examples of transformational destruction. It is transformational destruction that is closest to Schumpeter's meaning when he wrote about "gales of creative destruction"; he envisioned companies and even whole industries being replaced. Often transformational destruction is triggered by market events, such as the entrance of foreign competition (in the case of Intel's DRAM) or the emergence of oversupply. Transformational destruction is a totally different and far more permanent process than substantial destruction, since the changes are irreversible.

All three kinds of destruction are crucial for corporate health. As corporations grow and mature, they become more complex. The complexities manifest themselves in rules, design manuals, and bureaucratic growth. The corporation becomes encrusted with rules and procedures.

Destruction is the one sure way to eliminate this encrustation. It scours corporate systems clean, keeping them fresh. And the longer one waits to remove the crust, the more dramatic the act of destruction must be, as Cheyenne Software discovered after it was too late.

CHAPTER 6

Balancing Destruction
and Creation

I have the feeling that I am sitting at a campfire, late at night, and the embers are slowly going out. I can hear the sounds at the edge of the light, just beyond view, but I don't know what they are or what they mean.

CEO OF A FORTUNE 100 GLOBAL CORPORATION,
January 2000

In Chapter 3 we described the natural evolution of the key elements of a corporation's invisible architecture: mental models, information systems, decision-making systems, executional capabilities (actions), and control processes (which we called MIDAS), which can result in cultural lock-in. As we discussed, there is an inevitable evolution of corporations from the early passion of creation through the rational analysis stage and then into the trap of denial. This trajectory describes the great majority of American corporations over their lifetimes. A few corporations, however, have made attempts to break out of this pattern, and a few have succeeded—at least to a greater extent than the others.

The key to their success is the balance they have struck between creation and destruction—between continuity and change.

Often, we see a corporation beginning life as a result of a transformational innovation. As it matures, it begins to focus more on operations. The focus on innovation shifts, as we noted earlier, from transformational innovation to substantial innovation. Most corporations do not begin to focus on their need to destroy at this point. But a few do. Even at these early stages of development, those few companies begin to systematically break down the structures they have just built. If they do this too rapidly, of course, they destroy the basis of their existence—their current cash flow. If they do it too slowly, however, they will perform well in the short term but find themselves stuck in a cul-de-sac of mediocrity as time goes on. The corporation may still enjoy considerable success as it continues to improve through incremental innovation, but over the long term it is not sufficient to drive superior performance.

Eventually one of two things happens: either the corporation's performance begins to slow, or it attempts to revitalize itself. Companies can revitalize themselves by restarting the business, cashing out, simultaneous substantial creation and destruction, or simultaneous transformational creation and destruction. We will describe each in more detail.

One way companies try to revitalize themselves is by attempting to create transformational innovation without changing themselves to any degree. This is a difficult course to follow, and is usually unsuccessful. A second way is what we call "cashing out"—that is, liquidating the corporation through a sale of assets to another corporation, as Cheyenne had to do. This approach rewards current shareholders but clearly leaves the corporation moribund in the long run. It also leaves the company open for acquisition.

SIMULTANEOUS SUBSTANTIAL CREATION AND DESTRUCTION

A third approach companies can take is to attempt both creation and destruction on a substantial scale. Corning, which moved from cookware and diversified glass products into fiber optics, and Enron, which evolved from a natural gas pipeline company to a trader of natural gas and other commodities, have pursued this course. They demonstrate that management with vision and high executional skill can implement this approach. Both companies resolved not only to "destroy" their current business but to build the skills to produce new revenue streams. While each destroyed its current business, it was with some confidence that the new business was close enough at hand that the company would be able to survive the crossing. The stocks of both companies plummeted until the markets were convinced they were on the right track.

CORNING

In 1864, Amory Houghton, long an investor in glass companies, purchased the Brooklyn Flint Glass Company. Four years later it transferred operations to Corning, New York, attracted by ample coal for fuel and by good transportation. Houghton renamed the company The Corning Flint Glass Company in honor of its new location. The firm, which initially produced consumer products such as thermometer tubing, pharmaceutical glassware, railroad signal glass, and tableware blanks, was incorporated in 1875 as Corning Glass Works. In 1879, when Thomas Edison needed a glass bulb for his new electric lamp, he turned to Corning for assistance.

At first, the bulbs created by Corning were made by gaffers working gobs of molten glass on blowpipes, and production was very low. But a team of four glassworkers, capitalizing on the potential of molds, was eventually able to turn out more than 1,200 bulbs a day. By 1908, the year Dr. Eugene Sullivan established one of the nation's first industrial research laboratories at Corning, lightbulbs accounted for more than 50% of the company's business. Corning's bulb marked the beginning of a partnership between glass and electricity that grew broadly over the years and now has taken on increasing importance in the age of electronics.

In addition to its technological prowess, Corning's success stemmed from its joint ventures. Corning formed a glass construction company, Pittsburgh Corning, with Pittsburgh Plate Glass in 1937; a fiberglass company, Owens-Corning, with Owens-Illinois in 1938; and a silicone maker, Dow Corning, with Dow Chemical in 1943. Corning has always understood that performance was the issue—not control, but performance for shareholders. It has provided that continually, although at times its devotion to shareholders has come at the expense of increasing corporate size.

Following World War II, Corning expanded globally. The company's laboratories made it the undisputed leader in the manufacture of specialty glass, which it used at the time to develop consumer products. For example, the company developed the first chemically durable glass, borosilicate glass, which could withstand sudden temperature changes, for freezer-to-oven Pyroceram brand ceramic cookware. This glass made the company's products the leading cookware in the market and made Corning a household name.

In 1947, the company's research revolutionized glass-forming methods to mass-produce bulbs, making television affordable for millions. By

1949, the efforts of James W. Giffen, head of the laboratory's newly formed machine research group, had paid off with a new method for centrifugal casting of television funnels. At the same time, Dr. William H. Armistead, a Corning research chemist, developed a new lead-free glass composition specifically for television tubes that was both lighter and less expensive to produce. These television products dramatically increased Corning's sales and earnings growth. Investors responded accordingly with approval, bidding their stock to new levels.

But by 1983, James Houghton, the CEO, sensed that after a hundred years of excelling at the manufacture and sales of consumer goods, growth in that field was going to become increasingly difficult. Houghton initiated experiments with many different businesses. He narrowed the company's focus to high-growth industries and began buying laboratory services companies, such as MetPath in 1982, Hazleton in 1987, and both Enseco and G. H. Besselaar in 1989. The company also established international joint ventures with Siemens, Mitsubishi, and Samsung and dropped Glass Works from its name, representing a move away from consumer products and to technology.

Along with these efforts, which had only a slim connection with the core ceramic technical skills of the company, Corning began to work on the development of optical-fiber technology, thus entering a completely new arena. For years, the commercial use of optical fibers for voice and data transmission was impossible because of light loss over distance. In 1970, three Corning researchers solved the problem when they created the first optical waveguides—glass fibers made from fused silica—that maintained the strength of laser light signals over significant distances. The invention paved the way for the commercialization of fiber optics for long-distance telecommunications and other uses. In 1993, AT&T chose Corning to provide fiber-optic couplers for its undersea telecommunications system.

To enhance developmental efforts with optical fibers, in 1994 Corning undertook a joint venture with Siemens AG, forming Siecor and Siecor GMBH. Siecor GMBH then acquired several fiber and cable businesses from Nortel Networks, expanding the firms' presence in Canada. Corning also formed Biccor to invest in fiber-optic ventures in Asia.

Then Houghton retired and was succeeded by president and chief operating officer Roger Ackerman. As CEO, Ackerman decided to "double R&D spending . . . putting it into optical communications." The next year, demonstrating Corning's commitment to creative destruction, Ackerman tried to sell off the slowly growing housewares unit, Corning Consumer Products, which accounted for 50% of sales and 50% of the employees. He first attempted to sell the unit to AEA Investors, but the sale fell through. But the following year, Corning was able to complete the sale of CCP to Kohlberg, Kravis and Roberts, signaling the end of Corning's involvement with consumer products. By expanding its presence in telecommunication and other technologies and selling off its consumer division, Corning distinguished itself from the vast majority of traditional companies, demonstrating its willingness to actually "act like the market." Corning has shrunk to grow several times in its century-and-a-quarter history.

Nor did Corning stop there. In 1999, it bought UK-based BICC Group's telecommunications cable business, and in 2000 the company acquired Siemens AG's optical cable and hardware businesses and the remaining 50% of its joint venture, Siecor Corporation and Siecor GMBH. Also that year, the company acquired a communications components and mechanical control devices company, Oak Industries, and announced plans to spend some $750 million to double its optical-fiber manufacturing capacity. Later in 2000, Corning acquired NetOptix, a maker of optical filters, in a deal valued at about $2 billion.

These acquisitions are proving to be successful. For example, in early 1999, Corning introduced LEAF® Fiber, the first fiber and optical component capable of dramatically increasing the speed and information-carrying capacity of telecommunication networks. In addition, the company developed the first optical amplifier for telecommunication networks; the device can boost as many as eighty wavelengths of light through a single optical fiber. These inventions have enabled the company to dominate the market and rapidly increase sales growth.

Corning is now the leading provider of bandwidth, a market that is growing 30% a year. In 1999, Ackerman said Corning has "the largest position in the world in this particular technology [ultrahigh bandwidth], and we are continuing to invest aggressively in new plant equipment and, probably more importantly, in innovation." It has been Corning's steady commitment to creative destruction, without sacrificing its operational excellence, that has placed the company at the forefront of the lightbulb, television, and fiber-optics industries—and in investor returns.

Following this long-standing tradition, Corning is not satisfied in being in fiber optics alone. Ackerman said the company plans to go "well beyond optical fiber. We're spending a lot of money on R&D and doing very well in what I would call manipulating light information." Ackerman states that "Corning leads primarily by technical innovation and shares a deep belief in the power of technology. The company has a history of great contributions in science and technology, and it is this same spirit of innovation that has enabled us to create new products and new markets."

With more than 50% of sales coming from the fiber-optics unit and 30% of sales from the advanced material unit, which produces a variety of industrial and scientific products, Corning has a bright future based on the assumption of discontinuity, not the comfort of continuity. So far, Corning has been a master of the game.

ENRON

When Houston Natural Gas and InterNorth, two giants of the industry, merged to form Enron in 1985, Kenneth Lay, a former Federal Energy Regulatory commissioner, was selected to be the new CEO. Lay was recruited from a competitor to fight off the expected unwelcome advances of corporate raiders, since Enron had substantial debt when it was formed. Lay's first task as CEO was to aggressively eliminate layers of bureaucracy within the company while expanding the company's pipeline network. But even as he expanded the pipeline business, Lay saw that in the newly deregulated natural gas market, the highest long-term returns were likely to be generated not by selling or transporting gas, but by trading it.

Indeed, when the federal government deregulated the natural gas industry in the 1980s, it converted a stodgy, cost-based regulated industry into a competitive market. To supply that market, new companies, new networks, new financial channels, and new products had to be created. The possibilities for innovation were endless—but so were the risks. Sensing a market opportunity in this volatility, in the late 1980s, Enron began to build a gas bank business to serve as an intermediary between producers and consumers of gas. The "bank" would provide customers with a new form of stability—by custom-tailoring gas supply contracts according to quantity, time period, price index, and settlement terms.

It was Jeff Skilling, a senior partner at McKinsey at the time, who came up with the idea of creating a method to trade natural gas. He first presented his idea to the management committee of Enron Corp., who initially gave Skilling's idea a cool reception. But after further thought and more one-on-one discussions, CEO Lay and President and COO Richard Kinder championed Skilling's idea. In the end, Skilling left McKinsey to join Enron with the charter to create Enron Capital and Trade, now called Enron North America.

ECT was one of the first entrants into the free market for natural gas, operating as a trader—that is, buying gas from producers and selling gas to customers, such as power plants and industrial complexes. Previously, only regulated pipelines could purchase and sell gas, and the customers for natural gas had only one source of supply—their local utility.

When Skilling arrived at Enron, he inherited the old gas purchasing and marketing arm of the regulated pipeline business. Until deregulation, pipelines were engineering-oriented utilities that earned a fixed rate of return based on the amount of capital they had invested. Because the rate of return was fixed, buying smart or selling smart added nothing to the bottom line. Innovation was almost irrelevant. Skilling's first task was to change that.

Skilling rejected the conventional strategy of being the lowest-cost provider of a commodity product in favor of seeking to provide natural gas at the right time and the right price for a particular use. The trading model could not have been further removed from the traditional utility mind-set. In fact, Skilling wanted to change the traditional mind-set of the company from thinking of itself as a pipeline to thinking of itself as an energy store, closely following the approach MCI took when it entered the telecommunications business (deregulating along lines strikingly similar to the energy market). As Lay later commented: "[The energy market] will become just like the competing telephone companies, which offer a full line of telecommunications services today. You'll be able to call up and order all your energy from Enron."

In 1992, natural gas futures contracts began trading freely on the New York Mercantile Exchange, a discontinuity in which Enron led the pack. Practically from its inception, the new unit provided its parent company with 22% of its operating profits. As Skilling put it, "Selling natural gas is getting to be a real business, like selling washing machines. We're taking the simplest commodity there is, a methane molecule, and we're packaging and delivering it under a brand name, the way General Electric does."

To reach his objectives, Skilling dismantled the traditional hierarchy common in bureaucracies and created in its place a relatively flat pyramid with only three levels between the CEO and the lowest worker. He also replaced descriptive job titles with the kind found in professional service firms, titles that indicated the level of competency rather than describing the specific area of responsibility. Finally, Skilling and his team created a very high-risk, high-reward compensation system in which the base salary can be, for top performers, as little as one-third of total compensation.

As one executive said: "We hire very smart people and we pay them more than they think they are worth." This "Enron premium," a combination of higher-than-expected pay and the confidence of ECT personnel that they were continuously developing new knowledge and techniques and improving their skill sets, enabled Enron to retain exceptional people in the face of lucrative offers from competitor companies.

Skilling gave permission to young traders to commit up to $5 million on a deal without being obliged to seek upper-management approval. Performance criteria were broadened from simple revenue figures by establishing a system of "peer review" whereby teams of up to two dozen employees were given free rein to rank their peers on criteria like "ability to learn," "leadership of self and others," "connecting and leveraging," and, of course, "innovativeness," in addition to raw revenue figures. These evaluation and compensation systems allowed ECT to turn over the vast majority of the organization in the initial few years—hiring the new talent that would be able to design and negotiate sophisticated contracts, and encouraging those unwilling to shift their mental models and skills to move on.

The environment that management created at ECT bears little resemblance to the one that preceded it in the era of regulation of natural gas. Senior management actively supported new ventures, even when they might cannibalize existing businesses. "Nothing happens without people being willing to put flesh on the table," said one manager. For each of their new major ventures, someone in the leadership ranks was willing to put his or her reputation on the line and move away from lucrative activities to make the initiatives succeed. They were willing to do this not only because they believed in the idea, but also because they knew that if they succeeded, they would get major financial rewards *and* have the opportunity to run the new business.

ECT even changed its workplace environment, creating large, open work areas so that people would constantly interact with each other and exchange ideas easily. Since information is key to the success of the business, all information was made available to everyone. The company developed proprietary analytical tools that are available to everyone on a single IT system.

Perhaps the most interesting example of creative destruction was Enron's facility with managing exit—and its myriad consequences. In an attempt to anticipate and even drive the next wave of electricity deregulation (the retail market), the company rapidly spent in excess of $30 million to aggressively pursue first-to-market advantage in California and New Hampshire, two key states that had championed energy deregulation. But just as MCI had learned to launch multiple new business models into the market, with tight strings attached, Enron abruptly pulled back from the consumer market when customer response proved unexpectedly tepid. Rather than punishing Lou L. Pai, the head of that unsuccessful effort, Enron's response was to reward him for a successful management of the exit by promoting him. In fact, timely exit is a key element of the mental model at Enron.

Another variant of simultaneously pursuing creation and destruction can be seen in the efforts of General Electric, Hewlett-Packard, and Johnson & Johnson. At GE, for example, Jack Welch, within four years of taking over as CEO, divested 117 business units—from mines to Light N' Easy irons—totaling one-fifth of GE's 1981 $21 billion asset base. Welch was determined to mount a massive assault on GE's outmoded identity. The "new" GE that Welch envisioned would be a high-tech provider of large-ticket products and essential services, from mutual funds to jet engines, credit-card processing, medical imaging, and network television programming. By aggressively moving to sell off the prime symbols of the "old" GE, Welch advanced his case by years, if not decades. He had unambiguously demonstrated to all concerned that "nothing was sacred," that "change would be accepted as a rule, rather than the exception," and that "paradox is a way of life."

The key distinction between this third approach of simultaneously implementing substantial creation and destruction, and the previously mentioned strategies of restarting or cashing out, is that these companies have rejected the assumption of *continuity* and embraced the assumption of *discontinuity* as the primary driver of their performance. They are not trying to achieve excellence in operations, and only later deal with creative destruction as they have the time. They are first and foremost focused on achieving market levels of creative destruction; they then design their operating procedures to be compatible with that constraint.

Achieving this in the proper balance (given their "inverted' approach) is not simple. In each of the companies named above it raised practical problems (for example, how to redeploy once-productive people without creating so much resistance that the efforts are sabotaged from the start, or how to eliminate businesses that board members consider to be part of the heritage of the corporation). Careful thought and attention was given to these questions. But in the end, with sufficient leadership, these companies addressed and handled them. As a result of getting the balance right, these companies have provided returns to their shareholders that have matched the returns of the S&P 500, sometimes with a little room to spare.

SIMULTANEOUS TRANSFORMATIONAL CREATION AND DESTRUCTION

A fourth option is attempting *simultaneous* transformational creation and destruction. An example is Monsanto. CEO Dick Mahoney started Monsanto's transformation in the mid-1980s by divesting commodity chemical businesses, acquiring pharmaceuticals, and investing in biotechnology R&D. Robert Shapiro took over as CEO in 1995 and further accelerated the transformation. Shapiro understood that the markets wanted growth. As a former patent attorney, he also believed in the power of technological change. Shapiro launched a major growth initiative that led to shaping investments in biotechnology and genomics, in acquisition of seed companies to commercialize the biotech products, and in building a human nutrition business. As an example of Monsanto's technical success, the introduction of transgenic soybean seeds rendered the "chemical weeding" of fields so easy that in the first year after its introduction (1996) U.S. soybean farmers bought enough mutated soybean seeds to plant 35 million acres, or roughly half of the total acreage devoted to soybean production in the country.

Sensing the potential of Monsanto's invention, Shapiro boldly embarked on a wholesale transformation of the nearly century-old firm from a traditional chemicals-and-pharmaceuticals giant into a biotechnology company. He moved aggressively toward his goal by coupling a "deal-a-day" acquisition program for seed and smaller agricultural biotech companies with an exit from Monsanto's traditional core chemical businesses. In December 1995, he sold Monsanto's plastics business to Bayer AG for $580 million, then he spun off the $3 billion chemical company (under the new name Solutia) in 1997.

The idea was to allow the remaining $7.5 billion business to focus on the life science growth pillars: agricultural chemicals, seeds, pharmaceuticals, and food ingredients. On this base, he radically realigned the management structure that existed in the days when Monsanto was a "chemical company." Arguing that "things are moving too fast for traditional management," Shapiro created "two-in-a-box" management teams that pair relevant technology and marketing managers to make decisions about the business.

In 1999, in a bid to pay down the substantial debt incurred from an unprecedented number of acquisitions, the company put up for sale one of its most profitable products—the artificial sweetener NutraSweet—as well as the rest of its $1-billion-in-annual revenues food-ingredient business. The goal was to generate cash while conveying to shareholders and other stakeholders the sheer depth and conviction behind this massive strategic shift. While seeking to exit from a wide variety of businesses, Monsanto embarked on a cost-cutting program estimated to remove nearly 4,000 employees from the company payroll of 30,000 worldwide. As Shapiro said,

> *We're entering a time of perhaps unprecedented discontinuity. Businesses grounded in the old model will become obsolete and die. Years ago, we would approach strategic planning by considering "the environment"— that is, the economic, technological, and competitive context of the business—and we'd forecast how it would change over the planning horizon. Forecasting usually meant extrapolating recent trends. So we almost never predicted the critical discontinuities in which the real money was made and lost—the changes that really determined the future of the business.*

Monsanto's transformation was, instead, built on the belief that they could be the drivers of a discontinuity in their market. But they could do so only if they destroyed what they once had been.

Initially, the market appreciated what Shapiro was trying to do, more than doubling the multiple on Monsanto's earnings. In 1998, however, widespread consumer resistance started to develop to genetically modified foods, particularly in Europe. The prospects for longer-term earnings growth seemed very much delayed. The market lost confidence in Monsanto's vision. In the summer of 1999, Monsanto sought refuge in a merger with American Home Products, whose chairman, Jack Stafford, was, like Shapiro, a lawyer. As the summer progressed, it became clear that the two sides could not get along and the merger had to be undone.

At that time Monsanto entered negotiations with several companies. Ultimately, Monsanto ended up partnering with Pharmacia & Upjohn to become Pharmacia in a merger of equals. Shareholders of both companies were dismayed, at least initially. Both sets of shareholders had been expecting to receive a premium for their companies were they acquired by a larger pharmaceutical player. When the deal was announced, the combined market capitalization of the two companies was $54 billion. Shares of both companies dropped sharply after the announcement, but by the time the deal was complete, the market had recognized the potential synergies, increasing the combined market capitalization to more than $60 billion.

The merger was sold on the prospects of becoming a major pharmaceutical player, not the biotech company that Shapiro tried to create. Pharmacia has already divested several components that defined the company, including its Equal brand sweetener, sold for $570 million to Pegasus Partners, and its bulk NutraSweet business was sold to J. W. Childs Equity Partners for $440 million prior to the merger. Additionally, it spun off the agrochemical division of Monsanto in an IPO. The name of the small spin-off tells us who was the greater of the two merger "equals"—it is called Monsanto. Shapiro will remain as a non-executive chairman through 2001.

For a while it looked like Monsanto's transformational move was a stroke of genius. But in the end, too many things had to work perfectly for too long. Monsanto stumbled perhaps because the business it attempted to move toward was not yet an assured market. This is hindsight, however. At the time it looked like a reasonable strategy to almost everyone.

BALANCING CREATION AND DESTRUCTION IN PRACTICE: THE CASE OF SEQUENT COMPUTER

Maintaining the balance between creation and destruction is exceptionally difficult, even for those with exceptional credentials. The story of the life and death of Sequent Computer shows the full cycle of corporate birth, growth, and extinction over a short period of time. It gives us a quick movie of what really happens to companies on the ascent, as they reach the summit, and as they head down.

As we described earlier, Sequent Computer was an Intel spin-off born without much foresight in Intel's incubator in 1983. "We knew we were going to build a computer, we just didn't know what kind of computer it was going to be," Casey Powell, Sequent's first and only chief executive, said.

A few weeks after Intel's "Black Monday" in 1983, Sequent Computer Systems decided that it would produce a "parallel processing" computer, a new type of high-performance computer that used multiple processors manufactured by Intel or its competitors. Despite the technological risk and the uncertainty of an unproven management team, Sequent raised $5.2 million from several venture capitalists within months of Black Monday. Less than two years later, Sequent's first computer, the Balance 8000, was completed.

The Balance 8000 was the first commercialization of a technology referred to as symmetric multiprocessing (SMP), or parallel processing. Previously, mainframes and minicomputers used single central processing units (CPUs) to perform calculations for all of the users connected to the system. To provide greater computing capability, companies like IBM and Digital Equipment Corp. designed and developed their own complex CPUs. Sequent believed that it could design the software and hardware necessary to make several inexpensive, mass-produced CPUs work together as a single unit, cutting the cost of production enormously. In the Balance 8000, Sequent created a machine that could use up to twelve CPUs harmoniously. It was a substantial innovation in the industry.

When Sequent first announced its SMP computer, however, the industry barely noticed. "Of the six people who showed up at our first presentation, four were [the conference organizers]. They felt sorry for us," said Robert Gregg, a former chief financial officer of Sequent.

Initially, customers were equally unreceptive. Sequent had created the Balance 8000 to solve scientific and technical problems that required substantial, dedicated computing power. But it found the market small and difficult to penetrate; it sold fewer than fifty machines, capturing only $5 million in revenue in 1985.

Soon, however, the market began to discover Sequent. While the Balance 8000 could outperform much higher-priced computers on technical problems, it was even more effective for business applications that involved multiple users accessing and modifying a large database. In the first half of 1986, Sequent signed four-year deals with Siemens and Amperif to supply $70 million worth of computers to be rebranded and bundled with other office computing products. And Boeing Co., a company that Sequent had hoped to sell to for technical computing, bought a Sequent computer to store and manage a research database instead.

As sales grew, Sequent decided to go public, raising more than $25 million in April 1987. Sequent's product line also grew as it released the Symmetry models, which were based on up to thirty of Intel's new 80386 microprocessors and ranged in price from $85,000 to $800,000. In terms of MIPS (a simple measure of computing power), Sequent's top machine was on par with IBM's 3090 mainframe, which sold for $11.5 million. The Symmetry series led to an operating profit of $4 million on sales of $38 million in 1987, almost double the sales of 1986. This rapid expansion continued through 1990, with profits rising to $16 million on sales of $146 million in 1989.

Most of Sequent's sales were driven by database management needs. In early 1987, Sequent entered agreements with several independent database companies, including Oracle and Informix. It agreed to prepurchase software licenses and ship computers with the customer's choice of database. Working directly with software companies, particularly Oracle, helped Sequent draw attention to itself. In 1989, Oracle announced that the Sequent machines were the most cost-effective computers to use with its databases. For similar performance, customers would have to pay twice as much for a Digital Equipment VAX system, or six times as much for IBM's offering.

Sequent computers were an excellent value for database applications, and Sequent continued to sell computers in ones and twos, even to large clients. Coca-Cola, Radisson, and Boeing, for example, were customers, although they bought Sequent for specific database needs rather than for companywide distribution.

To reach customers looking for tens or even hundreds of machines, Sequent entered a five-year agreement in 1989 to supply Unisys with computers that Unisys would bundle with additional software and peripherals and sell under its name. It reached similar, smaller agreements with Siemens and Prime Computer.

While this approach paid off in the short run (original equipment manufacture, or OEM, sales accounted for 34% of revenues in 1989), it also concentrated Sequent's customer base at a time that it needed to be broadened. A year later the agreements unraveled. Prime Computer broke its agreement in order to pursue its own parallel system, and Unisys, which had bought more than 25% of Sequent's computers in the first half of 1990, began facing operational difficulties that led it to announce its intentions of phasing out all OEM agreements. The inevitable decline in market distinctiveness that Sequent had established early on was being eroded by competitors' imitations.

The pace of imitation accelerated, and Sequent's direct customers began to find that they had growing bargaining power, as several small computer companies such as Pyramid Technology and Teradata followed Sequent into the area of high-performance multiprocessor systems. IBM and DEC started to offer competing systems as well. Additionally, a slow-down in the overall economy resulted in more of Sequent's sales coming from its lower-end, lower-margin products. These events led to a decline in sales in 1991 and an operating loss. The honeymoon was over.

Scott Gibson, one of the company's original founders, who served as president, director, and co-CEO with Powell, attributed Sequent's problems to external causes: "It's pretty clear that the entire industry is going through a very difficult period. It has also become painfully clear that Sequent is not immune to the industry-wide effects of a severe slowdown in capital spending by end users." However, the comparison of total return to shareholders relative to industry performance indicates that Sequent's downturn in 1991 was primarily internal. Others within Sequent may have not shared Gibson's publicly stated view; in February 1992, it was announced that Gibson was resigning his positions, which would be taken over by Powell.

Sequent had found that after its original innovation—creating a successful SMP computer—its business relied on working with software builders to provide customers with systems that could address a specific need. This strategy was extended from database management to networking in late 1991. As PCs replaced mainframe terminals in the late '80s, companies began to shift to a client-server computer structure, where files could be maintained centrally and shared across the company. Novell had captured a sizable share of the networking software market with its NetWare software. Sequent worked with Novell to produce a version of NetWare that took advantage of the capabilities of the multiprocessor environment.

Sequent's file servers began selling immediately, returning the company to profitability in 1992. But its competitors, which had already caught up with Sequent by offering multiprocessor machines capable of running Oracle database software, were not far behind. The software that Sequent helped Novell develop would need only slight modifications to run on other multiprocessor machines, and Novell had a strong interest in licensing to Sequent competitors. Whenever the competition caught up, Sequent drove forward into new territory rather than defending the turf that it first claimed. "When other people offer the same capabilities, we have to go on to something new," Powell said. The spirit of substantial and transformational innovation was alive, but little attention was being paid to the right way to deal with the operations of the business, or how to oversee their decline.

The company's head start in the file server market was indeed fleeting, and with little new to offer customers, Sequent saw its growth slow again in 1993, while costs associated with the sales force grew, leaving Sequent with a loss on the year. Sequent's progress was also hampered by the delay of Intel's Pentium processor, which promised to double the speed of Sequent's Symmetry models.

In the wake of 1993, Sequent began to rethink its strategy and started focusing on larger clients, choosing to forgo competing for smaller contracts that they had chased in earlier years. While sales responded well in 1994, Sequent's success was in a larger part attributable to a weakened dollar that led to greater international sales, propelling Sequent faster than most of the industry, which was more reliant on domestic markets than Sequent. In the next two years, Sequent continued to grow and succeed in line with the industry as a whole, but now it faced an innovation challenge.

Until 1996, the increased computing performance of Sequent products was primarily due to improvements in Intel's processors, speeding along at the rate of Moore's Law, which states that the speed of microprocessors will double every eighteen months. The number of processors that Sequent had been able to lash together effectively remained capped at thirty-two. Beyond that, the CPUs simply began to get in one another's way when trying to share other components, such as RAM or the main disk drive. Stanford engineers proposed a new type of computer structure called non-uniform memory access, or NUMA, that would enable multiprocessor computers to share memory and disk space more efficiently. Several SMP computer manufacturers worked feverishly to perfect the first marketable NUMA computer, but Sequent was first again with its NUMA-Q system, which could link sixty-four Pentiums. The system was released for shipment in February 1997. Unlike many companies, Sequent had been able to achieve a second transformational innovation. But the cost was high.

While large customers responded positively to the NUMA-Q, including a $59 million order from Boeing, the stock market was far less responsive to Sequent's breakthrough than it had been to earlier innovation. Essentially, the capital markets did not believe that Sequent's latest advance would lead to higher cash flows for the company beyond the first year or two. In addition, the NUMA-Q emphasized Sequent's focus on the top end of the computer market, rather than the smaller dedicated machines that had been the source of its initial success. Powell was emphatic: "I'm big, big, big—I'm after the $5m to $40m space. If a [Sequent] sales guy goes to try and sell a four-way [an earlier, smaller system], not an eight-way [NUMA-Q 2000], he hasn't got a job."

From the start Sequent claimed that the performance of its top machines could rival that of mainframes. With a NUMA-Q built around Intel's next big chip, the Merced, projected for delivery in the middle of 2000, IBM began considering tendering an offer for Sequent. In July 1999, IBM agreed to pay $810 million for the company, which Sequent's board accepted. Sequent was an independent company no longer, although the NUMA-Q brand may well survive with an IBM logo on it.

In its sixteen years of independent existence, Sequent had consistently maintained a technological advantage, bringing concepts to market years ahead of other companies. But it was never able to claim and defend the high ground as it moved forward, as Corning and Enron did. Its operations side simply couldn't match its success at innovation. It was not a bad performance for a company, but it was not enough. The right balance between creation and destruction wasn't achieved. In the end, the market did the necessary cleaning.

What can we conclude from this? First, to create at the scale and pace of the market, one has to destroy at the scale and pace of the market. The destruction that is essential to maintain freshness in a capitalistic market economy is also essential within the corporation if it is to extend its prosperity. Yet destruction is as difficult to master as innovation, since it requires overcoming the emotional barriers of denial that are built into the natural evolution of the corporation. As a result, corporations often pay insufficient attention—or pay attention too late—to the task of destruction.

Second, striking the right balance between creation and destruction is extraordinarily difficult. In the popular 1991 movie *Other People's Money*, Danny DeVito was cast as "Larry the Liquidator," a workout artist who found and scavenged weak companies. Larry realized that his latest prey, New England Wire and Cable, could not survive competition from abroad. Near the end of the movie, Larry comes to town to tell the shareholders (who are also employees and townspeople) that the end is at hand. Larry's final comments are well-argued. "In the end," he says, "market forces will seal your fate, not me." While Larry does not get the girl (the brilliant lawyer who defended the company), neither does the town get a reprieve—it loses its company. The message of the movie mirrors the lessons of life: The markets always win.

We think back to the unnamed senior executive quoted at the opening of the chapter, who stares out past the light of the campfire and ponders the fate that awaits him. His worries are well founded, his fears are real. Night eventually will deepen, and the embers will cool. Predators do crouch beyond the light. Our only defense is to be well prepared.

CHAPTER 7

Designed to Change

Don't tell me about the flood. Build me an ark.

attributed to LOU GERSTNER, CHAIRMAN OF IBM

A s we indicated in Chapter 1, by the year 2025, the average length of time a company resides on the S&P 500 will be no more than ten years, compared to twenty years today. The pace of change is accelerating. Survival alone, as we have seen, is no guarantee of performance. Based on the historical record, even those companies that do survive to the year 2025 will likely underperform the markets.

Can the steel link between survival and underperformance be broken? Can today's companies avoid the fate of the East River Savings Bank and other companies that have slipped into obscurity? We believe they can. In fact, the prescription to do so is quite simple to state: "Act like the market."

What does "act like the market" mean? It means that corporations must strive to change themselves at the pace and scale of the market. But how does a company go about "acting like the market"? How does one, as Lou Gerstner put it, "build the ark"?

To build the ark, the concept of the corporation must change from the nineteenth-century view that managers must operate a company first and handle creative destruction when they can. It must establish a more dynamic view that mandates managing creative destruction first and operations second. But it must do so in a highly decentralized way that nevertheless does not sacrifice control. It is necessary for the corporation to become a creator, operator, and trader of assets, rather than a merely efficient operator of assets.

Specifically, companies must:

1. Increase the pace of change to levels comparable with the market
2. Open up their decision-making processes to make use of the collective talent of the corporation and its partners (and avoid cultural lock-in)
3. Relax conventional notions of control, but not to the detriment of operations

These are the critical elements of the new corporation—the corporation that will be able to successfully ride the waves generated by Schumpeter's "gales of creative destruction."

THE ARCHITECTURE OF CREATE, OPERATE, AND TRADE

In Chapter 2 we discussed the five elements of corporate architecture that shape and drive companies: mental models, information systems, decision-making systems, executional capability (actions), and systems of control (or MIDAS for short). Coordinating these elements is relatively simple in the operating corporation, which has one reasonably stable mental model. The mental model drives the structure of the information systems, which are perfectly stitched into the fabric of the decision-making and control systems of the corporation. Action (or execution) comes as a consequence of the decision-making systems, and is held in check by the control processes. It is all very neat and simple. But because the business environment is constantly changing, the system becomes vulnerable to cultural lock-in and eventually loses its effectiveness.

The increasing pace of change in the markets requires a new model. It is likely that this new model will be more complex, to accommodate the higher pace of change in the future. An operating model will still have to exist, but it will have to be joined by creating and trading, the essential functions of creative destruction. In other words, the five elements of MIDAS will be completely different for companies seeking effective creative destruction and successful operations.

CREATION VS. OPERATIONS

Companies seeking to foster creation must support multiple mental models—representing fundamentally different approaches to business—because such models are always present in the marketplace. Rarely is there such uniformity of thought in the marketplace that there is no dissension. That would constitute a monopoly, and there are precious few of those (even monopolies have their opposing interests, as OPEC and DeBeers illustrate). How does such thinking fit in with the mental models of typical companies focused on operations? Let's take a look.

In companies focused on operations, the essential information is known, and is presented when it is needed and in the form it is needed. In companies focused on creativity, it is often not clear what information is necessary or relevant. The information necessary for decision making can be ambiguous, difficult to obtain, or simply missing.

The decision-making processes in companies focused on creativity are equally unclear. Frequently, such processes evolve along with the decision to be made. One may discover problems only as the solutions become obvious. Only after the fact are the methods clear. Accordingly, the real-time measurement of the efficiency of decision making for the creative process is extremely difficult, if not meaningless altogether.

Control also takes on a different meaning in the organization focused on creativity. The precise nature of control systems at the heart of operational effectiveness are useless in the creative process. In the creative process control has more to do with the selection of people with talent, with having some sort of worthwhile objective, and with having a set of warning signals that can shut down the system before harm is done. But these are crude measures of control. More finely tuned control measures run the inherent risk of shutting down the creative process altogether. Here permission is more important to creative output than control.

Execution, too, takes on a different meaning. In companies focused on operations, execution is almost routine, made up of a thousand little tasks, executed one after the other until the job is done. Miss a few of these trivially simple tasks, and the overall operational effectiveness may be jeopardized. In the organization focused on creativity, execution may mean "thinking the right thought" as much as "doing the right thing." Creation is dependent on execution, certainly, but the nature of the process is entirely different.

TRADING VS. OPERATING

Trading—the "destruction" part of creative destruction—is more like operations than it is like creation. Yet there are substantial differences in the requirements for effective trading and effective operations as well. For example, in trading, the information needed is not routine. Most trades, at least at the corporate level, are one-time deals and have to be designed each time from scratch. Trading is the final act. There is no presumption of continuing activity. In trading, control also takes on a different meaning. Control implies achieving the desired outcome, then bringing the process to a stop with no loose ends. This is a different kind of control than that exercised in either operations or creation. In trading, the control system has to be designed for the individual trade, unless a routine commodity is being traded. Rarely, however, does the senior level of a corporation face routine trades. When 3M spun off Imation, when Hewlett-Packard spun off Agilent, when Siemens spun off Infineon, or when General Motors spun off Delphi Systems, the transactions were anything but routine.

Not surprisingly the invisible architecture of organizations that foster creation, operations, and trading is very different, and much more complex, than the invisible architecture of an organization focused on operations alone. (See Appendix B for a summary of the different requirements.)

Can any company maintain the balance between continuity and discontinuity as well as the markets? Yes, companies can, although simply trying to adapt the systems utilized in an operating organization will not often work. Rather, one has to start over and create systems built on discontinuity. We now turn to two companies that have successfully ridden "gales of creative destruction"—Kleiner, Perkins, Caulfield and Byers, and Kohlberg, Kravis and Roberts. These companies can not only claim to have successfully ridden through the gales—they can rightfully claim to have helped create them.

CONTINUOUS CREATION: KLEINER, PERKINS, CAULFIELD AND BYERS

Kleiner, Perkins, Caulfield and Byers is a leading venture capital company. Venture capital firms operate for the sole purpose of helping to launch small companies with new, potentially valuable ideas.

Kleiner Perkins, as it is commonly referred to, was formed in 1972 by Thomas Perkins, the first general manager of Hewlett-Packard's computer division, and Eugene Kleiner, a veteran of Bell Laboratories and a co-founder of Fairchild Semiconductor. Unfortunately, their timing could not have been worse: The United States was slipping into the longest recession the country had seen since the Great Depression. It was a terrible time to form a company for the purpose of funding technology start-ups. Still, the firm managed to raise $7 million. Soon after it raised its initial capital, Brook Byers, a specialist in life science businesses, and Frank Caulfield, a career venture capitalist, became partners, adding their names to the firm.

The firm's combined expertise in computers and biotechnology proved to be its competitive advantage, luring both investors and entrepreneurs to the fund. Its first major success came in 1976 when it decided to invest in Genentech, the first recombinant DNA technology company. Kleiner Perkins provided the capital and appointed Robert Swanson, a Kleiner Perkins associate, CEO. After producing the first human protein and then cloning human insulin, Genentech went public in 1980. Its stock price doubled the first day. By 1992, the $1 million that was originally invested in Genentech in 1976 was worth $372 million. Genentech remains one of Kleiner Perkins' most profitable companies to this day.

Kleiner Perkins also focused on computer companies. In the 1970s, it funded many firms including Tandem Computers and Lotus Development, followed by Sun Microsystems and Compaq. In the 1980s, it funded Intuit and Symantec. By 1982, Kleiner Perkins had become one of the largest venture capital firms in the world, with investments totaling $150 million. By 1998, Kleiner, Perkins, Caulfield and Byers' success had helped it raise more than $1.2 billion, which it had invested in more than a hundred private firms that subsequently offered their shares to the public. The total market value exceeded $80 billion in 1998.

The capital for Kleiner Perkins' funds came from large investors, including the endowments of the University of California, Stanford, Harvard, MIT, Georgia Tech, Yale, Vanderbilt, and Michigan. More recently Kleiner Perkins has brought in money from the pension funds of General Motors, the Rockefeller endowment, and the foundations of Ford and Hewlett-Packard.

Kleiner Perkins prefers to raise funds from institutions and very wealthy individuals because they can help finance portfolio companies in later rounds. Of the money that is invested, Kleiner Perkins receives a 2% management fee and 30% of all profits. The share holdings are distributed to its investors after the public offerings.

Today, Kleiner Perkins organizes its investment strategy around eight categories, which are divided between the life sciences (medical devices and diagnostics; drug discovery and therapeutics; and health care services) and information sciences (the Internet; enterprise software; consumer media; communications; and semiconductors).

Kleiner Perkins is selective in its investment candidates, and examines their management closely. "What we do is look for markets that are going to change at least by an order of magnitude, technologies that can make it possible, and great teams—because strategies are easy, it's execution that's everything," said L. John Doerr, who has served as leading partner since the '80s. When considering a company for investment, a single "no" from any one of the nineteen partners can stop the investment. In addition, two partners must be willing to sit on the company's board of directors. "The valuation process is not numbers-crunching. It's really based more on experience," said Michael Curry, who serves as CFO for Kleiner Perkins. "If you can't do the math in your head, it's probably not a venture deal."

Doerr believes that investment strategies should be built around specific market initiatives. "There are four hundred venture firms, right? So how can any one firm develop significant market share? Only by focusing on initiatives, which means several partners work together to help build companies and opportunities in specific areas."

Not all of Doerr's initiates have been successful. In the late '80s, for example, the company invested in several companies that were targeting the mobile computing market, including Dynabook Technologies. Although the market has since proven itself, at the time Kleiner Perkins and Dynabook were too far ahead of the technology and the market. Doerr admits he was slow to pull the plug. "We didn't execute, and we didn't shut it down," he recalled. "We thought the portable market was going to be so big." By the time Kleiner Perkins was able to off-load Dynabook to Unisys in 1990, it had cost the firm $8 million.

In the 1990s, Doerr was skeptical about the value of the Internet. "At first, I thought Al Gore was nuts when he talked about information highways, on ramps, off ramps, and roadkill. But I was wrong. We can use networks, not just to lower costs, but to improve communications and build communities." Now the companies that Kleiner Perkins has funded *define* much of the Internet. They include America Online (which bought Netscape), Amazon.com, and Excite (which merged with @Home).

Kleiner Perkins' 1995 investment in Netscape marked its shift from computer hardware to Internet investments. "In the 1980s, PC hardware and software grew into a $100 billion industry," Doerr said in 1996. "The Internet could be three times bigger."

The IPOs Kleiner Perkins have founded have been so successful that today the firm receives more investor interest than it needs. One effect of the firm's success has been mergers and acquisitions between companies that Kleiner Perkins started. In 1998, Compaq acquired Tandem Computers for $3 billion in stock, and AOL bought Netscape for $4.3 billion (after rumors that Sun was in talks with Netscape).

More recently, Kleiner Perkins has taken steps to form partnerships of its own, announcing plans in 1999 to join Charles Schwab, TD Waterhouse, Ameritrade, Benchmark Capital, and Trident Capital in an investment bank to underwrite Internet company offerings. In 2000, Kleiner Perkins continued the trend, forming eVolution Partners with Bain & Company and Partners of Texas Pacific Group.

Venture capital firms like Kleiner Perkins show that it is possible to operate a create-operate-trade model very effectively and over long periods of time. They also illustrate how different the "invisible architecture" of the corporation—the mental models, the information and decision-making systems, the executional capability and the control process—have to be to make the system work. Of course, venture capital companies are not an incremental step away from operating organizations. They are totally different. But they are not the only examples of successful, sustained approaches to the create-operate-trade organization. Principal investing firms are a second example.

CONTINUOUS TRADING:
KOHLBERG, KRAVIS AND ROBERTS

In 1988, Duracell, then a division of Kraft Foods, was a struggling, underperforming company trapped in its own operational processes, unable to break the cycle of cultural lock-in that engulfed it. It was at this low point that the leverage-buyout firm Kohlberg, Kravis and Roberts bought Duracell from Kraft Foods. Leverage-buyout firms such as Kohlberg, Kravis and

Roberts buy struggling companies and then seek to dramatically improve their operations through breaking the cycle of cultural lock-in by selling divisions without potential, providing incentives for extraordinary performance, and increasing the penalties for underperformance.

KKR paid $1.8 billion for Duracell ($1.45 billion in debt and $350 million in equity), believing that the company had substantial untapped growth potential, especially in international markets (which comprised 12 percent of the company's sales).

With help from KKR, Duracell began to transform itself by selling its underperforming divisions and consolidating production (in part to pay off KKR's debt, which had been incurred in making the purchase). Subsequently, Duracell diversified its product line, further decreased production costs, and added new advertising and marketing efforts. Contrary to the exploitative image some critics have associated with KKR, the firm strove to make Duracell stronger than it ever had been. And they were successful: Between 1989 and 1995, Duracell's cash flow increased at an annual compound rate of 17% (under Kraft, Duracell's cash flow had been flat).

Duracell's CEO, Bob Kidder, found that KKR was aggressive about the development of new technologies. "Not once did Henry [Kravis] or George [Roberts] ask, 'How can we cut R&D?'" Kidder recalled. "In fact, they asked just the opposite, 'Should we be investing more in R&D to ensure that we have a technological edge for the long haul?'" Duracell's R&D efforts led to the development of a mercury-free alkaline battery, a rechargeable battery, and a smart battery for laptops. Duracell had to destroy to create, and cultural lock-in prevented that from occurring while the company was owned by Kraft.

More innovation followed: Duracell introduced the freshness date code, battery multipacks, and the package battery tester. As a result of such brand-strengthening moves, the company became the market leader. With new advertising efforts and new distribution channels, the company added 500,000 retail outlets to its worldwide distribution network by 1996. Meanwhile, Duracell was able to dominate the European market and expand sales in South America, Africa, the Pacific Rim, and the Middle East. The original five-year plan targeted 15% annual growth, but Duracell was racing far beyond that. It had grown so fast, in fact, that within three years of the buyout, in 1991, KKR decided to take Duracell public.

Five years later, in 1996, Gillette bought Duracell for $2.8 billion in stock (KKR had already made more than $1.3 billion during the previous eight years as a result of Duracell's operations—a 39% annual compounded return on its investment). The $350 million that KKR had originally invested in Duracell had returned $4.22 billion. That was the amount Kraft had forfeited through poor management.

CREATIVE DESTRUCTION AND PRIVATE EQUITY FIRMS

Kleiner Perkins and KKR are both examples of private equity firms. Private equity firms are made up of a set of limited partnerships organized as investment funds. These firms operate under a special set of regulations established by the federal government in the '30s and '40s to regulate companies that choose not to offer their equity shares to the public. What is interesting to us is that, based on the historical evidence, private equity firms do a far better job of embracing the spirit of discontinuity than do the traditional operating companies that have been the backbone of the productive capacity of the United States.

Private equity has its origins in the Great Depression and against the background of the trusts of the late nineteenth century. Private equity companies were first provided for by the Securities Act of 1933 to protect the public from undue risk (or unscrupulous bankers) from certain financial ventures (e.g., backing newly formed firms). Congress recognized that "sophisticated" investors were in a better position than the general public to assess the risks of these ventures. The Securities Act provided an opportunity for wealthy individuals, in small groups (fewer than a hundred investors), to invest capital in more risky and less regulated ventures, all overseen by the Securities and Exchange Commission.

Even before the Securities Act was signed into law, venture capital had begun as a family affair with the formation of Venrock, the Rockefeller family venture capital fund and Bessemer, the Mellon family fund. By the early 1950s, other venture capital firms had formed, including American Research and Development, led by visionary investor and Harvard Business School professor Georges Doriot, which backed the formation of Digital Equipment Corporation (absorbed by Compaq Computer in 1998) and many other successful start-up firms. Another venture capital firm, J. H. Whitney, led by Benno Schmidt Sr., invested heavily in the early advances in medicine.

The Securities Act of 1933 was followed by the Investment Company

Act of 1940, which established regulated "investment companies" for small groups of "sophisticated" investors. Again the purpose of the act was to keep such companies separate to protect less sophisticated investors. The Investment Company Act defines an investment company as any company that has more than 40% of its assets invested in companies that it does not control (that is, does not hold a majority of the stock).

For forty years after this regulation was put in place, the potential of private equity went largely unrecognized. While some investors did place their funds in regulated investment companies, the amounts of money were not large compared to investments through the public markets. There were probably two main reasons for this. First, there was thought to be a great deal of potential left in exploiting the public equity markets, particularly in the "conglomerate boom" of the '60s. Financial entrepreneurs like Jimmy Ling (who built LTV) and Harold Geneen (who built ITT) were convinced that strong management could manage any business well, and that a well-hedged portfolio of tightly controlled public companies was the key to financial success. The idea was to use a combination of debt and ownership control to leverage earnings-per-share growth in initially weak companies. If this approach was successful, there would be no large-scale need to turn to private capital for funds.

The second reason private equity was dormant for so long was that the economy came under severe stress in the 1970s as inflation, created by skyrocketing oil prices, drove the economy into a decade-long period of "stagflation." Stagflation, and the high cost of debt, brought an end to the conglomerate idea. It also brought a significant slowdown to venture capital as the IPO market almost completely stopped. In 1974, there were seven IPOs in the United States; a mere $96 million was raised. The year 1975 saw only six. In 1999, by comparison, there were 527 IPOs, raising $69 billion.

As the nation emerged from the '70s, however, the conditions were ripe for a significant expansion of private capital. In the early '80s, as the country turned the corner from a period of high inflation rates and low growth, a new form of corporation was founded: the "leveraged buyout association," as George Baker, a professor at Harvard Business School, called it. Having seen what happened to the conglomerates of the '60s, the LBO association sought to avoid some of the problems that undermined the conglomerate concept from the '60s.

The LBO association was based on the concept of leverage and decentralized operational control. Moreover, control was based on contracts and the ownership structure of the corporation, rather than on managerial control as Ling and Geneen had practiced it. As Professor Baker points out, "The LBO association is not a *keiretsu*-like system, nor is it a conglomerate."

The leveraged buyout associations succeeded. At the same time, venture capital was also beginning to flourish. As stated earlier, Kleiner Perkins was formed in the early '70s, although it really began to be successful in the early '80s. General Atlantic Partners was another such firm. More established firms like Venrock and J. H. Whitney also were finding new opportunities.

As venture capital investment volume began to build, investors flocked to private equity. In 1999, for example, 4,006 venture capital deals took place, involving investments of $45.6 billion, or about $135 million per day. Roughly half of that money was invested in start-ups. Another $27 billion was invested in 1999 in companies by "principal investors" (formerly known as leveraged buyout associations). In fact, Professor Baker claims, "the principal investing association" movement was one of the most important reasons for the resurgence of the U.S. economy in the '80s. To put these numbers into context, there were about 11,000 mergers and acquisitions in 1999, accounting for $1.7 trillion. Twenty years ago, mergers and acquisitions would have represented virtually all the financial transactions that took place in the economy. Today, while M&A's still dominate the field, for every dollar represented by an M&A deal, 25 cents is traded in private equity markets. Moreover, returns in the private equity market have been substantially above those of the public equity markets since the early '80s, as the chart below shows.

Returns by Asset Category

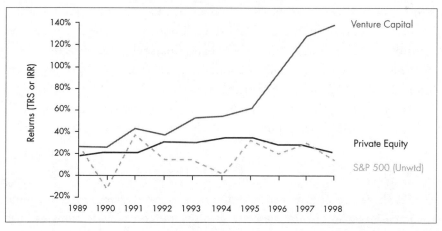

These two kinds of private equity firms, venture capital firms and principal investing associations, although different from each other in their focus, are successfully riding the waves of Schumpeter's "gales of creative destruction"—venture capital in the area of creation and principal investing in the area of trading or destruction.

How have they done this? Private equity firms are designed for change. They have replaced the traditional assumption of continuity with the assumption of discontinuity. In doing so, they have become critical players in shaping the processes of creative destruction in the U.S. economy. They are increasingly important drivers of change, and have also created enormous wealth for their shareholders. And in doing so, they have evolved a system of management and control that is far more suited to the management of discontinuity.

HOW PRIVATE EQUITY FIRMS OPERATE

Although private equity firms are very diverse, they have many similarities. We will look at their differences, their similarities, and what we can learn from them that can be carried over to public equity firms.

DIFFERENCES

There are significant differences between the venture capital and principal investing firms. The greatest difference between them is their investment focus. Venture capital firms focus on the early stages of a company's or industry's life, or what we call in Chapter 2 the beginning of the S-curve, where there is substantial growth potential. Principal investment firms, on the other hand, generally focus on companies that are nearing the slower-growth phase of their evolution, where there is substantial potential for restructuring and transforming them through operational and financial improvements.

Venture capital firms distribute money to the companies they own in small amounts, using the process to control the evolution of the company. Principal investing firms, on the other hand, make large single investments (supported by significant debt loads), and subsequently derive profits off the cash flow.

SIMILARITIES

While there are clearly major differences between venture capital and principal investing firms, there are also several common features of both

S-Curve and Private Equity

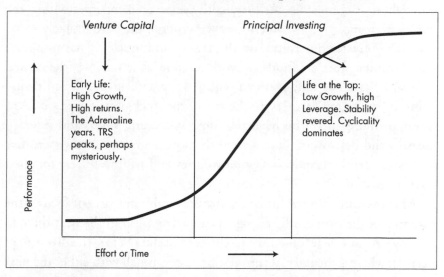

that distinguish them from public equity firms. Those features are an adoption of limited life investments, minimal corporate size, control based on contracts and incentives, and an obsession with decentralization. While some of these categories may seem to be similar to practices in public equity corporations, the extremes to which they are carried out by venture capital firms sharply distinguish these firms from most public equity firms. We have found that, collectively, these four differences constitute a superior approach to the management of discontinuity. Let's examine those four differences in more detail.

Limited-Life Investments

All investments made by private equity firms are assumed to have a "limited life"—typically ten to twelve years or less. At the end of that time they are required to sell their investments and return the capital to their fund investors. "Though the closing of any one limited partnership does not mean the close of the private equity firm, the requirement that it do so constrains the private equity firm to behave quite differently from the typical public equity company." Private equity firms invest only when they have a clear idea about how and when they will divest.

Many corporations are slow to divest unless forced to do so. As a result, history shows that corporations tend to be opportunistic buyers but reluctant sellers of companies. As long as divisions or companies within the corporation meet minimal performance criteria, they are unlikely to be sold. The private equity firm, on the other hand, not only has to put its equity capital from its funds to work as soon as is feasible (the capital generally has to be fully invested within six years), it also has to realize gains for its limited partners for the sale of the stock of its businesses. As a result, private equity firms have to be both systematic buyers and sellers—creators and destroyers. They are much more aggressive in their creative efforts to identify acquisition opportunities and to find buyers for their "transformations."

Moreover, the limited life of the private equity investment focuses the activities of the firm on the change it can accomplish in the next three to seven years (to give it some time to correct mistakes before the divestment occurs), whereas the normal corporation is consumed with either the next quarter's operating numbers or that of the very long term—say, beyond ten years (for example, in basic research programs). The intermediate time horizon for investments allows private equity firms more freedom in making fundamental changes to their investments than public companies can currently muster.

Minimal "Corporate" Staff

Private equity firms control staff size, and therefore involvement with their investments (due to time constraints), through a fixed management fee that typically runs about 2% per year of the assets under management. In addition, the general partners of the private equity firm share in the profits they make above some minimal level of return—say, 20%. This arrangement creates a clear standard of performance for the management of the private equity firm, so that it can judge its own performance independent of the performance of the companies it has invested in. If the costs of guiding and administering the private equity firm rise above 2%, the private equity general partners lose income. This fixed fee is a powerful incentive to keep the private equity general partnership small. Its small size and the financial structure of the partnership mean that the first priority of the management group has to be creating new investment opportunities and shedding old ones, rather than focusing on the day-to-day management of the companies they invest in.

Methods of Control: Contracts and Incentives

Private equity firms have a very different philosophy of control than most public equity corporations do. The control systems used by private equity firms give up the rights to day-to-day operational control in return for very clear contracts negotiated with the company receiving the investment. Because of the small staff size of private equity firms, they simply do not have the time to control the day-to-day process. The control processes invoked by private equity investors are tailored to the specific needs of the individual company and its future shareholders. Private equity firms do not attempt to control multiple businesses with a single management approach (or a single set of information reports or decision processes).

There are two key methods private equity firms use to control their investments: the contract with the company they invest in, and the incentives they provide to management for fulfillment of the contract. The key feature of contracts between private investment firms and corporations receiving the funds is the *restrictive covenant*. Restrictive covenants specify, and limit, the decisions that the private equity firm must be involved in. Everything else falls under the responsibility of management. The restrictive covenant approach gives the investor the "right to control," rather than a mandate to control. As such, private equity firms adopt a minimalist approach to operational control: They control what they must when they must, not what they can when they can. If problems arise, a private equity firm frequently has the right to interfere, but, in the absence of problems, they do not interfere.

The requirements for control generally include some of the following: decisions regarding the issuance of new shares; mergers, consolidations, or the purchase or sale of assets; and the award of stock and cash dividends. In addition, these covenants often specify balance sheet requirements (including working capital and net worth); restrictions on encumbrances and indebtedness; levels of managerial compensation; the use of proceeds; the issuance of preemptive rights and the rights of first refusal; mandatory redemption rights, registration rights, and so called drag-along and tag-along rights; charter amendments; and the nature of the business. While this list appears to be quite long, the entrepreneurial managers who accept the conditions set forth in the contract are free to run all other aspects of their business as they see fit. The list does not include any line item budget restrictions or the use of capital. It does not require approval of specific investments. It does not require involvement in the creation or changing of corporate strategy.

The second key method of control is through incentives. Private equity firms permit a much broader range of management incentives than do conventional corporations. While private equity firms seek very high levels of performance, they are also prepared to offer very high levels of rewards. Their target TRS is often at least double that of the conventional corporation. These high targets stimulate a greater sense of urgency. But if market-based performance measures are reached, managers can make many times their annual compensation. The range of compensation and risk is far greater in the private equity firm than in the conventional corporation. "Everything about the firm's structure and incentives are geared to increasing the long-term financial value of asset," says Baker.

Perhaps because of their comfort with the contract system and their own persuasive skills, private equity companies are more comfortable with minority ownership and a minority of board seats than are operating companies. Board meetings are often used to convey information, identify issues, and make decisions on behalf of the investors. It is a system based on permission more than tight control. While reporting is frequent and detailed, it is not as overwhelming as that in many traditional operating companies.

Conventional public equity firms depend far more on daily operational control, with a flexible set of criteria for action, than do private equity firms. Perversely, this greater flexibility often saps initiative taking on the part of the divisions within a large corporation, out of fear of second-guessing. The flexibility intended to provide options actually opens the door to defensive routines and cultural lock-in.

While many public equity corporations feel they see themselves as decentralized, they keep tight strings on strategy decisions, major (and often minor) investments, compensation structures, advancements and promotions, and information flow.

Obsessed with Decentralization

Integral to the concept of effective management by private equity firms is the notion of decentralization. Each of the companies that a private equity firm invests in is a legally separate company, with its own management structure and board. Decentralization, of course, has long been a primary organizing principle for many public equity companies. What is novel about private equity firms is the extent of decentralization, which often includes the decentralization of responsibility for the balance sheet as well as strategy and major investments.

Duracell, for example, was fully responsible for the health of its balance sheet, for paying the interest on its loans, and for raising more capital when it was needed. In a large public company, these functions are typically handled by a "corporate group," based on the argument that the corporation can negotiate better financial arrangements than any single division. That may be true, but it is also true that with the assumption of this responsibility for the balance sheet and additional financings, the corporation narrows the scope of thinking and responsibility of its operating company. For Duracell, these decisions are critical to company performance.

In general, the private equity firm does not make serious efforts to capture potential synergies among its operating companies. Private equity firms, and the companies they invest in, have neither the luxury nor the temptation to engineer the kinds of financial, technical, or talent synergies that are commonly sought in public corporations. Moreover, financial transfers from one company in a private equity portfolio to another are restricted by the provisions of the Investment Company Act of 1940. Talent transfers, in the name of information transfer (including technical knowledge transfer), are rarely sought because private equity firms would rather the companies maintain their focus on their goals, rather than be distracted with the effort required to realize profits from potential synergies.

We are not suggesting that private equity firms, because they have embraced the concept of "limited life," minimal corporate staff, control through contracts and incentives, and obsessive decentralization, have found the path to perpetual excellence. Despite their strengths, venture capitalists do miss markets, enter markets too early or too late, pick the wrong teams, and ride some investments longer than they should. Principal investing firms, too, blunder from time to time. Private equity firms are not infallible. Moreover, when the markets change again, and enough competition emerges, the weaknesses in their approaches may be exposed, and new corporate models will need to be found.

Nevertheless, private equity firms have performed well over the past twenty years, and at a pace that equals that of the marketplace. Moreover, they have evolved a system of management that is quite different in practice from the surviving incumbent publicly traded corporation. With this system of management, private equity firms have done as well as any group we have seen in finding ways to "create, operate, and trade" simultaneously.

Even with their faults and inevitable mistakes, they offer a useful model that companies can turn to when they are seeking guidance in learning how to adopt the assumption of discontinuity.

Private equity firms offer a way to deliver what only the markets have been able to deliver so far. They change at the pace and scale of the market, thrive on creative destruction and thus thwart cultural lock-in, and control through permission without putting operational excellence at risk. And in doing so, they have created substantial wealth for their investors.

CORPORATE EXAMPLES

None of the public equity firms we have examined in the McKinsey Corporate Performance Database "found the secret" of creative destruction. None has outperformed the market, or demonstrated excellence relative to the overall market over the long haul. As described previously, there are companies such as Enron and Corning that are beginning to demonstrate that they too can adopt some of the mechanisms of private equity investors for the benefit for their shareholders. And there are some diversified corporations that have done much better than most. GE and J&J are perhaps the two best examples. We discuss J&J in Chapter 11. Now we turn our attention to GE.

In a June 1999 interview in *The Wall Street Journal,* GE CEO Jack Welch philosophically observed:

> *I've talked about all the disadvantages of working at a big company, but there are a lot of advantages to being huge. Last year we made 108 acquisitions for $21 billion. That's 108 swings. Every one of those acquisitions had a perfect plan, but we know 20 or 30 percent will blow up in our face. A small company can only make one or two bets or they go out of business. But we can afford to make lots more mistakes, and, in fact, we have to throw more things at the walls. The big companies that get into trouble are those that try to manage their size instead of experimenting with it.*

GE has "created options" in broadcasting and financial services, to name a few; it has "traded options" in its sale of GE appliances. It has "operated" (in its high-performance management style) many businesses, including plastics and jet engines. In doing so, GE has completely reshaped its portfolio and achieved some of the rates of change seen generally only in private equity firms or in the indices of the capital markets themselves. During the past twenty years, GE has remained near the top of the normal performance band of the S&P 500 index.

Not all of the 108 acquisitions that GE made in 1998 were start-ups. But they did position GE well within the growth sectors of the economy. The businesses that GE traded, on the other hand, were those that Welch and his staff decided had no "economic function" within GE.

When Welch took over at GE in 1981, much of GE's management philosophy was based on the idea of "defend first; attack if you must." Welch's greatest contribution to GE employees and shareholders, in our view, has been turning this rule on its head. GE today clearly "attacks first, and defends when necessary." By engineering such a profound shift in strategic direction, Welch demonstrated that survivor companies can be successful in absorbing and applying the requirement for discontinuity. GE found a way to effectively integrate the functions of creation, operation, and trading close to the pace and scale of the maket. In doing so, it went from being a great innovative manufacturer to "a global services company that happens to make great products."

In GE's case, the "create, operate, trade" model is already in place. Copying GE's success is not easy, despite the fact that the company is willing to share its ideas and methods. Still, GE's success shows that such change can be accomplished in public companies, and that the capital markets will reward companies that can do it.

CURRENT EFFORTS

The heady progress of the stock market over the past decade has given rise to some new experiments attempting to capitalize on the potential of creative destruction. One of the most famous of these attempts is the "incubator," a company whose sole function is to generate new successful companies. In many ways, incubators are like venture capital companies, but they provide more than just capital and advice. They supply high-speed telephone lines, computers, office space, and, in many cases, access to executive search resources, accountants, consultants, and lawyers. While venture capital firms are typically partnerships, incubators often see themselves as public companies. Should they be able to do what they hope, they will likely reap substantial stock-market gains.

At this writing, there are at least seven hundred incubators in the United States, up from twelve in 1980. All of them are attempting a Schumpeterian task—balancing the management of creative destruction with the management of operations.

The new incubators have predictably offbeat, or "e-centric," names: Devine InterVentures (which has money from Dell and Microsoft); eCompanies (in Santa Monica, California, with money from KKR, Goldman Sachs, the Soros Fund, Sprint, and Walt Disney); e-Cubator (formed by investor Scudder-Kemper Investments); eFinanceworks in New York (formed by former principal investment firms CapZ and General Atlantic); eHatchery in Atlanta; Garage.com (founded by former Apple Fellow and chief evangelist Guy Kawasaki); I-Group HotBank (the Boston-based partnership between Softbank and the Intercontinental Group); IdeaLab (the Pasadena, California, firm founded by Bill Gross, backers of eBay, Citisearch, GoTo.com, and more than thirty other Internet start-ups in the past three years), and Ignition (founded by ex–Microsoft product developer Brad Silverberg).

Nor is the United States alone in the creation of incubators. Among the incubators in Europe are Starthouse and Speed.com, Gorilla Park, antfactory, and Earlybird. Hong Kong has Incubasia, and Japan Softbank.

Some of these high-talent agglomerations already sense a greater destiny. Devine InterVentures, for example, dreams of becoming a holding company on the scale of General Electric.

How many of these young incubators will become important institutions and last over the long term? At this point it is unclear. Many are starting to fail now. But we expect the best of them to last, modified in form and function but definitely different from the traditional survivor. They are attempting to design themselves for creative destruction.

Regardless of the type of company created, however, mastering creative destruction will be a prerequisite for strong, sustained performance. And as we've seen, there are already a few examples to look to. In the following chapters, we will look at what is needed to manage creative destruction in the operating corporation.

CHAPTER 8

Leading Creative Destruction

You implore us: Will you guys make up your mind? One day, it's SG&A. The next day it's top-line growth. The next day it's cost of goods. The next day it's Credo behavior. The next day it's innovation. Will you make up your minds? Well, the answer is no! We are not going to make up our minds, and you don't want us to make up our minds.

ROGER FINE,
Member of the Executive Committee of Johnson & Johnson, 1998

It was a typical late-fall Monday afternoon in northern Germany in the early '90s. The ten-person internal management committee, known as the Vorstand, was an hour into their regular meeting. As usual, no one other than the *Sprecher* (chairman of the management committee), Professor Schultz, had spoken. Schultz was signing capital authorizations. Although the company had more than the equivalent of $20 billion in physical assets to look over, and spent $2 billion per year, no member of the Vorstand was able to authorize an expenditure of more than $250,000. Consequently, during the year, several thousand proposals had to be authorized. Each had be scrutinized by the central planning department after it had been thoroughly prepared by the "responsible" department. With several thousand proposals a year needing the approval of the Vorstand, typically fifty to a hundred had to be approved each week. The approval process was straightforward. The *Sprecher* looked at each proposal to see if central planning had approved. If they had, he signed the authorization on behalf of the sitting Vorstand, unless he had personal knowledge that contradicted the recommendation of the central planning unit (in which case he made a unilateral decision to turn the proposal down). No discussion with the Vorstand was needed. None was expected. They simply sat and watched the *Sprecher* sign the requisitions. When he had finished, the great bulk of the meeting had been completed; other topics were briefly raised, and the meeting was adjourned.

Granted, the routine represented in this meeting, coupled with the utter lack of dialogue, is unusual. But the routine it represents is not. In some of the most advanced companies, routine dominates the agenda of the management committee (which is the name we will use for the corporation's most senior management group) meetings. Under the assumption of continuity, many top management groups interpret their primary purpose to be the stewards of operational excellence. They need to assure the shareholders that the operations are going well. The way to do this is to hold a "review." We call these meetings "presentation and response" meetings. Lower-level executives present their bulletproof plans to higher levels of executives to see if they can get them approved. The sessions are spent reviewing the plans of the divisions, reviewing capital appropriations, and reviewing recommendations for advancement. Dialogue is not sought. Winning the case is the objective. It is more like a court drama—with point and counterpoint—than a joint session in problem defining and solving.

In the normal life of many corporations, much of the management committee's time is spent in routine meetings, often at the request of others, rather than as a consequence of their own drive to manage. The management committee is extraordinarily responsive to the requests of others. They see their job as one in which they make decisions based on the options presented to them. It is not their job to generate alternatives. That is the work done by the organization "beneath" them. Rarely do they enter territory as murky as grappling with the balance between creative destruction and operations. It is not even clear how they would do that if they decided they wanted to. Once, when we suggested to a very senior and very talented executive member of a management committee that they eliminate the least important 20% of the routine agenda items from the management committee meetings, the question we received in response was "Well, then what would we do with our time?" Indeed. What would they do with their time!

Clearly, this system does not work. The failure of a company's leaders to challenge the very premises under which it operates is the source of much of the long-term lack of competitiveness one sees in corporations. This process leaves too many issues unspoken and too many opportunities unaddressed. The market has a much more robust dialogue, through thousands of "buy and sell" conversations every day. The market is constantly shaping new options and killing off programs that are just not progressing rapidly enough.

MANAGERIAL STALEMATE

In Chapter 4 we discussed lengthy conversations we have had with more than fifty executives from more than two dozen companies in the United States and Europe, in fields ranging from consumer products to high tech. All had the same sense of what it took to be successful—operational excellence—and all had problems with the same thing, change management, or what we call creative destruction. They could not do both at the same time. While the German company cited above demonstrates an extreme example of change paralysis, the same general problem, with perhaps milder symptoms, is widely felt.

There are two parts to the problem. The first is understanding the environment well enough to see opportunities—and to anticipate problems—in a timely way. Executives on both sides of the Atlantic have told us that strategic insight is needed for success. One of the most common phrases we heard was "You have to know where the market is going." Of course, such insight requires knowing future customer (and consumer) behavior, future channel behavior, future technology developments, future supplier capabilities, and future regulatory opportunities and restrictions. The executives found it very difficult to read the industry (very much as analysts have trouble reading the industry, discussed in Chapter 2).

In practice, these executives couldn't predict future customer behavior patterns. They misjudged competitors' reactions to their own moves, generally underestimating the ferocity of counterattack. Further, they misjudged their timing, either coming in too early (Kodak in electronic imaging) or too late (Pacific Bell and, until recently, AT&T in mobile telephony). They also failed to understand the different levels of skills required between two generations of technology (or between two business models). They found it difficult to generate the sense of urgency that is required to initiate and sustain change. Most of all, the executives found great difficulty in transforming future insights into an attractive business model.

The second part of the paralysis problem stems from the difficulty in implementing change that goes beyond the current mental models. Executives conceded that they found it very difficult to integrate both successful operations—the requirements for strategic management and change management. And most often it was innovation that suffered. The most common sentiment was "We're okay, but we have vast room for improvement. The incremental things seem to go well, but larger change eludes us; and we are worried about the future." Here are a few of the things executives said to us that underscore these points:

- "On a relative basis, and judging by our market success, I believe that we are effective innovators. However, on an absolute basis there is vast room for improvement, especially in meeting schedules. Our biggest issue is that we do not have a culture that values meeting deadlines. We need a more disciplined approach. The engineers would probably say that they are doing a great job, but the sales managers would probably say that they need more new products, and at a faster pace."
- "With our hands-on consumer goods characteristics, we are not sufficiently focused on more transformational options."
- "Salespeople would probably say that we were not quick enough in introducing new products and engineers would probably say that we don't use the best stuff."
- "With regard to our effectiveness at innovation, if we hit 20% we are lucky. It is very hard to guess ahead on what customers will want. It is like leading ducks—they go wherever they want. We need to figure out how to get our products close to customers' specifications and rapidly reach closure. Too often, we are guilty of developing too many products instead of basic technologies. I think that frontline engineers and salespeople would be more charitable in their comments, because they measure success one product at a time whereas I measure it as a business."
- "Our effectiveness at innovation troubles me greatly, because I believe that we are less and less innovative, perhaps as a result of size. Innovation for us has less to do with R&D or engineering than with how we serve our customers. Innovation either does not occur rapidly enough or does not bubble up to the resource controllers and decision makers. I guess that there are probably smart people down there seeing stuff, but the ideas are not getting to

the point where there is an ability to embrace, adopt, and execute."

- "Innovation is important to us, but we are not very innovative because our focus has been too much on the internal rather than on the external. There has been an inherent conservatism about reaching out for the future. Our group is a small and reasonably separate unit within the corporation, so we have had somewhat more success. We were the first of the print publishers to go aggressively to the Internet. If we were not under the constraints of the overall corporation, we could have gone even faster."

- "By everyone's standards, we are rated as the best at innovation in our industry. From a development point of view, I worry that in the older parts of the company we are stuck in the past. Getting agreement and then getting them to do something is the challenge."

It is clear that most executives feel they can do better. But they do not know how to proceed. Their specific questions ranged from "What will the value proposition be that could be so compelling as to change our behavior?" to "What are the first steps?" In some cases, the executives said they preferred to avoid these problems rather than address them, hiding the failure of a core business with acquisitions or even scurrilous accounting (none of which solved the real problem). Some resorted to denial: "Great innovations happen by accident," one company argued. "Some individuals come across a great idea and they exploit it. You cannot manage for that. The best you can do is to put people in touch with one another and see what happens. In our business all innovation is incremental in any case." (It should be noted that this large company has underperformed the markets for twenty years.)

The irony is that the executives making these comments and asking these questions are the corporate managers that most people would think have all the answers. But they don't. And most are not satisfied with the answers that they have at hand. They simply do not understand how to run their companies at the pace and scale that will match the markets without sacrificing operational control. They are frozen in the headlights.

TECHNICAL WORK VS. ADAPTIVE WORK

As we noted in Chapter 1, Ron Heifetz is one of the most reflective and effective thinkers in the country about the nature of leadership. Heifetz has thought extensively about the nature of authority and its relationship to leadership. His work is broadly consistent with the work of earlier pioneers, such as Chris Argyris and Dean Keith Simonton.

Heifetz makes a distinction in companies between technical work and adaptive work. Technical work is the work of experts. It is the exercise of authority, "a conclusive statement from a person in command." Adaptive work, on the other hand, is exploratory work. It is work where the answer is not known by the experts—any experts. Adaptive work is often creative work.

To function effectively, management committees must grasp and grapple with the difference between technical work and adaptive work. As Heifetz says,

> *In a complex social system, a problem will lack clarity because a multitude of factions will have divergent opinions about both the nature of the problem and its possible solutions. Competing values are often at stake. Furthermore, in a large social system the scientific experts often disagree even on the fundamental outlines of a problem, particularly in the early stages of problem definition. The critical strategic question becomes, "Whose problem is it?" And the answer is not so obvious.*

In times of distress, he claims, we turn to authority for:

Direction
Protection—scanning the environment for threats and mobilizing a
    response
Order—orienting people to their places and roles, controlling internal
    conflict, and establishing and maintaining norms

Both investors and employees seek answers to the questions of "direction, protection, and order" from the senior management of the corporation. In those cases where the nature of both the question and the answer is clear, an "authority" or "expert" can make pronouncements that will provide accurate direction, protection, and order. For many questions put to them, senior management is a qualified "authority." Most operations questions involve "technical" work, and thus are fully addressable this way. Technical work thrives on the desire to reduce or eliminate ambiguity.

But desire to eliminate ambiguity cannot be fulfilled in real markets. In real markets, authority and expertise are insufficient. Leadership is required.

By leadership Heifetz means "inducing learning by asking hard questions and by recasting people's expectations [in order] to develop their responsibility." Standard authority will not work in these cases, because there is no precedent yet. The hard work of learning has yet to be done.

Leadership of this type is often required of the management committee and chairman of a corporation. Managing the proper level of creative destruction demands this kind of "adaptive work." It requires management to ask expert questions rather than to fall into the more familiar pattern of providing expert answers.

For the executive committee, taking on this task amounts to a role reversal—a reversal for which it is generally not prepared. Most members of management committees are there because they have demonstrated their skill in operations—whether in production, marketing and sales, product development, or finance. They have not reached their position because they have demonstrated great skill at understanding the vagaries of future markets or the processes of capital (financial or human) allocation for the benefit of investors. Their skill is an expert's skill at answering questions, not the leadership skill of asking questions.

Adaptive work requires changing one's mind-set. In the case of a corporation, it is the mind-set of the management committee that has to change; doing so gives permission for the rest of the organization to change its mind-set as well.

When faced with an adaptive challenge, companies have to try to break down the problems requiring adaptive work into components that will yield to authoritative answers. "Yes, we need more creative destruction. Specifically, we need to invest over the next two years in mobile telephony as it applies to medicine. Moreover, we have to find a way to exit from our traditional hospital businesses without hurting our customers." These are ideas that can be turned into action plans. In this way the complexities of adaptive work have been reduced to the more familiar territory of technical work.

The evidence suggests that the economic environment will continue to ratchet up the rate of change. If we are right, the adaptive work of the corporation will only increase. As we go forward, then, the purpose of the management committee has to change; its primary responsibility in the future must be to identify the adaptive challenges facing the corporation and focus its attention on these challenges. No other group can do this. Should it fail to do this, the company will inevitably falter or stagnate.

The management committee must also modulate the level of adaptive stress it places on the organization (and it is capable of placing the organization under great stress!). Managing the stress level is closely associated with managing the pace of change. Management cannot randomly select the pace of change that best suits it, since, as we have seen, markets generally change faster than the corporations, leaving weaker players behind. There is a natural tendency to avoid changing too fast. But if management committees give in to that inclination, they place the long-term health of their employees and investors at risk.

The management committee must keep attention focused on the relevant issues until they are resolved, then move on to the next challenge, shifting responsibility for the last challenge to the next level. What is a technical challenge for the management committee, of course, may be an adaptive challenge for the next level of management. But at that point, the process simply repeats itself.

Changing a corporation's mind-set from the assumption of continuity to the assumption of discontinuity is an exceptionally difficult task. It involves moving from the comfort zone of technical work, with its dependency on authority, to the open-endedness of adaptive work and its requirements for leadership. Whether corporations are willing to do what it takes to adopt the assumption of discontinuity—to engage in creative destruction at the pace and scale of the market—is, we would argue, *the* prime test faced by management committees. Can the management committee eschew its traditional role as the monitor of the decisions of others—the challenge of technical work—and embrace the adaptive challenge of becoming the controller of the rate of creative destruction in the corporation?

The questions and issues real markets pose are not clear and certain. Real markets are filled with uncertainty and ambiguity. Old problems rarely present themselves in the same way a second time. The all-important problems are almost always new problems, just as all-important opportunities are new opportunities (as any venture capitalist can attest). In other words, real markets do not cater to problem solvers. They cater to the masters of adaptive work. They cater to leaders.

DEFLECTING THE ISSUES

The pain of dealing with the adaptive work that accompanies the assumption of discontinuity is often more easily avoided than addressed. As Heifetz says,

Authorities, under pressure to be decisive, sometimes fake the remedy or take action that avoids the issue by skirting it. In the short term, of course, this may quell some of the distress. If the [leader] succeeds in shifting . . . attention to a substitute problem . . . then the problem . . . may cause less discontent. Attention is deflected from the issue, which appears to be taken care of. We readily invite distraction because it lowers distress. In the long run some problems get worse, and then frustration arises both with the problem situation and with those people in authority who were supposed to resolve it. In response to the frustration we are likely to perpetuate the vicious cycle by looking even more earnestly to authority, but this time we look for someone new offering more certainty and better promises.

Heifetz claims that the flight to authority is particularly dangerous because of this avoidance of adaptive work, which occurs in response to the company's biggest problems, and because it disables key personnel and resources needed to accomplish that work.

FAKING IT

The executives we talked to revealed many examples of "faking it" or "skirting" the issue. We offered some examples above. Others include an excessive focus on short-term financial results (when it is quite clear that the short term contributes only in minor ways to the generation of wealth) and denial of the importance of innovation for long-term success (e.g., "Our brands make us strong. That is all we need."). A variation on that theme is a general acknowledgment of the importance of innovation, while at the same time only programs of incremental innovation that do not challenge the established mental model of the business are implemented (such as the clipper ship vs. steamship battles of the late nineteenth century, described in Chapter 4). The challenges of incremental innovation are easier to conceptualize and tackle. But genuine long-term competitive advantage comes only from substantial and transformational innovation.

SHIFTING ATTENTION TO OTHER ISSUES

Some of the executives we talked to blamed the parent company for the failure of divisions, or blamed failures in their corporations on middle management, when the real culprits were the corporate incentive systems that rewarded the short term and provided no parallel system for rewarding long-term performance. In short, it is quite easy to avoid adaptive work, and few executives really want to do it unless they are clear about its importance and the distinction between adaptive work and technical work.

LEADING ADAPTIVE WORK:
"MIXED SIGNALS"

Roger Fine, General Counsel at Johnson & Johnson, understands the difference between technical and adaptive work as well as anyone we have met. He had the opportunity to comment on this challenge in a speech he gave in 1996 to the top 800 executives of the corporation. Fittingly, it was delivered at an off-site meeting that J&J had dedicated to renewing the corporation's commitment to innovation. Roger Fine's speech crystallizes the challenge to leadership very clearly:

> *You know, over the past four years new words have crept into our vocabulary at J&J: Words like "ambiguity" and "complexity" and "paradox" and "multiple mental models." What these words and what the ideas behind them have given us is an enormous respect for the power of complexity and ambiguity. We need to embrace this. We need to turn this to a competitive advantage.*
>
> *It's a sign of the maturity of the individuals in an organization, a sign of the maturity of an organization that they welcome complexity, or what some people call "mixed signals." I'd rather change mixed signals to complexity and ambiguity to make the point.*
>
> *It's a habit of highly successful people that they welcome complexity and ambiguity and mixed signals. They take it as a challenge to be innovative. And what's so great about this company is that we have the experience to handle this better than anybody else.*
>
> *And why is that? Because we have the greatest example of mixed signals in the history of business, and we call it our Credo, which establishes the basic principles by which we operate. If anybody ever asks us the following question, we all know the answer: "When are you guys gonna make up your minds? What are your objectives? What are your*

core principles? Is it the customer? Is it the employee? Is it the commu-
nities and society? Or is it the stockholders?"

Our answer is "Yes, it's all of the above. We refuse to make up our
minds." The great strength of our company is in not making up our
mind, but of using our energy and intellect, not just to balance and rec-
oncile those principles of the Credo—that sounds passive—it's to take
each one of those and use them robustly. We will infuse each of those
abilities to the maximum of our ability and talent.

MANAGING THE CONFLICT BETWEEN ADAPTIVE WORK AND TECHNICAL WORK

How do Roger Fine's "mixed signals" look to someone seeking direction, protection, and order? They do not look helpful. If Fine's dictum is to be successfully applied, the organization itself has to come to realize that its desire for direction, protection, and order will not be met from above. Fine's message is that the organization has to deliver it to itself. Top management will err if it stands in the way of this realization. By taking the "expert" road, and thus eliminating the need for others to develop their own sense of direction, protection, and order, the management committee can thwart the accomplishment of the adaptive work it would like to see.

But if the management committee does not provide direction, protection, and order, what does it provide? The fundamental responsibility of the management committee is to ensure that the scope of inquiry of the corporation is sufficient to provide for its future. If the cause of the long-term degradation of performance is cultural lock-in, then it is up to the senior stewards of the business to prevent that from happening.

This is the message to be gleaned from the fall of IBM in the 1980s described earlier. The fault of IBM management in the '80s was not that they had lost operational control. Quite the opposite. They were the best in the world. What they had lost control of was the scope of inquiry on a scale sufficient to ensure their future. They had become so focused on operational excellence that the process of dialogue about the future had dried up. While the form of the meetings differed from the Vorstand meeting described at the beginning of the chapter, in effect, it was almost identical.

Our conventional notions of leadership are deeply rooted in the notion that the leader is able to lead because he is an expert. He or she has a clear vision of the future. But we cannot know the future, particularly today. Perhaps, based on our expertise, we can eliminate some possibilities, but that is all. The executives we talked to confirmed that fact. A general comment was "It is essential to be able to read our industry, but we don't know how to do that." All one can do is depend on our adaptive resources.

DESIGNING A PROCESS FOR INCREASING ADAPTIVE WORK

How can an organization accomplish adaptive work without losing control of its technical work, or operations? Over the past decade we have been working with many of our clients to find ways to more effectively achieve this objective. We have also worked intensely with private equity firms over the past decade on the same task. As a result of these experiences we have concluded that there are three responsibilities management must assume.

First, management must assume the responsibility for designing a process that allows adaptive work to flourish without losing operational control. This begins with shaping a broad vision of the processes of adaptive work that accommodates both divergent and convergent thinking and yet does not sacrifice operational control. The goal is to mimic the real-life processes of creativity (as we described them in Chapter 4) as closely as possible in order to maximize the chances of "mimicking the market." In carrying out this responsibility, the management committee has to provide sufficient time in the process to allow alternative mental models of the business to be conceptualized, for voices of opposition to be developed and constructively heard, and for a search for new solutions.

More often than not these processes are informal, invoking a series of temporary processes (e.g., meetings, discussions, visits, and "free time" to think through the implications of the ideas being discussed), involving the part-time activities of many people rather than the establishment of a new department or function staffed with full-time people. In this sense, these processes work at the interstices of the organization, rather than by interfering with existing processes, or by establishing new organization units. There are several ways to reach this objective. We will describe one recent example in depth in Chapter 11.

Second, management has to take oversight responsibility for the conduct of the process so that it reaches a useful outcome that matches the pace and scale of the market, yet does not threaten the loss of operational control or create unproductive levels of stress and conflict in the organization. The key tool management has to achieve this result is the pace at which it introduces new thinking to the organization. If new challenges and ideas are added too quickly, the result will be stress, conflict, and a collapse of productivity. If the pace is too slow, then competitiveness will be lost, as we have seen in many cases in this book. A key task for management is reviewing the pace of the process of managing adaptive work, reaching a judgment about whether it is too fast or too slow, and responding accordingly.

Third, management should take responsibility for several supporting, yet critical, activities in the management of adaptive work. These include: framing issues for discussion, selecting the people to participate in the discussion of the issues, and overseeing the required implementation—specifically, by setting the standards and goals for performance and by assigning responsibility for execution.

Collectively, these three responsibilities are aimed at managing the transition from divergent to convergent thinking, and at managing the balance between thinking and acting.

ADAPTIVE WORK IN PRIVATE EQUITY

As we discussed in Chapter 7, adaptive work thrives within the world of private equity. The leaders of private equity firms have extensive experience in balancing divergent and convergent thinking, and in balancing thought and action, although they rarely call these activities by these names. They also have a great deal of experience in the design (and redesign) and oversight of the processes to achieve these balances. The biggest difference we see between private equity firms and public equity companies is the amount of time and energy senior managers in private equity firms spend on revising their worldviews and thinking through the implications of those changes for companies they should buy and sell, compared with corporate leaders, who spend their time thinking about how to improve their present operations.

The private equity firm, because of the rapid pace of change of the assets it owns, is continually assessing its progress; questioning its fundamental direction; thinking of the next wave of change. As a result, successful venture capitalists become excellent analysts of future opportunities, and principal investing firms become exceptionally talented at tearing apart a business to understand its potential and vulnerabilities. Neither skill is used as often in public equity firms, where new business proposals often come out of R&D rather than out of a new business development function run by partners with personal funds invested. The difference in these two approaches can be astounding in terms of their results. The differences in the capacity for adaptive work can be even more fundamental.

Today there are a number of important early attempts being made to bridge the gaps between the approaches of private and public equity, combining the approaches of private equity with the rigors of public equity ownership (for example, continually having to meet "mark-to-market" tests, which compare how well these companies are doing relative to the general stock market indices).

It can be rough going, as all these firms have discovered. Many faced extreme financial pressures in the second half of 2000 after the Nasdaq markets collapsed, and their market valuations declined by as much as 90%. Moreover, the market is skeptical that these companies are different from mutual funds and thus are reluctant to offer high multiples for these companies at this writing. Yet, if these companies succeed in their attempts to find practical, sustainable ways to blend the managerial approaches of private equity with the requirements of public equity corporations, they will represent an attractive model that other companies will want to emulate. For the time being, these are interesting companies worth paying attention to given how skilled they are at adaptive work. As one of the oldest of these companies, Safeguard Scientifics provides a detailed study of the processes of adaptive work in the challenging environment of public markets.

SAFEGUARD SCIENTIFICS

In 1953, three years out of college, Warren "Pete" Musser left his job as a stockbroker to form a $300,000 investment fund called Lancaster. With no specific industry focus, expertise, or investment strategy, Musser initially invested in a wide range of young companies in industries that he believed had long-term growth potential. Investments were made in real estate, office automation, medical services, cable television, robotics, and automobile parts. The results were strong. The company's first investment, for example, was in a cable television firm called Comcast, now the fourth-largest cable company in the country.

Musser changed Lancaster's name to Safeguard Industries after a successful early investment in a business called Safeguard, which Musser renamed Safeguard Business Systems. SBS made check printers that wrote payment amounts by perforating the paper. Benefiting from Safeguard's managerial and financial support, Safeguard Business Systems grew to provide computerized information systems and successfully promoted its services to more than 650,000 small businesses. The Safeguard Industries investment in Safeguard Business Systems became the company's largest source of income, leading to the initial public offering of Safeguard Industries in 1965. Switching from cable companies to check-perforating machinery companies to computerized information systems companies began to develop Musser's adaptive work abilities.

Although Safeguard Business Systems was profitable, the concept of Safeguard Industries was vulnerable, as demonstrated by its other holdings, including a remanufactured auto parts business. Losses in the remanufactured auto parts business forced the company into debt.

The financial losses resulting from the slow-growth businesses ultimately spawned a new investment strategy. In 1977, Musser decided to identify and invest exclusively in high-growth businesses. Musser had learned the lessons of the assumption of continuity the hard way.

Nonetheless, the timing of the move was unfortunate. Safeguard Industries' mounting debt forced it to spin off Safeguard Business Systems to its shareholders in 1980. Under the plan, shareholders of Safeguard Industries received shares of Safeguard Business Systems. But by splitting the profitable unit away from the parent, Safeguard Industries was able to transfer some of the burdensome debt of the company to the more profitable entity, thus stabilizing the finances of the remaining businesses and generating capital to invest in new areas of the economy with high potentials for growth. The company renamed itself Safeguard Scientifics, reflecting its intention to invest in high-tech firms.

As a consequence of spinning off Safeguard Business Systems, Musser realized that separating the interests of the companies at an appropriate point led to a tremendous return for the shareholders. "We noticed that a

$4 stock went to the equivalent of $50 if you added up both resultant companies," Musser said. "All we had done was split the assets. That left a visible impression on us." The adaptive strategy that he intuitively pursued was paying dividends.

Musser decided that once an acquired growth company was on solid financial and managerial footing, Safeguard would split it off as a separate public company through a program that would sell portions of Safeguard's holding directly to Safeguard stockholders. This would be a theme that was to generate superior returns over the years, although the timing and nature of the spin-offs differed considerably. The former investment company would come close to taking over some operating responsibilities, but it never crossed the line to day-to-day operations.

Before Safeguard Scientifics had an opportunity to implement its novel plan on a broader scale, however, the company was nearly destroyed by a totally unrelated event. An Iowa stockbroker, Gary Lewellyn of Des Moines, owner of a small brokerage, in an attempt to manipulate the Safeguard stock to his own benefit, began to accumulate Safeguard stock in late 1981. By November, he had accumulated about 7% of the outstanding shares. Lewellyn had purchased the stock in small daily increments on margin through Swiss American, the U.S. Branch of Credit Suisse. To finance his purchases, Lewellyn misappropriated $2.8 million of government securities from an account he managed for the First National Bank of Humbolt, Iowa, the bank where his father presided.

Over the next five months, he continued to buy the stock, trying to force a run-up (and preventing a call on his previous margins); by March of 1982, he "owned" 58% of the company. When Swiss American and Merrill Lynch stopped extending him margin, he set up accounts in the names of his Des Moines clients and continued to buy, even from himself, to create an illusion of demand.

On March 17, Lewellyn informed Swiss American that he couldn't fulfill his obligations and went into hiding. After a spending spree in Las Vegas, Lewellyn turned himself in to the FBI.

The results were disastrous for all involved: Safeguard saw its stock price plummet, followed by a ten-day suspension of trading by the SEC. Swiss American and Merrill Lynch found themselves owning the majority of Safeguard; the First National Bank of Humbolt was declared insolvent and was liquidated by the FDIC. Lewellyn received twenty years in federal prison for embezzlement.

Although Swiss American wanted to sell the 1.6 million shares it was left holding, Musser was able to convince the firm to hold the shares for a year. Musser was also able to assure his other investors that the recent fiasco had nothing to do with the underlying business plan of Safeguard, and in 1983, shareholders agreed to a secondary public offering of the 1.6 million shares to rid Swiss American of its unwanted ownership. Fortunately, Safeguard's first attempt at a rights offering was a blockbuster.

In February 1981, Musser spent $2.5 million of the money Safeguard made for 51% of Novell, Inc., at the time a struggling software maker. By the end of 1984, Novell was growing rapidly as the market for local area networking (LAN) hardware and software developed, and Safeguard decided it was time to spin Novell off. In February 1985, Safeguard stockholders were given the right to purchase a share of Novell for $2.50 for every two shares of Safeguard they held; a total of 2.3 million shares were distributed in this fashion. By allocating stock to its shareholders, Safeguard's ownership of Novell fell to 23%, and it relinquished direct control. Subsequent to the offering, Novell grew by more than 200% in 1985, on its way to a peak value of over $500 a share in the '90s. By 1990, Safeguard had reduced its ownership of Novell to less than 5%, reaping capital gains of nearly $100 million over three years. Some of these sells may have been required by the Investment Company Act of 1940, which would have declared Safeguard Scientifics a mutual fund and exposed it to ordinary earned-income tax liabilities, rather than capital gains, had it not sold its interest. The provisions of the law can help force these companies to value adaptive work even when they do not want to.

While spinning off a company at the height of its achievements might not seem surprising for a financial intermediary, it would be exceptionally surprising for an operating company to take such action. Traditionally, the operating company will hold on to the company rather than realize gains in the public market. The rationale is based on the assumption of the strong link between control and performance. "We cannot give up control of the enterprise, because if we do, performance may suffer." Such a decision is based on the assumption of continuity. The opposite logic was used at Safeguard, which was eager to find other new opportunities. It relinquished control, profited from its transaction, and provided a stunning opportunity to investors, freeing Safeguard to move on to the next opportunity.

Unlike the traditional venture capitalist, though, Safeguard was prepared to hold a stake in a company for years beyond the IPO if it needed to strengthen the company. For example, in the late 1980s, Safeguard held a minority 15% block of the stock in Machine Vision, a maker of optical systems for industrial applications. In November 1985, Safeguard reduced its holding from 15% to 11% through an offering at $2.75 per share. Machine Vision performed poorly in its early days. Rather than sell its position, Safeguard decided to increase its ownership to 70% through a warrant that it held in 1985, and by purchasing shares on the open market in order to help Machine Vision through hard times. Working with Machine Vision, Safeguard changed the direction of the company to a focus on reselling computer hardware and software to businesses and institutions, changing its name to CompuCom to commemorate the shift. This proved to be a successful strategy. CompuCom grew by 45% annually from 1988 to 1992, providing substantial returns for Safeguard shareholders. In this case the traditional assumption of the link between performance and control proved to be correct. Safeguard demonstrated its ability to use either assumption to its advantage, depending on the circumstances.

Safeguard did not restrict its investments to only small start-ups. In the late '80s, as many companies found difficulty in raising the capital necessary to expand, Safeguard provided unsecured credit in exchange for substantial stock warrants. Again, their direct lack of control is notable. Through this mechanism, Safeguard obtained equity in QVC, the television shopping channel, and Infotron, a manufacturer of communications networking equipment. In addition, in 1988, Safeguard formed Radnor Venture Partners, a venture capital group. Radnor and the other venture capital firms that Safeguard started later on were designed to allow Safeguard to invest in companies that didn't meet its strict criteria for joining the Safeguard fold but were nevertheless promising. Safeguard has been relentless at finding new ways to create value through changes in its approach to ownership and control.

In the '80s, Safeguard Scientifics decided computer hardware and software were the areas with the largest growth opportunities. In the '90s, its focus began to turn to information technology, showing its determination to change at the pace and scale of the market. It began to develop companies offering consultation and implementation services, such as Cambridge Technology Partners, which Safeguard took public through a rights offering in May of 1993. By buying in at the IPO price of $5 per share for Cambridge Technology Partners, Safeguard shareholders were able to realize a fifteenfold increase in their investment over the following three years.

Safeguard's focus on shareholder return drives its involvement with companies that it has taken public. "We are active in the management of these companies. We aren't just passive investors, so we can influence their strategies and their directions. We can help to pick the management, and that gives us better knowledge on how the company is doing," said Musser. Each company is assigned a team of experienced Safeguard professionals in the areas of operations, finance, legal, and business development. But Safeguard is focused on giving support rather than establishing standards for control.

In the case of Safeguard Scientifics, less control did not compromise performance or the aspiration for high performance. Quite the reverse was true. Those chosen by Safeguard to serve on the board of directors of partner companies push strongly for high levels of return for shareholders. In July 1999, after Cambridge Technology Partners failed to meet estimated earnings, for example, Musser disposed of CEO James Sims for failing to move the company forward: "We asked Jim to excuse himself," said Musser. Days later, Safeguard forced Edward Anderson, a former Safeguard executive, out of his position as CEO of CompuCom Systems (Safeguard still owned 54%).

As the IPO market accelerated with the growth of Internet-related start-ups in the late 1990s, Safeguard realized that its method of rights offering was limiting the potential of its offerings. By allocating all of the shares on offer directly and proportionately to shareholders of Safeguard, small investors, who account for 70% of all Safeguard investors, were able to participate, but investment banks were often unable to offer large blocks of shares to the institutional investors. To provide large blocks of shares to institutions (and thereby increase demand and share price), Safeguard developed a second method of taking companies public, called a *directed shares subscription program*. With this method, a smaller portion of the shares is distributed to Safeguard stockholders at the IPO price (typically higher than that for a rights offering), allowing those interested to buy at the same rate as larger institutions. The directed shares subscription program is a recent example of Safeguard's determination to innovate to allow itself the flexibility to move into and out of businesses.

The first company to be offered in this way was the Internet Capital Group, in August 1999. Two Safeguard executives helped form ICG in 1996 as an Internet holding company actively engaged in business-to-business e-commerce through its own network of partner companies. The formation of ICG corresponded to the passing of the National Securities

Markets Improvement Act, which relaxed some of the constraints on the number of investors that could participate in a venture capital company.

Providing operational assistance and capital support, ICG intended to maximize the long-term market potential of its partner companies. Safeguard shareholders were allowed to buy a share of ICG at the offer price of $12 for every 10 shares of Safeguard held. The strategy increased interest in the offering and yielded higher returns for initial shareholders, as ICG's stock price ended the year up over fourteenfold, making it the most successful IPO of 1999 (although it has since fallen off substantially). Safeguard Scientifics' 13% interest in ICG, bought in two transactions for a total of $29 million, was valued at about $150 million as of December 2000.

ICG's success contributed to Safeguard Scientifics' shift in focus from information technology businesses to Internet businesses. It was the third fundamental shift Safeguard had made in twenty years. And the shift was not at all marginal. When Safeguard changes its spots, it changes them to stripes. The company is now moving again. In 1999, it announced that it planned to target e-commerce, e-business, and e-communications companies. "In the early '90s, we helped define and implement client server architectures in enterprise computing environments through Cambridge Technology Partners. Now, we are helping build the Internet as a new medium for business and consumer interactions and transactions through a number of our partnership companies," said Musser. Safeguard is riding the waves as the gales of creative destruction blow.

This investment strategy is intended to increase shareholder return and optimize the deployment of resources by building on Safeguard's portfolio of high-growth companies while sharpening its investment focus. Safeguard's partner network has grown to forty directly held partner companies and 210 companies held indirectly through its private equity funds. Musser's decision to focus on Internet companies has enabled Safeguard to build a larger network and take more companies public. Between 1990 and 1998, Safeguard took nine companies public, compared to four companies in 1999 alone. This is adaptive work at its best.

Shareholders of Safeguard are in many ways buying the opportunity to participate in the public offerings of its partner companies. Although Safeguard's stock has not performed above average, the nine rights offerings that have been completed between 1992 and 1998 have on average resulted in a 67% internal rate of return for the Safeguard shareholder, substantially above even the very high levels of return achieved in the public markets. Musser believes that "shareholders should be evaluating Safe-guard on its value creation, not on earnings." It seems hard to argue.

Safeguard Scientifics is a clear example of how a firm can operate as the creator, operator, and trader of options. It is also a clear example of the power of adaptive work. Safeguard would not have produced the returns it did if it had limited itself to technical work. Musser and the senior people at Safeguard provided the function of the market, but so far have not gotten caught up in cultural lock-in. While they certainly do not for-mally talk about managing the rate of creative destruction or about how to innovate and eliminate at the pace and scale of the market, these notions are clearly part of the tacit knowledge of the organization. The essential role of the management committee at Safeguard is to manage the pace and scale of creative destruction, and to do it in a way that does not jeopardize operational control. Management has developed a process to manage the transition from divergent to convergent thinking, and to manage the balance between reflection and action, techniques Musser and his colleagues learned and applied in the markets of the '80s.

Safeguard's ability to continually generate substantial and perhaps even transformational innovation, while not losing control of its operations, is one of its core strengths. The key is its focus on people and its willingness to tighten up control when things are not working well. Its primary lever for control, once it has made an investment, is people selection (or elimi-nation). Once that is done, control is truly delegated to the (often public) operating company.

Recently Safeguard has had to go through some hard times—some due to misjudgments it have made and some due to the late-2000 Nasdaq col-lapse. And it will undoubtedly have to go through hard times in the future. But it has made it through these times without sacrificing longer-term per-formance. In the end the challenge may be for Safeguard to maintain its methods as it goes through the inevitable change in senior leadership. Maintaining as fine a balance as Safeguard has is not easy. Many people can read music, but few can play like Glenn Gould.

L'ORÉAL

The world of American venture capital is a very long way from life in high-fashion France, but L'Oréal and Safeguard Scientifics share a management philosophy of creative destruction. Liliane Bettencourt, as the primary shareholder of the French cosmetics company L'Oréal, is not only the wealthiest woman in Europe (the most recent *Forbes* Richest list, Summer 2000, lists her as the richest woman in the world), but also the beneficiary of one company that for the time being has found the secret of perpetual economic youth.

L'Oréal was started by Madame Bettencourt's father, Eugene Schueller, in the early 1900s. Schueller, a chemist by training, developed a synthetic dye that could be used on human hair and began selling it in the streets of Paris in 1907. Within two years, he was calling the dye L'Oréal, based on the French word *aureole* ("aura of light"), and selling it to local hairdressers. Schueller extended his product line to include soaps and perfumes, and after World War II, he convinced his compatriots to follow the American hair care trend of putting down soap bars in favor of shampoo.

When her father died in 1957, Bettencourt inherited the company, which continued to grow and expand internationally until 1963, when it was taken public. Bettencourt maintained a majority stake until 1974, when she traded 49% of her share to Nestlé in exchange for 3% of the food giant, although she maintained 70% of the L'Oréal voting rights in the exchange. This deal, along with additional stock purchases later, made Bettencourt the largest shareholder of both companies.

Lindsey Owen-Jones became CEO in 1988 when L'Oréal was one of the largest companies in France, with nearly $4 billion in sales. It was a blue-chip company that the market considered unlikely to grow. However, since Owen-Jones took over at L'Oréal, the company share price has risen tenfold, while the S&P 500 has appreciated sixfold, roughly at the same pace as that of the consumer products industry. L'Oréal has also been paying out consistent dividends over the period, making its return to shareholders even higher.

What did L'Oréal, a large, old company, do to generate such strong performance? Before Owen-Jones, L'Oréal had expanded by acquisition: It had bought Lancôme in 1965, Ralph Lauren and Gloria Vanderbilt cosmetics in 1984, and Helena Rubinstein in 1988. This approach had produced growth, but not high returns to shareholders. In those days L'Oréal was quite restrictive in terms of product and brand territory definition. Owen-Jones saw this restrictiveness as the primary constraint on L'Oréal's performance.

Accordingly, Owen-Jones decided that L'Oréal should adopt a much more expansive mind-set by enlarging the category where it competed and the markets that its key brands had to cover. This mind-set would allow L'Oréal to become a more potent competitor in the marketplace by increasing the pace and scale of change. Owen-Jones decided that there was a very broad market for beauty concepts that came from outside the home market, wherever that was. While Lancôme, for instance, remained closely connected to the concept of French beauty, Georgio Armani perfumes sold to consumers desiring Italian fashion, and Gloria Vanderbilt and Ralph Lauren Polo represented New York style and wealth. Most of the sales of fragrances and cosmetics were outside the country they represented. Polo did particularly well in England, while Gloria Vanderbilt became the top-selling fragrance in Europe only four years after its release.

Under Owen-Jones, L'Oréal accelerated its pace of internationalization, increasing sales by equating different brands with different national identities. "To me, being truly international is to find a new way in which brands can be extremely coherent internationally and yet in which each country can bring something to the overall international picture," said Owen-Jones. Given this concept, L'Oréal is constantly looking for a transfer of ideas between regions and businesses, and thus leverage of its innovations on a global scale. For example, its Japanese office developed a hair color product for teenagers that has become a very significant product line across the world. In addition, this has helped to enhance L'Oréal's skills in the area of hair colors, which the company leverages successfully for women's products.

The engine of this process is creative destruction. First, L'Oréal is "obsessed" with being more innovative. This is an objective widely shared by the organization. Innovation is at the center of L'Oréal's most important internal processes. Each global division has to target a certain amount of innovation (share of sales achieved), and over the last ten years, the percentage of innovation-driven sales has increased significantly. Every brand manager has to be able to define precisely (and present it to the top management) what new product plan they are working on and what potential impact they expect from their efforts. As a consumer goods company, L'Oréal is obsessed with being faster in the marketplace, reducing time to market, and being sure that it presents interesting concepts and not just new products.

Second, beyond innovation per se is a strategy to let innovations evolve in a way that mimics the dynamics of the market. This is the heart of L'Oréal's creative destruction process. For example, in 1986, before

Owen-Jones took over, L'Oréal released a Lancôme-brand liposome cream to hide wrinkles at $50 per jar. When the competition matched L'Oréal's product three years later, L'Oréal added liposomes to its lower-priced Plenitude line, allowing customers to buy the cream for $8. Many companies would not consider this move, fearing the effects of cannibalization. L'Oréal saw it the other way around: Adding liposome to Plenitude was part of mastering the game of creative destruction. Having different brands for different markets allows L'Oréal to introduce new technology to the high-end products first, and over time allows it to migrate to the lower-priced markets and eventually be replaced. In many ways this is the cosmetic equivalent of the "chip wars" that occurred in the semiconductor industry, with each generation moving down in price performance to allow the next generation to enter.

For this strategy to work, Owen-Jones has to be certain to have a new improvement waiting for Lancôme before it sends its innovations down to the low-price brands. This is the essence of managing the pace of creative destruction. Owen-Jones says: "Our labs have a basic rule—they're not allowed to let anything trickle down until they've provided something hot which will be the next new thing. That's my call."

L'Oréal has worked hard to make certain there always is a "next new thing," increasing research in line with profits and producing more patents on a yearly basis than any other French company. Owen-Jones controls the pace of creative destruction through this process. Needless to say, while Owen-Jones calls the pace, if the pace falls behind the market, if the labs cannot successfully come up with the "next new thing" at the pace of the market, L'Oréal will fall behind.

This strategy became successful almost immediately after Owen-Jones took over. The company grew sales and, significantly, margins through the late '80s and early '90s. In addition, Owen-Jones demonstrates the same savvy in dealing with the capital markets as Bill Gates did at Microsoft, and John Chambers did at Cisco, when he underplays the long-term significance of short-term performance. In 1990, for instance, after a strong annual performance, the company attributed much of the increase to one-time adjustments. Additionally, L'Oréal typically refused to provide earnings estimates throughout the year, and Owen-Jones dismissed the value of quarterly reports, saying that only an American investor could be interested in such a thing. Nevertheless the performance increases have continued to come, causing continual upward revisions in analysts' estimates and delighting shareholders.

The implicit strategy of creative destruction is leveraged by a program of acquisition. Owen-Jones acquired Maybelline in 1996 for $758 million. Although the acquisition doubled L'Oréal's U.S. sales figures and made L'Oréal the leader in market share, the deal had an overriding global strategic rationale. L'Oréal immediately began to market Maybelline as American urban chic in Europe and Asia. It also served to fill out the lower end of L'Oréal's offerings. With its premier brands like Lancôme being offered in department stores, L'Oréal wanted to extend its cosmetics offerings to drugstores and discount stores such as Wal-Mart, where Maybelline and its major competitor, Revlon, are sold.

Through the mid-'90s L'Oréal continued to grow solidly, always building revenue and usually growing its margin. L'Oréal's new trajectory became apparent to the market in 1991. As Europe began to slide into a recession, revenue and profit growth continued to accelerate. Over twelve months starting in June 1991, L'Oréal's share price doubled. During the period, profits continued to grow, and Owen-Jones continued to explain much of them away, either as fluctuations in exchange rates or as one-time capital gains.

Through the strategy of globalizing its operations while relentlessly engaging in creative destruction, L'Oréal has proven itself to be not only a tough competitor but also a rewarding investment for shareholders. It has demonstrated over the past fifteen years that the ability to operate and change at the pace and scale of the market can be accomplished, even in a larger corporation, if the leadership is present and sufficiently visionary.

Moreover, L'Oréal demonstrates that it is possible for a company to change from a focus on operations to a simultaneous focus on operations and creative destruction. As we have seen time and again, however, strong past performance does not imply strong future performance. It only buys the opportunity to make the next step. The pace of change is accelerating and will continue to do so. It has been the secret to L'Oréal's strong economic performance for the past decade and half. L'Oréal knows how to play the game of creative destruction; it knows how to lead adaptive work.

CHANGING THE RATIO OF ADAPTIVE TO TECHNICAL WORK IN THE CORPORATION

Setting the proper—that is, market-based—balance between adaptive work and technical work, as we have said, is the responsibility of the management committee and the CEO. No other group has sufficient scope of authority to both see the need and command the attention to get the job done. The tool for initiating the change in balance of adaptive and technical work is really quite straightforward—it is the annual calendar of management committee meetings, and agendas for each of these meetings. It is sometimes difficult to imagine that the prosaic act of setting the calendar, a task often delegated to support staff, is at the heart of some of the most important decisions management has to make. But it is nonetheless true. The calendar of meetings determines which issues will be addressed, which conversations will be held, who will and will not have a voice in challenging the existing mental models, and who will have a voice in proposing and establishing new mental models. In the end, the pace of change in the corporation can be set by the pace of these meetings and the issues that are accepted for inclusion.

In addition to the calendar, the agendas for the individual meetings are also critical. The more traditional agenda calls for the exchange of information and the ratification of strongly recommended decisions. Generally there is not much dialogue at these meetings, and what dialogue there is centers on the exchange or clarification of information. These meetings usually take place near the end of a convergent thinking process. The agenda setting for these meetings can generally be assigned to staff, with periodic review. No special skill is needed to run the meetings other than that of a convener.

A different type of meeting involves a real conversation, where people exchange "views of the world" (i.e., mental models) to identify, clarify, and resolve issues and to convert general notions of direction into a rough sense of action. These meetings are typically nearer the front end of a divergent thinking process. They are much more open-ended, and correspondingly have rather loose agendas. The sequence of the issues on the agenda is often important as well. It should be designed by someone senior enough to have an overall sense of what is trying to be accomplished, and a hypothesis of how the conversation in the meeting should flow. The idea is to get the best ideas on the table and discussed in an open way. Avoiding premature closure is an important art in these meetings, and often it is useful to assign someone the role of keeping the meeting on track so that it lingers and speeds up at appropriate times.

We are not suggesting that the management committee address itself *only* to adaptive work. That would be a major error and would send an unproductive signal to the corporation. Clearly the management committee does have to continue to review key operating decisions, change-of-ownership decisions, budgets and resources, talent reviews, and external relations. However, it is essential that the committee make a conscious decision about the balance of time and attention that is spent on each of these issues. This time allocation should not just happen, as it often does. It should be entirely premeditated. If the outcome of premeditation is worse than the unmanaged outcome, it should be seen as an opportunity for reflection and improvement. To abdicate this responsibility is to abdicate responsibility for the balance of adaptive versus technical work, and to abdicate the responsibility for the longer-term performance of the corporation.

SETTING THE STANDARDS FOR MANAGEMENT EFFECTIVENESS

Setting the standards of effectiveness for these tasks helps to establish standards by which management committees should be judged by the CEO and the board. Typically, the CEO is the architect of the activities of the management committee. It is with his or her leadership, and permission, that the management committee sets its agenda, mobilizes the company's resources, carries out its tasks, establishes standards, and evaluates its performance. The CEO is both the chairman of the management committee and a member of that committee. In his role as a member of the committee, he participates in the dialogue along with the others. If the management committee fails to ask and answer the questions about the responsibility for managing creative destruction and operations, only the CEO can be found to be at fault.

The task of setting the proper balance between the company's focus on creation and trading versus operations is at the core of what the management committee and the chairman value. Accordingly, the committee should be evaluated based on its ability to set and adjust this balance properly. In the end, the management committee must take responsibility for both operational effectiveness and managing the rate of creative destruction to match the markets. This is the standard by which it should be judged and to which it should be held.

• • •

Throughout this chapter we have been addressing the following questions: What is the role of the management committee when the corporation has to change at the pace and scale of the market? What value does it add? How can it address the requirements of direction, protection, and order? How effective is it? We think these questions are at the heart of long-term future corporate performance. We have come a long way from the Vorstand meeting in Germany described at the beginning of the chapter. Often these questions are not asked. Unless a company can answer these questions clearly and pragmatically, performance will ultimately suffer.

CHAPTER 9

Increasing Creation by Tenfold

Arun Gupta is the founding entrepreneur of NeuVis, which is one of the newly formed companies currently on the periphery of the decision support software industry, a several-hundred-billion-dollar, rapidly growing industry meeting companies' changing information needs. NeuVis was established five years ago to take advantage of new programming tools (Java Beans) to bring more flexibility to the process of changing corporate decision support systems. Before forming NeuVis, Gupta was the chairman of DataEase International, a successful software developer that was sold to Symantec in 1992. While at DataEase, Gupta had begun wrestling with the problem of how to improve the efficiency of changing major elements of the software that underpins most corporate decision support systems today. Changing a key element of these programs—say, the program that manages the general ledger—is a very costly and often time-consuming process, since the software that controls the flow of information across the interface between the general ledger and the systems it interacts with, such as the accounts receivable system, has to be completely rewritten. While Gupta could visualize what needed to be done to cut the time and cost of these switchovers, he could not see technically how to do it. When DataEase was sold to Symantec, Gupta was given a multiyear contract, but he had no real job. However, he was not idle. He took advantage of the two years of free time to develop his ideas for met-alevel software language. Based on the ideas he developed during that time, Gupta formed NeuVis in 1994. After five years of development, which Gupta personally financed, NeuVis had gotten successful first-round financing managed by Goldman Sachs.

If you ask Gupta what he did for those two years of "incubation," he cannot really say, other than that he was playing with ideas and talking with lots of people. In fact, this time was critical in creating his ideas and testing the robustness of his conclusions. Gupta was intensely engaged in the process of divergent thinking, simultaneously drafting problems and solutions until they fit together. The toggling between observation, reflection, and conversation served to juxtapose ideas, until at one point Gupta arrived at the business concept and direction he was searching for.

Gupta's story is typical of those founding new companies. Often the founder starts the new company after years of reflection and preliminary testing. Sometimes the necessary reflection takes place at a university, sometimes on the open road. But it rarely takes place in the corporation. There are simply too many other pressures to allow that kind of reflective time. Whether Gupta and NeuVis will be one of the successful attackers from the periphery is not knowable. But what is certain is that Gupta required the time for conversation, observation, and reflection before he could create his company. This is time that is normally not available in an intense operating environment.

THE REQUIREMENTS FOR
DIVERGENT THINKING

As we showed in Chapter 4, the capital markets produce substantial and transformational innovations at ten times the rate of the established cor-poration. The story of NeuVis is one of thousands of similar stories that are being played out in the capital markets.

To reach the level of innovative power of the market, corporations that have excelled in operations will have to master the skills of divergent thinking just as they mastered convergent thinking. For divergent think-ing, as we have pointed out, is at the heart of the creative process.

Also in Chapter 4, we discussed that the purpose of divergent thinking is to discover new ideas at the pace and scale of the market. Achieving this purpose requires focusing on significant problems (unmet needs) and identifying promising solutions, just as Arun Gupta did. The divergent-thinking process does not require that the solution be developed in detail, nor that the solution be proven effective. These critically important steps, although necessary, are better treated as part of the convergent-thinking process. The purpose of divergent thinking is to define the possibilities and propose a promising solution that can be validated to the point of creating a business plan that will attract external investors. Search, incubation, and collision, as we saw in Chapter 4, are the core elements of divergent thinking. These processes are essential if discontinuity is going to be embraced.

Divergent thinking, as seen through search, incubation, and collision, may seem ungovernable. But our experience has shown us that there are some techniques that can stimulate divergent thinking. To a great extent, however, current corporate processes thwart the pursuit of search, incubation, and collision at the pace and scale of the market.

THE FAILURE OF STRATEGIC PLANNING, RESEARCH AND DEVELOPMENT, AND CORPORATE VENTURE CAPITAL

There are three processes in most corporations that are relied upon to provide a search, incubation, and collision, all resulting in a flow of new ideas: research and development, corporate development, and corporate planning. However, in our view, none of these processes seems to be working particularly well. Collectively these three functions, operating as they have been, have not produced change within survivor corporations at the pace and scale of the market.

STRATEGIC PLANNING

Strategic planning was originally conceived of as a mechanism for identifying major opportunities facing the corporation and developing the plans to capture those opportunities. Today there is widespread dissatisfaction with strategic planning. As one senior manager confided to us about his company's strategic planning processes: "Our planning process is like some primitive tribal ritual: There is a lot of noise, dancing, waving of feathers, beating of drums, and no one is sure exactly why we do it, but still there is an almost mystical hope that something good will eventually come of it, and it never does." Another disappointed manager noted, "Our annual planning process is like the office Christmas party: We feel obliged to have one, even though no one seems to really enjoy it."

Often today's strategic planning does not attempt to collect information that could challenge existing mental models. It focuses on reanalysis of the existing businesses and the analysis of similarly sized competitors, rather than attempting to understand what is happing at the periphery of the business and how it might change. Often strategic planning has become a paper exercise, devoid of direct observation in the marketplace. Junior planners are sent off to write plans without much dialogue with the senior executives who might have the necessary insight and perspective to spot real opportunities. The process gathers new information infrequently, offers few new experiences, and does not allow time for reflection or conversation among thoughtful people. It has been reduced to a pure numbers exercise, rather than an exercise in thinking. (A self-administered test of the adequacy of a corporation's strategic planning processes is provided at the end of this chapter.) To be successful, strategic planning must be designed to incorporate the principles of divergent thinking.

RESEARCH AND DEVELOPMENT

Research and development (R&D), which most people think is charged with the responsibility for renewal, is also often disappointing. An examination of the companies in the McKinsey Corporate Performance Database shows that there is no general correlation between R&D spending (either funding level or growth of resources) and total return to shareholders. The results vary considerably by industry. In the pharmaceutical industry there is a reasonably strong correlation between R&D and total return to shareholders. This is the conventionally assumed relationship. These companies spend on R&D to create new products, which helps maintain growth. In the pharmaceutical industry the process seems to be working.

This same positive relationship is seen in several other industries as well, if to a lesser extent: pulp and paper, commodity and specialty chemicals, aerospace and defense, and oil extraction. But in three of the industries we analyzed—soaps and detergents, medical and surgical equipment, and telecommunications—there is no correlation at all. Perhaps soaps and detergents can be intuitively understood, since they are in a "low-tech" industry.

But medical products and telecommunications are far from low tech. That is not to suggest that if R&D were stopped the result would not be a loss for the shareholders. One would expect that to be the case, actually, since both these industries depend on new products for their growth. It is just that the R&D expenditures in these industries do not create enough "surprise" to provide excess rewards to shareholders.

There is a third group of industries, however—computer hardware, software, and semiconductors—where the correlations are actually negative! The more that the companies spend on R&D, the lower are the total returns for shareholders. This occurs because the primary source of new products and innovation in these industries is not internal R&D, but rather technology licensed from the rest of the industry (there is extensive cross-licensing in these industries) or from acquisitions.

On the whole, our analysis indicates that investors expect more from R&D than they actually get. There are two reasons for this. First, technological change is only broadly correlated with total return to shareholders. Total return to shareholders is a result of the corporation's current performance and expectations about its future performance. Technological change is only one of the ways in which either current performance or expectations about future performance can be affected. Other ways include having preferred supplier or customer relationships, holding a unique market niche, or having access to special resources. It would be surprising if technological change were equally important in all industries.

Second, even in those industries where technological change is important, the most important technological advances may come either from inside the company, as a result of R&D, or from outside the company as a result, say, of the purchase of a license for the use of technology developed by another company, or through an acquisition. We would expect a correlation between R&D and TRS in those industries where cross-licensing of patents is rare, such as in the pharmaceutical industry. But in those industries where cross-licensing is more common—for example, semiconductors or computer hardware—there is not much of a relationship.

The decision whether to use internal R&D to develop the technological information required to create surprising new products or services, or to use licensed technology or to acquire a company that owns the needed technology, is the technological equivalent of a traditional make-or-buy decision, although one does not normally think of R&D in this context. In testimony to the practical nature of this observation, Cisco has penned this credo: "Most innovations don't happen in your company."

CORPORATE VENTURE CAPITAL

Perhaps out of frustration over the ineffectiveness of internal efforts to develop important new technologies, many U.S. corporations have recently stepped up their spending on venture capital. The first wave of such spending reached a peak in 1989 at about $1 billion per year, an amount that accounted for more than 20% of all venture capital raised in the United States. By the early '90s, corporate spending had fallen off to less than $300 million as profit pressure mounted during the recession. Today, however, corporation spending on venture capital has risen to a level in excess of $10 billion per year (compared, however, to about $160 billion on R&D)—once again more than 20% of all the venture capital raised. Many leading companies are pursuing this route: AOL–Time Warner, AT&T, Intel, and Lucent, to name a few. European companies are also providing venture capital funds; Siemens and Deutsche Telekom are examples. According to Dan Case, CEO of investment company Hambrecht & Quist, "Of the 100 largest companies in the United States, two-thirds are doing [corporate venture capital], think they are doing it, or are thinking about doing it."

Corporations are flocking to venture capital because they sense the potential for financial returns and the strategic growth options that venture capital has recently come to represent. As one company executive says, "Investments of $2 to $5 million are not much, compared to our R&D budgets. But the benefits and insights we get are significant." The efficiency of using corporate venture capital to gain insight into the periphery may turn out to be substantial, and more effective than traditional R&D.

But for corporations to be effective with these investments, they are going to have to learn to be effective private equity investors, and as we discussed in Chapter 7, there are four reasons why that is difficult. First, corporations often, at least inadvertently, apply the same rules to their venture capital investments as they do to their normal investments—for example, no cannibalization, no channel conflicts, and no dilution. Under these circumstances, they perpetuate their current mental models, rather than wrestle, in marketlike fashion, with new opportunities. Second, corporations often require majority ownership, which is contrary to the general style of venture investing. Third, corporate venture capital groups are often led by individuals without proven venture investing records. Rather, these individuals have strong operating records, and so may find it hard to compete successfully with lifelong investors. Fourth, the compensation for the leaders of many corporate venture capital groups is more like the internal compensation structure of the corporation than that of traditional venture capital firms. Consequently, the corporate groups rarely attract the quality of talent the traditional venture capital firm does. There are exceptions, of course—like Cisco, Dell, or Intel—but such exceptions are rare. Thus it is far from clear that corporate venture capital is going to provide the opportunities necessary to fill the gap left by R&D or strategic planning.

The collective failure of these three processes—strategic planning, R&D, and corporate venture capital—has contributed to the inability of the corporation to match the pace and scale of change in the marketplace. We believe that it is possible to improve all three processes sufficiently to bring survivor corporations more into line with the pace and scale of change in the capital markets. But to do so, the fundamental assumptions underlying these processes will have to change. The old assumption of continuity and the unrivaled importance of operating excellence will have to be replaced by an assumption of discontinuity and the importance of mastering creative destruction.

IMPROVING STRATEGIC PLANNING, R&D, CORPORATE VENTURE CAPITAL

Among the first stars to appear on a winter night are the three that make up Orion's belt. The bright light of these stars does not reveal all that could be seen, however. Near the center star of the belt is the vast Horsehead nebula, the birthplace of future stars. The nebula of economic activity, however, rather than at the center, is at the periphery of current industries. It is at the periphery that new companies are forming to exploit unmet customer needs and to capitalize on new capabilities, new technologies, and new ways of doing business. The periphery is a vital part of Schumpeter's "gales of creative destruction."

DEFINING THE PERIPHERY

The periphery can be visualized as the edge of the vortex of creative destruction, caused, in the simplest case, by competition between a maturing business and a new one. In this vortex, attacking companies, seeking to fulfill hitherto unmet or unknown needs (as in the case of Enron), or to exploit new and potentially valuable capabilities (as in the case of Cisco), occupy the periphery, while the defenders occupy the core of the vortex, focusing on the evolutionary improvement of the existing business.

In some very mature industries, such as airlines or steel, the vortex spins slowly, bringing only infrequent challenges to the existing order. In other industries, such as broadband communications or corporate decision support systems, the vortex spins so rapidly that the periphery is about all that one can observe. Moreover, in some cases the speed of the vortex is dramatically changing as a result of external forces. This is currently occurring in the electric power industry as it is being deregulated.

One pragmatic way to define the periphery is the earliest point in time that private capital can be attracted to support an idea. Arun Gupta is at the periphery of the decision support software business. In a few years, many of the key positions in this round of the decision support software business will be taken. But in a few years there probably will be another major discontinuous change in the decision support software industry, due to advancing computer hardware and software technology and continually changing customer needs. Accordingly, there will be a new periphery.

For now, however, NeuVis is part of what may become the future decision software support business. If Gupta is successful, his approach will change the structure of that industry. If he can establish a preemptive position in the periphery, he has a good chance of surviving and prospering for a while in the core. Competitors, unaware of what he is trying to accomplish and how he is going about it, will find themselves defending their positions in the future, if Gupta has it right and if he can successfully execute against his vision.

Understanding the Periphery

To understand the periphery one has to understand the unmet needs waiting for fulfillment, as well as the capabilities that may be used to fulfill them. The knowledge itself may be difficult, or expensive, to get and maintain. Moreover, access to the required information may only be available in exchange for access to information that others feel is valuable for them. Accordingly, companies also have to invest to develop their stores of exchangeable information.

Understanding the companies forming at the periphery is necessary to gaining strategic insights into the future possibilities of the industry, but it is also important for revealing the most pressing unmet customer needs. Each of the companies operating at the periphery is selling products, or exploring selling products, to some group of currently dissatisfied customers. It is important to know who they are, what they are dissatisfied about, and what other approaches they are pursuing to meet their unmet needs.

Understanding the periphery can also provide insight into the *actual* cutting edge of corporate capabilities, rather than the theoretical edge. For example, today one reads a lot in the press about new drugs that will come from understanding the genome. However, when one looks on the periphery of the biotech industry, it is virtually impossible to find companies pursuing clinical development of new drugs based on new genomic insights. Companies are pursuing bioinformatics (DoubleTwist, Ingenuity Systems, DNA Sciences, or Spotfire), software products that allow scientists to make sense of the genome, protein analysis that allows scientists to make sense of the proteins that are made by the genome (including Protogene Laboratories, Ciphergen Biosystems, Zyomyx, Mycometrix), new medical diagnoses, and new drug-screening technologies, but almost none are pursuing new drugs at the clinical stage. In a few years it will be different. There will be clinical efforts going on; the periphery will have moved.

Alternatively, by focusing on the periphery one can identify companies that are forming to exploit new opportunities or skills in hitherto unknown ways, as Enron did when it entered the natural gas trading business. There is no better way to understand the cutting edge of new business possibilities than to understand the periphery.

Understanding the Evolution of the Periphery

While it would have been interesting to know what Gupta was thinking a few years ago, it was not worthwhile trying to replicate it or to invest with him then, because there were so many unanswered questions about his approach. Gupta himself was uncertain about how his efforts would turn out, and in any case he was unwilling to give up some of his control over the pace of development to others. Moreover, a few years ago, the decision support systems business was dominated by a few competitors, including EDS in the United States and SAP in Germany. The conditions were not ripe for entry.

But customer needs have changed, and new technology is available. Support for entrepreneurs aspiring to pursue ideas that may eventually compete in the periphery is provided by universities with government support, or by larger corporations, or inadvertently by companies like Symantec, which house entrepreneurs like Arun Gupta yearning to realize their own dreams. Incubation takes place most commonly in this noncorporate environment. Consequently it is important to understand, as best one can, what is happening in the nebula of new ideas before the ideas arrive at the periphery. By understanding something about what is happening in these places, one can more accurately describe how the periphery might evolve.

At the point that ideas appear to have a chance of becoming economically successful, private capital takes over the support role. Because of the great amount of capital now available for venture investing (aided by the U.S. Department of Labor's 1979 clarification of the Employee Retirement Income Security Act's "prudent man" rule to allow pension funds more latitude to invest risk capital), this point is moving toward increasingly uncertain ventures.

Implications of Evolution

To foresee the economic implications of evolution of the periphery, one has to divorce the idea of company failure from the notion of a business concept failure. In any industry, there will be many companies on the periphery. It is likely that several companies will be pursuing almost identical strategies. They focus on the same customers, with the same value proposition and the same marketing approach. While some of the companies will fail, a few, perhaps only one, might succeed. However, if even one company survives, then the business strategy pursued by that single company will survive, even if most of the companies pursuing that strategy do not. Consequently it is the potential of the business concept, rather than the potential of an individual company pursuing the concept, that should be the focal point for understanding the periphery.

Most business concepts that make it to the periphery will not survive. The point of attempting to understand the implications of the evolution of the periphery, however, is not to find a foolproof way to predict the future. It is to find a way to identify the real possibilities for the future, so that a more intelligent choice can be made about strategic direction, research programs, venture investments, and acquisition candidates. Cisco, for example, has used its skill in understanding the periphery to decide which companies to acquire to extend its franchise in the hopes of gaining a sustained competitive advantage and substantial returns for its shareholders.

Most corporate analysts find it easy to dismiss the power of new approaches because they associate these approaches with a single company, rather than a class of companies all pursuing the same strategy. This error inevitably leads to a more pessimistic assessment of the future possibilities for change than is warranted. This flawed approach is a variant of the defensive routines we discussed in Chapter 3.

The Importance of the Periphery

In our view, a central focus of a corporation's strategic planning, advanced research, and corporate venture capital activities should be on understanding the evolution of periphery and the potential implications of that evolution for wealth generation. Focusing on the evolution of the periphery helps ensure that the focus of innovative activity within the corporation will be on substantial and transformational change, since these are the dominant types of change found on the periphery. Moreover, focusing on the evolution of the periphery, as Enron did when it conceptualized newly emerging needs in the natural gas business, or as Corning did when it focused on fiber optics, helps ensure that the timing and focus of new business development efforts will be neither too early nor too late. The periphery provides an external market benchmark for the pace of change in the economy. Appropriate use of this benchmark can help focus strategic planning or research efforts so that they don't become too abstract or narrowly focused. Because the periphery constitutes a standard being set by thousands of venture capitalists, it is a pragmatic test for the adequacy of corporate focus.

DEFINING THE PERIPHERY

Here are a few questions that can help define and interpret the periphery:

1. Which companies define the periphery of your industry today?
2. What business strategies are they pursuing? How are those strategies different from the ones you are pursuing today? Which approaches offer the greatest potential? Which represent the greatest threat?
3. If one examines the periphery from the point of view of the customer, what new benefits do companies competing at the periphery bring to customers? When will it become economically feasible to provide these benefits?
4. If one examines the periphery from the point of view of competitors currently occupying the core, which are most vulnerable to attack? How will the attack take place? When will it occur? What will be the consequences of an attack to key customers? To prices? To profits and value created? To talent? Are there opportunities for retaliation?
5. After examining the implications of the periphery from the perspective of customers and competitors, which competitors from that arena are likely to succeed? Which are likely to lose, and why?
6. What are the economic implications of any changes in the competitive order in terms of your industry market share, prices, profits, talent, and value creation?
7. What are the implications for *your* company? What options do you have?

Answering these questions will require new information. Pondering the implications of the newly gathered information will take time. New concepts will have to be given a chance to flourish. The key question one needs to keep in mind is not which of these new efforts will fail, but which will succeed.

Today, while there is some effort within long-term-survivor corporations to meet this test, the efforts are far too small or sporadic to match change at the pace and scale of the market. For example, today in the United States, about $3 of private venture capital is being spent for every

$5 on R&D, yet few of the venture activities of corporations could come close to this ratio.

The need to understand the evolution of the periphery as a basis for change has grown as the pace of change in the economy has grown. As the pace of change accelerates further in the future, gaining the skill to understand the periphery will become even more important. Understanding the evolution of the periphery was much less important in the past, as the current systems of strategic planning, research, and corporate development were being shaped. But it is vital today. Accordingly, it must become a core concept in the restructuring of strategic planning, research, and corporate ventures.

RETHINKING STRATEGIC PLANNING AS EXTENDED DIALOGUE

Strategic planning has too often become a dry, lifeless enterprise in today's corporations, as we indicated earlier. We believe drawing on the evolution of the periphery, combined with a spirit of divergent thinking, can bring it back to life.

A great deal is already known in most corporations about the periphery and its likely evolution. The employees of the corporation already have a great deal of this knowledge, if it could only be brought to light. Rarely, however, is this knowledge gathered or utilized, because the strategic planning process is so rigidly structured and narrowly focused on next year's plans, rather than on the economic long-term implications for the corporation. Cultural lock-in has inadvertently prevented the talent of the organization from addressing the issues of creative destruction. The objective of the redesign of the strategic planning process is to unlock the talent of the organization so that it can identify and address the issues of creative destruction.

If the corporation were quite small—say, one or two people—the task would not be difficult. The involved people would simply get together for a meal to discuss the options in front of them. In this kind of conversation, nothing is sacred. During this dinner discussion all are equal, limited only by their cognitive and verbal abilities; no inhibitions are respected. Under these circumstances, there is no given order to the conversation. The issues are raised spontaneously. The parallel question to be asked by the senior management of long-term survivor corporations is If you could assemble the fifty to a hundred most talented, thoughtful, and creative people inside or outside your organization, regardless of tenure or position, who would they be, and what would you talk to them about?

Imagine that you can bring these people together—a few at a time—for an intimate conversation similar to one you might have with friends in your living room after dinner. The conversation will run for three hours, but beyond that there are no deadlines, or end products due. The agenda is yours. This is the environment we would like to create for the senior management of the corporation. It is an exercise in divergent thinking. This is the exercise that Arun Gupta went through over a two-year period as he worked on the concept of NeuVis. We will discuss this in more detail in Chapter 11.

APPLYING DIVERGENT THINKING

Can the processes of divergent thinking, which are so essential for the generation of new businesses, be replicated in established corporations? What would it have taken to create an environment inside the corporation where Gupta could have succeeded?

From our research and experience we believe there are five requirements to realizing the potential of divergent thinking in matching the pace and scale of the market:

1. **Pick the Right People**

   Not everyone is capable of divergent thinking. The process of divergent thinking is characterized by the lack of clear goals, inherent ambiguity, and recursive problem solving. Engaging in divergent thinking can frighten and discourage some people who are comfortable only with the proven pathways of convergent thinking. Senior management has to be able to distinguish those with talent for divergent thinking from those who do not have it.

   Divergent thinkers tend to be energetic and have high aspirations. They are passionate, impatient, self-motivating individuals who are complex, smart, and comfortable with ambiguity and risk. One of the most distinctive characteristics of divergent thinkers is their tolerance for (Teresa Amabile would say "love for") ambiguity and uncertainty. Csikszentmihalyi's people with a "sunny pessimism" believe that the problems are exceptionally hard (they are pessimists about solving the problems), but they believe that if the problems can be solved, they are the ones to solve them. Divergent thinkers thrive on dialogue, challenge, interchange, new people, new tools, new experiences. Unlike most of us, divergent thinkers believe they can "fill in the blanks" in the information they are given to solve problems. When they do, they experience the rush of the "ah-ha!" collision. They seek that rush. Divergent thinkers like risk. They will innovate only when they face risk. Yet while divergent thinkers like risk, they also personalize failure. They need to be in a position where, if they do fail, they will be able to recover. If the dialogue is properly conducted, the collective community offers a hedge against individual risk. That is the kind of corporation divergent thinkers flock to.

2. **Allow Adequate Preparation Time**

As we discussed in Chapter 4, the time required for the divergent thinking process to reach fruition is unpredictable and often rather lengthy, as the story of Arun Gupta's journey to NeuVis illustrates. The unpredictability is a consequence of the complexity of the problem, the need to understand what resources exist, and how these resources might be combined in an effective manner through an iterative process. Often, "suspending disbelief" is necessary to avoid premature closure, or entrenchment in existing concepts and approaches. Suspending disbelief means temporarily accepting data and observations that do not seem to make sense. The ability to suspend disbelief helps to ensure that the chances for finding a fresh view are maximized. Suspending disbelief is an unnatural act for an operating organization, but essential to an innovative organization. Adequate preparation time is needed to lay the groundwork for ideas to form and be shaped in sufficient detail to allow a credible plan to be developed. As Csikszentmihalyi noted, artists who spent the longest time getting familiar with their materials before they painted, painted the most important works. There must be time in the dialogue process for the artists to become familiar with their materials if important outcomes are sought. Divergent thinkers need time to wander and wonder. The cadence of observation, reflection, and conversation has to be right. Incubation is required for productive divergent thinking. One of the most valued opportunities management can give to divergent thinkers is the time to prepare and the time to let ideas and insights collide.

3. **Set High Aspirations**

Many entrepreneurs, including Arun Gupta, want to "change the world." This is what distinguishes them from conventional, or incremental, problem solvers. Divergent thinkers seek tough and important problems to solve, or they will lose interest. We have observed that many times the difference between an incremental and transformational outcome in business is the result of the aspiration level of the leaders.

4. **Provide Resources, Flexibility, and Deadlines**

Divergent thinkers want to work in an environment rich in alternative resources, data, and access to the information and information-processing tools they need to do their work. They do not expect to be controlled in any detailed way. They have trouble with routines and schedules. They want to be free to seek the most interesting people to work with. They dislike being isolated, or having limited access to the resources and people they feel they need. They like to be in environments where they can discover new things. But they also need deadlines, as we will discuss further below.

5. **Provide Senior Coverage**

Someone in leadership has to be willing to put his or her reputation on the line in order to make the dialogue a success. As one Enron manager bluntly put it, "Nothing happens without people being willing to put flesh on the table." There will be many challenges along the way. Senior management has to be available to sort them out.

If the strategic dialogue process can pass these five tests, the chances of success are high.

DESIGNING THE STRATEGIC PLANNING PROCESS

We have used the principles laid out above to redesign the strategic planning process. There are four steps in the redesign process. The first step is for top management to plan the overall process. The second step is to prepare for the first dialogue. This preparation is different from the preparation required in classical strategic planning processes, since it involves more senior management time; is generally longer than the typical strategic planning process, since it is intended to provide time for "incubation" to take place; and depends on the direct experience of the periphery by top management. The third step in the process is to force the collision of perspectives and develop recommendations for specific action steps to be taken. This step is designed to replicate the process of collision as we described it in Chapter 4. The fourth step is for the results to be summarized for top management, who will then decide which of the recommendations to pursue.

The following sections cover in more detail each of the steps in redesigning the strategic planning process.

Step 1: Overall Process Design

The first step in reconceptualizing the strategic planning process is to design the overall process. Top management's objective in this step is to select the issues for discussion over the next year or two, pick a leadership team to prepare and lead the discussion, and establish the timing and venue for the first discussion.

Senior management should select the issues after appropriate discussion. We recommend that this discussion not last more than a day. Each member attending should prepare a list of the most important issues or opportunities facing the corporation over the next five to seven years. They should focus on the pace of creative destruction in some aspects of the business, and on understanding the economic implications of the evolution of the periphery. (We offer examples of these issues and approach in Chapter 11.) We have found it productive to conduct this session after members of the senior management have taken a foreign trip, or visited a series of customers, or attended a major trade show or a major industry meeting—some event to help open their thinking to the challenges of creative destruction in their industry. Trips abroad, or visits to customers, help ensure that the management team adopts an external rather than internally focused mental model.

Having selected the issues the company intends to address, the leader of the first dialogue should be chosen. Generally the leader should be selected from among the top management team that developed the slate of issues necessary to ensure continuity of thought and intent. The role of the leader is to select the participants in the dialogue (from the fifty to one hundred of the most knowledgeable people), lead the dialogue-development process and chair the dialogue itself, and make recommendations to the senior management group after the dialogue. This process is designed to observe the principles of divergent thinking and to best leverage the insight and judgment of senior management.

Step 2: Preparing for the First Dialogue

Observing the requirements for divergent thinking means that sufficient time has to be allowed for the participants in the dialogue to gain a first-hand understanding of the periphery, as opposed to reading the views of others. Nike's senior managers, following in the footsteps of CEO Phil Knight, have developed a keen sense of the importance of direct experience. Nike organizes "inspirational trips" for key employees and managers charged with the responsibility for a product line—for example, basketball. These trips give managers an opportunity to visit with pro players to understand what is working and what is not. Often it is the leading customers, like pro players, who see unmet needs first or most clearly. Occasionally these lead customers will also have very good ideas about how to meet these needs. The trips also give managers a chance to hang out at schools, mix with the street ballplayers, and still have enough incubation time to mull over the insights they've gathered along the way.

A second example of Nike's focus on understanding the evolution of the periphery (although they do not call it that) through direct experience is their investment in NikeTown stores. They operate them not as retail profit centers (or as competition with key customers like Champs, Foot Locker, and Athlete's Foot), but as a way to achieve greater insight into consumers' unmet needs. Nike sees NikeTown stores as "retail laboratories" that provide insight not only into product needs but also merchandizing needs. Many credit Nike with leading the way toward branded stores-as-entertainment, an approach now followed by Warner Brothers, Disney, Levi's, Coke, Harley-Davidson, and others. Because NikeTown stores are enormously popular, Nike gets a good sense of the range of emerging customer needs. In fact, Nike's second NikeTown, placed in Chicago, has become one of Chicago's most popular tourist sites.

Preparation on this scale ensures that sufficient new information will be brought to the process to maximize the chances of novel insight. Traditional strategic planning processes, which rehash old or secondhand data, cannot be expected to generate new ideas with the same frequency. While this process takes longer than the conventional process, the costs can be spread out over a longer period of time, and the value of insights created are much greater than those found in the conventional strategic planning process.

Step 3: Design and Conduct the First Conversation

After the preparation has been completed, the team is ready to begin the dialogue. Generally the dialogue occurs over two days, with a very light agenda to allow ample time for discourse. The only constraint on the dialogue meeting is that a clear set of objectives has to be developed, such as determining the best opportunities to pursue, developing the case for pursuing those and not other opportunities, the sequence of their pursuit, and the details of the next steps to take.

The fact that there is a light agenda for the dialogue does not imply that the dialogue is loose. But the dialogue should be managed by a well-prepared leader rather than follow a prearranged agenda. The job of the dialogue leader is to encourage the creative thought of the other participants in the dialogue. At McKinsey, our partners have developed a tool kit of questions for use by the leaders of the dialogue to stimulate better ideas. These questions are drawn from a database of questions developed by "reverse-engineering" actual innovations with which we have been involved. The questions posed nudge workshop participants out of their usual ways of looking at the world. It is a technique that has been successfully used in more than 125 applications across a broad array of industry sectors and company situations.

As we stand back from our experience with these meetings, we see that there are four tricks we have learned over the years, in addition to the bank of questions that our partners at McKinsey have developed that improve the productivity of the actual dialogue:

1. **Changing the Context:** Mihalyi Csikszentmihalyi observed that positioning an individual at the intersection of different cultures or disciplines can stimulate creativity: "In cultures that are uniform and rigid it takes a greater investment of attention to achieve new

ways of thinking. In other words, creativity is more likely in places where new ideas require less effort to be perceived."

There are several ways to change the context. The first is to change the social context of the dialogue—say, by providing a rich mix of senior and junior executives, researchers and marketers, Europeans and Americans to improve the productivity of the meetings (as long as all have shared the same preparation steps).

The second way to change the context is to change the mental context of the problem. For example, William McGowen, founder and chairman of MCI, was known for "reverse thinking"—thinking the opposite of what everyone else at the time was thinking. Sir James Black, as we noted earlier, calls such thinking "turning the question around." If you believe you need a small molecule to build a new pharmaceutical drug, try a large one, as well. After all, you cannot always anticipate what will work.

An alternative to reverse thinking is to employ the "zoom-in, zoom-out" approach favored by some chess champions. Zooming in reveals the fine details of each part of the game and the short-term trends. Zooming out shows the relationship among the parts and how they are changing over long time scales. Juxtaposing the perspectives gained by zooming in and zooming out often results in novel insights, insights that form at the "intersection" of these two perspectives.

A fourth trick is to change the physical context simply by getting away.

2. **Visualization:** Visualization—forming a visual image in the "mind's eye"—can help to stimulate connections. Astronomer Vera Rubin doodled to discover her thoughts on the structure of the universe; Jonas Salk claimed that it was his efforts to visualize the viral process that led to his discovery of the polio vaccine. Visualization can be used during "collision" meetings by attempting to draw a picture of the relationships that are being discussed, rather than relying on verbal cues alone. For this reason, it is sometimes helpful to have a graphic designer at some of the meetings—or perhaps an artist—to capture different ways of expressing common thoughts.

3. **Using a Muse:** Many creative people need a muse—someone to play off of, to converse with, to argue with. Einstein, for example, had

Besso in developing his special theory of relativity. "When Einstein burst in on Besso in May 1905, three and a half years [after their last discussion], it was time, light, and the ether that were on his mind. Sure enough, talking with Besso worked. 'Trying a lot of discussions with him,' Einstein wrote in 1922, 'I could suddenly comprehend the matter. Next day I visited him again and said to him without greeting: Thank you. I've completely solved the problem.'"

As Paul Valéry, the French poet and essayist, said, "It takes two to invent anything. The one makes up combinations; the other chooses, recognizes what he wishes and what is important to him in the mass of the things which the former has imparted to him."

The same technique can be used in dialogue meetings, by having the participants pair up to discuss their thinking: placing a researcher with a marketing expert, or a senior executive with a junior one, or an executive from the hardware business with one from the software business. If the chemistry is right, and the muse relationship develops, the results can be very impressive.

4. **Slowing Things Down:** We have often observed that the dialogue meeting leader can increase the productivity of the meeting by consciously slowing things down, rather than speeding them up (as one typically does in business). As Valéry said about poetry, "Poetry is about slowing down, I think. It's about reading the same thing again and again, really savoring it, living inside the poem. There's no rush to find out what happens in a poem. It's really about feeling one syllable rubbing against another, one word giving way to another, and sensing the justice of that relationship between one word, the next, the next, the next."

Nothing could be more contrary to the accepted ways of doing business in corporations focused on operations than to slow things down. Yet this may be precisely what is necessary. Allowing long immersion in the details of the data, combined with personal reflection—letting the parts of the business "rub together"—increases the probability that significant new insight will be born. Using this technique forces the meeting leader to develop a fine sense of when to push and when to hold off, since the final deadline does have to be met, but the most important objective of the session is to develop potentially successful new directions.

Step 4: Post-Dialogue Reflection and Decision Making

After the dialogue has been completed, it is the task of the dialogue chairman or leader to summarize the results for top management, who will decide which opportunities to pursue given the other demands on the corporation. These decisions should be taken rather quickly, within a few weeks of the completion of the dialogue, since it is important for the credibility of the process that the participants know the results of their hard work have been used. Some favor making the decision to proceed on some of the ideas at the conclusion of the dialogue, but we have found that often senior management needs time to reflect on the implications of the recommendations before proceeding.

Once the first issue and dialogue have been completed, the senior executives can proceed to pick the leader for the second dialogue, and then the third, and so on. Since the design of all conversations are conceptually the same, having done one, the others follow in step. The pace can vary according to the needs of the marketplace and the capacity of the organization for change. Controlling the pace of these meetings, as we discussed earlier, is one of the most direct ways management has to control the pace and scale of change in the corporation.

These four steps, taken together, can provide the basis for a new strategic planning process, one that has proven to be much less bureaucratic than traditional processes. The four steps we outlined are not new. They mimic the processes in the marketplace, they focus on the periphery, and they bring the process of strategic planning to the point of application for capital. We have designed several successful processes along these lines for our clients. In Chapter 11 we will discuss in detail the longer-term use of these techniques at Johnson & Johnson.

RECONCEPTUALIZING R&D

Given the evidence presented earlier in this chapter, we believe "R&D" is a dysfunctional phrase. The classic phrase "R&D" inadvertently emphasizes the unity between research and development, rather than the unity of the need for technical information useful for generating new businesses.

In light of our research on the increasing importance of creative destruction, we believe the goal today within corporations should be new business creation—not research and development. Research is one way to acquire some of the information needed for new business formation. Technology licensing is another. The acquisition of small companies, perhaps as part of the job of the corporate venture capital department, is a third. If the objective is to acquire the information needed for business building, then all three of these functions—classical research, licensing, and small-company acquisition through corporate venture capital—may be more productively linked than kept separate. In many ways this is already happening today in an informal way. Acquisitions, particularly of smaller companies, are increasingly a core element of rapidly changing and highly innovative industries. Cisco alone made fifty-one acquisitions between 1993 and April 2000 in the course of gaining access to technology.

Development, on the other hand, is concerned with the effective use of technical information rather than its acquisition. We feel that "information acquisition" and "information application," both in the service of new business generation at the pace and scale of the market, are more useful concepts than R&D.

While the day-to-day activities of research, licensing, and small-company acquisition are totally different, they share the same purpose: providing technical options for the creation of new businesses to the corporation. Linking research, licensing, and small-company acquisition is no different in principal from linking material "make-or-buy" decisions in the manufacturing department. Research "makes" the needed technical information, and licensing and acquisitions "buys" the information. If it is cheaper to make the needed component or subassembly, then it is made. If it is cheaper to buy the needed component or subassembly on the open market, then it is purchased. It is a very efficient system. This logic holds for technology information acquisition as well.

J&J's Approach

We can see an illustration of this integrated approach at Johnson & Johnson, a very large manufacturer of pharmaceuticals, medical equipment, and consumer products. J&J has long been skilled in riding the waves of creative destruction, and in doing so it has provided exceptional long-term total return to shareholders. Part of their secret is the close link between research, licensing, and corporate venture capital. J&J did not set out to design the system this way; nonetheless it has evolved in very much the way described above. To complement their internal R&D efforts, J&J has a corporate venture capital group called Johnson & Johnson Development Corp. (JJDC). This is a small group that looks a lot like the venture capitalists of Silicon Valley. They, along with more than a hundred vice presidents of business development (or VPs of licensing and acquisition) around the world in the different J&J operating companies, spend all of their time scanning the market for viable new technologies both in start-up companies and within other major corporations.

Having been in existence now for more than twenty-five years, JJDC is one of the longest-running examples of corporate venture capital. One of the reasons JJDC was successful is that they were given the time they needed in the early years to get the fund over the investment-stage hump. According to Jim Utaski, who was the president of JJDC between 1990 and 2000, "Having only two bosses over twenty-five years who were both very growth oriented helped. We needed at least a ten-year horizon to realize returns. This patience level does not exist for most corporations."

Established in 1973 by CEO Jim Burke, JJDC received "air cover" from Burke's long-term vision. Burke's successor, the current chairman of J&J, Ralph Larsen, has shared this commitment. Utaski says, "Our cost-neutral position eliminated all critics; it is difficult to dismantle the unit now."

This freedom has allowed JJDC, with its eclectic team of senior executives, technologists, and lawyers, to pursue an appropriately varied portfolio of technologies (often in competition with each other), provide a window on technology to J&J's operating companies around the world, and measure success according to venture capital–like criteria (Utaski would rank JJDC among the top-performing second-tier venture capital firms). They "do deals," bringing the technologies into the corporation (usually into one of the decentralized operating companies) to be developed and launched through the highly capable worldwide sales and distribution channel the corporation has developed. Most of these technologies are already in some stage of development.

To make sure that J&J does not miss out on scientific breakthroughs before they become viable technologies, the corporation has another group called the Committee Office of Science and Technology (COSAT). This group of eight to ten Ph.D.s stays in touch with the top researchers around the world, tapping into breakthrough research and connecting it with the internal R&D efforts around the corporation. They come quite close to a real understanding of the evolution of the periphery as it applies to J&J.

Because both of these groups are sponsored at the corporate level rather than in the operating companies, they have the flexibility to maintain longer time horizons on their activities, often nurturing researchers or small start-ups for years before the technology can be licensed or the company acquired.

An acquisition can stimulate a brilliant new idea in its core business, just as an in-house idea can spark an acquisition. Johnson & Johnson is one example of a company that pursues both paths—and reaps the significant rewards. The J&J leaders believe that the only way to act like the market is to be deeply immersed in it.

RECONCEPTUALIZING CORPORATE VENTURE CAPITAL

Few companies have had the success J&J has had with corporate venture capital. While small investments have been successfully made by a few firms, the great majority of these efforts are insufficient to match the pace and scale of change in the market. One alternative to focusing solely on corporate venture capital is that provided by J&J, but there is another option that has become increasingly well developed in Europe.

This alternative approach—internal "business plan contests"—capitalizes both on the employees' knowledge of the periphery and on the traditional corporate venture capital strength of understanding the new companies. Together these functions may work in a fashion superior to that of traditional corporate venture capital, according to the work of our McKinsey colleagues who developed the concept. At one European electronics firm, a business plan contest led to the identification of more than 180 new business concepts, which, after a period of refinement, elimination, and incubation, resulted in four new start-ups within the corporation. The impact was greater than that of long-standing corporate venture capital activities in the corporation that did not leverage the knowledge of the employees.

To begin the process, the company established a cross-functional senior review team that was supported by the corporate venture capital department. The team solicited ideas, emphasizing people in the lower ranks who had traditionally been excluded. The business plans were reviewed and winners were selected. Winners were awarded prizes as well as seed money to move forward. More important, the winners were coached on how to develop and iterate their ideas. Through this process of iteration and staged decision making, the number of quality ideas grew over time.

AddVenture! at Infineon

Other companies have created similar programs. A clear example is Infineon Technologies, the former Semiconductor Group of Siemens. Infineon launched a business plan/idea generation competition in 1997— the AddVenture! Program, which was open to all employees.

The program was structured so that ideas were developed step-by-step into comprehensive business plans. The program ran over several months, accompanied by workshops and coaching sessions at company locations worldwide. More than two hundred teams submitted proposals. Several dozen were developed into detailed business plans. A jury of senior executives and experts on technologies and markets selected a final set of teams that entered into negotiations for funding. The evaluation criteria largely matched those a venture capitalist might look for in a winning start-up concept—but also took corporate strategic interest into account.

Five new growth businesses have taken off so far, all targeting market opportunities of several hundred million dollars each. The Group has established a unit called Infineon Ventures, which nurtures these businesses and helps identify other new business opportunities inside and outside of Infineon. It is more successful than traditional corporate venture capital activities are.

Infineon's experience shows that corporate competitions do more than simply generate ideas: They help change a company's culture by motivating employees to reach outside their daily responsibilities. Competitions also teach employees to think about building businesses around their ideas.

Business plan competitions are now a proven tool. In Germany alone, regional competitions have tapped venture capital of several hundred million euro, and have stimulated thousands of new jobs.

It is not clear whether enough Arun Guptas can be created within the environment of long-term-survivor corporations to make a difference. But the need to do so is clear, as well as the conditions that will have to be met: the need to swap the assumption of continuity for the assumption of discontinuity; the need to balance the focus on operations with the focus on creative destruction; the need to understand the likely evolution of the periphery; and the need to provide time for ideas to incubate if the efforts are going to be successful. If the corporation is going to become an active creator, operator, and trader of options, at the pace and scale of the market, it must learn to mimic the methods of Arun Gupta. Moreover, as we have discussed, there are significant options available for reconceptualizing the key change processes of the corporation: strategic planning, R&D, and corporate venture capital. The key requirement in the end is the will to change. The Guptas of the world, if they can find a way to prosper in the survivor corporation, can give senior management the option to change at the pace and scale of the market. But management still has to make the decisions, as we discussed in Chapter 7. The dilemma is how to accomplish this degree of change without undermining operational excellence. The answer to that dilemma lies in the details of the control processes of the corporation, the focus of the next chapter.

DIAGNOSTIC QUESTIONS TO EVALUATE THE QUALITY OF A COMPANY'S STRATEGIC PLANNING

Are you satisfied with your strategic-planning efforts?

1. Do you feel that enough good ideas emerge from your strategic-planning efforts?
2. Have your businesses missed opportunities that they regretted?
3. Are you concerned that your strategic-planning process is mainly a paper exercise?
4. Are there two parallel processes in your organization—the effort to develop the plan "for corporate" and the real planning process in the business?
5. Has the annual planning process become a rote exercise where last year's plan gets updated on the word processor?
6. Are your strategic plans more tactical than truly strategic?
7. Do you tend to be more reactive than proactive in shaping major issues for your business?
8. Are you satisfied with the quality of feedback for your strategic plans?
9. Are your budget, capital allocation, compensation, and succession planning guided by the themes in your strategic plan?
10. Does the strategic-planning process link strategies to an understanding of the future of the industry?

CHAPTER 10

Control, Permission, and Risk

Give us a proposition we can't say yes to.

CEO OF A MID-SIZED HIGH-TECH ATTACKER

I f corporations are to be a creators-operators-traders of options, they will have to learn to accommodate and balance the assumption of continuity and the assumption of discontinuity. They will have to accommodate and balance divergent and convergent thinking. To do that, they will have to learn to balance control and permission.

In his classic 1946 work *The Concept of the Corporation,* Peter Drucker commented on the underlying tension at General Motors at the time between freedom and control:

> *General Motors could not function as a holding company with the divisions organized like independent companies under loose financial control. On the other hand, General Motors could not function as a centralized organization in which all decisions are made on the top, and in which the divisional managers are but little more than plant superintendents.*

The tension was resolved, Drucker argued, through GM chairman Alfred P. Sloan Jr.'s concept of decentralization, which was developed between 1923 and the mid-1940s. Decentralization was

> *. . . not merely a technique of management but an outline of a social*
> *order. For Mr. Sloan and his associates, the application and further*
> *extensions of decentralization are the answer to most of the problems of*
> *modern industrial society.*

Decentralization ensured the accountability of the organization's operating divisions and, with the tightly specified accounting systems it required, allowed GM's central management to determine which of its divisions was operating well and which was operating poorly.

On the other hand, GM employees told Drucker that their greatest cause of job dissatisfaction was not inadequate pay but excessive interference from senior management in the operational details of their jobs. On balance, Drucker felt that decentralization, as practiced, sapped the spirit, independence, and the initiative to be more productive of lower-level managers and workers. Accordingly, he advised GM management that decentralization should be carried to its "logical conclusion"—that is, to enhance the independence and initiative of the workers and foremen. He further recommended that GM's central governing policy should be reoriented toward "developing . . . a 'responsible worker' with a 'managerial aptitude' [operating in the context of] a 'self-governing plant community.'"

GM management rejected Drucker's recommendations, arguing that the decision would abrogate the "expertise" of senior management. The truth is, the "top men"—as they were known—who ran General Motors during the '30s conceived of decentralization not as a means of relinquishing control but of extending it over their far-flung empire. Perhaps more surprisingly, the leadership of the United Automobile Workers union also rejected Drucker's recommendations, insisting that financial reward, not psychological gratification, was the only factor worth considering in the compensation-and-control equation. The opinions of workers and foremen were ignored by both management and the unions.

The tension between central control (an assertion of continuity) and local initiative (in the spirit of discontinuity and change) was resolved in favor of continuity.

BALANCING CONTROL AND PERMISSION

As in the '40s at General Motors, the essential tension between control and the permission to take local initiative continues within many corporations today. To balance control and permission, we will first have to describe the key features of each way of thinking.

CONTROL

Control is the outward expression of convergent thinking. As Kenneth Merchant, dean of the Levanthal School of Accounting at USC, said, "Control, which essentially means 'keeping things on track,' ranks as one of the critical functions of management. Good control means that an informed person can be reasonably confident that no major, unpleasant surprises will occur."

As Robert Simons pointed out, the purpose of control is to eliminate surprise. The purpose of divergent thinking is to create surprise. Control needs a stable environment to work. Divergent thinking fosters a dynamic one. Control systems squelch divergent thinking and creativity. Adaptive, divergent-thinking environments celebrate it.

In the practical everyday world of business, control is valued by investors, senior managers, midlevel managers, and specialists (e.g., scientists, salesmen, planners, controllers, etc.). It is sought out by individuals in their own lives. Formal systems for gaining control include processes for setting standards; collecting, processing, and delivering information; and the design of evaluation and reward systems. Informal control systems, which are often unrecognized as "control systems," include conversations among managers and subordinates, physical presence, and calendar and agenda setting. In the corporation, control is required at four levels: the corporate level, divisional level, functional level, and project level. Controls are required to help avoid profit shortfalls and to prevent the assumption of excessive risk.

In response to these complex needs and processes, most corporations have developed hundreds of subordinate control systems within the corporation. Sometimes they are in conflict. We asked the senior management of one company to name the five most important systems for maintaining control over operations and the five most important processes for ensuring the effectiveness of technology development. Ten systems were identified in all. No system that was identified as being important for controlling operations was also important for controlling the flow of innovation. Moreover, often the systems that were important for ensuring operational excellence (e.g., systems designed to keep the production processes running at high speeds) undermined efforts to introduce innovations (which would require disrupting the existing manufacturing processes).

Conflicts, if they were spotted (and often they were not, since even the recognition of the problem was discouraged), were resolved on a case-by-case basis. Even though these systems were in perpetual conflict, no reasonably enduring solution could be found. The differences were often resolved "politically," with the victory going to the most senior person. Moreover, control systems, once in place and running, were difficult or costly to remove or change. It was difficult to argue that these systems mimicked the market.

Control systems may not only be in conflict with one another; they can also inhibit performance in a number of ways. They can:

- Distort the information they are meant to interpret, as has been discussed previously. The control system can reject information that does not fit the preestablished requirements of the system (e.g., form, timeliness, or accessibility). Novel information that could offer clues to new opportunities—or risks—is difficult for the system to accept.
- Emphasize issues that are easily understood, rather than issues that may be equally important but less apparent and more complex. "What gets measured, gets done." To which we could add, "What does not get measured, does not get done."
- Emphasize issues that were important when the control systems were built, rather than those that exist now or those that will exist in the future.
- Inadvertently inhibit adaptive work and dampen creativity and innovation. The more novel the system, the more difficult is the job of designing control systems.
- Contribute to a false sense of security if they are not designed to be adapted to changes in the environment. Control systems are generally self-renewing, and regardless of their gradual ineffectiveness, remain in place because of the cost and complexity of changing them. Once in place, control systems have advocates who are reluctant to change them.
- Can be abused by "gaming the system."

As a result, companies that are focused on tight control systems as an integral part of their effort to be operationally excellent risk not being able to anticipate or cope with a changing competitive environment. Realizing the limitations of tightly controlled corporations, Bill McGowan of MCI decided to cultivate a corporate culture based on freedom and flexibility. As McGowan recalled:

> *If people have a standard procedure for everything, when does anybody learn to make decisions? Are you supposed to follow the manual all the way to the top and then one day suddenly start thinking for yourself? I used to get up once a year before all the employees, and say, "I know that somewhere, someone out there is trying to write a manual of procedures. Well, one of these days I'm going to find out who you are, and when I do, I'm going to fire you."*

Capital markets are the opposite. Capital markets do not establish goals, in the performance sense of that word. Moreover, capital markets are silent on the issue of the need to eliminate surprise. Effective capital markets are designed to provide for admission of new competitors and the elimination of weak ones, and thus increase, not decrease, the chances of surprise. Capital markets control the process of entry and exit, not operations per se. Capital markets establish standards for the quality and timeliness of information about operations, and they enforce adherence to standards. But they do not control results. As a result, capital markets generally introduce new options more quickly than corporations, and eliminate old and weak ones without remorse.

To foster this kind of discontinuous behavior within corporations, control has to be balanced with permission to engage in divergent thinking. As our former colleague at McKinsey, Tom Peters, observed in 1991, "We need to give up control, and lots of it, to stand even a chance of gaining control in these tumultuous times."

But what controls should be given up? How can they be given up without losing control over operations? What do we replace them with, if anything? Before we move on to these crucial questions, we need to understand the flip side of control: permission.

PERMISSION

In management, the counterpoint of control is permission. For most managers, permission means having the freedom to act without first having to check, and perhaps justify, their actions with higher levels of management. Freedom to act also implies that they are free to do what is right in their eyes to meet the goals of the business. Managers seek freedom from interference from senior management, just as the General Motors workers did. But granting this freedom is difficult for executives who feel an obligation to maintain control. Permission, they argue, is just one step closer to recklessness. Control-oriented executives are like the farmer who pulls the carrots up each morning, "just to see how they're doing." Striking the right balance between control and permission has long been a dilemma for management. As the pace of change in the economy accelerates, the importance of balancing the tension between control and permission will increase.

Permissions Sought

What kinds of permissions do managers seek? There are several. The permission to explore to the same extent that exploration takes place in the capital markets. The permission to pursue their goals without undue interference from the operational control systems, which, by requiring unnecessary information or review cycles, or requiring useful information too frequently, drive up the cost of compliance and drive out the time needed for exploration. The permission to take risks—that is, experiment with new business concepts at the pace and scale of the market, without higher-than-market costs (e.g., bankruptcy, loss of health, loss of job). Finally, the permission to seek external funds for valued ideas if the parent corporation decides not to pursue the idea. If these four permissions were granted, many managers would feel that they have sufficient freedom to "do what is right."

Permission is not a decision. It is an enabling concept. If one is granted permission, one is granted an option to act. Permission does not imply a lack of responsibility, or recklessness. Rather, it implies increased accountability. Permission granted by senior management or investors transfers control to the second group. It is not uncommon for a group that has just received an increase in permission to hoard it by not passing it along to their subordinates (thus reinitiating the unwanted system of control).

Some companies have learned the lessons of permission management very well. At J&J, for example, explicit performance targets are avoided, giving employees in the business units permission to "do the right thing." Chairman Ralph S. Larsen says, "I don't want to set financial targets for the growth of the businesses within J&J. Either I shoot too low and the businesses don't reach their potential, or I shoot too high and they are forced to pursue bad business practices to make the numbers." To Larsen, company aspirations are not about numbers—they are about generating new growth businesses that will change the face of the health care market. With sales of $27 billion dollars in 1999, J&J is a leading global provider of health-care products. But it did not get to be so big by doing it "by the numbers."

Similarly, MCI did not set a growth target and then figure out how to reach it; it focused its thinking on the entire "opportunity space" it had, then extracted as much value from it as it could. And MCI has grown rapidly as a consequence.

The markets grant enormous permission, of course, to everyone who enters it—permission to try, permission to risk, permission to fail, and permission to succeed.

Permission Conundrums

The shift within corporations from control to permission is not easy. Giving permission is tantamount to giving up control. One must deeply trust those to whom control is relinquished. In the private equity world, control is relinquished only after long, and often arduous, negotiations. And when it is granted, a "term sheet" (a short summary of the key provisions of an agreement that is a prelude to a binding and detailed contract) faithfully records the details of the exchange. Permission (granted by the capital holders) for control (received by the operating team) is drafted and signed. Often this term sheet includes "flip" clauses, specifying that should standards slip, control reverts to the originating party.

Permission without the resources to exercise those liberties, of course, is disingenuous. Permission requires the obligation to provide either the resources (money, talent, equipment, time) or the time and wherewithal to get them.

The Failure to Grant Permission—The Collapse of Intrapreneuring

At the time of publication in 1985 of Gifford Pinchot's *Intrapreneuring: Why You Don't Have to Leave the Corporation to Become an Entrepreneur,* "intrapreneurship" was hailed as "one of the great social inventions" by *The Economist.* The source of this enthusiasm is not hard to understand. "Intrapreneuring" appeared to offer a practical solution to one of the most vexing challenges facing the managers of large corporations: how to release the entrepreneurial talent of the organization.

Yet, despite its apparent theoretical soundness, extensive publicity, and a significant degree of interest in putting his provocative notions to work, Pinchot's work has failed to make a dent in how most corporations operate. Pinchot, in an interview with *INC.* magazine, ventured a guess as to why that was the case.

INC.: Perhaps the most surprising suggestion you've made is that [intrapreneurs] be managed the way venture capitalists manage entrepreneurs, right down to offering them the chance to accumulate a substantial amount of corporate money—intracapital, you call it—to spend as they choose. What is it that venture capitalists do right?

PINCHOT: Venture capitalists tend to be very careful in selecting the people who are to be involved in a business. But having been very rigorous in the selection process, they are then in a position in which it makes a certain amount of sense to trust the entrepreneur to make the kind of lightning maneuvering decisions required in a start-up . . . [O]nce the entrepreneur has the money, he has a great deal of freedom to spend it however he thinks is best.

INC: As opposed to how a typical corporation handles the would-be intrapreneur?

PINCHOT: Corporations do just the reverse. You ask for two years and they give you a year and a half. "Couldn't you do it faster?" they ask. "Couldn't you do it with less money?" But if the intrapreneur is doing his job right, he has already pared his estimates to the bone. And companies tend to have people signing off on each request for a capital expenditure, with each one treated as a separate item. But that extra scrutiny doesn't produce a better investment; quite the reverse. It causes the would-be intrapreneur to pad his budgets and to spend it all right now. After all, if you can't take money out of an engineering budget and put it in marketing, then the intrapreneur has only one solution: overinflate the hell out of every budget, and then, by God, spend it that year, because you may need the slack next year.

So despite the initial enthusiasm about intrapreneuring, it was never implemented. Permission was not granted.

SETTING THE BALANCE BETWEEN CONTROL AND PERMISSION

Balancing risk and reward has been one of the most useful and durable principles of economic decision making. But setting this balance requires grappling with the issue of the balance between control and permission, because the decision about who assumes risk and who receives rewards is intimately connected to the questions of who is in control. In this regard, it is important to have a common understanding of the meaning of risk.

The Nature of Risk

If the future were known, while there would certainly be unfavorable news, risk would evaporate. But since we don't know the future, risk will always be a part of practical decisions. The word *risk,* in fact, comes from the Italian *risco,* a word used by sailors to express the chances of ending up on the rocks.

Risk is not absolute. It implies probabilities. Furthermore, what one person perceives as risk may not be seen as risky by another (who may have special knowledge and experience, or simply a stronger ability to recover from failure). A CEO who risks billions on behalf of his company, but has a long-term contract, is not risking as much as the lower-level project manager who may lose his job if the project fails.

Risk-Taking Behavior and Goals

How do decision makers choose between alternatives? First, decision makers use "expected value" to compare alternatives. Expected value refers to the level of benefits (or costs) multiplied by the probability that they will occur. So if there is a 20% chance of a $10 gain, that is the same as a 40% chance of a $5 gain. Both bets have the same expected value: $2. In the first case the expected value is 20% of $10. In the second case the expected value is 40% of $5.

Which choice will most decision makers take? Kahneman and Tversky, two academic psychologists who have made great contributions to our understanding of this question, say the answer depends on how close the return is to the "target return" that the decision maker has in mind. Richard Bernstein, in his book *Risk,* summarizes Kahneman and Tversky by identifying four different regimes:

1. "When decision makers are in the neighborhood of their goals and confront a choice between two items of equal expected value, decision makers tend to choose the less risky alternative if outcomes involve gains, and the more risky alternative if outcomes involve losses."

   If the expected value of $2 is close to what the decision maker hoped to gain, he would chose the less risky alternative; he would choose the opportunity with the $5 gain.

2. "When individuals find themselves well below the target, if they are falling further and further behind the target, they tend to take bigger and bigger risks."

   If the $2 was much less than the decision maker wanted, he would take a flier on a 20% chance of gaining the $10, the logic being "what do I have to lose, I am already so far behind."

3. "As [corporations] come closer and closer to extinction, they tend to become rigid and immobile, repeating previous actions and avoiding risk."

   If, having lost several prior bets, the decision maker is faced with the same choice as above, he will choose whatever he has been choosing previously. He has passed from a rational state into an irrational, emotional state. Some corporations find themselves in this state from time to time, particularly those that have maturing industries and have failed at prior diversification efforts.

4. "When individuals find themselves well above the target, they tend to take greater risks."

In other words, if our decision maker feels the $2 he or she has won initially is so far above what he or she expected to achieve in the first place, the person may next take a shot at the opportunity for the riskier $10 gain. He or she is willing to risk more at this stage.

These results, which have been verified many times since Kahneman and Tversky first published them, are important in understanding risk and the balance of permission and control. When management presents options of uncertain values to either investors or managers, they need to understand how the payoffs compare to the individual's "targets." If the payoffs are about what one expects, investors or management will likely choose the less risky venture. If they are a reasonably long way from their targets, on either the high or low side, they will often choose the riskier venture. And if the choices are presented to someone who has experienced a long string of losses, that person will make a decision independent of what the facts suggest, simply responding to prior experience. Management, then, can affect the outcome of a decision by adjusting the risk/reward parameters to fit expectations.

Designing to Encourage Creation and Trading

If change is perceived as more valuable than continuity (often the case in venture capital or principal investing), change will be made. But if change is perceived as bringing in less value (which is often the case in corporations), continuity is chosen.

When the values are perceived as very similar, the choice is more complex. If the corporation and its shareholders are satisfied with its rates of return, for example, making significant change is difficult to justify. This is indeed the situation today for many companies despite the market's gyrations. Today, more than in many periods, we would argue, it's important that senior management make a conscious effort to give permission to the organization to explore options for creating future value.

Leadership is essential in setting the balance between continuity and change. To match the pace and scale of change in the markets, corporate senior management should ensure that the economic and personal rewards for those who take risks finding new business opportunities are at market levels, even if the opportunity is not pursued at the end of the day. This is what the private equity community has done over the past two decades. Through a continuous flow of insights into new opportunities, private equity firms have actually reduced their risk, while boosting the pace of change and their rewards.

Fear of Risk; Fear of Failure

Fear is the sharp edge of risk. Many people and many institutions can't take it—they are risk averse. Their fear of risk restricts the free flow of new information and enhances the natural propensity to disconfirm unwelcome data. In one Fortune 500 company we surveyed, we found that fear was the number-one barrier to innovation. At the corporate level the fear is the fear of cannibalization, channel conflict, or earnings dilution as we described. At the individual level, fear is often the fear of unrecoverable economic harm done to one's career.

When asked what the most significant factor in his company's declining performance was, one Fortune 500 CEO replied, "We lack a culture of risk taking." Because of this, he explained, the company's engineers and business managers were unable to work together to create innovative products that would succeed in the marketplace.

Perceived Barriers to Improving Innovativeness

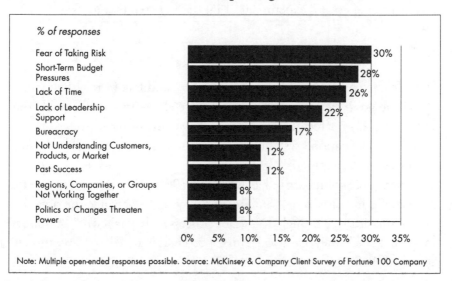

Note: Multiple open-ended responses possible. Source: McKinsey & Company Client Survey of Fortune 100 Company

To understand this issue better, we asked six hundred individuals at that corporation, spread across several businesses, functions, and countries, whether the corporation tolerated different ways of thinking. Fifty-six percent felt the corporation did. Then we asked if they felt failing on a project would set back their careers. Some 57% felt it would. In other words, the perceived cost of failure was relatively high. Finally, we asked employees if they felt they would be rewarded proportionately for the risks they might take. Some 89% said no. The company may have tolerated and even encouraged different ways of thinking, but the low rewards for risk taking, and the unrecoverable costs of failure, explain why so little real innovation emerged from the corporate ranks.

Ideas are fragile things that must be handled carefully. As Michael Faraday, the British discoverer of electromagnetism, once pointed out,

> *The world little knows how many thoughts and theories which have passed through the mind of a scientific investigator have been crushed in silence and secrecy by his own severe criticism and adverse examinations; that in the most successful instances not a tenth of the suggestions, the hopes, the wishes, the preliminary conclusions have been realized.*

Risk aversion kills even the best ideas. As Roy Vagelos, former CEO at Merck, said, "There is only one sure road to failure that I've seen many wander down: Some people become so afraid of failing that they are unable to do a critical experiment or take a first step in a market."

PERMISSION VS. CONTROL AT ENRON

How do the concepts of control, permission, and risk fit together? Enron offers one good example of managing these elements to a favorable outcome. The Enron formula balances control (instituted through its performance evaluation system) and permission (encouraged through employee incentives).

When Jeff Skilling arrived at Enron in 1990, the company fit the traditional gas industry mold. Skilling and Lay had to change the organization dramatically. Through a series of processes they labeled "facilitators" and "enablers," they gave aggressive permission to the organization to innovate in new markets and cannibalize existing businesses where necessary. Here are the facilitators and enablers created at Enron:

FACILITATORS	ENABLERS
Initiated a compensation system that provided monthly compensation of only one-third of expected annual compensation but provided potential for higher-than-normal annual compensation if risks were assumed and results were achieved.	Cut organization layers, and eliminated specific job titles and delinked job titles from job responsibilities, making titles more like those in professional service firms.
Created a performance evaluation system driven by a committee of peers that used the same criteria for everyone in the organization.	Removed career staff positions and created an associate pool to do needed analytical work.
Cut back the control system to a few key variables that were closely monitored. The rest of the activities ran without intensive involvement from top management.	Hired large numbers of exceptionally highly qualified people. Changed information flow so that everyone had ready and easy access to all information.
Established open-plan work areas to allow people to constantly interact with each other, thus removing some uncertainty about what was happening.	Made information access free.

Almost immediately, there was a great deal more energy at Enron among its employees. As one junior manager described it, this was due to:

1. Support from upper management.
2. Loose organizational structure. "People take a lot of ownership because no one is telling you what to do."
3. The personnel review process. "It is more than the monetary

reward. It is reassuring that a consensus was developed about you and that you are getting good feedback."

4. Investing significantly in recruiting and hiring smart people.
5. Being nimble and able to quickly adapt to change.

Enron sought out employees willing to take control of their own careers and that of the company. To help promote this attitude, technical and corporate information is available to everyone throughout the organization through a proprietary IT network, one configured for loose distribution. Moreover, as was pointed out in Chapter 6, Enron uses compensation as another lever to encourage creativity.

Enron North America has even reinforced the message in the design of its executive offices. At its headquarters, you will not find the cubicles of a conventional energy company, but a great open space that not only tells the visitor this is an energy *trading* company, but that it is a place where people can gather and communicate. The office of the CEO is glass-walled and placed near the action. Passersby are likely to be invited into Jeff Skilling's office for an impromptu chat.

Through its actions, Enron has dramatically changed the balance of permission and control. While this is only part of Enron's story, its impact on the creative productivity of the corporation is clear. Enron has transformed itself from an operating organization into an organization dedicated to create-operate-trade.

PERMISSION RUN AMOK: THERMO ELECTRON

Permission, however, doesn't always work. The story of Thermo Electron, one of the most interesting experiments in corporate design to emerge over the past two decades, is a case in point. After a rocky start, for much of its history Thermo looked like it might become the new model of the modern organization. The corporation was almost entirely based on what we have called "permission." But the particular way Thermo chose to grant permission contained a time bomb, as we will explain.

Thermo Electron was founded in 1956 by George Hatsopoulos with $50,000 borrowed from a friend, in an attempt to capitalize on his Ph.D. research in the field of thermionics, a method of converting heat to electricity. In 1965, natural gas producers contracted with Thermo Electron to develop industrial equipment that ran on gas rather than electricity, and in 1968, Ford Motor Company provided funds to build a low-emission automobile engine. Thermo Electron's growth as a research lab allowed it to go public in 1967.

Thermo Electron's first major financial success was in supplying chemical-analysis equipment to auto companies. In 1971, Congress passed a law requiring car makers to report the amount of nitrogen oxides their cars were emitting. Ford, with whom Hatsopoulos was still working, was scrambling to find a supplier since there were no such devices on the market. Hatsopoulos seized the opportunity. "I said, 'Give me an order for ten instruments and we will deliver.' They said, 'What instruments? You don't make instruments.' I said, 'We'll develop it,'" Hatsopoulos recalled. Thermo Electron was able to produce the instruments a year ahead of the competition, prompting orders from the other automakers. "Then all hell broke loose," he recalls. "Then you don't need a marketing force. You need a telephone operator to take orders."

By 1980, the Waltham, Massachusetts, company was registering about $200 million in annual sales, generating $7.5 million in net income for its shareholders. But the lingering effect of the '70s recession began to take its toll on large equipment orders from industry, and Thermo Electron's profits declined to $2.5 million in 1982 and fell to $50,000 in 1983. At the same time, Thermo Electron was investing heavily in R&D, building new applications for its existing technology.

With Thermo Electron having grown into a mid-sized corporation, management issues began to appear. In order to fund some of its development, Thermo Electron decided to partially spin off one of its divisions, Thermedics, which held patents for medical applications, to the public. Hatsopoulos referred to the partial spin-off as a "spin-out." In August 1983, the spin-out was completed, raising $4.7 million for the new company. Thermo Electron maintained an 80% stake in the new company, but the spin-out did provide cash for additional research and relieved pressure on its earnings (which had been exacerbated by Thermedics). This accidental organizational innovation was soon to become the core of Thermo Electron's management philosophy. "Our purpose," Hatsopoulos said, "is to found and grow new companies."

A crucial component of the spin-out idea was also to provide a reward mechanism for the leadership of the new company. Hatsopoulos and his brother John were concerned that those developing new ideas for the company's technologies would choose to leave the company and form their own ventures. The brothers found that they were unable to properly reward the leadership of small, high-growth-potential areas of the company with stock options because of the relative size of Thermo Electron. The spin-out mechanism, born of desperation, proved to be a very attractive solution. As George Hatsopoulos reflected tens years after the idea was born, "There's no better way to stimulate creativity than to see a guy next to you get $500,000 in options for a great idea."

Thermo Electron repeated the spin-out twice in 1985. In August it took Thermo Analytical (which provided hazardous waste and nuclear contamination analyses) public, raising $9.6 million for one-third of the company, and in September it organized Tecogen, the company's cogeneration division, which generated $1 million for a 5% stake that Thermo Electron sold privately. (It took the company public in 1987.)

By 1986, Thermo Electron was growing rapidly again, profiting from its spin-out strategy and the general improvement in the economy, which left it with $250 million in back orders for its electricity-generating equipment. And from 1977 to 1987 it yielded a 12.2% return on average to shareholders, at a time when the broader market returned 9.3%. Giving permission to the operating companies through the mechanism of the spin-out was working beautifully.

Thermo's share price continued to climb in 1990, helped along by its majority stakes in its spin-outs (among them Thermo Cardiosystems, a 1989 spin-out from Thermedics, Thermo Electron's first "grandchild"). But the market was beginning to have its doubts about the sustainability of Thermo's strategy. By 1990, Thermo Electron was valued by the market at 23% less than the value of its holdings in its spin-outs (and their spin-outs), in spite of the fact that Thermo Electron had several strong divisions of its own that it had yet to spin out.

While the approach worked well for Thermo Electron and its "children," the increasing complexity of the system as it grew larger was beginning to have an effect. In 1993, Hatsopoulos made the decision to stop serving on the board of directors of Thermo Electron's "grandchildren." "There's a physical limit to the number of board meetings one man can attend in a single week." John Hatsopoulos, however, continued to serve as CFO to all of the Thermo companies.

As Thermo grew, the various spin-off offspring began to lose contact with one another. Conversations and chance meetings that occurred easily when the corporation was smaller were less likely to happen as the size and complexity of the corporation increased. Some of the freedom that had been the foundation of Thermo was beginning to be sacrificed in the name of efficiency and managerial control. As the company continued to grow, it was increasingly difficult for even Thermo's talented top management to stay on top of what was going on, which proved to be unnerving.

In 1997, as some of the share prices of Thermo companies began to sag, Thermo Electron stepped in and used its cash to extend its ownership of the companies. Hatsopoulos explained these steps as good investment practice. "The first reason we buy back all of these shares of spin-offs is very simple—we buy them when we think they are undervalued." By 1998 shareholders of Thermo Electron were complaining that the company's structure was too complex and was holding it back. Trying to satisfy its corporate shareholders and the minority shareholders of its twenty-two Thermo companies was proving impossible.

Additionally, financial troubles in Asia were dragging down the company's sales. In July 1998, Thermo Electron's stock fell 17% after it announced it would miss its earnings estimate due to a delay in a new spin-out. The company responded in September 1998 by announcing a reorganization that would cut seven hundred jobs. It also announced that John Hatsopoulos would be replaced as president of Thermo Electron by Arvin Smith, CEO of Thermo Instruments. At the end of 1998, John Hatsopoulos stepped down from his nearly two dozen CFO roles.

But shareholders were not satisfied that significant changes had been made, and on the back of a boom in U.S. share prices, Thermo Electron's share price continued to fall to $12.50 a share in April 1999, from $40 a share a year earlier. In March 1999, the company announced that founder and CEO George Hatsopoulos would retire, to be replaced by Richard F. Syron, chief executive of the American Stock Exchange.

Within months, Syron announced that he would begin to simplify the company, indicating that "the risk is [that] the complexity of the structure can deflect management attention." Syron announced that it would reduce its family of companies down from twenty-three to eleven, by "spinning in" some units, divesting others, and closing some entirely, including ThermoLase. By February 2000, Thermo Electron extended the plan, announcing that its divestment would exceed $1 billion in assets by year end, and increase the number of "spin-ins" to nineteen, effectively eliminating the family structure altogether. In response to its increasing complexity, Thermo Electron has opted for control.

For a long time, Thermo Electron appeared to have a winning formula. It produced very strong results for almost twenty years. But ultimately the increasing complexity of the organization overwhelmed management capacity. While the strategy of permission helped the company weather early crises and grow at a rate that it might not otherwise have been able to achieve, in the end the company simply could not find a way to both allow for the entrepreneurial spirit that had been its foundation and control operations as the corporation grew larger.

As earnings began to slip, so too did Wall Street's confidence. Hatsopoulos's strategy clearly had the advantage of retaining creative and entrepreneurial talent—yet perhaps oddly in this environment of entrepreneurial encouragement, because Thermo management were unwilling to give up full control (by spinning *out* companies rather than spinning them *off*) and they created excessive organizational complexity as the parent grew larger. In this case, the battle between permission and control was won, at least for the time being, by control. The future will tell whether Syron's simplification will allow Thermo to create and grow again.

MAKING CHANGES WORK

How, practically, can these ideas be implemented? Thermo Electron shows us that despite the best intentions, the job of balancing permission and control is quite complex. The key questions concern where to minimize classical controls and where to increase permission, how much permission to give, what mechanisms to use, and how to reserve the right to take it back if things don't work out. The model for making these decisions is always the market, rather than some internal notion of control. If in doubt, one should ask: what processes take place in the market? We think there are six key guidelines to use in answering this question:

1. **Determine What to Measure and Control**
   There are five levels to examine when seeking to minimize controls: corporate, business unit, functional (e.g., marketing or operations), project, and general coordination and control (finance). The task at each level is unique to itself.

   At the corporate level: As discussed in Chapter 8, a substantial portion of the management committee agenda should be devoted to ensuring that the pace and scale of creating and trading matches the pace of change in the market. The amount of time the management committee spends on these issues should be at least equal to the amount of time spent on operating issues. For example, the management committee might regularly review the rate of entry and exit of new companies at the periphery. Among the questions the committee might focus on are: Is the company as a whole moving at the pace and scale of the market in these areas? Should it move more aggressively? What is the key information needed to assess the answer to this question? Which divisions are pursuing business models that may have long-term economic potential? What is the minimum amount of control required to exercise oversight? What processes can be totally eliminated without cutting the effectiveness of oversight?

At the business level: Most of the managerial effort of existing business units is expended on operations. The business unit leaders are the ones who "own" these P&Ls. On the other hand, business units cannot abdicate the responsibility for growth. Quite obviously, they need to understand their future sources of growth and understand how they are going to attain them. In some ways, making room for growth is more difficult at the business unit level than it is at the corporate level. In addition to traditional operations-oriented questions, one should ask: Are growth plans realistic? Are companies at the periphery well enough understood (e.g., does senior management personally know the top management people of the most powerful peripheral companies?). What customers are buying the products from peripheral companies, and what value do those customers see in the products? Does senior management personally know the lead customers for the peripheral companies? Do we understand their vision for the evolution of the business? Does it conflict with ours? Under what circumstances could our company become vulnerable to attack from these peripheral players? Typically, these are very difficult questions for existing businesses to answer objectively.

At the functional level: The functions (e.g., marketing, sales, production, procurement, development) have operating responsibility for execution, and thus are in charge of achieving excellence. But that excellence can be elusive. Expertise may become rapidly obsolete. New areas of expertise may be required to develop and launch new business models. Thus, performance at the functional level must be understood both in terms of the daily operating level (upon which traditional benchmarking is based) and in terms of the corporation's ability to adapt to an ever-changing market.

In addition to traditional questions about cost competitiveness, one might ask: How "fresh" is our skill base? Do we know what new approaches are being tried? Do we understand new emerging areas with growth potential? Do we have the expertise we need in these areas? What do we plan to get rid of over the next two years? What new expertise do we need? What are we doing to get such expertise? Are we making enough progress in those areas?

At the project level: At the project level, ask managers to design their own control and review processes. What are the key variables to watch? What are the critical milestones? What is the earliest time at which progress should be measured? How will they know if things are on track or not (most normal project-tracking systems are notoriously inadequate)? How frequently should the manager hold reviews? What are the two or three goals that must be accomplished? Are they being realistic about costs, timing, and results? What would it take to cut the complexity of this project in half?

At the coordination and control level: The finance and information management groups are traditionally responsible for oversight of the metrics in the corporation—that is, for gathering data in specific formats at specific times, evaluating budgets, and helping steer capital allocation and set performance standards. Finance also plays a critical role in the control and permission systems of the corporation—and that's why it must be at the center of the redesign effort.

2. **Measure and Control What You Must, Not What You Can**
   Clearly, control systems are required. The task is to make the required necessary control systems as simple as possible. Harvard's Robert Simons points out, "The information processing systems of our contemporary world swim in an exceedingly rich soup of information, of symbols. In a world of this kind, the scarce resource is not information; it is the processing capacity to attend to informa-

tion. Attention is the chief bottleneck in organizational activity, and the bottleneck becomes narrower and narrower as we move to the top of organizations." Adopting the slogan "measure and control what you must, not what you can" directly addresses the dilemma Simons identifies.

To implement this guideline, the corporation will need to take an inventory of the existing control processes and document how they work (what data they require, when they require it, how the data is analyzed, what decisions are enabled by the data and analysis, what the system costs to gather the data, analyze the data, distribute the data, and make changes based on the data) and the benefits they bring. The analysis of the costs and benefits of current control systems should be conducted by the people who are expected to produce the results and those who carry the "official" responsibility for the results. This guideline for redesign—"measure what you must, not what you can"—should be applied to each control process of the corporation. It should be applied to the scope of measurements taken, the frequency of measurement, the breadth of distribution of the data, the frequency of required feedback once the data is reported, and the extent of data review.

Additionally, key managers with control responsibility should be selected with great care. Their understanding of the need to balance divergent and convergent thinking in their areas of responsibility should be probed before they are selected.

3. **Increase Flexibility of Information Systems**

One of the greatest barriers to change is the cost and time required to update information systems. The systems for gathering, transforming, transmitting, and using information are often quite expensive. Although new technologies are reducing the costs, switching costs are still high.

This has significant implications for competitive adaptiveness. New companies forming at the periphery don't have the burden of old information systems. These companies have no switching costs. Management should ask itself about how the corporation is positioned in terms of information management. What information is likely to be permanent and which may change? Which is likely to become obsolete? What new information might be required, and how can the architecture of the system be accommodated to provide that? Does the firm have the skills to make full, intelligent use of the new information?

4. **Increase Permission for Experimentation**

   As discussed above, the corporation needs to provide permission and resources for experimentation at the pace and scale of the market. Specifically, this means permission to explore to the same extent that exploration takes place in the capital markets, permission to pursue a goal without undue interference from control systems, permission to experiment with business concepts at the same rate as the market, and permission to raise funds externally if strong ideas are developed and subsequently turned down by the corporation.

5. **Change the Range of Reward and Risk in the Incentive System to Reflect and Amplify Permission**

   There are two elements of the incentive system that have to be thought through in addition to the standard monetary elements. They are the nature of nonmonetary rewards and the existence of risk with the associated possibility of failure.

   Nature of rewards: Redesigning the evaluation and compensation systems are examples of useful "enablers." But many executives feel that compensation is not the most important part of the incentive system—that more important is creating passion around innovation in the company. As one executive observed: "The type of people who really drive innovation don't do it because of rewards, they do it because they strongly and passionately believe in the idea."

   Indeed, at the average start-up, particularly a high-tech firm, one will more likely hear people speaking about "dreams," "passion," "trust," "degree of freedom," and "autonomy" than money. Monetary compensation, whether delivered in the form of bonuses, options, and other equity-participation plans, is just one among many factors driving decisions.

   Risk and failure: The existence of risk (the unknowability of the future) and the possibility of failure that accompanies it, is the second element that has to be thought through for incentive systems.

Nike uses a team approach to syndicate risk. When an employee has an idea, he or she recruits others to further it. Once others sign on, they share the risk. No one gets credit for a major success or takes the blame for a failure alone.

A few years ago, for example, Nike attempted a foray into the rough-and-tumble arena of street hockey, a far cry from the more traditional sports Nike had become extraordinarily adept at supporting. The company assembled a team to go out and learn about the market, develop some concepts, and test them out. Despite the best of intentions, the team couldn't figure out a way to win. So Nike withdrew the effort. A failure? Nike regarded the effort as part of the learning process. In fact, one of the key players in this "failure" was promoted.

Thinking through how to deal with failure is an important element in the design of incentive systems. As Roberto Goizueta, former chairman of Coca-Cola, noted, "We became uncompetitive by not being tolerant of mistakes. The moment you let avoiding failure become your motivation, you are going down the path of inactivity. You can stumble only if you are moving."

Nike president Tom Clark noted that teams help people "learn from the past, admit mistakes, and then move ahead. Nothing happens to people who fail," he added. "I don't think Phil Knight ever trusted anyone entirely who didn't suffer through a significant failure on his or her watch."

As Henry Ford noted a half century ago, "Failure is only an opportunity to begin again more intelligently."

These approaches can be used to increase the range of risk and reward permitted in the corporation without sacrificing adequate controls.

6. **Establish a process for ongoing senior support, with a Focus on Its Impact on Divergence and Creation**
To get the foregoing measures accepted by employees at the more junior levels, top management will have to convince them that they are serious, and that the penalties for blocking change are greater than the penalties for trying new ideas and failing.

At Pepsi, for example, Chairman Roger Enrico holds sessions with junior members of the organization, listening to their ideas and assuring them that he stands squarely with them in their aspirations. The goal is to encourage risk taking in the middle-management ranks, and to break down the self-censorship that often blocks good ideas. Of course, holding such sessions in and of itself is not magic. The magic comes in the content of the sessions, and Enrico is widely admired for his ability to make them interactive and intimate.

Opening up conversations between senior management and the rest of the organization is, in fact, one of the most powerful mechanisms for giving permission. This is not "presentation and response," the closed conversations that are simply another form of control. (There are many linguistic devices for "controlling" individual conversations—e.g., "Now, really, let's be practical." Translation: "I am tired of what you are talking about, let's talk about what I want to talk about.") Instead, Pepsi fosters real conversation.

These six guidelines provide a starting point for rethinking how the corporation could work if assumption of continuity were replaced with the assumption of discontinuity.

The dilemma facing General Motors in the 1940s—how to manage the tension between centralized control (an assertion of the importance of continuity) and local initiative (in the spirit of discontinuity and change)—is strikingly similar to the dilemma facing many large and successful companies today. The question is whether today's corporation, with the evidence of long-term performance before it, will choose continuity or change as its operating paradigm. Is it willing to transform itself from an operating model to a "create-operate-trade" model? If it is to do so, it will have to adjust its control systems. A corporation cannot declare itself in favor of decentralization and then refuse to give up control. It will not work.

Now that we have a better grasp on the needs of the new corporation, the question remains how we go about delivering them. We address that question in the next chapter.

CHAPTER 11

Setting the Pace and Scale of Change

All learning is rooted in conversation.

JOHN SEELY BROWN,
president of Xerox's Palo Alto Research Center (PARC)

A long with General Electric, most analysts would consider Johnson
& Johnson, one of the world's largest health-care companies, to be
a very well-managed corporation. Lauded in the press as the role model
company for entrepreneurial decentralization, J&J is a symphony orches-
tra of operating companies competing aggressively in the marketplace.
Over the past twenty years, J&J has increased sales by more than tenfold,
has doubled the number of its employees, has entered many multi-
hundred-million-dollar businesses such as blood glucose monitoring
and disposable contact lenses, has exited such businesses as disposable
diapers, ocular lenses, and CT scanning, has survived and triumphed over
the 1982 and 1986 Tylenol scares, has expanded sales internationally, and
has, in general, shifted from a mainly consumer-products company to
one whose profits are dominated by a rapidly growing pharmaceutical
business.

The source of J&J's strong sustained performance is the industries it
has chosen to compete in (consumer health care products, medical products, and pharmaceuticals), the countries it has chosen to compete in, and
its strong performance in each of those sectors and countries. J&J is well

known for their values, as expressed in their Credo, first penned in the mid-'40s by Robert Wood Johnson.

The 1972 Annual Report laid out some of the principles of that credo that are present more than twenty-five years later:

- "It has always been our management philosophy to look beyond the immediate problems of running a business so that our broader vision would include the backdrop of changing social conditions that reflect the interests and concerns of our customers as well as our employees."
- "Johnson & Johnson has typically grown over the years by creating new companies built around a particular technology or group of products. These companies, often previously units of a larger organization, are able to concentrate on a special area of business. [This approach allows the new companies to focus on] its own specific and identifiable market, which it can respond to more quickly than a larger organization."
- "The Company is organized on the principles of decentralized management and conducts its business through operating divisions and subsidiaries, which are themselves integral, autonomous operations. While direct line management of these units is maintained through the Executive Committee of the Board of Directors of the Company, operational responsibility lies with each operating management."

J&J's keen sense of the need to balance operational excellence as well as to change at the pace and scale of the market, goes a long way in explaining why it has done as well as it has. J&J is always on the lookout for both opportunities and sources of potential trouble, and then is ready to take action to either capitalize on the opportunities or avert the dangers.

But how does J&J do it? How does it set the pace and scale of change necessary to keep up with the markets? Answers to this question are instructive as other corporations seek to mimic J&J's record of performance.

Perhaps no example of the J&J approach to setting and managing the pace and scale of change is better illustrated than the history of the evolution of the "FrameworkS" process at J&J. The story begins with a call that

Chairman Ralph Larsen gave one of us early in 1993 when he had become concerned about "clouds on the horizon."

ASKING THE QUESTION

The focal point of Larsen's concerns was the collapse in IBM's performance. John Akers, well-known chairman of IBM, had resigned. Lou Gerstner had been brought in to salvage what had once been viewed as the blue chip of blue chips. Like J&J, IBM was for years everybody's favorite company. It represented technological virtue. Innovation. An aggressive American spirit. It was an American juggernaut. Not only had IBM failed, but DEC, Unisys, and Sperry Rand had failed before it; NCR, Siemens, and even Toshiba had lost considerable ground in the 1980s and early 1990s. What had happened at IBM seemed much bigger than the company itself. When James Burke, former chairman of J&J, was appointed head of the search committee for a new CEO at IBM, it would have been hard for the J&J top team not to wonder if what had happened to IBM might not also be possible at J&J. After all, IBM had been caught in the downdraft of the computer hardware industry, and now J&J was facing a new Democratic administration with a clear focus on reforming health care, not unlike the reform that the market had forced on the computer hardware industry. Moreover, the increase in political risk was matched by an increase in managed care. Managed care companies were the hot companies of the early '90s. The parallels with the rise of software companies in the computer industry were not hard to make. These factors and others made Larsen question the impact of health care reform on J&J. Could J&J's valued principles be sustained? Did they need to be reinterpreted or applied in new ways, given the challenges of the '90s? Did these principles still work for a company that had grown to the size of J&J? These were some of the fundamental questions on Larsen's mind. Larsen possessed an essential skill of a strong divergent thinker—the ability to ask the right questions, no matter how disturbing.

Knowing that McKinsey was studying long-term corporate performance during discontinuity, Chairman Larsen asked us to work with him, along with Roger Fine (then VP of administration, and now general counsel) and members of the Johnson & Johnson Executive Committee. Larsen wanted us to help him assess and reduce the threat facing J&J.

SETTING THE INQUIRY INTO MOTION

In our ongoing discussions with Larsen and Fine, we suggested that the dangers facing large companies as a result of discontinuity are not those that are unknown but those that are undervalued. But few corporations provide a forum to talk in an extended and exploratory manner about the potential impact of future discontinuities. Because there is no forum for dialogue, there is little possibility of changing one's mental model (which we then called one's mental frameworks) about the future evolution of the industry. No matter how many rounds of presentation and response one goes through, it is not the same as a personal exploration of the issues over an extended period of time. We explained that the conventional presentation-and-response approach afforded no time for the search for new ideas, for new ways of looking at the future. Nor does presentation and response allow sufficient time for incubation—for new patterns to fall into place. Without changing its mental models, changing its dialogue, changing the information available to it, there could be no changes in systems or action. Accordingly, the first thing to do was to meet with the Executive Committee, the highest managerial committee at J&J, to lay out this diagnosis of the problem, agree on an approach to fixing it, and lay out a plan for getting started. Larsen agreed that the analysis made sense, and suggested that the ideas should be exposed to, and discussed with, the Executive Committee at a retreat they were planning to have a few months later.

DESIGNING THE DESIGN PHASE

To prepare the Executive Committee for this meeting, individual discussions were held with each member to determine their agreement or disagreement with the basic line of thinking we were pursuing, as well as to hear the issues they thought the corporation faced in the next three to five years.

Armed with these insights, we, along with Fine, developed an agenda—really a sequence of conversations—for the Executive Committee meeting. The meeting would begin with a few case studies of other corporations that had faced this dilemma, discuss how they dealt with it, assess the results of their efforts, and then draw lessons from those cases. Among the specific questions we agreed to discuss were these:

How did these companies come to the danger point? Did they simply become too big? Did they become too bureaucratic? Did their technology lose its edge? Did their sales force lose its edge? Did the company lose touch with its customers? What happened?

Why couldn't the company management see the risks emerging until they were in the vortex of discontinuous change? How could so many intelligent and accomplished individuals, individuals not unlike the J&J team, misread the situation for so long? Why could the leadership not shape an effective program to deal with the problem when it did see the threat?

Finally, fully anchored in the thinking about the successes and failures of others in dealing with this issue, the Executive Committee would address their perceptions of the most pressing issues facing J&J over the next five years that could have potentially similar effects if not dealt with. The vehicle for doing this was a set of questions for discussion, selected to meet the test of the defining question mentioned below:

Identify in your mind the 100 most talented, thoughtful, and creative people in the organization, regardless of tenure or position. Now imagine that you can bring them together a few at a time for a conversation, an intimate conversation similar to one you might have with friends in your living room after dinner. In this conversation, nothing is sacred. All taboos are off. Everyone is equal, limited only by his or her cognitive and verbal abilities. The agenda is yours. You can raise any issue you want to raise to this august and candid group of experienced advisers. What would you ask them? What are the six most important issues to raise with the most intelligent people you can find in your organization?

At the end of the meeting, an action program would be sketched out, but the intent was not to design the long-term future. It was only to determine the topic, timing, location, and chairman for the next session.

The purpose of the "design" meeting was to set the stage for changing the mental models of the corporation. The criteria for success for the meeting was to be the openness and range of topics discussed. The criteria did not include "closing" on issues, but rather the opposite. The intent was to "suspend disbelief" about what the "right" answers might be. The focus was on finding the right questions.

The discussion was intended to have only the lightest architecture. It was intended to be very open, and only loosely moderated. The agenda contained a great deal of "white space," unprogrammed time to spot and discuss issues. We anticipated that many of the issues identified could not be resolved during the meeting, because there would be insufficient data or expertise among the members of the Executive Committee to address them. Such questions would simply be tabled. The fact was, we knew that if all the questions raised could already be answered so easily, the right questions were not being asked. The intent of the meeting was simply to pick issues for later resolution.

THE DESIGN MEETING

The design meeting was held a long way from the J&J headquarters to increase the chances of devoting every available moment to the conversations. It is hard to have this kind of conversation when faxes are being delivered, people are stepping out to take phone calls, and side meetings are being held. Meeting at a remote site gave us a chance to control those risks.

The meeting was judged a success, and resulted in unanimous agreement on a specific action program that addressed the most basic concerns of the Executive Committee. The feeling at the meeting was both positive and collegial. There was little pressure, since current performance was strong and was forecast to remain strong (the forecasts turned out to be accurate) for the coming quarters. It was more like an informal gathering of interesting, intelligent peers cross-stimulating each other with their insights, speculations, and stories. During the meeting, the Executive Committee was able to reach some conclusions about key risks and opportunities for the future. The greatest risk was to stay exclusively focused on operations, fixed on one mental model of how the industry would evolve and how the position of the lead competitor would evolve along with it, rather than to recognize that there were many possible ways the industry could evolve. Rather than look to "expertise" for the answer, the real answer was to be found in observation, reflection, and conversation. Vice Chairman Robert Wilson captured the spirit of the meeting when he observed that J&J needed to think about multiple frameworks for the future rather than just one idea. So central was this idea to the spirit of the task that Wilson suggested the process be known as the "FrameworkS" (the capital *S* was added to emphasize the multiplicity of future possibilities) process, and everyone quickly agreed.

Given this general conclusion, the Executive Committee identified and selected a series of critical issues that had the potential to alter the competitive environment of their industry. Among the issues were the implications, both long and short term, of managed care on health care suppliers; the impact of the European Union on health care in Europe; growth in emerging markets; the use of advanced information technology—and in particular the Internet—on the delivery of health care; and the changing perception by consumers of their role in the delivery and evaluation of that care. The intent was to construct a "conversation" around each of these issues after there had been sufficient observation and reflection. Moreover, the participants in the conversation would be picked from all parts of J&J, independent of their position in the corporate hierarchy, dependent only on their ability to contribute to the discussion and the changing FrameworkS of the corporation.

At the end of the meeting, Ralph Larsen summarized by saying, "We need to think about running the business in a different way. We don't want to be the management group that presides. We want a process that makes sure we don't miss the boat." General Counsel George Frazza put it this way: "I think of it in family terms. We are a family of companies. What are our aspirations for our children? We want them to exist, be successful, and be creative. We need to create the environment where our children can be successful. We must not become too specific. The seven of us can't come up with the answer for the other 83,000. We have to make it more likely for the other 83,000 people to contribute. We want to remain a great company. We want to be the challenger, not the challenged. We have to think the opposite of the 'great man' theory of history. It is more likely that the key insights for the future lie out in the corporation than it is that they lie here in the EC. . . . My biggest concerns are the ABC's of failure: A = Arrogance, B = Bureaucracy, C = Complacency. They can be the dark side of success."

In addition to the specific issues and the general sense of commitment to the effort, the Executive Committee committed to some basic principles. First and foremost, it wanted a process that got the Executive Committee started on its basic role of "looking though the eyes of others" and putting a structure to it. The idea would be to generate multiple frameworks for viewing the market, the competition, and the company.

Moreover, a series of objectives were laid out for the process:

1. Ensure that J&J's direction for its future is based on a realistic, up-to-date view of the world, and especially of its customers and markets.
2. Identify the key business imperatives for coping with the next three to five years (i.e., cost reduction, more innovation, proposed government reform, the emergence of the Internet) rather than a longer-term future, and build the consensus needed for addressing these imperatives in a decentralized environment.
3. Identify the areas where J&J's existing or potential core skills/competencies and major health needs can intersect to provide an element of renewal and synergy for J&J. In particular, identify those areas that might otherwise fall through the cracks because of J&J's decentralized organizational structure and management philosophy.
4. Build a generation of J&J executives who are better equipped to think widely, to recognize discontinuities early in their development, and to seek out, understand, internalize, and act on new ways of viewing J&J's markets and customers.
5. Disseminate a real understanding of J&J's direction and underlying perspective on its markets and customers (and how they will evolve) widely enough to ensure that J&J executives and managers in all sectors and geographies can pursue it independently yet appropriately.

Given the design principles laid out in the initial Executive Committee meeting, a template for future meetings was developed. The template included three phases, each with its own objectives:

Phase 1: Discovery. This phase, devoted to search and incubation, sought to replicate the fairly lengthy search for anomalies in select sets of issues. Its purpose was to expose J&J executives to a wide range of perspectives on health care; open up issues that had been discussed in private; expose J&J executives to a wide range of cultures, political beliefs, and market structures, leading to a more insightful view of J&J's current and future markets and customers; the collection of relevant demographic, social, and market facts whenever feasible, while allowing for intensive periods to collect, disseminate, and discuss information as well as periods of "gestation." And, importantly, J&J should focus on searching the periphery for insight. The Executive Committee knew that it would not generate any bold new visions or plans just sitting in "The Tower" in its world headquarters in New Brunswick. It had to go to the source. If the subject was growth in China, then the session should be held in China. If it was to examine innovation, then the members had to go see how other innovative companies really worked.

Members of the Executive Committee chaired the discussion sessions. The session chairman personally lined up outside speakers who were experts in their fields, and briefed these speakers beforehand on the meeting's objectives. These premeeting sessions served the important function of grounding the official sessions in current data, whether it was pleasant or unpleasant.

Phase 2: The "Forcing Event" The conversation itself becomes the equivalent of the "deadline," where all the divergent thinking is brought together in the context of the group. The goal is to obtain that "collision of perspectives" that may produce the "ah-hah!" moment. Meetings should therefore be as open and nonhierarchical as possible, to ensure that the best ideas and conceptual frameworks are brought to light and considered as the process unfolds; involve as many of the key leaders (present and future) of J&J as possible; and seriously and visibly wrestle with the most fundamental, gut-wrenching issues. To achieve this purpose, a somewhat artificial but effective device was used: For the purposes of the FrameworkS meetings, all participants (roughly twenty in number) were designated members of the Executive Committee. As members of the Executive Committee they could not use the FrameworkS process as a bully pulpit for their own points of view. They had to adopt the corporate point of view. And with this, the official meeting concluded.

Phase 3: Synthesis During this phase, which occurred after the meeting, the thinking and insights developed in the first two phases are reduced to practice. The focus there is on both short-term actions and long-term issues. Task forces would take charge of making things happen.

J&J had known about the dangers of management excessively focused on operations. Now it set out to create a continually self-transforming company, one that thrived on its own creative destruction.

THE EARLY YEARS

Once committed to this new process, the J&J Executive Committee began what has turned into a series of focused dialogues examining the changing U.S. health-care marketplace. The first meeting was called FrameworkS 1, the second FrameworkS 2, and so on. There have been more than a dozen FrameworkS altogether.

THE FIRST FRAMEWORKS

The first FrameworkS, FrameworkS 1, produced a more urgent and more specific understanding of the threats to J&J's businesses. In order to look ahead over the next five years, the Executive Committee and other FrameworkS task-force members sought to put the next few years in a longer-term context. They asked themselves: What will the demographics of 2010 look like? What might the customer look like in twenty years? What will a typical doctor's office look like? What role will governments play? What will be the role and power of the payors in 2010? If regulatory models change to a much more regional approach, it could change all of our prior assumptions. What should we do? What will the technology look like in 2010? Who is on the cutting edge of change now? What unconventional approaches are being tried—for example, wiring the doctor's office? Who are the leaders?

After the session, they concluded that

the traditional ways of doing business are eroding. We used to rely on doctors and nurses as our customers. Now those positions are being taken over by managers whose role is to negotiate with us. In our consumer business we are faced with a shift in power between the manufacturer and the retailer. There is a dramatic power shift going on in all of our businesses, which will deeply affect the way we do business in every way.

I'm worried about the issue of complacency. With our profit margins and growth, we have a credibility gap with our own employees who do not understand we are under attack and that the profits we have could get shot very quickly. We have to become more efficient and effective. Being the low-cost producer has historically been tough for us.

A lot of us realize the way the world is going, but are we preparing ourselves for it?

FIRST STEPS IN THE TRANSFORMATION: LAUNCHING BUSINESSES AND CUTTING COSTS

Three themes came out of the FrameworkS 1 effort.

1. *Understanding the "new American customers"*: Who are they? How do they think? What drives them? What drives their economics? What drives their customers? How can J&J sell to them? How can it develop new products for them? How well positioned are we to meet their future needs compared to other suppliers/partners?

2. *Reducing the cost of doing business* throughout the corporation so that the products delivered to the "new American customers" will be both low-cost for them and profitable for J&J. A great deal of work seemed to be ongoing in this area. Thus it was incumbent only to make sure everything that could be done was being done.

3. *Improving innovativeness* throughout the corporation—both to meet the needs of the "new American customers" and existing customers, and to increase the speed and competitive impact of innovation in the corporation. In particular, pursuing new business opportunities, especially those relating to the "new customers" and "new technologies" emerging in the United States.

The primary focus resulting from this first FrameworkS session was building "new businesses for the new marketplace." One of the conclusions teams reached was that J&J's largest customers, such as hospital networks, managed-care plans, and government organizations, were increasingly pressing for a single J&J contact to coordinate purchases from its diverse operating companies. As a result, just three months after the task forces met to review their findings, J&J combined several U.S. operating companies to create Health Care Systems, Inc., the coordinating point customers were asking for. "It's a truly unique and innovative structure, the perfect vehicle to address customer needs while retaining the culture of autonomous operating companies," wrote David Cassak, editor of *In Vivo: The Business and Medicine Report*, a magazine that tracks the medical industry. Duke University's integrated health-care-delivery network was one of the J&J customers whose feedback led to the creation of Health Care Systems. "We are thrilled with the result of that dialogue," said Duke's Peter Nyberg, assistant operating officer for the corporate program. "Health Care Systems help us be more efficient, to make the most of our resources. That ultimately benefits our patients."

At the same time, a consensus emerged to undertake a massive reengineering and cost-avoidance effort. This was not the first time that J&J executives had talked about improving cost performance, but it was the first time they were able to make such radical progress on the issue. Over the course of the next eighteen months, J&J quite rapidly extracted some $2 billion in cost savings that went straight to the bottom line. Some of the savings involved elimination of jobs, but much of it came from doing more with the same, using assets more efficiently to grow. What made the difference this time? First, the entire Executive Committee aligned itself around the challenge. Through the process of discovery in FrameworkS 1, they were each deeply, personally committed to the fact that something had to be done. Second, Vice Chairman Bob Wilson took on the mantle of leader of the cost-reduction effort, holding regular meetings with designated managers from each of the major franchises, demanding each business set targets (though not specifying what those targets should be), pushing people to consider nonincremental solutions, and, in general, keeping the sense of urgency and importance high. During those eighteen months, Bob Wilson saw to it that cost avoidance and cost reduction never left the radar screen.

At the outset, we had conceived of the process as largely a creative effort. Destruction would be, we believed, at best an afterthought. One of the most important pieces of information that we took away from implementing the process was that it naturally produces both creation and destruction, because it produces *change*.

Ralph Larsen said at the time, "Health-care reform will be one of the greatest energizing forces we have ever had." Fear of the potential negative consequences of health-care reform had become an energizing force for the future of J&J.

NEXT STEPS

Following this initial success, the Executive Committee launched several more FrameworkS efforts, covering such diverse areas as the New American Consumer (a follow-up from the FrameworkS 1 effort), information management, organization, leadership, and several focused efforts on regional growth in Europe, China, Korea, and Japan (each held in the relevant region). The results of these conversations varied by topic. In Europe, the primary outcome was the launching of seventeen pilot businesses. In these, J&J would step out of its traditional role as a product supplier and involve itself in health services. In China, investments increased dramatically and an Executive Committee liaison for China was appointed. In regard to finding talented people, J&J set up J&J Standards of Leadership. Henceforth, management teams in each of the approximately 175 operating companies would use these standards to evaluate their own record of leadership development. The discussion on information management led to the creation of the chief information officer position on the Executive Committee.

These accomplishments proved that the FrameworkS process was anything but formulaic. By breaking the mental models and seeing the world as others see it, J&J created a striking diversity of solutions to the most fundamental challenges facing the corporation.

In 1995, stepping back from a few years of considerable change, the Executive Committee felt a sense of accomplishment. FrameworkS by this time had become a new managerial process within J&J. It had, by design, a very light architecture. It was designed to draw the best from the entire organization. It was neither top-down nor bottom-up nor middle-out; rather, it was infused throughout the entire corporation. It required people to think deeply rather than simply to respond in some standard way, and it gave them the time and permission to do this thinking.

As a result of FrameworkS, time was spent differently, old information was used in new ways, new information was used in practical ways, and the evaluation of ideas was conducted based on new criteria. The elaboration and implementation of these ideas at J&J followed a radically different path from that practiced in most corporations today.

Changing the old mental models was an emotionally charged experience for the J&J Executive Committee and the other highly successful, effective, intelligent people involved. Denial, defensive routines, rationalization, and avoidance were part of the arsenal brought to bear against the often uncomfortable facts and disconcerting, even disorienting, conclusions that emerged from the process. Yet these reactions did not prove insurmountable. Part of the importance of FrameworkS at J&J was in creating a forum where participants could overcome their prior conceptual frameworks. In the end, FrameworkS gave "permission" to the organization to break out of old thinking habits and to create new habits. The

Executive Committee explicitly relinquished some of its power and authority—even if that power and authority was more in the eyes of the operating company management than in the eyes of the Executive Committee itself—to the operating management of the corporation.

Persuading participants to allow sufficient time for incubation was sometimes an uphill struggle. It was critical that the company induce participants to shrug off years of training, to abstain from seeking closure or a rush to judgment, to seek questions, not answers. Participants had to learn to refrain from planning an outcome, and from defining "action steps" based on decisions they felt obliged to make, based on information that had been gathered years before.

Most of the credit for overcoming these obstacles was due to the support provided by Ralph Larsen and Bob Wilson, the chairman and vice chairman, who remained enthusiastic proponents of the program even in the face of resistance. For example, the first geographically oriented FrameworkS dealt with the challenge of growth in Europe. While the first conversation generated a sense that real growth opportunities existed, six months later little had happened. European management had not had the true "wake-up call." They felt that they could cover the growth expectations within their existing plans. In this case, the Executive Committee proved willing to go to the mat in their insistence that such a response was not sufficient. They asked the European management to organize a second session. And again they found resistance. But three was the lucky charm: This time the European executives realized the Executive Committee meant business, that they were not going to accept incremental solutions, that henceforth they must think about their businesses differently. And this time they came up with seventeen ideas for new growth businesses that would take J&J far beyond the realm in which it had operated until then—away from being a pure product company and into services that would be part of the transformation in health-care delivery in Europe. Europe went from being the laggard to being a bed of experimentation for the entire corporation. But it was a nearly four-year process and took the undying commitment of the Executive Committee to make sure real change happened.

At the same time, Larsen and Wilson stressed that participation was strictly voluntary. They knew that if they had attempted to make it mandatory, they would have encountered a whole new set of difficulties. They went to some lengths to stress that taking part in FrameworkS wouldn't be easy, efficient, or comfortable. It would not be a process for which success or failure would be easily determined.

And yet the participants were deeply engaged in the process. Despite having very full plates, executives made room for FrameworkS. In some cases, this meant getting on a plane and traveling across the Atlantic, and in one case from China, in order to attend.

Fortunately, both the chairman and the vice chairman were prepared to wait for the results to come in. While they did insist on evaluations of the FrameworkS process at the end of each conversation, they did not force a broader assessment of the impact in the early days. It could have been tempting for them to pull this particular carrot out of the ground every day to ask, "How's it growing?" Instead, they proved willing to wait eighteen or even twenty-four months for results—at which point a few visible successes could be ascribed to insights achieved through the program.

LATER YEARS

Two years after the first FrameworkS sessions, J&J's Executive Committee realized that some of the original issues raised in the FrameworkS design session—increasing innovation and improving operational effectiveness—remained unsolved. Despite specific progress on growth in various regions, despite some marked success in launching new businesses, and despite some profound cultural changes related to leadership, they felt that the corporation needed to push itself further on both the innovation and operations fronts. The low-hanging fruit had been plucked, and the Executive Committee had the sense that this next round of efforts would be more daunting.

STIMULATING INNOVATION

The ninth FrameworkS was thus focused entirely on innovation and aimed at uncovering some of the deeper mysteries about what it takes to up the innovation ante. By surveying executives across the corporation, holding focus groups of employees, conducting intensive diagnostics of three critical businesses, gathering the input of leading academics and experts, and, most important, visiting innovative companies in very different industries (Nike, Pepsi, and Enron), the participants in FrameworkS 9 challenged some of the institutionalized patterns of innovation in the corporation—incremental innovation in the operating companies, reliance on licensing and acquisition for more substantial innovation, focus on product innovation at the expense of other dimensions, and heavy reliance on a few "big bang" innovations for sales growth. There was a general sense that the past pace of innovation, while admired externally and appropriate for the size and scale of the corporation, would no longer be adequate in the changing health care marketplace as J&J continued to grow larger and more complex.

The members of the "extended Executive Committee" (the participants in this newest FrameworkS project) developed a strong understanding of the challenges Johnson & Johnson faced in achieving higher levels of innovation. And they became highly committed to meeting this challenge. They clarified their understanding of the different levels of innovation and made substantial innovation *the* major upcoming challenge. Next, they mapped out a set of behaviors and actions that are conducive to top innovation performance. And they gained a sense of what it would take to make individual operating companies and franchises more innovative.

There was an electric excitement coming out of that meeting. The participants, having gone on the site visits, having participated in the innovation diagnostics, having held discussions with people across the corporation, had a personal, tangible, firsthand understanding of the issues. Many described the experience in nearly religious terms.

Their next step was to translate this understanding and commitment to the broader management in the corporation. The task Johnson & Johnson executives faced was by no means simple. They were challenging themselves to sustained levels of growth and innovation that have rarely been achieved in the business world. They were seeking to change at the pace and scale of the markets in which they had chosen to compete. And they rightly saw themselves as but thirty (admittedly senior) people in a corporation of more than 87,000. Could they imbue the rest of the businesses and the rest of the workforce with the same feeling of commitment and the same personal understanding of innovation?

It was eminently clear that improving innovativeness was not simply an intellectual issue, a matter of understanding the definitions of innovation and the principles of innovativeness better. The participants in FrameworkS 9 were just that—participants. They had personally engaged in the experience. They had seen how other companies worked from the inside. They had seen for themselves how their employees talked about their fear of risk taking. One might argue, in fact, that none of the concepts or principles was particularly new. While it was certainly useful to have all the facts in one place and the principles articulated clearly, this was not what made the difference. The difference was the experience.

At the end of the FrameworkS 9 meeting, the discussion turned to how to make an impact on the corporation given this newfound commitment. One member of the Executive Committee suggested that they re-create the experience for the entire corporation—for all of the presidents or managing directors and the boards of all of the operating companies around the world. It seemed a fairly audacious suggestion, but the more they discussed it, the more they liked it.

They named the project What's New? as a symbol of the different kind of dialogue they were hoping to engender in the corporation. It was the question that Dr. Paul Janssen, a prolific inventor and founder of J&J's Janssen Pharmaceutica, asked of his people as he walked around the lab. It also echoes the sentiments of former CEO and chairman Jim Burke:

> *When I visit our companies around the world, I try to discourage managers from telling me what the business is like today. I'm not really interested. It's only natural for people to want to tell me how things are going at the moment, but I tell them to talk about the future. This is hard for them, but by my taking this attitude, I am sending a signal that we are primarily interested in long-term growth, and we want to know how it is going to be achieved. This focus on the future forces our managers out of the rut of simply running the business as it is today. We must keep moving on to new things. If we are going to have a future, then we must concentrate on it.*

Scaling a thirty-person event to an eight-hundred-person event was not simple, but a year later, in 1997, more than eight hundred leaders at J&J met in Los Angeles for three days, the largest event of its kind in the company's history. All of the participants did prework—assessments of their own businesses, reading about other innovative companies, and surveying their organization for perceptions about the effectiveness of current innovation processes. At the meeting itself, they held small group FrameworkS-style discussions about what they had learned. Since not everyone could go on a site visit, the organizing team brought the site visits to the executives, using elaborate multimedia presentations so that the presidents and CEOs of these leading companies could talk about their businesses and re-create some of the feel of the company itself.

The Executive Committee members spoke about the importance of innovation for the continued success of the corporation. And, by all accounts, it was a successful meeting: Most came away energized and committed. They understood that the team at the top was universally supportive of innovation efforts and they felt new freedom to press their growth agendas in their own businesses.

The meeting generated a great deal of excitement about the future. Some businesses went aggressively forward in making changes. However, not all businesses were able to translate their enthusiasm into action. For those companies, it was business as usual, perhaps because in the following year, 1998, these businesses faced some short-term performance challenges (e.g., falling sales-growth rates) and much of the advocacy for investment in the long term was crowded out by the desire to get the most out of the short term. Not surprisingly, J&J, as a large and complex corporation, has successes and failures just as the market has.

In an effort to keep the energy alive, the Executive Committee asked Group Operating Committees for each sector to appoint a person to take the lead in assuring implementation; all businesses were supposed to report to their groups about the progress that they had made. In an effort to further institutionalize the importance of innovation, the strategic planning requirements, widely criticized as disconnected from the actual running of the business, were revamped. While the intent was to encourage more FrameworkS-style dialogue and challenge in the planning process, the effort to transmit that intent to all of the businesses around the world led to a degree of formality that detracted from the impact. For example, the planning team put a tremendous amount of energy into creating a tool kit with a wide range of options that individual operating companies could use to stimulate innovation in their organizations. Available in hard copy and online, the tool kit was intended to help the companies through the process of self-discovery and change in order to dramatically up the innovation ante.

There were "wake-up call" tools, such as detailed instructions on how to conduct a site visit—ways to identify potential site visit companies, how to draft introduction letters, suggested discussion guides. There was a diagnostic tool complete with a self-evaluation survey, central data processing support service, and suggested formats for workshops to discuss the findings. There were guidelines for using science advisory councils, for accessing the J&J quality management knowledge network, for setting up "innovation cells" to protect and accelerate the development of innovative new business ideas, for conducting post-audits of innovation efforts to understand what worked and what did not. All in all, nearly forty different suggestions were initially included. The idea was to help jump-start the process in the operating companies, to share the insights that had come from the FrameworkS 9 site visits and internal discovery of innovation's best practices.

In many ways, the tool kit was intended to be the linchpin of the implementation effort after the What's New? launch meeting. Concerned about assuring that something happened after the launch, executives planning the meeting hoped that this tool kit would give J&J executives in the nearly 175 operating companies around the world some handholds, some ideas for actions, that could be developed and tailored to the specific situations in each company. No one thought for a moment that there could be a universal process that would work in all situations. And even if there were, J&J was not the kind of company that would set such guidelines top-down. Instead, the idea was to spark a passion and urgency among the more than eight hundred attendees at the launch meeting and then give them a menu of ideas for making a difference once they got home from Los Angeles.

But the impact of the tool kit has been limited so far. In the end, tools are not the issue—what is critical is the *passion* to innovate. J&J learned that ad hoc, unstructured, exploratory processes are a more powerful force for change than are formalized programs.

Where the program had the most effect, it was because the executives took it upon themselves to encourage their organizations to generate their own process, design their own metrics, and develop their own aspirations for success. In these situations, the tools provided through the What's New? effort—such as the innovation diagnostic, and the videos from the What's New? meeting in Los Angeles—proved helpful starting points. Indeed, the diagnostic survey probably got the most traction of any of the tools. Fueled by the generally self-critical culture and curiosity of managers around the world, and facilitated by a central support system that processed the surveys confidentially and produced management reports of the findings quickly, the vast majority of operating companies or worldwide franchises used the diagnostic survey in a process of discovery about their organizations. Some used the findings as support for quite radical changes; others found the results helpful in adjusting existing efforts.

The real lesson seems to be that best practices discovered by others are not as meaningful to organizations as the discoveries they make themselves. Attempting to codify the insights that generated so much excitement in FrameworkS took the "ah-hah!" out of them. The diagnostic survey gave managers a chance to make their own discoveries about their organizations. But we (and they) found that real change happened only when organizations generated their own tools and approaches.

IMPROVING OPERATIONS

Having focused on innovation for several years, the Executive Committee decided it was time to turn to the other side of the coin—operations—particularly because the initial reengineering effort sparked from the initial FrameworkS meeting seemed to have produced much of its potential benefit. The goal of the next FrameworkS session was to seek out ways to improve operations in the context of balancing operations with innovation, although a simple focus on operations effectiveness probably won out. Not only did this FrameworkS session have a profound cultural impact—the operations executives felt valued in a way that they had not previously been in a marketing- and sales-dominated culture—but it also got a lot of traction throughout the organization. Restructuring major manufacturing quickly followed, which resulted in closing 36 out of 158 plants and reducing 4,100 jobs and taking a significant write-off.

REFLECTING ON THE PROCESS

No one imagined in March of 1993 what the FrameworkS process would become to J&J. While there were many successes, there were also the inevitable bumps in the road. But each bump was squarely addressed by the senior management group and overcome. Without executive intervention, a willingness to take a stand against sources of resistance, and increased visibility on critical change efforts, FrameworkS would not have had the impact that it has had.

Looking back over those years, the following observations stand out:

1. **The pace**. Since 1994, the J&J Executive Committee has conducted thirteen different FrameworkS conversations (including the initial design session). When we first began, we expected that perhaps three of these sessions could be done per year. And J&J sustained that pace for the first two years. But eventually it had to slow things down. Part of the reason is that the preparation for the next session began to overlap with the follow-up task forces from the previous one. People found themselves committed to multiple FrameworkS-related task forces, to the point that it was beginning to crowd out too much of their normal operating responsibilities. In addition, they discovered that the process demanded more, rather than less, preparation time. Every time they talked about making the process somehow more "efficient" by shortening preparation time, or by having other people go on the site visits and report back, they concluded that efficiency was counter to the objectives of FrameworkS. So even though J&J would have liked FrameworkS to take less time out of people's schedules, they realized that such a change would kill the process. Finally, each of the FrameworkS led to significant change efforts, whether it was cost reduction, innovation, or growth businesses in Europe. Each of these demanded real leadership attention and energy (and political capital). With each succeeding FrameworkS, the number of change efforts demanded multiplied. In some sense, leadership capacity became the scarce resource.

   Time and again, we asked: Should we stop FrameworkS? Is J&J's organization exhausted? Are there too many other things to do? And time and again, after serious debate and consideration, the answer came back: No, we can't afford *not* to do FrameworkS. In the early days, it was necessary to hold several in quick succession to get the critical issues on the table, to deal with the rapidly changing health-care environment, to signal to the organization that the Executive Committee was serious about making change. But after the first few catalytic years, a more measured pace seemed to make sense.

   In the end, FrameworkS turned out to be a direct expression of the pace and scale of change that can be tolerated within the corporation. FrameworkS increased that pace and scale to the point where management felt J&J was changing at least as rapidly as the markets in which it participated.

2. **The evaluation process**. We collectively went into the FrameworkS process not knowing what would result. The Executive Committee believed that an effort like this was essential if J&J was to avoid the fate of IBM in the early 1990s. But short-term attempts to evaluate the efficiency and effectiveness of FrameworkS, had they been attempted, would have been inconclusive. The earliest we were really able to evaluate the process was two to three years into it; before that the benefits would not have been obvious enough to justify continuing the process. Several years later, people began to see what the payoffs really were.

What saved FrameworkS from being evaluated prematurely—this natural tendency by managers everywhere to measure and monitor processes across relatively short time frames—was the early and sustained commitment of Ralph Larsen, Bob Wilson, and Roger Fine. They maintained the company's commitment through the vulnerable first two to three years. They accepted only shorter-term evaluations that were focused on the process of the conversation itself: Have we raised critical issues? Have we challenged our current assumptions? Have we developed aspirations that are orders of magnitude different from those we started out with? Without their willingness to accept the ambiguities of such a nontraditional management process, it would have been prematurely closed down, rather than continue as it has for more than six years.

3. **Sources of resistance**. There were, not surprisingly, people who resisted the FrameworkS process. As we pointed out, resistance came in many forms—regional executives who wanted to run their own shows in the way they had always done it; operating company presidents who were convinced intellectually of the need to change, but who could not reinforce such change through behavior; corporate staff members who wanted to create institutional processes for change rather than support widely varied ad hoc efforts in various companies; even members of the Executive Committee who, once charged with leading change on a particular issue, found themselves unwilling to break down organizational rigidities. These barriers are not unique to J&J. What characterized the FrameworkS process was the unwavering insistence by Larsen, Wilson, Fine, and later Russ Deyo (when he took over administration of the process) that they find a way over or around the barriers.

4. **Going to the source**. Many of the barriers were overcome by "going to the source" in each of our FrameworkS sessions. The European FrameworkS sessions occurred in Europe, China's in China, Japan's in Japan. The analysis of innovative companies meant having to go to see innovative companies. In the end, we learned that experience is more convincing than analysis no matter how compellingly presented. This was key, and quite a hard sell in the beginning. But it was, in the end, what made FrameworkS real. "Being there" increased the sense of urgency that in turn increased the passion to implement. It took the subjects covered by FrameworkS out of the intellectual realm and put them into the visceral, emotional realm. This was the way to "sense the periphery" firsthand.

   Going to the source meant that preparation took longer—but that preparation was more effective. It meant that Executive Committee members were less concerned with formal evaluations of the FrameworkS process because they personally experienced the changes and impact themselves. Going to the source helped break down the sources of resistance and build up commitment. And it allowed the Executive Committee to overcome some of the emotional barriers to changing their mental models.

5. **Bringing the rest of the organization along**. If "going to the source" was critical for the participants in the FrameworkS process, then the challenge was in bringing FrameworkS to the rest of the 87,000-employee organization (or the more than eight hundred top managers of J&J's far-flung businesses). The answer came in many forms. Perhaps most dramatically, in what we called FrameworkS 9 and ultimately the What's New? effort, it meant bringing the top eight hundred to Los Angeles to experience things for themselves. It also meant broadcasting the events of the conference back to the operating companies around the world on a daily basis. In terms of formal method, Chairman Ralph Larsen set up a series of regular communications to employees: quarterly video broadcasts about key issues in the company that never failed to highlight FrameworkS efforts; a regular companywide newsletter devoted to FrameworkS; specific attention to FrameworkS in the annual meeting with shareholders. Even more important, Ralph Larsen, Bob Wilson, Jim Lenehan, Roger Fine, Russ Deyo, Bob Darretta, and

Ron Gelbman, as well as many other members of the Executive Committee and many of the Company Group Chairmen, who became critical players in the FrameworkS process, spent time in one-on-one conversations with their colleagues, in speeches to their employees, in discussions of strategic plans, in tours of their plants. They passed on the insights generated in the process throughout the organization. They incorporated the company's new aspirations into the ways they managed the businesses they oversaw. And it is mainly in this way that FrameworkS has changed how J&J works.

ASSESSING THE RESULTS

What has been the impact of FrameworkS? Looking back at the progress since the 1992 "wake-up call," Ralph Larsen, Bob Wilson, and their other senior J&J executives have made J&J into a very different place. Their willingness to reflect on critical, tough issues has played a crucial role in their success.

GENERAL ACCOMPLISHMENTS

Among J&J's accomplishments are:

- Highly tangible results, such as the launch of a corporationwide cost-competitiveness effort that eliminated more than $2 billion from the bottom line and created or helped to acquire several new multimillion-dollar businesses.
- Less intangible results include increased cross-functional and cross-division teamwork, greater risk taking, broader participation in addressing key strategic challenges, increased cohesiveness among senior managers, and better management development.
- Initiation of high-profile corporate-change initiatives focused on such areas as leadership building and innovativeness.
- A changed attitude about the pace of change. The rank and file now believe that change is the essence of competitiveness. J&J is more aggressively seeking change in all areas of its businesses—cost structure, products, organization, and people. The role of creative destruction stands alongside operating excellence as the twin pillars on which J&J's success is built.

There are other ways to look at the impact, however. One is to see it through the eyes of J&J executives and employees; the other is through the eyes of the outsider.

HOW THE J&J EXECUTIVES SEE IT

As the FrameworkS process unfolded, here are a few of the comments and assessments J&J's CEO and other members of the top team have made:

- "FrameworkS is not a finite project designed to produce a single new strategy or business venture by a certain date. Rather, it is an open-ended, ongoing process that is changing the way we think about our businesses, changing the way we relate to and work with one another, and encouraging the confidence and commitment that will be necessary for us to renew ourselves and remain a great and growing enterprise."

- "My reaction is that it has brought hundreds of executives into dealing with the complicated and profound issues we've got to deal with. FrameworkS has built a broad base of support for change. FrameworkS has changed my job as chairman. I've moved from a role of being a pusher and shover to the role of encouraging. I've never seen anything like it. I've never seen an organization as driven and self-motivated as the organization is today, and I attribute a lot of that to FrameworkS."

- "We are now looking much more across the corporation as a global entity versus staying within our silos. This is a chance for participants to step back and look at the whole competitive scene, and also to learn from executives within other parts of the organization. We are more likely to identify synergies. It finally puts the spotlight on key areas of opportunity. When you put a spotlight on it, turn it upside down, and look at it more closely, you get more insights."

- "FrameworkS has brought a fresh awareness of the implications of fundamental changes in industry structure—for example, increasing consolidation of competitors and increasing power of purchasers to the corporation. People are electrified by these changes, and they are willing to cooperate in ways they were unwilling to just a year ago."

- "It was very exciting to see people at all levels of the organization actively involved in shaping, and reshaping, the company."

Among the comments from participants who were not members of the Executive Committee:

- "Without FrameworkS, we wouldn't take much of a risk. What this has done is raise the risk profile at the top, and the perception of the [company's] willingness to take risks lower down—as a middle manager, I will be willing to put something forward now."
- "FrameworkS increased learning among the business heads and greatly increased communication. I learned things during FrameworkS that I just did not learn over my prior twenty years with the company. It empowered—a word I hate—the general managers a lot. Having the Executive Committee lay out what they expected was very helpful. It raised expectations a lot. It was a very motivational experience."
- "FrameworkS is a means of communicating with the Executive Committee and injecting reality into the decision-making process. The Executive Committee went out of touch five years ago, and FrameworkS has brought it into touch. Some terrific people need to be heard out on key issues, and this is a way to do that."
- "A collateral benefit is exposure to the Executive Committee, and vice versa. This makes other business interactions easier."
- "The cross-functional dialogue that has started and continues is fantastic. The Executive Committee's stock has gone up because of this. This has been very good for them. Their willingness to listen and take action has been seen by everybody."

OUR VIEW

We have been very pleased with the overall impact FrameworkS has had on J&J, although perhaps J&J's executives have expressed the impact more poignantly than we could. This has been a long journey. Certainly the efforts aimed at improving the adaptability of the corporation have had some measure of success. That is not to say, however, that there is not more to do. There is. The effort to dramatically increase the pace and scale of creative destruction, without sacrificing operational effectiveness, will remain a difficult balance to strike. More has to be done, particularly to stimulate substantial and transformational innovation. Perhaps some of the difficulty can be attributed to the difficulty of leading adaptive work.

As Ralph Larsen said, "The last thing they need is someone at headquarters telling them what to do." It will take more time to perfect the skills of leading adaptive work.

From the experience at J&J, however, we see that change is most effective when the people who drive the change have been personally engaged in generating urgency and in determining the shape and aspirations for change. We feel convinced that the semi-structured, open-ended nature of the FrameworkS process is the kind of jumping-off point that is necessary for companies like J&J that want to revolutionize the corporation and alter the pace and scale of both creation and destruction.

Intellectual stagnation is the great problem of large organizations. It is paramount to increase fertility in the field of ideas. The greatest responsibility of modern management is to develop the human intellect in order that it may express its talent.

ROBERT WOOD JOHNSON, 1959

Ralph Larsen summarized the impact the program has had in an assessment for *Chief Executive* magazine: "Is FrameworkS a single, simple approach to equipping an organization to deal with change? Absolutely not. But within the decentralized management structure of Johnson & Johnson, it has become a proven means of releasing energy throughout the corporation and focusing the eyes of the organization and its leadership on the two most important issues central to our future innovation and growth."

FrameworkS can be an important step in "increasing fertility in the field of ideas," a critical step in helping the corporation make the transformation from an operating organization to one that creates, operates, and trades at the pace and scale of the market, remaining fresh and vibrant for the future.

CHAPTER 12

The Ubiquity of
Creative Destruction

Joseph Schumpeter's ideas about the central role of entrepreneurism came into public debate in the 1930s but were drowned out by the vision and hope of Lord John Maynard Keynes. The rivalry between Schumpeter and Keynes was intense and well known. As the Great Depression sucked half of the GDP out of the United States and left a quarter of its workforce unemployed, Schumpeter's concepts were not seen as being as productive for reviving the weakened economy as were Keynes's proposals to use strong fiscal policy to cure the Depression. Schumpeter was bitterly disappointed that his voice had not been more widely heard.

But that was seventy years ago. Keynes's ideas, formed in the crucible of the depression, found their métier in the middle of the twentieth century. Most nations have now absorbed Keynes's lessons. Today, general economic conditions are quite different from those that dominated thinking during the Depression. Then companies remained on the S&P for a half century or more. Now companies remain on the list for two decades on average—and the average is rapidly falling. Investment in venture capital funds is at an unprecedented high level, as are venture capital expen-

Merger & Acquisition, 1890–1998

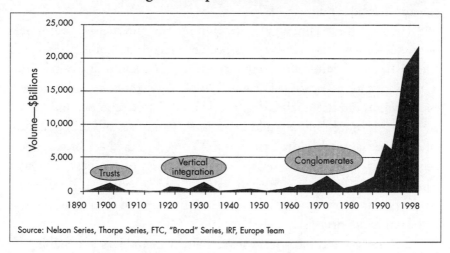

Source: Nelson Series, Thorpe Series, FTC, "Broad" Series, IRF, Europe Team

ditures. The level is so high, in fact, that one wonders whether the nation has sufficient talent to productively use these expenditures. Other signs of change are at all-time-high levels, as well, including the rate of mergers and acquisitions and the rate of corporate spin-offs.

While this pace of change probably will not be sustained in the long run, neither will it return to the levels of the '70s. There is simply too much potential for productive change for that to happen. The game of creative destruction will continue—and probably quicken in pace—in the United States.

THE FUTURE OF THE NEW ECONOMY

The New Economy is the dramatic manifestation of Schumpeter's ideas. We doubt that even Schumpeter anticipated a rate of change as extensive as the one we are currently experiencing.

The revolution is far from over. The economic and technological forces are working to accelerate it. In the key technologies driving the economy forward, each advance provides the basis for future advances. The cycle will last for a very long time. We are on the front end of a broad curve, which will continue to accelerate through our lifetimes. The Internet represents the most visible example. It has already begun to change virtually all industries in a permanent way. It has created the potential for both more efficient markets (as the 2,000 or so exchanges that have been established in the past five years indicate) and the more effective marketing of consumer goods and services.

Moreover, the technology underpinning the Internet—communications, computers, and software—is not yet nearing its limits. Broadband and wireless communications will increase the pace and utility of telecommunications for many years to come. It will take decades to build the necessary communication systems in the United States, Europe, and Japan, and perhaps more time to build them in the countries of Latin America, Southeast Asia, the Middle East, and in China. On the back of these new capabilities will come new services and new levels of business efficiency. The cost of interaction—that is, the cost of buying, selling, and delivering products among businesses and between businesses and their consumers—will continue to decrease.

Based on the advances in genetics (which themselves are enabled by better computer and software technology) we can expect substantial advances in health care, probably starting with diagnostic businesses and later involving whole new families of pharmaceuticals. The flow of new devices, drugs, and businesses coming from these advances can be expected to continue over several decades at the very least.

The path from where we are to where we will go will not be smooth, as we have pointed out many times. New companies will bring new ideas to the marketplace, and with them the inevitable reversal of fortunes that first attracted them. Losses will be an inevitable part of the march to a higher standard of living. The increasing pace of change, coupled with the increasing complexity of our society and our inability to accurately forecast the future, will assure that. Investors and managers can expect more turbulent markets as a permanent feature of the future. We have already seen spectacular price increases and decreases in many Internet stocks, such as Priceline.com and Amazon.com. More will certainly come. As a consequence, it will be more important than ever to find ways to hedge our investments, perhaps through the increasing use of derivative financial instruments such as options. But in the long run, enormous new value will be created in the economy as the new technologies are developed, combined, and exploited.

THE FAILURE OF INCREMENTALISM

The United States is not the first, or only, place where innovation has flourished, but it is the place where the processes of creative destruction have been maintained for the longest period of time and have affected the most people. The two are not the same. Japan is an instructive example. In the late nineteenth century and again in the mid–twentieth century, Japan rose to the ranks of a great power with breathtaking speed by determinedly applying Western technologies and methods. Once Japan became a world-class manufacturer in the late 1970s, however, further economic success demanded that it embrace creative destruction at the pace and scale of international markets. Japan attempted to compete by encouraging incremental innovation in important economic sectors, such as steel, shipbuilding, automobiles, and electronics. While they have been very successful in these areas, no one would claim that the Japanese have embraced the spirit of creative destruction. Quite the opposite. They have gone to great lengths to consolidate the power of the great companies and maintain the status quo. They are still wrestling with the issue today. They have aggressively tried to protect the assumption of continuity rather than embrace discontinuity. The Japanese approach, which couples a yearning for centralized control with incremental change, will be increasingly vulnerable. Now the world has moved ahead, and the Japanese are having trouble keeping up. It may take them decades to sort this out and reach a "new way."

South Korea provides a similar story. One of us attended a small breakfast a few years ago with former South Korean prime minister H. K. Lee, who made the point that the number-one issue facing South Korea, in his view, was increasing South Korea's innovativeness. He pointed out that the Korean "miracle" was based on copying the Japanese industrialization strategy. That strategy had now reached its limits. Korean labor rates had reached world levels, but productivity was below world-class levels, and technology access was being denied by non-Korean companies (most technology these days is traded for other technology rather than bought and sold). Moreover, Korean companies were extremely highly leveraged as a result of government-subsidized interest rates that were well below real market rates. The dam was bound to burst at some point, and Prime Minister Lee felt that innovation was the only way out. Since that time, the dam has burst, and many Korean companies had to seek bankruptcy protection. The failure to provide for indigenous capacity for creative destruction undermined the Korean miracle.

Lee recalled being present in the early days after the Korean War, when the economic policy of the country was being shaped. He said, "We felt that if we only achieved world-scale operations we would have a seat at the table. We would be respected members of the international economic community, and that was our goal. We were successful in reaching our goal." He went on, "Our strategy of industrial organization gave us the scale we sought. But when we got to the table, we found we had no seat. We were not welcome because we had copied what others had done. We had not built a capability to contribute to further advances, because we did not know how to innovate. Now we must learn." Since that time Korea has made progress in learning how to innovate, but to be competitive in the future, Koreans will have to do more than innovate—they, too, will have to learn to become masters of creative destruction.

Until now, developing countries seeking to bolster their economic standing have adopted the strategy of replicating existing innovations rather than attempting to develop the capability to nurture and develop new ones. While this strategy has proven temporarily successful, it has failed in the longer term, as the cases of Japan and Korea illustrate.

THE AMERICAN SYSTEM— DESIGNED FOR CREATIVE DESTRUCTION

In the United States we have been more aggressive in adopting the assumption of discontinuity. We have been much more willing to give up the reins of control to the individual. Why?

There are several policies that have been effective in providing a more permissive environment in the United States that encourages economic development—and thus fosters creative destruction. First, our capital markets are the most transparent and developed in the world. Investors have confidence in the information provided by our companies, and that gives them the confidence to invest. Without honest corporate reporting, there can be no honest investing. Second, our trade policies, by and large, encourage foreign competition, perhaps more so than many other countries' policies do. Foreign competition exposes our companies to the realities of global competition and keeps the incentives aligned for continual improvement. Third, we have, for now, a series of government policies—for example, tax policies that encourage capital investment, and provide tax credits for R&D expenditures, as well as patent laws—that encourage risk capital investment and establish the value of intellectual capital more aggressively than other countries' policies do. In addition, we have bankruptcy laws that provide for an orderly process of disposal of assets in the event that a company cannot continue to operate successfully. Moreover, our labor laws provide a safety net for our workforce, but also provide for more labor mobility than is seen in other countries. Finally, as difficult as our legislative processes are, they do allow for more rapid adjustment of our legal framework than is seen in other countries.

While improvements can be made in all these areas, the collective effect of the laws is a more aggressive acceptance, perhaps even encouragement, of creative destruction and the assumption of discontinuity than is seen in any other country in the world. The economic system that has evolved in the United States confers an advantage on U.S. corporations that other countries find difficult to match.

Economic systems that tie up or centralize the access to capital, or that have an insufficient base of scientific knowledge, or that try too hard to maintain continuity of employment or protect themselves from the force of external competition, find that in the long run their national economic productivity falters. This has been the case in many European, Asian, and Latin American countries. Releasing the forces of creative destruction is neither simple nor often sought by those in control.

The changes coming to Europe may rock current social and economic institutions to the core, including labor. Trying to hold off the inevitable pressure will not work; the capital markets are too powerful. Even with vast changes in the tax structure of Germany, it may be years yet until investors are convinced that the change is real and values are bid up accordingly. When this does take place, one can look forward to a rapid change in the established competitive order in Germany—and perhaps the rest of Europe.

In the developed world, we are in a time when a country's capacity to innovate has become one of the most important sources of its national power. The ability to accommodate creative destruction as a central element of national economic policy, whether explicitly or implicitly, has become one of the major drivers of economic growth. It will only increase in importance in the future.

COVERING THE COSTS OF
CREATIVE DESTRUCTION

The benefits of creative destruction are apparent: the potential for low inflation, low unemployment, and budget surpluses. But the forces of creative destruction, as we know, can also wreak havoc. In the '30s, the great objection to Joseph Schumpeter's ideas was that they did not deal with the consequences of the social upheaval they implied. And indeed that was the case. If the pace of change is going to increase, and it seems that it inevitably will, the social costs of industrial disruption—the number of people "left behind"—could also increase. Issues of retirement benefits, educational costs, medical costs, and social "safety nets" could all increase in intensity. We will need approaches to these problems, and today there is no agreement on these policies.

THE UBIQUITY OF
CREATIVE DESTRUCTION

We believe that all institutions benefit from the refreshing processes of creative destruction. We also believe that the forces of creative destruction are impossible to resist in the long term.

Failure to provide avenues for sufficient continual change—to create new options and to rid the system of old processes—eventually results in organizational failure, whether at the national, institutional, or individual level. If the forces of creative destruction are suppressed for long periods, the resulting ruptures can destroy institutions and individuals with astonishing speed and cruelty, as political and military revolutions have taught us consistently—from the time of the Reformation to the most recent revolutions in the Soviet Union and Serbia.

The benefit of legitimate capital markets is that they coordinate the wishes and capabilities of millions of individuals and through their relatively peaceful processes set an appropriate pace and scale of change. Legitimate capital markets allow divergent thinking to flourish if there is the potential for it. Without an active market, entrepreneurship can be suppressed, sometimes for decades.

This requires all organizations and institutions to think through how they will create a "place" for divergent thinking—how they will allow the competition between new and old ideas to take place. It will also require these institutions to determine when and how to let the forces of destruction act.

We believe that the lessons that hold for our organizations hold for the individual as well. Finding the time for divergent thinking while still holding a job or mastering a discipline at school is at least as difficult on the personal level as it is on the institutional level. Remaining open to new ideas without prematurely rejecting existing ones; maintaining a bias toward change rather than the status quo; changing at the pace and scale of our environment—all are personal challenges that we face as individuals. There are no easy prescriptions to offer, apart from recognizing and accepting such change and finding ways to adapt and respond to it.

In 1939, Schumpeter observed that "it is not [price and output] competition which counts, but the competition from the new commodity, the new technology, the new source of supply, the new type of organization." His observation, however, went unheard by policy makers concerned with the Depression and the onset of war. Today the importance of his insight cannot be overstated.

Whether we like it or not, we live in the discontinuous age. Corporate position and prestige are increasingly fleeting; cannibalization is critical; turnover is normal. We are a long way from the 1930s, when the ideas of Schumpeter and Keynes fought for attention. Long ago we learned the lessons of Keynes. Today we have to learn and digest Schumpeter's lessons.

Some object to applying Schumpeter's economic ideas to individual corporations, arguing that one should leave to the markets that which they do best—reallocation of resources. Corporations, such thinkers argue, not only cannot do this but should not do this, since it will divert their attention from the corporation's central task of managing or administering the operations of highly efficient companies.

We cannot accept this argument. It is an argument first made in Keynesian times, a time of continuity. Under the assumption of continuity, the lifeblood of the corporation was efficient operations. Corporations gave up very little if they abdicated the allocation of resources to the markets. Today the reverse is true. It is no longer good enough simply to operate well. Corporations have to operate and manage creative destruction at the pace and scale of the market, without losing control, or they will falter and fade. Managing for creative destruction is a substantial challenge that will increase in intensity in the coming years. Those corporations that abdicate the responsibility for resource reallocation to the markets are cooperating in their own demise. Companies unwilling or unable to play the game of creative destruction will inevitably be replaced. Like it or not, the age of continuity is forever gone. The very forces that make our capital economy so vibrant and resilient are the same forces that spawn discontinuity and creative destruction. Rather than simply acting as custodians of operational excellence, and being buffeted by the winds of change, we urge corporations and their leaders to be the captains of their fate, the masters of the forces of creative destruction that shape and renew the markets into the new millennium.

Appendix A
List of Companies

AEROSPACE AND DEFENSE

ATLANTIC RESEARCH CORP.
AVONDALE INDUSTRIES INC.
BANGOR PUNTA CORP.
BOEING CO.
CESSNA AIRCRAFT CO.
CORDANT TECHNOLOGIES INC.
FAIRCHILD INDUSTRIES INC.
GATES LEARJET CORP.
GENCORP. INC.
GENERAL DYNAMICS CORP.
GRUMMAN CORP.
GULFSTREAM AEROSPACE
HALTER MARINE GROUP INC.
HEICO CORP.

HOWMET INTERNATIONAL INC.
LOCKHEED MARTIN
MARTIN MARIETTA CORP.
MCDONNELL DOUGLAS CORP.
NEWPORT NEWS SHIPBUILDING
NORTHROP GRUMMAN.
RAYTHEON CO.—CL B
ROCKWELL INTL CORP.
ROHR INC.
TEXTRON INC.
TRACOR INC.
TRIUMPH GROUP INC.
WOODWARD GOVERNOR CO.

AIRLINES

AIRTRAN HOLDINGS INC.
ALASKA AIRGROUP INC.
AMERICA WEST AIRLINES INC.
AMR CORP.—DEL
ASA HOLDINGS
ATLANTIC COAST AIRLINES HLDG.
COMAIR HOLDINGS INC.
CONTINENTAL AIRLINES INC.
DELTA AIR LINES INC.
EASTERN AIR LINES
MESA AIR GROUP INC.

MIDWEST EXPRESS HOLDINGS
   INC.
NORTHWEST AIRLINES CORP.
PAN AM CORP.
PEOPLE EXPRESS AIRLINES INC.
PIEDMONT AVIATION INC.
SOUTHWEST AIRLINES
TIGER INTERNATIONAL
TRANS WORLD AIRLINES
UAL CORP.
USAIR GROUP

CHEMICALS, COMMODITY

AIR PRODUCTS & CHEMICALS INC.
AIRCO INC.
ALBEMARLE CORP.
ALLIEDSIGNAL INC.
ARCO CHEMICAL CO.
ARISTECH CHEMICAL CORP.
BORDEN CHEM&PLAST—LP COM
CALGON CARBON CORP.
CYTEC INDUSTRIES INC.
DOW CHEMICAL
DU PONT (E.I.) DE NEMOURS
ETHYL CORP.
GEON COMPANY
GEORGIA GULF CORP.
HERCULES INC.
LAWTER INTERNATIONAL INC.
MILLENNIUM CHEMICALS INC.
MINERALS TECHNOLOGIES INC.

MONSANTO CO.
NL INDUSTRIES
OLIN CORP.
OM GROUP INC.
PENNWALT CORP.
PRAXAIR INC.
QUANTUM CHEMICAL CORP.
REICHHOLD CHEMICALS INC.
ROHM & HAAS CO.
SCHULMAN (A.) INC.
SOLUTIA INC.
STAUFFER CHEMICAL CO.
STERLING CHEMICALS INC.
UNION CARBIDE CORP.
VALHI INC.
VISTA CHEMICAL CO.
WELLMAN INC.
WITCO CORP.

CHEMICALS, SPECIALTY

AGRIUM INC.
AKZONA
BAROID CORP.
BEKER INDUSTRIES
BETZ DEARBORN INC.
BUSH BOAKE ALLEN INC.
CABOT CORP.
CAMBEX CORP.
CELANESE CORP.
CHEMFIRST INC.
CK WITCO CORP.
DE SOTO INC.
EMERY INDUSTRIES INC.
FERRO CORP.
FOSTER GRANT INC.—CL A
FREEPORT MCMORAN INC.
FULLER (H. B.) CO.
G-I HOLDINGS INC.
GRACE (W.R.) & CO.
GREAT LAKES CHEMICAL CORP.
IMC GLOBAL INC.
INMONT CORP.
INTL FLAVORS & FRAGRANCES
INTL SPECIALTY PRODS INC.

LILLY INDS INC.—CL A
LOCTITE CORP.
LUBRIZOL CORP.
LYONDELL CHEMICAL CO.
MACDERMID INC.
METHANEX CORP.
MISSISSIPPI CHEMICAL CORP.
MOORE (BENJAMIN) & CO.
MORTON INTL INC.
NALCO CHEMICAL CO.
NATIONAL STARCH & CHEMICAL
PETROLITE CORP.
PHOSPATES RES PARTNERS—LP
PPG INDUSTRIES INC.
RPM INC.-OHIO
SCOTTS COMPANY
SEQUA CORP. -CL A
SHERWIN-WILLIAMS CO.
TERRA CHEMICALS INTL.
THIOKOL CORP.
VALSPAR CORP.
VIGORO CORP.
WD-40 CO.

COMPUTER HARDWARE

AMDAHL CORP.

APEX INC.

APOLLO COMPUTER INC.

APPLE COMPUTER INC.

ASCEND COMMUNICATIONS INC.

AST RESEARCH INC.

BAY NETWORKS INC.

CABLETRON SYSTEMS

CASCADE COMMUNICATIONS
    CORP.

CHIPCOM CORP.

CIPHER DATA PRODUCTS INC.

CIRRUS LOGIC INC.

CISCO SYSTEMS INC.

COMMODORE INTL LTD.

COMPAQ COMPUTER CORP.

COMPUTER CONSOLES

CONNER PERIPHERALS

CONVEX COMPUTER CORP.

CRAY RESEARCH

CREATIVE TECHNOLOGY LTD.

CYLINK CORP.

DATA GENERAL CORP.

DATAPOINT CORP.

DATAPRODUCTS CORP.

DELL COMPUTER CORP.

DIALOGIC CORP.

DIGI INTERNATIONAL INC.

DIGITAL EQUIPMENT

DYNATECH CORP.

DYSAN CORP.

ELECTRONICS FOR IMAGING INC.

EMC CORP./MA

EMULEX CORP.

EXABYTE CORP.

FLOATING POINT SYSTEMS INC.

FORE SYSTEMS INC.

GATEWAY INC.

GOULD INC.

HEWLETT-PACKARD CO.

HMT TECHNOLOGY CORP.

INTELLIGENT SYSTEM CP.

INTERGRAPH CORP.

INTL BUSINESS MACHINES CORP.

IOMEGA CORP.

ISC SYSTEMS CORP.

JTS CORP.

LEXMARK INTL GRP INC.—CL A

MAXTOR CORP.

MAXTOR CORP.

MICRON ELECTRONICS INC.

MINISCRIBE CORP.

MIPS COMPUTER SYSTEMS INC.

MMC NETWORKS INC.

MTI TECHNOLOGY CORP.

NCR CORP.

NETWORK APPLIANCE INC.

NETWORK EQUIPMENT TECH INC.

NETWORK GENERAL CORP.

NETWORK SYSTEMS CORP.

QANTEL CORP.

QUANTUM CORP.

ROLM CORP.

RSA SECURITY INC.

S3 INC.ORP.ORATED

SANDISK CORP.

SCI SYSTEMS INC.

SCM MICROSYSTEMS INC.

SEAGATE TECHNOLOGY

SECURE COMPUTING CORP.

SEQUENT COMPUTER SYSTEMS
    INC.

SILICON GRAPHICS INC.

SPERRY CORP.

STANDARD MICROSYSTEMS CORP.

STORAGE TECHNOLOGY CP

STRATUS COMPUTER INC.

SUN MICROSYSTEMS INC.

SYMBOL TECHNOLOGIES

SYNOPTICS COMMUNICATIONS
    INC.

TANDEM COMPUTERS INC.

TANDY CORP.

TELEX CORP.

TERADATA CORP.

TSL HOLDINGS INC.

UNISYS CORP.

VERBATIM CORP.

WANG LABS INC.

WESTERN DIGITAL CORP.

WYSE TECHNOLOGY INC.

XIRCOM INC.

XYLAN CORP.

COMPUTER SOFTWARE

ACCLAIM ENT INC.
ACXIOM CORP.
ADOBE SYSTEMS INC.
ADVANTAGE LEARNING
   SYSTEMS INC.
ADVENT SOFTWARE INC.
ALDUS CORP.
ALLERION INC.
AMERICAN SOFTWARE—CL A
ARDENT SOFTWARE INC.
ASHTON-TATE CO.
ASK GROUP INC.
ASPECT DEVELOPMENT INC.
ASPEN TECHNOLOGY INC.
AUTODESK INC.
AUTOMATIC DATA PROCESSING.
AVANT CORP.
AVT CORP.
AXENT TECHNOLOGIES INC.
BANYAN SYSTEMS INC.
BBN CORP.
BDM FEDERAL—CL A
BEA SYSTEMS INC.
BISYS GROUP INC.
BMC SOFTWARE INC.
BOOLE & BABBAGE INC.
BROADVISION INC.
BRODERBUND SOFTWARE INC.
CADENCE DESIGN SYSTEMS INC.
CCC INFORMATION SVCS GRP INC.
CHECK POINT SOFTWARE
CHEYENNE SOFTWARE INC.
CITRIX SYSTEMS INC.
CLARIFY INC.
COGNOS INC.
COMPUTER ASSOCIATES INTL INC.
COMPUTERVISION CORP.
COMPUWARE CORP.
CONCORD COMMUNICATIONS
   INC.
CONTINUUM INC.
COREL CORP.
CSG SYSTEMS INTL INC.
CULLINET SOFTWARE INC.
DAISY SYSTEMS CORP.
DAVIDSON & ASSOCIATES INC.
DENDRITE INTERNATIONAL INC.
DISCREET LOGIC INC.

DOCUMENTUM INC.
DST SYSTEMS INC.
EDWARDS J D & CO.
ELECTRONIC ARTS INC.
ENGINEERING ANIMATION INC.
EPICOR SOFTWARE CORP.
FILENET CORP.
FISERV INC.
FORTE SOFTWARE INC.
FTP SOFTWARE INC.
GENESYS TELECOMM LABS INC.
GT INTERACTIVE SOFTWARE
HARBINGER CORP.
HBO & CO.
HENRY (JACK) & ASSOCIATES
HNC SOFTWARE INC.
HOGAN SYSTEMS INC.
HUMMINGBIRD COMMUNICATNS
   LTD.
HYPERION SOFTWARE CORP.
HYPERION SOLUTIONS CORP.
I2 TECHNOLOGIES INC.
IDX SYSTEMS CORP.
INDUS-MATEMATIK INTL
INFORMIX CORP.
INPRISE CORP.
INSO CORP.
INTEGRATED SYSTEMS INC.
INTUIT INC.
LANDMARK GRAPHICS CORP.
LEARNING COMPANY INC.
LEGATO SYSTEMS INC.
LEGENT CORP.
LHS GROUP INC.
LOTUS DEVELOPMENT CORP.
MACROMEDIA INC.
MANAGEMENT SCIENCE AMERICA
MANUGISTICS GROUP INC.
MAPICS INC.
MEDIC COMPUTER SYSTEMS INC.
MENTOR GRAPHICS CORP.
MERCURY INTERACTIVE CORP.
MICROS SYSTEMS INC.
MICROSOFT CORP.
MIDWAY GAMES INC.
NATIONAL INSTRUMENTS CORP.
NETMANAGE INC.
NETSCAPE COMMUNICATION

COMPUTER SOFTWARE *(continued)*

NETWORKS ASSOCIATES INC.
NEW ERA OF NETWORKS INC.
NOVELL INC.
ORACLE SYSTEMS CORP.
PANSOPHIC SYSTEMS INC.
PARAMETRIC TECHNOLOGY
PEOPLESOFT INC.
PLATINUM TECHNOLOGY
   INTL INC.
PROGRESS SOFTWARE CORP.
PROJECT SOFTWARE & DEV INC.
QAD INC.
QUADRAMED CORP.
RADIANT SYSTEMS INC.
RATIONAL SOFTWARE CORP.
REALNETWORKS INC.
REMEDY CORP.
SABRE HLDGS CORP.—CL A
SAGA SYSTEMS INC.
SANCHEZ COMPUTER ASSOCS INC.
SAPIENT CORP.
SHARED MEDICAL SYSTEMS CORP.
SHL SYSTEMHOUSE INC.
SIEBEL SYSTEMS INC.
SOFTWARE PUBLISHING CORP.
SPYGLASS INC.

STERLING COMMERCE INC.
STERLING SOFTWARE INC.
STRUCTURAL DYNAMICS
   RESEARCH
SUNGARD DATA SYSTEMS INC.
SYBASE INC.
SYMANTEC CORP.
SYNOPSYS INC.
SYSTEM SOFTWARE ASSOCIATION
SYSTEMS & COMPUTER TECH
   CORP.
TECHNOLOGY SOLUTIONS CO.
THQ INC.
TOTAL SYSTEM SERVICES INC.
TRANSITION SYSTEMS INC./MA
TRNSACTN SYS ARCHTCTS—CL A
TSI INTL SOFTWARE LTD.
TYMSHARE INC.
UCCEL CORP.
USWEB CORP.
VANTIVE CORP.
VERITAS SOFTWARE CO.
VIASOFT INC.
VIEWLOGIC SYSTEMS INC.
VISIO CORP.

CRUDE OIL EXTRACTION AND REFINING

ADOBE OIL & GAS CORP.
ADOBE RESOURCES CORP.
ALBERTA ENERGY CO LTD.
AMAREX INC.
AMERAC ENERGY CORP.
AMERADA HESS CORP.
AMOCO CORP.
ANADARKO PETROLEUM CORP.
APACHE CORP.
APACHE PETROLEUM—LP
APCO OIL CORP.
ASAMERA INC.
ASHLAND OIL INC.
ATLANTIC RICHFIELD CO.
ATWOOD OCEANICS
BARRETT RESOURCES CORP.
BELCO PETROLEUM CORP.
BELCO OIL & GAS CORP.
BERRY PETROLEUM—CL A
BJ SERVICES CO.
BOW VALLEY ENERGY INC.
BROWN (TOM) INC.
BURLINGTON RESOURCES INC.
CABOT OIL & GAS CORP.—CL A
CHESAPEAKE ENERGY CORP.
CHEVRON-GULF
CHIEFTAIN INTL INC.
CITIES SERVICE CO.
CLARK OIL & REFINING CORP.
CLIFFS DRILLING CO.
COASTAL CORP.
CONOCO INC.-OLD
CONSOLIDATED OIL & GAS
CREOLE PETROLEUM CORP.
CROSS TIMBERS OIL CO.
CROWN CENTRAL PETROL—CL B
CRUTCHER RESOURCES CORP.
CRYSTAL GAS STORAGE INC.
DEVON ENERGY CORPORATION
DIAMOND OFFSHRE DRILLING
   INC.
DIAMOND SHAMROCK INC.
DOME PETROLEUM LTD.
DYCO PETROLEUM CORP.
EARTH RESOURCES CO.
EEX CORP.
ENERGY RESERVES GROUP

ENRON CORP.
ENSCO INTERNATIONAL INC.
ENSTAR CORP.-DEL
EOG RESOURCES INC.
EQUITY OIL CO.
EXXON CORP.
FALCON DRILLING COMPANY INC.
FELMONT OIL CO.
FINA INC.—CL A
FORCENERGY INC.
FOREST OIL CORP.
FREEPORT MCMORAN OIL & GAS
   CO.
FRONTIER OIL CORP.
GEARHART INDUSTRIES INC.
GENERAL AMERICAN OIL CO-TX
GETTY-SKELLY
GLOBAL INDUSTRIES LTD.
GLOBAL MARINE INC.
GLOBAL NATURAL RESOURCES
   INC.
GREAT BASINS PETROLEUM
GREY WOLF INC.
GULF CORP.
HALLIBURTON CO.
HAMILTON OIL CORP.
HELMERICH & PAYNE
HOLLY CORP.
HOME OIL CO LTD.
HOUSTON OIL & MINERALS CORP.
HOWELL CORP.
HUDSON'S BAY OIL & GAS CO.
HUGHES TOOL CO.
HUSKY OIL LTD.
INEXCO OIL
KELLEY OIL & GAS PTRS—LP
KERR-MCGEE CORP.
LEVIATHAN GAS PIPELINE—LP
LOUIS DREYFUS NAT GAS CORP.
LOUISIANA LAND & EXPLORATION
LOUISIANA LAND OFFSHORE EXPL
MAPCO INC.
MARINE DRILLING CO INC.
MAXUS ENERGY CORP.
MCMORAN OIL & GAS CO.
MESA INC.
MGF OIL CORP.—COM

CRUDE OIL EXTRACTION AND REFINING *(continued)*

MITCHELL ENERGY & DEV—CL B
MOBIL CORP.
MORAN ENERGY INC.
MURPHY OIL CORP.
NABORS INDUSTRIES
NATOMAS CO.
NEWFIELD EXPLORATION CO.
NICKLOS OIL & GAS CO.
NOBLE DRILLING CORP.
NOBLE AFFILIATES INC.
NUEVO ENERGY CO.
NUMAC ENERGY INC.
OCCIDENTAL PETROLEUM CORP.
OCEAN DRILLING & EXPLO-
  RATION
OCEAN ENERGY INC.
OCEANEERING INTERNATIONAL
OKC CORP.
ORYX ENERGY CO.
PACIFIC RESOURCES INC.
PARKER DRILLING CO.
PATTERSON ENERGY INC.
PENNZ ENERGY CO.
PETRO-LEWIS CORP.
PHILLIPS PETROLEUM CO.
PHOENIX RESOURCES CO.
PIONEER NATURAL RESOURCES
  CO.
PLAINS PETROLEUM COMPANY
POGO PRODUCING CO.
PRIDE INTERNATIONAL INC.
PRODUCTION OPERATORS CORP.
QUAKER CHEMICAL CORP.
QUAKER STATE CORP.
R & B FALCON CORP.
RANGER OIL LTD.
REMINGTON OIL & GAS CP—CL B
RIGEL ENERGY CORP.
ROWAN COS INC.
ROYAL DUTCH PET—NY REG
SABINE CORP.
SAGE ENERGY CO.

SANTA FE INTERNATIONAL CORP.
SANTA FE ENERGY PRTNRS—LP
SANTA FE SNYDER CORP.
SCEPTRE RESOURCES LTD.
SCHLUMBERGER LTD.
SEDCO INC.
SKELLY OIL CO.
SNYDER OIL CORP.
SOLV EX CORP.
SOUTHLAND ROYALTY CO.
STANDARD OIL CO.
STONE ENERGY CORP.
SUN ENERGY PARTNERS—LP
SUNOCO INC.
SUPERIOR OIL CO.
SUPRON ENERGY CORP.
TALISMAN ENERGY INC.
TELECO OILFIELD SERVICES INC.
TESORO PETROLEUM CORP.
TEXACO-GETTY
TOSCO CORP.
TOTAL PETROLEUM OF
  N AMERICA
TRANSCO EXPLORATION—LP
TRANSOCEAN OFFSHORE INC.
TRANSTEXAS GAS CORP.
TRITON ENERGY LTD.
ULTRAMAR DIAMOND SHAMROCK
UNION PACIFIC RESOURCES GRP.
UNION TEXAS PETRO HLDGS INC.
UNITED CANSO OIL & GAS LTD.
UNITED MERIDIAN CORP.
UNOCAL CORP.
UNOCAL EXPLORATION CORP.
USX-MARATHON GROUP
VALERO ENERGY CORP.
VASTAR RESOURCES INC.
VINTAGE PETROLEUM INC.
WEATHERFORD ENTERRA INC.
WESTERN ATLAS INC.
WESTERN CO OF NO AMER
WISER OIL CO.

ELECTRIC UTILITIES

AES CORP.
ALLEGHENY POWER SYSTEM
ALLIANT CORP.
AMEREN CORP.
AMERICAN ELECTRIC POWER
ATLANTIC ENERGY INC.
AVISTA CORP.
BEC ENERGY
BLACK HILLS CORP.
CAROLINA POWER & LIGHT
CENTERIOR ENERGY CORP.
CENTRAL & SOUTH WEST CORP.
CENTRAL HUDSON GAS & ELEC
CENTRAL VERMONT PUB SERV
CILCORP INC.
CINERGY CORP.
CIPSCO INC.
CITIZENS UTILITIES
CLECO CORP.
CMP GROUP
CMS ENERGY CORP.
COMMONWEALTH ENERGY SYSTEM
CONECTIV INC.
CONSOLIDATED EDISON INC.
CONSTELLATION ENERGY CORP.
DESTEC ENERGY INC.
DOMINION RESOURCES INC.
DPL INC.
DQE INC.
DTE ENERGY
DUKE POWER CO.
EASTERN UTILITIES ASSOC.
EDISON INTERNATIONAL
EL PASO ELECTRIC CO.
EMPIRE DISTRICT ELECTRIC CO.
ENERGY EAST CORP.
ENOVA CORP.
ENTERGY CORP.
FIRST ENERGY CORP.
FLORIDA PROGRESS CORP.
FPL GROUP INC.
GPU INC.
GULF STATES UTILITIES CO.
HAWAIIAN ELECTRIC INDS
HEIZER CORP.
IDACORP. INC.
IES INDUSTRIES INC.

ILLINOVA CORP.
INTERSTATE POWER CO.
IOWA RESOURCES INC.
IOWA SOUTHERN INC.
IOWA-ILLINOIS GAS & ELEC
IPALCO ENTERPRISES INC.
KANSAS CITY POWER & LIGHT
KANSAS GAS & ELECTRIC
KU ENERGY CORP.
LG&E ENERGY CORP.
LONG ISLAND LIGHTING
MADISON GAS & ELECTRIC CO.
MAGMA POWER CO.
MIDAMERICAN ENERGY
    HOLDINGS
MINNESOTA POWER & LIGHT
MONTANA POWER CO.
NEW CENTURY ENERGIES INC.
NEW ENGLAND ELECTRIC SYSTEM
NIAGARA MOHAWK POWER
NISOURCE INC.
NORTHEAST UTILITIES
NORTHERN STATES POWER/MN
NORTHWESTERN CORP.
OGDEN PROJECTS INC.
OGE ENERGY CORP.
ORANGE & ROCKLAND UTILITIES
OTTER TAIL POWER CO.
PACIFICORP
PECO ENERGY CO.
PENNSYLVANIA POWER & LIGHT
PG&E CORP.
PINNACLE WEST CAPITAL
PORTLAND GENERAL CORP.
POTOMAC ELECTRIC POWER
PSI RESOURCES INC.
PUBLIC SERVICE CO. OF N. MEX
PUBLIC SERVICE ENTRP.
PUGET SOUND POWER & LIGHT
RELIANT ENERGY INC.
ROCHESTER GAS & ELECTRIC
SCANA CORP.
SIERRA PACIFIC RESOURCES
SIGCORP. INC.
SOUTHERN CO.
SOUTHWESTERN PUBLIC SVC CO.
TECO ENERGY INC.

ELECTRIC UTILITIES *(continued)*

TEXAS UTILITIES CO.
THERMO ECOTEK CORP.
TNP ENTERPRISES INC.
UNICOM CORP.
UNISOURCE ENERGY CORP. HLD CO.

UNITED ILLUMINATING CO.
UTAH POWER & LIGHT
WESTERN RESOURCES INC.
WISCONSIN ENERGY CORP.
WPS RESOURCES CORP.

PULP AND PAPER PRODUCTS

ACX TECHNOLOGIES INC.
AMERICAN BUSINESS PRODS/GA
BEMIS CO.
BOHEMIA INC.
BOISE CASCADE CORP.
BOWATER INC.
BOWATER PULP & PAPER
BROOKS-SCANLON INC.
BUCKEYE TECHNOLOGIES INC.
CARAUSTAR INDUSTRIES INC.
CHAMPION INTERNATIONAL
    CORP.
CHESAPEAKE CORP.
CONSOLIDATED PAPERS INC.
CROWN ZELLERBACH
DENNISON MFG CO.
DIAMOND INTERNATIONAL CORP.
FEDERAL PAPER BOARD CO.
FORT HOWARD CORP.
FORT JAMES CORP.
GAYLORD CONTAINER CP
GLATFELTER (P.H.) CO.
GREAT NORTHERN NEKOOSA
    CORP.
HAMMERMILL PAPER CO.
INTL PAPER CO.

KIMBERLY-CLARK CORP.
LONGVIEW FIBRE CO.
LOUISIANA-PACIFIC CORP.
MEAD CORP.
OLINKRAFT INC.
PENTAIR INC.
POPE & TALBOT INC.
POTLATCH CORP.
RIVERWOOD INTL CORP.
ROCK-TENN COMPANY
SAXON INDUSTRIES
SCHWEITZER-MAUDUIT INTL INC.
SCOTT PAPER CO.
SMURFIT-STONE CONTAINER
    CORP.
SOUTHWEST FOREST INDUSTRIES
ST REGIS CORP.
STONE CONTAINER CORP.
TAMBRANDS INC.
TEMPLE-INLAND INC.
UNION CAMP CORP.
WAUSAU-MOSINEE PAPER CORP.
WESTVACO CORP.
WEYERHAEUSER CO.
WILLAMETTE INDUSTRIES

PHARMACEUTICALS

ABBOTT LABORATORIES
ADVANCED TISSUE SCI—CL A
AGOURON PHARMACEUTICALS
   INC.
ALLERGAN INC.
ALLIANCE PHARMACEUTICAL CP
ALPHARMCA INC.—CLA
ALZA CORP.
AMERICAN HOME PRODUCTS
   CORP.
AMGEN INC.
ANESTA CORP.
AVIRON
BARR LABORATORIES INC.
BIO TECHNOLOGY GENERAL
   CORP.
BIOCHEM PHARMA INC.
BIOCRAFT LABORATORIES INC.
BIOGEN INC.
BOSTON LIFE SCIENCES INC.
BRISTOL MYERS—SQUIBB
CATALYTICA INC.
CENTOCOR INC.
CHATTEM INC.
CHIRON CORP.
CIRCA PHARMACEUTICALS INC.
COLUMBIA LABORATORIES INC.
COOPER LABORATORIES
COR THERAPEUTICS INC.
COULTER PHARMACEUTICAL INC.
CYTOGEN CORP.
DIAGNOSTIC PRODUCTS CORP.
DURA PHARMACEUTICALS INC.
FOREST LABORATORIES—CL A
GELTEX PHARMACEUTICALS INC.
GENENTECH INC.
GENETICS INSTITUTE INC.
GENZYME CORP.
GILEAD SCIENCES INC.
HUMAN GENOME SCIENCES INC.
HYBRITECH INC.
ICN PHARMACEUTICALS INC.-DEL
ICOS CORP.ORATION
IDEC PHARMACEUTICALS CORP.
IDEXX LABS INC.
IMMUNEX CORP.
INHALE THERAPEUTIC SYSTEMS

INTERNEURON PHARMACEUTI-
   CALS
ISIS PHARMACEUTICALS INC.
IVAX CORP.
JONES PHARMA INC.
KEY PHARMACEUTICALS INC.
LIFE TECHNOLOGIES INC.
LIGAND PHARMACEUTICAL—CL B
LILLY (ELI) & CO.
LIPOSOME COMPANY INC.
LYPHOMED INC.
MARION MERRELL DOW INC.
MEDICIS PHARMACEUT CP—CL A
MEDIMMUNE INC.
MERCK & CO.
MILES LABORATORIES INC.
MILLENNIUM PHARMACTCLS INC.
MOLECULAR BIOSYSTEMS INC.
MYLAN LABORATORIES
NBTY INC.
NORTH AMERICAN VACCINE INC.
PARKE DAVIS & CO.
PATHOGENESIS CORP.
PERRIGO COMPANY
PFIZER INC.
PHARMACIA & UPJOHN INC.
PHARMACYCLICS INC.
PROTEIN DESIGN LABS INC.
QLT PHOTOTHERAPEUTICS
REGENERON PHARMACEUT
REXALL SUNDOWN INC.
RHONE-POULENC RORER
RICHARDSON-VICKS INC.
ROBERTS PHARMACEUTICAL CORP.
ROBINS (A.H.) CO.
SANGSTAT MEDICAL CORP.
SCHERBER (R P)/DE
SCHERING-PLOUGH
SEARLE (G.D.) & CO.
SEPRACOR INC.
SEQUUS PHARMACEUTICALS INC.
SEROLOGICALS CORP.
SICOR INC.
SIGMA-ALDRICH
SQUIBB CORP.
STERLING DRUG INC.
SYNERGEN INC.

PHARMACEUTICALS *(continued)*

SYNTEX CORP.
TECHNE CORP.
THERAGENICS CORP.
TRANSKARYOTIC THERAPIES INC.
TWINLAB CORP.
U S BIOSCIENCE INC.

VERTEX PHARMACEUTICALS INC.
WARNER-LAMBERT CO.
WATSON PHARMACEUTICALS INC.
XOMA LTD.
ZENITH LABORATORIES

SEMICONDUCTORS

ADVANCED MICRO DEVICES
ALPHA INDUSTRIES INC.
ALTERA CORP.
AMERICAN MICROSYSTEMS
AMKOR TECHNOLOGY INC.
ANALOG DEVICES
ATMEL CORP.
BENCHMARK ELECTRONICS INC.
BURR-BROWN CORP.
CHIPS & TECHNOLOGIES INC.
CREE RESEARCH INC.
CTS CORP.
CYPRESS SEMICONDUCTOR CORP.
CYRIX CORP.
DALLAS SEMICONDUCTOR CORP.
DII GROUP INC.
FLEXTRONICS INTERNATIONAL
GALILEO TECHNOLOGY LTD.
GENESIS MICROCHIP INC.
INTEGRATED DEVICE TECH INC.
INTEL CORP.
INTL RECTIFIER CORP.
JABIL CIRCUIT INC.
JDS UNIPHASE CORP.
KEMET CORP.
LATTICE SEMICONDUCTOR CORP.
LEVEL ONE COMMUNICATIONS
   INC.
LINEAR TECHNOLOGY CORP.
LSI LOGIC CORP.

M/A-COM INC. .
MAXIM INTEGRATED PRODUCTS
MEMC ELECTRONIC MATRIALS
   INC.
MICREL INC.
MICROCHIP TECHNOLOGY INC.
MICRON TECHNOLOGY INC.
MONOLITHIC MEMORIES INC.
MOSTEK CORP.
NATIONAL SEMICONDUCTOR
   CORP.
NEOMAGIC CORP.
PLEXUS CORP.
PMC-SIERRA INC.
POWER INTEGRATIONS INC.
REMEC INC.
SANMINA CORP.
SDL INC.
SEMTECII CORP.
SIPEX CORP.
SMART MODULAR TECHNOLGS
   INC.
SOLECTRON CORP.
TEXAS INSTRUMENTS INC.
TRANSWITCH CORP.
UNITRODE CORP.
VITESSE SEMICONDUCTOR CORP.
VLSI TECHNOLOGY INC.
XILINX INC.
ZILOG INC.

SOAPS AND DETERGENTS

ALBERTO-CULVER CO—CL B
AVON PRODUCTS
BLOCK DRUG—CL A
CHESEBROUGH-POND'S INC.
CHURCH & DWIGHT INC.
CLOROX CO/DE
COLGATE-PALMOLIVE CO.
DIAL CORP.ORATION
ECOLAB INC.
FABERGE INC.
FACTOR (MAX) CO—CL A
HELENA RUBINSTEIN INC.

HELENE CURTIS INDS.
LANVIN-CHARLES OF THE RITZ
LAUDER ESTEE COS INC.—CL A
MARY KAY CORP.
NCH CORP.
NEUTROGENA CORP.
NOXELL—CL B
PROCTER & GAMBLE CO.
PUREX INDUSTRIES INC.
REVLON INC.—CL A
SHULTON INC.

SURGICAL AND MEDICAL PRODUCTS

ACUSON CORP.
ADAC LABORATORIES
AFFYMETRIX INC.
AMERICAN HOSPITAL SUPPLY
AMERICAN STERILIZER CO.
AMSCO INTERNATIONAL
ARROW INTERNATIONAL
ARTERIAL VASCULAR ENGR INC.
ATL ULTRASOUND INC.
BALLARD MEDICAL PRODUCTS
BARD (C.R.) INC.
BAXTER INTERNATIONAL INC.
BECTON DICKINSON & CO.
BIOMET INC.
BOSTON SCIENTIFIC CORP.
CLOSURE MEDICAL CORP.
COLLAGEN AESTHETIC INC.
CONMED CORP.
CORDIS CORP.
CUTTER LABORATORIES INC.—CL A
DATASCOPE CORP.
DENTSPLY INTERNATL INC.
DEPUY INC.
GRAHAM FIELD HEALTH PDS
GUIDANT CORP.
GULF SOUTH MED SUPPLY INC.
HAEMONETICS CORPORATION
HEART TECHNOLOGY INC.
INSTRUMENTATION LABS INC.
INVACARE CORP.
KENDALL CO.

MARQUETTE MEDICAL SYS.
MAXXIM MEDICAL INC.
MEDTRONIC INC.
MENTOR CORP.
MINIMED INC.
MIRVANT MEDICAL TECHNOLO-
    GIES
NARCO SCIENTIFIC INC.
NELLCOR PURITAN BENNETT INC.
OEC MED SYS INC.
PATTERSON DENTAL CO.
PERCLOSE INC.
PHYSIO-CONTROL INTL CORP.
PSS WORLD MEDICAL INC.
PURITAN-BENNETT CORP.
RESMED INC.
RESPIRONICS INC.
SCIMED LIFE SYSTEMS INC.
SCOTT TECHNOLOGIES INC.
SHERWOOD MEDICAL INDS INC.
SOFAMOR/DANEK GROUP INC.
SPACELABS MED INC.
ST JUDE MEDICAL INC.
STERIS CORP.
STRYKER CORP.
SUMMIT TECHNOLOGY INC.
SUNRISE MEDICAL INC.
TECNOL MEDICAL PRODUCTS
    INC.
THERMEDICS INC.
THERMO CARDIOSYSTEMS

SURGICAL AND MEDICAL PRODUCTS *(continued)*

THERMOTREX CORP.
U S SURGICAL CORP.
VENTRITEX INC.

VISX INC./DE
VITAL SIGNS INC.
XOMED SURGICAL PRODS.

TELEPHONE AND TELECOMMUNICATIONS

ACC CORP.
ADVANCED TELECOMMUNICA-
TIONS
ALC COMMUNICATIONS INC.
ALIANT COMMUNICATIONS INC.
ALLTEL CORP.
AMERICAN TELE & TELEGRAPH
AMERITECH CORP.
BELL ATLANTIC CORP.
BELLSOUTH CORP.
C TEC CORP.
CALL-NET ENTERPRISES—CL B
CENTEL CORP.
CENTURY TELEPHONE ENTER-
PRISE
CINC.INNATI BELL INC.
CONTEL CORP.
E SPIRE COMMUNICATIONS INC.
ELECTRIC LIGHTWAVE—CL A
EXCEL COMMUNICATIONS INC.
FRONTIER CORP.
GTE-CONTEL
ICG COMMUNICATIONS
IDT CORP.
INTERMEDIA COMMUNICATNS
INC.
ITC DELTACOM INC.
IXC COMMUNICATIONS INC.
LCI INTERNATIONAL INC.
MCI COMMUNICATIONS

MCI WORLDWIDE COMMUNICA-
TIONS
MCLEODUSA INC.—CL A
NEXTLINK COMM INC.—CL A
NTL INC.
NYNEX CORP.
PACIFIC GATEWAY EXCHANGE INC.
PACIFIC TELECOM INC.
PACIFIC TELESIS GROUP
PRIMUS TELECOMM GROUP INC.
QWEST COMMUNICATION INTL.
INC.
ROSEVILLE COMMUNICATIONS
RSL COMMUNICATIONS—CL A
SBC COMMUNICATIONS
SOUTHERN NEW ENG TELECOMM
SOUTHERN NEW ENG TELEPHONE
SPRINT (CENTEL)
STAR TELECOMMUNICATIONS
INC.
TALK.COM INC.
TELEGLOBE INC.
TELEPHONE & DATA
TELEPORT COMM GRP—CL A
U S WEST INC.
VIATEL INC.
WINSTAR COMMUNICATIONS
WUI INC.

TRUCKING AND AIR COURIER

AIRBORNE FREIGHT CORP.
AMERICAN FREIGHTWAYS CORP.
ARKANSAS BEST-NAVAJO
ARNOLD INDUSTRIES INC.
CAROLINA FREIGHT CORP.
CON FRGHTWY-EMERY-PURLTR
CONSOLIDATED FREIGHTWAYS CP
EMERY-PUROLATOR
FEDERAL EXPRESS CORP.
HEARTLAND EXPRESS INC.
HUNT (JB) TRANSPRT SVCS INC.
IU INTERNATIONAL CORP.
KNIGHT TRANSPORTATION INC.

LANDSTAR SYSTEM INC.
LEASEWAY TRANSPORTATION
    CORP.
LEE WAY MOTOR FREIGHT INC.
M S CARRIERS INC.
MCLEAN TRUCKING CO.
OVERNITE TRANSPORTATION
PUROLATOR COURIER CORP.
ROADWAY SERVICES INC.
SWIFT TRANSPORTATION CO. INC.
USFREIGHTWAYS CORP.
WERNER ENTERPRISES INC.
YELLOW CORP.

Appendix B
Managerial Approach of
Principal Investors

	Typical Corporations	LBO Association
Purpose and Structure	Organized in perpetuity (long holding times— several decades; divisional structure)	Organized for limited life of fund (short holding time—several years; corporate structure with boards)
Control	Controls, often from senior levels. Single management approach; focus on information flows. Old rules hold; rules slow to change. No responsibility for finance and tax at manager level. "Understanding" rather than contracts. Stability in positions.	Monitors, not controls. Multiple approaches; focus on compensation, key crisis points, and key financings. Managers obliged to assimilate new rules of the game. Responsible for finance and tax. Written contracts. Focus on changing people if they don't perform.
Decentralization	Corporate headquarters; extensive staff	No corporate headquarters. Very small staff. (Paid for by fee of 2% of assets under management.)
Synergies	Essential to concept of leverage. Cross-subsidization possible. Consolidated accounts.	Not considered; ignored. Cross-subsidization impossible. No consolidated accounts.
Compensation	Complex system using surrogates for market value but often based on assets under management. Narrow range of increases. No decreases.	Simple system, tied to market. Wide range of increases possible. Decreases possible.

Appendix C
Dynamic Performance Analysis (DPA)

Dynamic Performance Analysis, or DPA, is a set of analytic techniques designed to reveal the underlying dynamics of companies, industries, and capital markets. DPA is specifically designed to avoid some of the implicit—and, we believe, limiting—assumptions of conventional analysis, which we will call Static Performance Analysis, or SPA.

We believe that DPA gives a more accurate portrayal of the state of the economy, an industry, or a company than do the conventional SPA analyses, on which DPA builds. There are two essential differences between DPA and SPA. First is the focus DPA places on understanding dynamics—that is, time-dependent cause-and-effect relationships. Unlike SPA, DPA does not presume equilibrium, although equilibrium can be revealed if it is present. Second, DPA explicitly does not assume that the distribution of results from competitive market processes are normally distributed around an average, as often SPA implicitly assumes. DPA goes to great lengths to observe the actual distribution of results from large samples over extended periods of time. Given these two differences, we believe that SPA is a special case of DPA.

The need to understand dynamic performance is clear, but until now most of the methods used extensions of static analysis rather than seeking to develop dynamic methods from the beginning. As a consequence of using DPA, we have reached conclusions about the nature of corporate performance and the forces driving that performance that are different from many others.

LIMITATIONS OF SPA

SPA is the common set of analyses used to diagnose historic corporate performance, and it is sometimes used as a basis for forecasting future corporate performance. Many of these techniques use rules of thumb based either on the past or on simple extrapolations of the past. These techniques are not designed to detect discontinuities or substantial changes in longer-term performance. As a consequence, SPA rarely does detect these discontinuities. Failure to detect discontinuity can lead to forecasting failures, because past relationships between cause and effect are erroneously expected to hold into the future.

SPA analyses typically cover periods of two to five years, and may occasionally extend to ten-year periods, neglecting what we call "The Minimum Unit of Analysis," or the business cycle. Generally, the time periods are selected with a reference to the current year, so they may go back two, five, or ten years from today, independent of the economy's or industry's position in the current economic cycle. Such comparisons are often misleading about the causes of past performance and therefore misleading about future possibilities and probabilities.

SPA implicitly presumes continuity and thus may produce results that confirm the embedded assumption. SPA can falsely reveal outstanding (or exceptionally poor) corporate performance, which is in fact not due to company actions but to industry or national economic effects, or the time period selected. Classic examples of "excellence" often err in this way, identifying, for example, SmithKline Beecham or Bristol-Myers Squibb as outstanding performers, when in fact their performance is indistinguishable, in a statistical sense, from that of the pharmaceutical industry overall.

The traditional SPA can misanalyze cause and effect either because a particularly good or bad period in the economic cycle is selected, or because the duration of the period examined is too short to be economically significant. Often SPA techniques fall into the trap of assuming the future will be more like than unlike the past. In making this assumption, SPA ignores the dynamic feedback loops in the economy (for example, between buyers and sellers, or between corporations and their investment analysts or regulators).

SPA is also powerless to explain such phenomena as the regular variation in the returns to investors in cyclical businesses, even though the cycle of the business is relatively well known. Nor does SPA provide a compelling rationale for the existence of "bubbles" in stock prices and their driving forces. DPA can readily offer explanations for both these phenomena and other complex phenomena like them. As a result, DPA dramatically reduces the rate of false-positive conclusions that are an artifact of the analytic method selected.

Finally, when SPA tackles the topic of statistics they often assume a normal bell-shaped distribution of results. We know, however, from a great deal of experience that often results are not distributed in a bell shape but rather some other shape. These different shapes result in different views on the probability of events occurring (how does the "once-in-a-century" hurricane occur twice in a decade in the United Kingdom, for example), or different views on the risk one faces or even the potential rewards.

DIFFERENCES BETWEEN DPA AND SPA

DPA does not seek to reject conventional economic analysis, but it does not rely totally on them. Specifically, DPA is built to enhance the understanding of rivalry, barriers to entry and exit, the relationship between industry structure, corporate conduct, and corporate performance, and the role of analyst expectations in influencing outcomes. DPA seeks to place all these effects in an explicitly dynamic context, not in a static context.

DPA is not proposed as a substitute for SPA, just as nuclear physics is not a substitute for Newtonian physics. Indeed, the basic framework for DPA analyses is the same as that for SPA—for example, the key balance of power between suppliers and buyers, the price-setting role of the marginal producer, the importance of barriers to exit and entrance. Rather, DPA builds on SPA and puts it into context. There are many situations where the simpler techniques of SPA will suffice. DPA is most useful in uncovering causes of long-term change and alerting the analyst to potential sources of long-term risk. DPA provides context for SPA.

There are six primary differences between DPA and SPA:

- First, DPA's primary focus on investors and their expectations as an explicit part of the analysis of the potential for perhaps temporary value creation.
- Second, DPA explicitly acknowledges the potential importance of feedback and has developed methods to detect its possible presence. DPA techniques seek to avoid making the assumption of continuity; in fact, they are designed to spot discontinuities such as the oil shocks of the '70s, or the rapid deterioration of the computer hardware industry of the early '80s, or the emergence of a restructured telecommunications market after the breakup of the Bell System. DPA finds continuity if it is there. If it is not, then discontinuity is revealed.
- Third, DPA focuses on the cycle of TRS returns as the basic time unit of analysis. DPA acknowledges that the selection of time period can dramatically affect the conclusions drawn from SPA. For example, if two companies in the same industry are competing but one is early in its cycle and is improving in performance, while the other is late in its

cycle and watching performance deteriorate, DPA will not judge one as better than the other until the two are compared at similar points in their cycle. SPA may not consider this possibility, and thus may conclude that one company is inherently superior to the other.

- Fourth, DPA seeks to put performance analysis in a dynamic statistical context so that one may easily understand whether, if a change is seen, the change is likely to be meaningful. SPA often does this as well, but there are special problems that have to be solved if one is going to attempt this in a dynamic fashion with a small number of companies. For example, non-bell-shaped (Gaussian) distributions and year-to-year changes in the shape of the distribution itself can play havoc with using common measures such as averages and variations from those averages.

- Fifth, unlike static performance analysis, DPA looks at a wide range of performance periods and examines them from many different perspectives.

- Sixth, DPA does not presume a normal distribution of results but rather uses empirical methods to gauge the most probable shape of the distribution.

SPA seems as if it were designed to focus on more mature businesses, operating in a slowly changing environment. SPA is well suited for value investors. DPA is more focused on growth investors—their concerns and their risks. By focusing on the interaction of linear and nonlinear systems, DPA provides more insight into longer-term sources of risk than does SPA.

More advances will be made in DPA techniques over time, since DPA is at a relatively early stage of development.

ORIGINS OF DPA

DPA is an outgrowth of the S-curve and discontinuity analyses that were fashioned in the mid-'80s as a result of the work done to support the writing of *Innovation: The Attacker's Advantage.* Our family of analyses developed incrementally/organically as the needs emerged. We did not know at the beginning that we were going to need to invent a new analytic method.

These analyses suggested that there were regular patterns of performance and these patterns were not straight-line projections of the past. Rather, industries start up and follow a very regular pattern of initially slow progress, then a rapid acceleration for a while until the maximum rate of progress is reached, and then a steady decline until equilibrium (either static or dynamic—e.g., cyclical) is established, as their potential or limit is approached. The pattern is shown in the following exhibit:

S-Curve

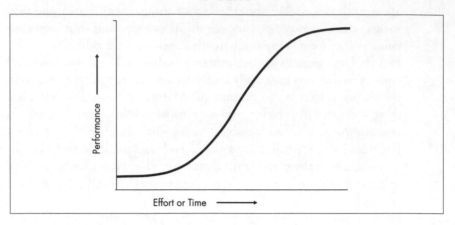

One of the implications of the S-curve is that productivity, a key determinant of economic success, varies in a regular but perhaps unexpected way. Productivity is nothing more than output, or performance, divided by input. Put another way, it is the slope of the curve above. It begins at a low level as everyone learns the new approach, then accelerates rapidly as the easier problems are solved, and then begins to collapse, just at the point some expect it to accelerate, because the limits of the S-curve are being reached and only the very tough problems remain to be solved. As the limit is being approached, the problems are getting harder faster than the problem solvers are getting smarter. The result is a dramatic fall-off, which sets up the opportunity for an attacker to enter the field if a better, and often different, approach can be found.

Productivity

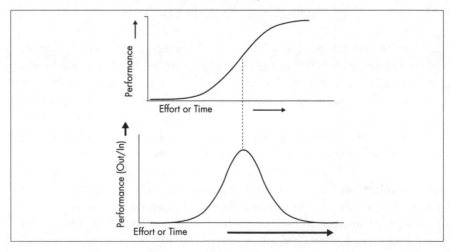

As the evolution begins to approach maturity, a discontinuity can result, changing the basic competitive structure of the industry. This has been the case many times in electronics, pharmaceuticals, consumer products, transportation, and other fields. Discontinuities are the vortex of the "gales of creative destruction" that Schumpeter described half a century ago. We represent the discontinuity as shown in the following exhibit:

Discontinuity Between S-curves

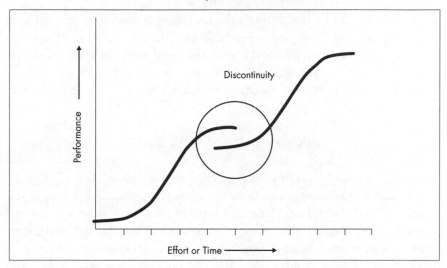

These analyses are not always relevant (for example, in analyzing the performance of the oil industry) because of exogenous events that overwhelm any regular economic process. But if the techniques are not appropriate they automatically demonstrate nonsense results, which indicates to analysts that they have to look elsewhere for answers.

BASIC QUESTIONS DPA SEEKS TO ANSWER

DPA seeks to see the company in an industry context and an industry in a national context.

As with SPA, DPA seeks an answer to the question How much of the observed company performance is due to managerial action and how much is due to other factors, such as industry or national economic conditions? The question is key, because it underpins the performance evaluation and reward systems (the internal feedback/control systems of the corporation). The answer to this query also shapes the key question management must ask: Should we focus on improving our internal operations or should we be seeking an adjustment in our portfolio (to make an investment or a sale)? If the answer is internal, management can control it. If it is external, management cannot directly control it other than through affecting the industry structure (merger or spin-off) or political action.

The basic question of the sources of performance gives rise to other key questions of concern to management, such as:

- Where is the power—with the attacker or the defender? How has the power changed over time, and why?
- Will the leader lose during a discontinuity, as has often been the case historically? How and when will the transition from defender to attacker occur? What are the economics to the attackers and defenders? What are the economics of attack, and how does profit flow?
- How will the effects of analysts' forecasts affect our strategy?

BASIC DPA ANALYSES

SPA often implicitly imagines relationships in business as "linear" relationships—that is, the more one puts in, the more one gets out. The proportion does not change over time. These relationships are simple to understand and communicate. They are also simple to analyze, since they involve straightforward, low-level mathematics. Often these simple relationships give rise to rules of thumb—for example, multiply the earnings by a price-to-earnings multiple to get the stock price.

There are some situations in business where these relationships and the shortcuts built on them provide accurate answers, particularly in the very short term. But as the period of analysis extends to multiple years, the probability that relationships will follow these simple linear patterns is greatly reduced. More likely the relationships are more complex, and the complexity confounds accurate, unambiguous interpretation. In the longer term, substantial feedback often exists. For example, analysts begin to expect stocks to outperform and they build these expectations into their models. At some point, the company cannot keep up with the constantly expanding expectations and it underperforms. As it begins to underperform, analysts change their models to reduce their expectations. Feedback between expectations and performance has emerged.

Feedback can, and often does, lead to cycles that are much more complex to analyze than are simple linear relationships. Examples of these more complex patterns include the way in which a new product substitutes for an old one, the way product prices react to the announcement of the construction of a new plant, and the way stock prices react to the emergence of a new category of products (the Internet bubble). Feedback systems can be very complex to analyze, since the strength of the feedback itself can change. Feedback—and the changes in feedback over time—is the explanation behind the admonition to leaders everywhere: "Beware: the organization you lead contains the seeds of its own destruction." The job of DPA is to find those seeds early on and to understand how they work in order to enhance their chances of success or to dull them.

Specifically, DPA is a baker's dozen set of basic analyses that are capable of revealing and understanding these underlying patterns and complexities.

1. S-CURVE ANALYSIS

S-curves represent the relationship between input (e.g., either resources or time) and output (e.g., product performance, or sales, or earnings). These relationships show a classic pattern of slow initiation, followed by rapid progress, which is then followed by deceleration as an asymptote, or limit, is reached. These patterns are called S-curves after their shape, which is an S tacked at the bottom left and drawn out to the top right.

Key questions include: What limits the present approach? How quickly will that limit be approached? What alternatives are available that might exceed the present limit? Who possesses the power to implement those approaches? When are they likely to use that power?

The mathematics of S-curves were best described in 1971 by Fisher and Pry, who asserted that all products grow by substitution for existing products. They imagined that the rate of substitution was proportional to the amount of product that had already been substituted and the proportion of the total product yet to be substituted for. If the amount of product was very small, the rate of substitution would be very small, even though the amount to be substituted for was large because there was so little experience in the art of substitution. As that experience grew, the amount substituted for would be greater and the rate of substitution would rise. Near the end of the cycle the rate would slow.

The approach Fisher and Pry developed has been repeated in many other fields—for example, epidemiology. Diseases spread in exactly the way Fisher and Pry imagined one product substitutes for another. Networks grow this way as well—for example, networks of facsimile machines or Internet sites. In the very early days, there is no one to hook up to so the rate of penetration is slow. After a while, when there are more and more people hooked into the network, the utility of hooking into the network increases, and so does that rate of hookup. Eventually, nearly everyone who is going to hook up has hooked up, and the rate of increase slows again. This is the classic S-curve, which combines both positive and negative feedback systems in its structure.

In verbal mathematical terms the basic (differential) equation is written as:

The rate of change = constant * (the proportion of the total substitution that has occurred) * (the proportion of the substitution that has not occurred)

The constant in this equation relates to the rate of substitution. It is called a rate constant. If it is high, the substitution is fast. If it is low, the substitution is slow.

Since the total amount of substitution is 100%, the proportion not yet substituted for is 100% minus the proportion that has been substituted for.

If the proportion substituted for is X, the constant is k, and time is t, then the mathematical equation is:

$$dx/dt = k * (x) * (1 - x) \qquad \text{Equation 1}$$

This equation can be solved to show the relationship between the proportion substituted and time. That equation is written as:

$$x = .5 * \{1 - \tanh[(t - t_{mid})/t_{crit}]\} \qquad \text{Equation 2}$$

t_{mid} and t_{crit} are two time constants that result from solving the equations. t_{mid} is the year the substitution is half completed. t_{crit} is the time it takes for the substitution to go from 10% complete to 90% complete. It is a rate constant. By including t_{mid} and t_{crit}, the rate constant "k" is eliminated. "tanh" is the "hyperbolic tangent," a basic geometric function that is strange to most people who are not engineers. It is a mathematical *function*. A function is an explicit relationship between two quantities. For example, we can define a function that we will call 2X. What 2X does is convert any value of X into a value of 2*X. If X = 5, then the function is equal to 10. If X = 200, then the function is equal to 400. "Tanh" works in exactly the same way, although the results would be different from 2X. In the case of Equation 2, the value for the quantity inside the brackets that come immediately after "tanh", $[(t-t_{mid})/t_{crit}]$, plays the role of X in 2X. If a value is provided for $[(t-t_{mid})/t_{crit}]$, "tanh" will give a number that can then be used in Equation 2 to find the answer. All computers have "tanh" built into their mathematical tables, so the function is easy to use. Equation 2 is the mathematical expression of the S-curve.

Given this equation, the analyst's job is to determine the constants t_{mid} and t_{crit}. Once this is done, the history of the S-curve can be used to forecast the future, if one believes the S-curve forecast will represent the future.

To test the robustness of the S-curve approach, we have determined t_{mid} and t_{crit} for evolution of sales in each industry. The overall fit of the industry experience is quite good, as shown in the following graph:

Sales Evolution Patterns

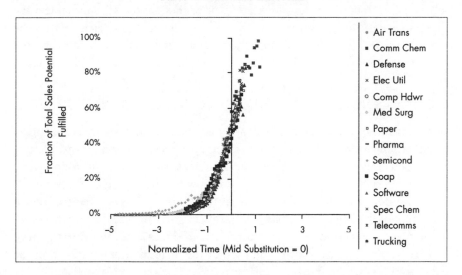

We have not included the oil industry in this analysis, since its prices—and therefore sales—have been so strongly affected by the formation and evolution of OPEC.

The overall pattern is quite clear. It is also clear that the model is not a perfect fit, at least with the constants we used. The semiconductor industry had a bit of a faster start than normal, and the chemical industry in its maturity is acquiring a cyclical pattern, which is not unexpected, rather than the straightforward "topping out" that the simple Fisher-Pry model assumes.

The time constants that were used to develop these curves tell us something about the rate at which the industry is changing. It is not surprising that the slowest evolution comes from commodity chemicals and the fastest from software. This is in accord with our intuition.

One final point should be made about this formulation of the S-curve: The slope of the S-curve, as pointed out above, is very similar to the bell-shaped curve commonly associated with random processes. The curve derived from an understanding of randomness is known as a normal distribution, referring to the expected distribution of outcomes if a process is normal. If one assumes that the various companies in the economy are each at some state of their own S-curve, then it is not unreasonable to assume that their growth patterns will be distributed in proportion to the slope of the S-curve. By examining these distributions, one should in principle be able to easily determine whether the underlying processes in the economy derive from random processes or an S-curve. The complication is that the normal distribution and the slope of the S-curve are almost impossible to differentiate, in any practical sense, from one another. Thus it is almost impossible to differentiate between the possible underlying mechanisms producing the results being observed from these distributions alone, since they are indistinguishable. One has to resort to other analyses to argue the differences. We believe that the great weight of the evidence supports the S-curve hypothesis rather than the randomness hypothesis.

2. DISCONTINUITY AND LONG-TERM-RISK ANALYSIS

S-curves often end in discontinuity. Discontinuity analysis seeks to understand when a new S-curve is about to begin, and estimates how and when it will interact with the existing S-curve. Discontinuities can occur for a variety of reasons, including the emergence of a new technology (e.g., the Internet, or computer software); a new approach (e.g., hub-and-spoke reorganization of airline traffic patterns); a change in industry structure (e.g., a merger of two large players; governmental intervention, as in the case of the Department of Justice breaking up the old Bell System; or the formation of a cartel, as in the case of OPEC in the '70s).

Discontinuities can lead to nondiversifiable risks for the investor and for management. DPA also seeks to identify and classify long-term risks (sudden changes from an apparently regular pattern) rather than shorter-term variations in performance, as is often the case with SPA.

While the discontinuities are wild, they are not without their own predictable characteristics. We believe that discontinuities occur when they do, last as long as they do, and have the effects that they do for fundamental economic reasons—often, at present, discoverable only after the fact, but nevertheless discoverable.

At the simplest level, discontinuities occur when the costs of the attacking business become equal to, and then less than, the costs of the defending business. It is at that moment that cash is being transferred out of the bank accounts of the defenders and into the accounts of the attackers. In reality, one has to consider the specifics of two different costs. The first is the *full cost* necessary to reach the target levels of returns—for example, a 15% return on invested capital. These costs include all the cash costs for supporting the business (including the costs of developing, making, selling, distributing, and servicing the product) as well as depreciation of capital equipment, amortization of goodwill, and profit for the bond and equity holders.

The second cost is the *cash cost*. This is the "rock-bottom" cost needed to avoid losing cash. Cash costs are always less than the full costs. They do not include depreciation, amortization, and profit for the equity holders (although interest for the debt holders is part of the cash cost in the vast majority of cases). The difference between the cash costs and the full costs is called the *margin*.

In practice, the definition of costs—a seemingly straightforward exercise—can become a bit more complicated. If one is running a nationalized industry, from the point of view of the government, taxes that in a normal business are considered part of cash costs can be, if required, considered part of margin. The government can decide to forgo these payments from the company in order to meet other objectives. This is happening in the United States, where local authorities give tax abatements to companies to encourage them to locate their facilities in the area. Another example is provided by Internet equity providers, who do not ask that cash costs be returned in the short run, hoping that the company they are investing in will establish such a strong position that it will be able to eventually operate in the black. Normally, an equity provider would insist on profitable operations at the full-cost level, but so eager are investors to capture the value implied by the growth potential of the Internet these days, they are willing to gamble that the payoffs will eventually be there. And for some, but not all, they will be.

In the vast majority of commerce, however, we can understand the essence of what is going on only by considering full and cash costs. These costs are generally declining for both the attacker and the defender, but they are falling faster for attackers, who are earlier in the evolution of their business than are the defenders. On the other hand, the attacker's costs are generally higher in the beginning than the defender's, since the attacker is just getting started. The result is a crossover point, the point where the attacker's cost becomes equal to, and then less than, the defender's cost. Since the attackers and defenders are both concerned with cash and full costs, there are actually four points of intersection, as the following graph shows:

Discontinuity Timing

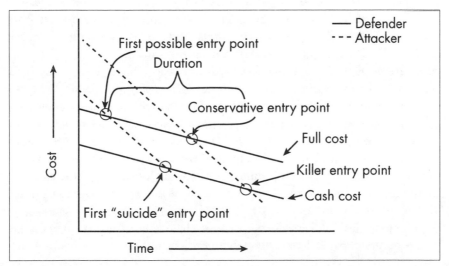

The simplest point to understand in this exhibit is the "conservative entry point." This is the point where the full cost for the defender and attacker are equal. At this point, if the defender wants to defend, it can do so by cutting prices (or the equivalent move of increasing the value of the product or service to the customer with no increase in price), and thus cut into its margins. To meet this defense, the attacker will have to reciprocate by cutting prices and cutting into its margins. It is a rough game, and the ultimate winner is the competitor with the lowest cash costs.

The earliest point at which it makes conventional economic sense to attack is when the cash costs of the attacker are equal to the full costs of the defender. We call this the "point of naked attack," because the attacker is economically quite vulnerable at this point. The attacker will sacrifice all profit margin but will not be losing out-of-pocket cash as long as the defender does not react, which is highly unlikely. The defender is much more likely to retaliate by cutting prices without risking negative cash flows, thus bringing real economic harm, and perhaps death, to the attacker. There are few successful attacks at this point, but many are attempted nevertheless.

For the extremely conservative attacker, waiting until full costs are less than the cash costs of the defender is a safe strategy. Few get to pursue it, however, because the game is often over by this point. There is one other significant point at which an attacker can attack, and that is where the cash costs of the attacker are equal to the cash costs of the defender. The full cost of the attacker at this point is usually no less than the full cost of the defender. Often it is more. But the attacker, if it is willing to not recover its full cost, can compete at the defender's price. The defender's main weapon, reducing price to its cash costs in order to bleed the attacker, cannot work at this point, because the attacker has the same cash costs as the defender. The deep-pockets defense is still applicable here, since the defender can subsidize its cash costs from another division or the corporate coffers. But unlike the point of naked attack, the defender will bear real pain here, and thus may be less likely to be as aggressive. There is still plenty of risk and exposure for the attacker here, but less so than at the first, naked, point of attack.

When the discontinuity is over, it will have taken an amount of time roughly equal to that between the points of naked and killer attack. To the customer's benefit, prices will have fallen substantially, by an amount roughly equal to the defender's original margins plus the value of the relative productivity improvements over the duration of the discontinuity. So it can be a meaningful amount—often 25% or more of the price at the beginning of the discontinuity.

Our empirical market evidence suggests that the transformation of market shares occurs in parallel with the process of price change:

Discontinuity Timing

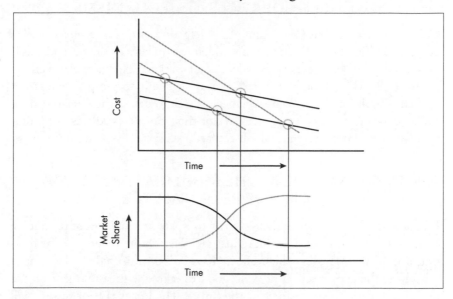

Of course, in real commerce, matters are rarely this simple (if the foregoing discussion can be called simple). First there is lack of information about the present. The defender and attacker rarely know each other's cost structures. They rarely know each other's productivity rates and how they will play out. They rarely know the proclivity of the other side to take the risk of a price war. Neither knows how the customer will react, and neither can predict the degree of cross-subsidization, willingness to deplete reserves, and cleverness in shifting some of the costs onto others (e.g., suppliers). So the principles outlined above may be hard to apply in practice. Nevertheless, it might be comforting to know that at least there are some principles at work, that they do explain what has happened, and that they can be used to predict what might happen in the future. Having these principles, if not a tool kit for their application, is better, we think, than believing that the discontinuity and its effects cannot be understood. They can be.

While there are no systematic statistics that we know of, we believe that one-third of all attackers die in the attack because they attack too early. They underestimate the resourcefulness and resiliency of the defender. We think another third die because they attack too late. In their efforts to avoid risk, they take the ultimate risk. They wait until positions have been established by others. Of the remaining one-third, the majority fail because while they have a vision of what they would like to accomplish, they cannot put that vision into practice. Most attackers fail. But the attack succeeds. The wave after wave of attackers constitutes Schumpeter's gale.

3. FEEDBACK ANALYSIS: THE EVOLUTION OF CYCLES AND SELF-CORRECTING MECHANISMS

Each effect has a cause that can ultimately undermine the effect. Prices become too high or low, resources are added too quickly or slowly, and this is what leads to the basic cyclical behavior of all markets. The nature and effects of this feedback cannot be ignored, but are difficult to grasp if one is not trained to look for them. Feedback analyses seek to detect these relationships and understand their consequences, if not their causes. Feedback is ubiquitous because control systems, which are feedback systems, are ubiquitous.

4. UNDERSTANDING THE MINIMUM DATA UNIT— CYCLES OF PERFORMANCE

Feedback, and the processes that give rise to it, are responsible for producing cycles in the economy and within industries. These cycles determine the minimum unit of time over which effects have to be measured. Unless one is measuring the cycle itself, it does no good to take one measurement on the upside of a cycle to try to forecast the future. The linear rule of thumb will not work. Thus the minimum unit of analysis in DPA is determined by the length of the business cycle, since this is the only unit that can give insight into the nature of the system. Since, in the United States, the TRS cycle has varied between three and four years, this is the minimum unit of time one must use to draw any conclusions about performance. Analyses that look at shorter periods of time run the risk of mistaking random variation in the system (noise) for meaningful effect. To be safe, one has to look at two cycles, since one cycle can be aberrant. We have used a seven-year period as the basic unit of analysis, since this covers two full cycles of TRS variation.

5. NOISE-REDUCTION ANALYSIS

Noise (randomness) is always present along with the regularities that the system contains. The noise has to be filtered out before an analysis of the regularities can be made. The trick is to sort out one from the other without confusing them. What is random is dependent on the decision one has to make using the data. What is noise to the CEO is signal to the day trader. A basic filtering method is to use seven-year averages, since this will filter out the noise of the variation in the business cycle. There are other methods available, but they are not explored in this study.

6. RENORMALIZATION ANALYSIS: THE ECONOMY, THE INDUSTRY, AND THE COMPANY

To understand the sources of a company's performance, one has to understand the contributions to the company's performance that are made by the overall state of the economy and industry in which the company participates. Industry performance can—and often does—ride on general economy conditions, and one has to account for this. Company performance can—and often does—ride on industry performance, so this gap has to be understood as well. Renormalization analysis allows a visualization of these complex relationships.

7. INVESTOR EXPECTATIONS ANALYSIS: THE CREATION OF BUBBLES

DPA takes the investor's perspective, seeking to understand how companies create value over time, not just once. Unlike traditional SPA, DPA focuses as much on the investment community and its expectations (and the changes in its expectations) as it does on the company and industry, since the expectations of future free cash flow influence important strategic variables for the corporation, such as market cap, P/E ratio, and TRS. There are two specific attributes of DPA that distinguish it:

1. First, DPA focuses on TRS. As a result, DPA can result in a perspective different from that of methods focused just on EPS, mutiples, growth rates, or market capitalizations.
2. Second, DPA focuses attention on investor forecasting methods, since these methods are intimately related to the values of equities and how those values change over time.

One particular application of our understanding of investor forecasting methods is the way analysts forecast price-to-earnings ratios. This is particularly relevant to the understanding of attacker performance that comes directly from an understanding of the inevitable evolution of industries and companies.

Let us apply this approach to the evolution of "bubbles." First, assume that the evolution of an industry follows the S-curve that we have described above. Second, assume that analysts, unable to credibly forecast the long-term future of an industry, fall back on "accepted" approaches—say, multiples analysis—based on current earnings and the short-term forecasts for these earnings. Essentially these analysts forecast the future based on the near-term past. This approach has a long history.

The graph below shows the S-curve. If one assumes, for the moment, that this curve is both knowable and known, one can use it to calculate the present value of the future cash flow streams of the corporation. This value is conventionally assumed to be equal to the market value of the corporation in any given year. Given the S-curve, the Net Present Value (or NPV) can be calculated for each year, resulting in a new curve, the NPV curve, which is similar to, but not the same as, the S-curve. The difference between the curves stems from the discounting process itself.

Evolution of Earnings and Market Value

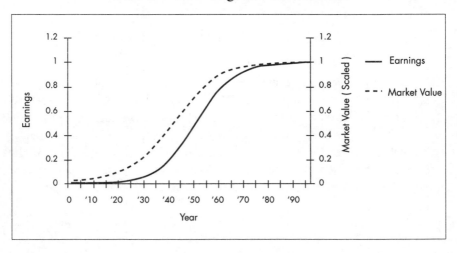

The important point is that the discounting process accelerates the evolution of market value. Market value is expected to develop more rapidly than earnings growth due to the discounting process alone.

Given the evolution of market value, it is easy to calculate the total return to shareholders in this situation where the analysts have accurately forecasted the future. In this case, as the next graph shows, the total return to shareholders will always be exactly equal to the cost of equity—which, in this example, is assumed to be 10%.

This result often surprises executives, many of whom may not believe it is realistic. The TRS should reflect the growth, but this is not the case. Rather, if analysts can correctly foresee the future, they can value it—and in so doing, they can make sure that at all points in time the annual returns will be equal. The implication is that the price-to-earnings ratio will be very high in the early years. After all, no matter how small the sales base is, if the next fifty years of sales could be accurately foreseen—because that is our assumption in this case—then the value would be very high, as the graph on the bottom of the next page shows.

Evolution of Earnings, Market Value, and TRS
with Perfect Forecasting

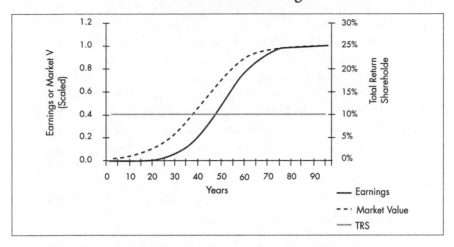

Evolution of Earnings, Market Value, TRS, and P/E
with Perfect Foreknowledge

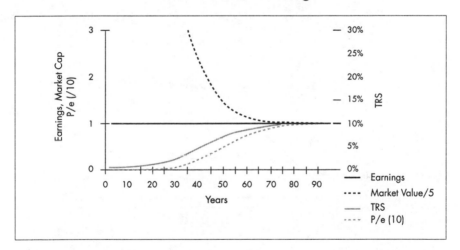

But this is clearly not a reasonable case. No analyst ever gets it right for the future of the industry, much less the company. Analysts are human, with all the failings of any other human. Recency and anchoring are two of them. *Recency* is the error that most of us make when we pay more attention to recent data than all the data. *Anchoring* is a state of mind that makes it difficult for us to change our minds once we make a choice about how we think the world works. These two well-known cognitive errors often combine to produce an analysis method that takes the present and applies it to the future.

This method is often eminently reasonable at the time but inconsistent with knowledge about the S-curve.

We call this forecasting approach the LINE approach, because it asserts that the investment analyst forecasts in a straight line from the past into the future. LINE stands for Linear INvestor Expectations. How does LINE work? At the beginning of the curve, the analyst forecasts a low rate of growth. The forecast will turn out to be very low—an insight we gain because we understand how the S-curve evolves. As time passes, the analyst forecasts higher growth because the business has evolved more quickly than expected. This happy situation persists until the midpoint of the S-curve, where the extrapolated growth of the business starts to exceed the actual potential of the business. Saturation has been reached. After this point, analyst forecasts are in excess of the actual evolution of the business, causing persistent disappointment (often called the "hockey stick" curve). This scenario is illustrated by the following graph:

Evolution of Bubbles

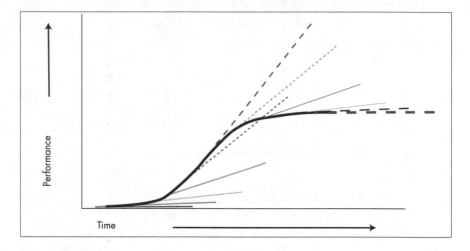

The evolution of systematic, if complex, forecasting errors can easily be seen in this exhibit.

What is the impact of these changes on the evolution of market capitalization (net present value)? Let's refer to the top graph on the next page.

The low early earnings forecast turns into lower net present value forecasts until the midpoint of the market capitalization cycle, which evolves earlier than the earnings, at which point the market capitalization forecasts begin to exceed the "perfect foreknowledge" case. One might think of the gap between the "accurate foreknowledge" case and the actual (if "actual" is adequately represented by the LINE methodology) as a "bubble." After the midpoint of the

Evolution of Earnings and Market Capitalization with and without Accurate Foreknowledge

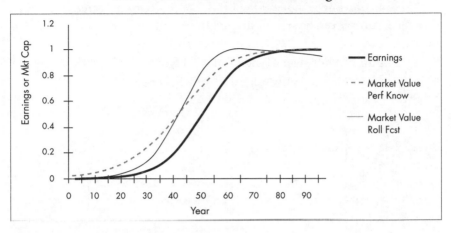

market value curve, the bubble is positive—that is, the estimated value is in excess of the fair value. Before the midpoint the bubble is negative—the estimated value is below the fair value.

Of course, the gaps between estimated and fair value translate into changes in the observed total return to shareholders. The "perfect foreknowledge" case and the LINE case are compared in the graph below.

As this graph demonstrates, with LINE forecasting, the TRS is above the levels of "perfect foreknowledge" until the midpoint of the earning evolution (not the market value), and then it dips slightly below the "perfect fore-

Evolution of Earnings, Market Value, and TRS with Perfect Foreknowledge and LINE Estimates

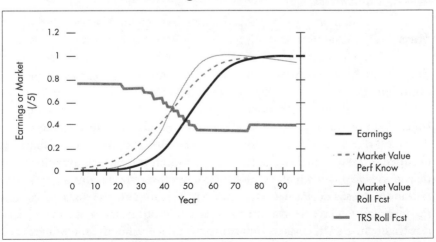

knowledge" case, at least in this case, where we assume that fifteen years has elapsed between 10% saturation and 90% saturation.

What are the implications of the LINE approach for the price-to-earnings ratio? The answer can be seen in this graph:

Evolution of Earnings, Market Value, TRS, and P/E with Perfect Foreknowledge and LINE Forecasts

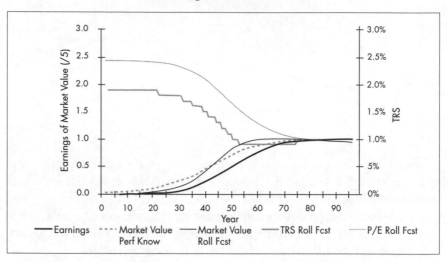

Here we see that P/E is much lower than that in the "perfect foreknowledge" case. In fact, this case would look much more reasonable to the typical senior executive, except that it forecasts long periods when high TRS is associated with high P/E, a case the typical value investor would not recognize. LINE forecasts do support the intuitions of the growth investor more than those of the value investor.

The case that we have developed above has assumed, as we have said, a fifteen-year transition time. However, as we have seen, transition times have been shrinking. What happens if the transition time is, say, three years rather than fifteen? The answers are as follows: First, with perfect foreknowledge the evolution of market value occurs, as before, sooner than the evolution of earnings, but the differences are more pronounced. (See the top graph on the next page.) Second, when fast transitions are combined with LINE forecasts, the evolution of market capitalization shows the formation of a very dangerous situation—the existence of a period of time when the estimated market capitalization is substantially in excess of the long-term-equilibrium market capitalization. This is depicted as the peak in the bottom graph on the next page. In this particular case, with a three-year transition time, the peak is more than double the final market value, indicating that at some point there will be a col-

Evolution of Earnings and Market Value with Fast Transitions Time and Perfect Foreknowledge

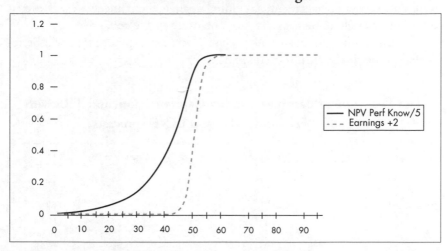

lapse of stock price of 50% or more. This is a period of great risk for shareholders and for management, which can be caught unawares.

The period has a substantial duration—about ten years in this case—and occurs before market saturation has occurred. In fact, the initial period of risk occurs at about the midpoint of the earnings evolution. It is important to note that this bubble is entirely due to forecasting errors about the unknowability, at least at this point in time, of what the future will bring. These behaviors have been seen in our case studies, and we have described and analyzed them.

Fast Evolution of Earnings and TRS with Perfect Foreknowledge and LINE Forecast

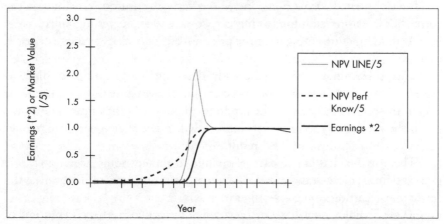

Now, however, we are able to say that these behaviors may result directly from forecasting inadequacies rather than from managerial action. This may have implications for management, including management incentives, if executives come to believe that it is, in fact, the cause of the collapse.

Of course, this sinuous development of market capitalization will be reflected in the total return to shareholders:

Fast Evolution of Earnings, Market Capitalization, and TRS with Perfect Foreknowledge and LINE Forecasts

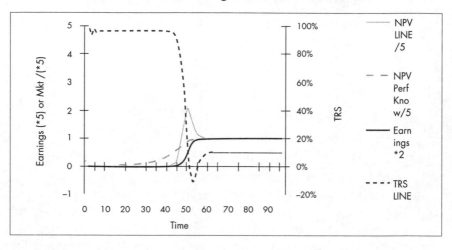

Initial TRS is very high, as all venture capitalists know, and then crashes well into negative ranges. The risk for new investors here is extreme. Not only is past performance not a guarantee of future performance, but if past performance has been strong, it is a warning signal—although, due to the long duration of high TRS, an ambiguous warning signal—of impending trouble. The period of consistently declining returns can last for several years, as many high-tech investors know. Someone who is very adventurous can "buy on the dip," but laser-precision forecasting is necessary to avoid getting killed.

A similar picture emerges for the price-to-earnings ratio, as the next graph shows.

Price-to-earnings ratios in the early days can be exceptionally high, as recent events show, but they too come crashing down as realistic expectations begin to set in. In fact, it is the crashing price-to-earnings ratio, combined with the moderately slowing earnings growth rates, that squash the market capitalization and historic TRS results.

The point is that as the pace of change in the economy accelerates, one can anticipate more of these "risks"—which are really inevitabilities unless the state of forecasting changes—rather than less.

These bubbles, then, are an inevitable consequence of the evolution of

Fast Evolution of Earnings, Market Capitalization, TRS, and P/E with Perfect Foreknowledge and LINE Forecasts

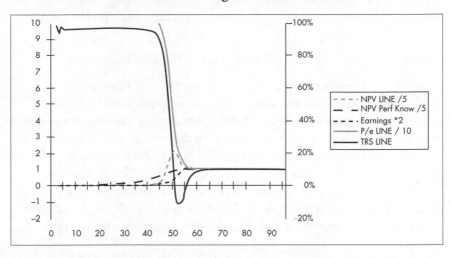

industries and the inability of analysts to correctly forecast the future. Understood in this way, a bubble actually has some analytic value. When the bubble is bursting, it may be a strong signal that the S-curve of the present business model is coming to an end.

8. ENTRY AND EXIT ANALYSIS: AVOIDING SURVIVOR BIAS

Determined to avoid the problems of "survivor bias" that often plague analysts, DPA explicitly focuses on rates of entry and exit. These dynamics are crucially important in determining or reflecting (it is not yet clear which) industry performance. In doing so, DPA places more emphasis on understanding the entrants and leavers in an industry.

9. PERIPHERY ANALYSIS: ANALYZING THE PRACTICES OF ENTRANTS

We characterize entrants as being at the periphery of an industry. Entrants have been found to account for most of the excess performance in an industry or an economy. Hence the periphery is extremely important to an understanding of the economics of industry dynamics. The periphery is a vital part of Schumpeter's "gales of creative destruction." Understanding how companies at the periphery create value, how long they are able to create value, and why they cease creating excess value is at the heart of DPA.

10. BARRIERS TO ENTRY ANALYSIS

Not all industries welcome new entrants. Understanding which industries welcome new entrants, and which do not, is an important part of DPA.

11. CONFIDENCE ANALYSIS

This is a set of analyses developed to determine the confidence one has that the results being observed are real and are not due to an artifact. These analyses will be explained in more detail below. There is, we think, an analogy in the science of meteorology. What is "normal" weather for this time of year, or for the year in general? This question, as we all know in this era of global warming, is not unimportant. Governments are spending millions of dollars trying to tease the answer out of nature. New evidence is being gathered that, in addition to helping resolve this environmental debate, may also illustrate the difficulty in understanding "normalcy" in the capital markets. As *Science* magazine reported in mid-1999,

> *George Washington's winter at Valley Forge in 1777–78, when temperatures fell as low as –15 degrees C, was relatively mild for those days; some years, New York Harbor froze solid. Indeed, so bitter were the centuries from about 1400 until 1900 that they have been dubbed the "little ice age." But new evidence appears to confirm that the long cold snap was nothing exceptional. Instead, it was only the most recent swing in a climate oscillation that has been alternately warming and cooling the North Atlantic region, if not the globe, for ages upon ages.*

Just as meteorologists and earth scientists have to sort out the "normal" weather cycles to determine what portion of global warming is due to nature and what is due to man, so we have to be able to take into account the "normal" oscillations of the capital markets to sort out what is extraordinary. What do these "normal" oscillations or cycles look like? Our technique for addressing this question is the confidence analysis.

12. NON-GAUSSIAN ANALYSIS: THE REAL FREQUENCY OF EVENTS

Unlike the distribution of events in the natural world (e.g., distribution of intelligence around the average), events in the capital markets can often be distributed in unusual patterns—with many more events occurring above or below the average than one might suspect. Moreover, these distributions themselves can and do change over time. Understanding these distributions and the way they change is critical to an accurate interpretation of representative statistics such as averages and standard deviations.

13. DYNAMIC FINANCIAL ANALYSES:

DPA focuses on the standard SPA financial analysis (EPS growth rates, margins, EBITDA, free cash flows, etc.), but also on more dynamic variables such as the reinvestment ratio (and its stability), the growth return on capital investment, and the amount of EBITDA growth that results from each new dollar of capital.

USEFULNESS OF DPA

DPA allows one to clearly see the periods of continuity and to distinguish them from the periods of change. It helps one to separate the "random from the regular," to quote Murray Gellmann, Nobel Prize–winning physicist and student of complexity.

DPA is helpful in determining and understanding the historic context (envelope) in which change has taken place, and thus setting limits on likely change in the future. It allows one to make judgments about the probable sustainability of long-term performance based on a clear understanding of the precedents of the past. It provides us with an automatic control sample—the market as a whole—which minimizes the chances of false attribution of cause and effect.

We believe that DPA is useful to CEOs and CFOs who want to understand how their investors are looking at their results—both the corporate results and the stock market interpretation of those results. These corporate officers also want to understand the forces at work on their industries.

WHAT DPA HAS TAUGHT US

We focused in Chapter 2 on some of the lessons of DPA. The following is a snapshot of our conclusions:

- Over the period of our analysis the economy has been in two regimes: one before 1974–75, and one since. Since 1976, the TRS cycles of the economy have been quite consistent.
- Most industries do not differ statistically from the overall economy. Only those industries in which there has been substantial change demonstrate any statistically significant superior performance. However, there are industries that have consistently underperformed the economy.
- Exceptional performance, as determined by long-term (two-cycle) total return to shareholders, is driven by earnings growth and ROI to a much greater extent than can be explained by p/e's.

- Exceptional performance is never sustained. Whether it is an industry that is outperforming or a company, high performance always comes to an end. The end of excellence is a good proxy for long-term risk to the investor.
- Company performance deteriorates over the longer run because the market is more dynamic than the corporation.
- Companies don't outperform the market except in rare nongeneralizable situations like Berkshire Hathaway.
- Rates of entry and exit from an industry are very strongly correlated with industry performance. What is cause and what is effect is not always clear. Usually both play a role.
- The best chance to beat the markets is early on, when the potential of a change is far greater than the market estimates.
- The difficulty of understanding the future, along with the difficulties in executing a program of change within a corporation, makes leadership the key resource.

Notes

INTRODUCTION
The Game of Creative Destruction

1   "The farther backward": There is some doubt that Churchill actually said this, but it is broadly attributed to him. According to Richard M. Langworth, editor, *Finest Hour,* The Churchill Center, "I've heard it often but have never been able to attribute it. I suspect it's one of those generic quotes ascribed to many people."

2   We selected: See Appendix C for a list of the variables covered in our data collection effort.

CHAPTER 1
Survival and Performance in the Era of Discontinuity

4   The capital markets provide: The objective of the regulators of the capital markets is to provide for a "level playing field," that is, no unfair informational advantage to any one player. A key mechanism for achieving that objective is to establish and enforce standards for information quality and transparency—that is, clear definitions of standards for the information, and clear rules for its access, use, and dissemination. Compliance with these standards is often carefully monitored and enforced. Compliance is enforced by a (hopefully) neutral judicial system reporting to or operated by the state. The rules governing the capital

markets can be changed through discussion and dialog among legislative, judicial, and executive bodies reporting to the state. The discussion about change will often solicit the opinions of players in the capital markets. The change processes can extend for decades or more.

4   "Control, which essentially means": Merchant, Kenneth A. *Control in Business Organizations.* Boston: Pittman, 1985.

4   "Measurement focuses": Simons, Robert. *Levers of Control: How Managers Use Innovative Control Systems to Drive Strategic Renewal.* Boston: Harvard Business School Press, 1995.

7   As a group: Throughout the book we will define the long-term return to investors as the total return to shareholders, or TRS. This measure, which is common in finance, is the sum of the annual increase in stock price for the corporation plus the dividends and special payments distributed to investors. It is the single best measure of the increase in wealth of the investor.

8   One reaches: The original S&P index was formed in 1926 and was made up of ninety companies.

15   "When the millennium arrived": Reston, James. *The Last Apocalypse: Europe at the Year 1000 A.D.* New York: Doubleday, 1998.

18   "theoretical frameworks": Munger, C., "A Lesson in Elementary, Worldly Wisdom As It Relates to Investment Management and Business," *Outstanding Investor Digest,* 1995, as cited by Mauboussin, *On the Shoulders of Giants—Mental Models for a New Millennium,* Vol. 2. Credit Suisse First Boston, Nov. 16, 1998.

19   Unfortunately, conventional: Merchant, 1985.

21   They keep the pipeline: It is true that these partnerships, because of the special laws under which they operate (as we will discuss in Chapter 7), also operate outside of the day-to-day scrutiny of the capital markets, giving them valuable time to focus on the fundamentals of their businesses without having to continuously worry about how the capital markets will interpret their actions. That being said, at some point all these intermediaries sell their properties to others—sometimes through a well-orchestrated auction among publicly traded companies, and sometimes through a public offering of the securities (known as the initial public offering, or IPO). At the time of the sale, they realize their gains and calculate their returns, just as an investor in a public company would.

22   "The test of a first-rate": F. Scott Fitzgerald, "The Crack Up," cited in Collins, J., and Porras, J., *Built to Last,* Harper Business: A Division of HarperCollins Publishers, 1994.

24   "The adaptive demands": Heifetz, Ronald A. *Leadership Without Easy Answers.* Cambridge: Belknap Press—Harvard University Press, 1994.

CHAPTER 2
How Creative Destruction Works: The Fate of the East River Savings Bank

27   The new name reflected: "East River Savings' New Name," *The Wall Street Journal,* Oct. 18, 1988.

27   "The Marine Midland Bank": Allon, J., "Neighborhood Report for the Upper West Side," *The New York Times,* Nov. 9, 1997.

27   Six months later: When it became clear that the bank was going to become a drugstore, local conservationists swung into action, gaining a landmark designation for the exterior of the building. The fate of the building's interior has not yet been decided. But according to one local resident, the outlook was not favorable: "What are they going to do, landmark the Tylenol?"

28   Yet in light of the numbers: This is not the only indicator one could use. We have also tracked the number of companies on the major stock exchanges, and similar, if a bit less dramatic, patterns have been observed. Another indicator is the number of companies in our sample of fifteen industries. This has increased from about 250 per year, in the beginning of our database, to more than six hundred in 1998.

30   "the . . . process of industrial": Schumpeter, Joseph A. *Business Cycles: A Theoretical, Historical and Statistical Analysis of the Capitalist Process.* 2 vols. New York and London: McGraw-Hill Book Co., Inc., 1939.

31   The exact position: The exact formula is:

$$Ii = (Pi—Pe)/Ce$$

where:

Ii = Performance Index
Pi = industry or company performance
Pe = economy or industry performance
Ce = 90% confidence interval for the economy or industry

39   Interpreting these potentially: *Standard and Poor's Industry Survey of Computer and Office Equipment,* 6/6/85, p. C83.

53   "The real trouble": G.K. Chesterton as sited by Bernstein, Peter L. *Against the Gods: The Remarkable Story of Risk.* New York: John Wiley & Sons, Inc., 1996.

54   Here is a distillation of Sterman's findings: Sterman, John D. *Business Dynamics: Systems Thinking and Modeling for a Complex World.* New York: Irwin/McGraw-Hill, 2000.

CHAPTER 3
Cultural Lock-In

61   "Things should be": As cited in Medio, Alfredo, and Giampaolo Gallo. *Chaotic Dynamics: Theory and Applications to Economics.* Cambridge: Cambridge University Press, 1995.

61   "When John Akers took over": "What Went Wrong at IBM: The Toughest Job in American Business," *The Economist,* Jan. 16, 1993.

64   "Man seeks for himself": As cited in Medio, Alfredo and Giampaolo Gallo. *Chaotic Dynamics: Theory and Applications to Economics*. Cambridge: Cambridge University Press, 1995.

64   "Small scale models": Kenneth Craik as cited by Johnson-Laird, Philip N. *Mental Models*. Cambridge, MA: Harvard University Press, 1983.

65   "If there is one gift": Virginia Woolf as cited by Ippolito, Maria F., and Tweney, Ryan D. "The Inception of Insight." *Nature of Insight*. Eds. Robert J. Sternberg and Janet E. Davidson. Cambridge, MA: MIT Press, 1995, pp. 433–462.

66   "We have limitations": Johnson-Laird, 1983.

66   "Mental models play": Johnson-Laird, 1983.

66   "A tight analogy or model": Simonton, Dean Keith. *Scientific Genius: A Psychology of Science*. Cambridge: Cambridge University Press, 1988.

67   "Language is used to create": March, James G. *A Primer on Decision Making: How Decisions Happen*. New York: The Free Press—Macmillan, 1994.

70   "Consequently, if the existing": See Johnson-Laird for experiments with Wason cards that demonstrate this point.

70   "The NASA scientists' belief": March, 1994.

71   "To give up one's": Simonton, 1988.

71   "Do we have to change?": Leonhardt, David. "McDonald's: Can It Regain Its Golden Touch?" *Business Week*, Mar. 9, 1998, p. 70.

72   "A mental model changes": Forrester, Jay W. *World Dynamics*. Cambridge, MA: Wright-Allen Press, Inc., 1971.

72   "myths, symbols, rituals": March, 1994.

72   "They give context": March, 1994.

73   "Active modeling occurs well before": Sterman, 2000.

73   "The constructive process": Johnson-Laird, 1983.

73   Language, visual imagery: This may be tautological. Beliefs are themselves mental models. But they can be the machine tools of mental models, useful for assembling other mental models, just as machine tools are useful in assembling other machines.

80   "In the start-up phase": Simons, 1995.

82   "In mature firms": Simons, 1995.

83   Often, the only real: See Appendix C for an analytical description of the economics of transition.

84   "Everyone is too damned": Markoff, John. "I.B.M.'s Chief Criticizes Staff Again," *The New York Times*, June 19, 1991.

84   "We know from common sense": Vail, Priscilla L. *Emotion : The On/Off Switch for Learning*. Rosemont, NJ: Modern Learning Press, 1994.

87   "When a problem arises": Cited by Sterman, 2000.

87   The capital markets: "Manage" comes from the Italian *maneggio*, which means "to train a horse!" Source: WWWebster.

88   "Every individual is continually exerting": Smith, Adam. *The Wealth of Nations: An Inquiry into the Nature and Causes*. (1776) New York: Everyman's Library, 1991.

CHAPTER 4
Operating vs. Creating: The Case of Storage Technology Corporation

90   "To compete with IBM": "A Corny (But True) Story," *Forbes*, Oct. 15, 1977.

92   His new goal: "Buying Magnuson and Its Problems," *The New York Times*, Dec. 21, 1981.

93   "We said to ourselves": Blumenthal, Karen. "At a Crossroads: Storage Technology, In a Slump, Pins Hope On New Data Device—Firm's Woes Show Hazards Of Battling With IBM; It Pushes Optical System—Technological Glitches Hurt," *The Wall Street Journal*, Aug. 16, 1984.

93   "Maybe that made us": Blumenthal, Karen. Ibid.

94   "I want to bring": Atchison, Sandra D., Mary J. Pitzer and Marilyn A. Harris. "Storage Technology Found Its Iacocca?" *Business Week*, Feb. 4, 1985.

94   Poppa's approach didn't: Ivey, Mark. "Storage Technology Is Turning Around—But Where's It Headed?" *Business Week*, Feb. 24, 1986.

96   Poppa was so impressed: Lancaster, Hal. "Storage Technology to Launch Its Vaunted Iceberg—Many Rave About the Data-Storing Device, but Some Doubts Linger," *The Wall Street Journal*, Jan. 24, 1992.

96   "I told Dick Egan": Lancaster, Hal. Ibid.

99   In a recent series: These discussions were conducted in cooperation with the Center for Corporate Innovation, Inc., 10835 West Olympic Boulevard, Suite 835, Los Angeles, CA 90064, (310) 575-1444.

100 In this sense, innovation: These views are wholly consistent with Schumpeter's original thinking. Although Schumpeter did not use the word "innovation" directly, he attributed the economic effects he saw to "the introduction of a new good, the introduction of a new method of production, the opening of a new market, the conquest of a new source of supply of raw materials or half-manufactured goods, and the carrying out of the new organization of any industry, such as the creation or breakup of a monopoly." Certainly technical and product advance was part of Schumpeter's concept, but was only a part.

104 "Measurement focuses on": Simons, 1995.

104 Once the variables are selected: Simons, 1995.

106 As the cellular: See box on the definition of innovation at the end of this chapter (p. 124).

113 Transformational innovations: Tushman, Michael L., and Philip Anderson. "Technological Discontinuities and Organization Environments." *Administrative Science Quarterly*. Sept., 1986, pp. 439–468.

115 But the word *creativity*: Modern reflection on the nature of creativity begins in the mid to late nineteenth century as Europe was going through an explosion of creativity in the arts, and the beginnings of the second real revolution in the sciences in Europe. In art, Impressionism was on the rise. Monet settled in Giverny in 1863. De Maupassant and other writers were actively thinking and writing about the essence of creativity. In music, Bruckner, Bartok, Mahler, Satie, and Sibelius were all in their ascendancy. Verdi and Wagner were battling to see who could sit at the pinnacle of

operatic achievement. In science, Darwin was newly popular, and the theory of electromagnetism was capturing the imagination of more than a few entrepreneurs. In mathematics, number theory, which eventually helped pave the way for quantum mechanics, was getting its start in Vienna through the work of Cauchy and others.

115   "Instead of thoughts": Simonton, p. 24.

115   "To say that Thomas Edison": Csikszentmihalyi, Mihaly. *Creativity: Flow and the Psychology of Discovery and Invention.* New York: HarperCollins, 1997.

116   They are trained in diverse: Epstein, Robert. *Cognition, Creativity and Behavior.* Westport, Connecticut: Praeger, 1996.

117   "It is evident that": Simonton, p. 43.

117   "These anomalies provide": Csikszentmihalyi, Mihaly, and Keith Sawyer. "Creative Insight: The Social Dimension of a Solitary Moment." *Nature of Insight.* Eds. Robert J. Sternberg and Janet E. Davidson. Cambridge, MA: MIT Press, 1995.

117   "Fleming was not the first": Simonton, 1988.

118   "the accumulation of anomalies": Simonton, 1988.

118   "I keep the subject": Ippolito and Tweney.

119   "where beliefs, lifestyles": Csikszentmihalyi, 1997.

119   "irrational and rational aspects": Csikszentmihalyi, 1997.

119   "What is so difficult": Csikszentmihalyi, 1997.

120   Chess masters call this: Winsemius, Peter. "The Emotional Revolution," Amsterdam: McKinsey & Company, 1999.

120   "constricted scan that screens": Amabile, Teresa M., et al., eds. *Creativity in Context : Update to the Social Psychology of Creativity.* Boulder, CO: Westview Press—Perseus Books, 1996.

122   "While many would be": This is wholly consistent with the observations of Kahneman and Tversky that the relationship between creativity and risk is U-shaped. When people are operating near their targets they are risk averse. When they are far behind or far ahead of their targets, they employ more creative strategies. This seems to fit the creative personality closely, since they are rarely at a point of satisfaction.

122   "In innovation you have": Csikszentmihalyi, 1997.

124   "conversion of a creative idea": Isaak, M. I., and Just, M. M. "Constraints on Thinking in Insight and Invention." *Nature of Insight.* Eds. Robert J. Sternberg and Janet E. Davidson. Cambridge, MA: MIT Press, 1995, pp. 281–326.

CHAPTER 5
The Gales of Destruction

127   "This deal will get done": Hardy, Quentin. "Technology & Science: McAfee Will Lobby Stockholders in Bid to Get Cheyenne," *The Wall Street Journal,* Apr. 17, 1996.

127   "absolutely inadequate": Ibid.

127 "The long-term prospects": Ibid.

127 "false and misleading public statements": "Technology & Telecommunications: Cheyenne Sues McAfee, Chief on Fraud Charges," *The Wall Street Journal*, Apr. 19, 1996.

127 "Sanjay called and said": Weber, Thomas E., and Steven Lipin. "Computer Associates to Buy Cheyenne—Pact for $1.2 Billion Comes Half Year After Target Spurned McAfee's Offer," *The Wall Street Journal*, Oct. 8, 1996.

129 By 1972, Intel's: "Strategic Exit and Corporate Transformation: Evolving Links of Technology Strategy and Substantive Generic Corporate Strategies," Robert A. Burgelman, George W. Cogan, Bruce K. Graham, Research Paper Series, Graduate School of Business, Stanford University, No. 1406, Sept. 1996.

131 "As the debates raged": Ibid.

131 Grove turned to Moore: Ibid.

131 After a few moments: Ibid.

132 "Intel equaled memories": Ibid.

132 It was a classic case: Ibid.

132 The company had: Ibid.

133 "fabrication facilities in": Ibid.

136 "The difficulty lies not": Winsemius, 1999.

136 "Our organizations tend": Winsemius, 1999.

137 "a normal, healthy one": Kübler-Ross, Elisabeth. *On Death and Dying*. New York: Collier Books—Macmillan, 1969.

137 Egyptian and Greek history: The range is from 250 years, as asserted by Tacitus, to 1500 years, according to Lipsius. The historic average range of dynasties in Egypt and Rome was closer to 300 years.

142 Closing down a heritage product line: While from time to time major companies do go bankrupt, in the United States the bankruptcy laws slow this process down. The major source of transformational destruction is acquisition.

CHAPTER 6
Balancing Destruction and Creation

146 As CEO, Ackerman decided: CNNfn, 3/6/00.

147 "the largest position in the world": CNBC, 12/6/99.

148 "well beyond optical fiber": CNNfn, 7/20/99.

148 "Corning leads primarily": Corning's website.

151 "nothing was sacred": All statements drawn from a "values document" prepared at the time by Welch's strategic team.

155 "We knew we were going": Anderson, Michael A., and Gordon Bock. "Information Processing: Sequent Discovers Talents It Didn't Know It Had—Its Fast-Thinking Computer Hasn't Done Well In The Scientific Market—But It's A Surprise Hit In Offices," *Business Week*, May 19, 1986.

155   "Of the six people": Heins, John. "Many Hands Make Light Work. (Sequent Computer Systems Inc.)," *Forbes,* May 29, 1989.

157   "It's pretty clear": "Sequent Computer Posts Quarterly Loss, Cites Major Charge," *The Wall Street Journal,* Oct. 21, 1991.

158   "When other people": Hof, Robert D. "Information Processing: Just When Sequent Thought It Was Safe . . . The Computer Maker's Once-Cozy Turf Is Being Invaded," *Business Week,* Nov. 9, 1992.

159   "I'm big, big, big": "Sequent Goes It Alone In Bid For Top Spot: Ignores The Industry Trends Of Volume And Commodity," *Computergram International,* Mar. 17, 1997.

CHAPTER 7
Designed to Change

166   "What we do is look": Peltz, Michael. "High Tech's Premier Venture Capitalist," *Institutional Investor,* June, 1996.

166   "The valuation process": Ibid.

166   "There are four hundred": Perkins, Anthony B. "The Thinker—Interview with John Doerr, General Partner in Charge of Investments in Information Technology at Kleiner Perkins Caufield & Byers," *The Red Herring,* Mar. 1, 1995.

166   "We didn't execute": Rutter, Nancy. "Fastest VC in the West," *Forbes,* Oct. 25, 1993.

166   "At first I thought": Perkins, Anthony B. "The Thinker—Interview with John Doerr, General Partner in Charge of Investments in Information Technology at Kleiner Perkins Caufield & Byers," *The Red Herring,* Mar. 1, 1995.

167   "In the 1980s, PC hardware": Peltz, Michael. "High Tech's Premier Venture Capitalist," *Institutional Investor,* June, 1996.

168   "Not once did Henry": Baker, George P., and George David Smith. *The New Financial Capitalists: Kohlberg Kravis Roberts and the Creation of Corporate Value.* Cambridge: Cambridge University Press, 1998.

169   The Securitites Act of 1933: Now amended by the National Securities Markets Improvement Act of 1996.

170   the "leveraged buyout association": Baker and Smith, 1998.

171   Roughly half of that: Pricewaterhouse Coopers MoneyTree® survey.

173   Though the closing: Baker and Smith, 1998.

179   Should they be able to do: The Street.com.

180   At this writing, there are: According to the National Business Incubator Association.

CHAPTER 8
Leading Creative Destruction

186 "In a complex social system": Heifetz, 1994.
186 Order—orienting people: Heifetz, 1994.
189 "Authorities, under pressure": Heifetz, 1994.
195 "We noticed that": Hall, Cheryl. "When the parts are greater than the sum;
       Some of Safeguard Scientifics' spinoffs reap big rewards for investors,"
       The Dallas Morning News, Mar. 12, 1995.
199 "We are active": CNBC/Dow Jones Business Video, 03/16/1999.
199 "We asked Jim": Bulkeley, William M. "Tech IPOs Put Unsung Backer In the
       Limelight," *The Wall Street Journal*, Oct. 14, 1999.
200 "In the early '90s, we helped": Press Release from website, 5/26/99.
201 "Shareholders should be evaluating": CNBC/Dow Jones Business Video,
       03/16/99.
203 "To me, being truly": Born, Pete. "Lindsay Owen-Jones: a world vision for
       L'Oreal," *Women's Wear Daily*, Oct. 12, 1990.
204 "Our labs have a basic rule": Barrett, Amy. "L'Oreal's Pretty Face Veils
       Growth Drive—Research Arm Helps Maintain Its Global Position," *The
       Wall Street Journal*, Jan. 16, 1998.

CHAPTER 9
Increasing Creation by Tenfold

218 more latitude to invest risk capital: Lerner, Josh, *Venture Capital & Private
       Equity*, New York: John Wiley, 2000.
227 At McKinsey, our partners: First developed by Kevin Coyne and others in the
       McKinsey Atlanta Office in 1996.
227 "In cultures that are uniform": Csikszentmihalyi, 1997.
228 A fourth trick is: Smith, Steven. "Getting into and out of mental ruts: A
       theory of fixation, incubation, and insight." *Nature of Insight*. Ed. Robert
       J. Sternberg and Janet E. Davidson. Cambridge, MA: MIT Press, 1995.
229 "When Einstein burst in": Everdell, William R. *The First Moderns: Profiles in
       the Origins of Twentieth-Century Thought*. Chicago: University of Chicago
       Press, 1997.
229 "It takes two": Simonton, Dean Keith. "Foresight in insight? A Darwinian
       answer." *Nature of Insight*. Eds. Robert J. Sternberg and Janet E. Davidson.
       Cambridge, MA: MIT Press, 1995, pp. 465–494.
229 "Poetry is about": Csikszentmihalyi, 1997.
233 Together these functions may work: The work was originally led by Lothar
       Stein in the McKinsey Munich office.

CHAPTER 10
Control, Permission, and Risk

236   General Motors could not: Originally published in 1946 by John Day
        Company; 1993 edition Transaction Publishers, New Brunswick, NJ.

238   "Control, which essentially means": Merchant, 1985.

238   The purpose of divergent: Simons, 1995.

239   can be abused by "gaming the system": In one study of the budgeting
        practices of more than four hundred U.S. firms, almost all respondents
        stated that they engaged in one or more budget games. Managers either
        did not accept the budgetary targets and opted to beat the system, or they
        felt pressures to achieve the budgetary targets at any cost.

240   "If people have a standard": *Business Month,* Dec. 1989, p. 33, and
        Management Review, 1986, p. 49.

240   Capital markets are the opposite: We are not making a case here for not
        planning and controlling, we are simply trying to clarify the differences
        between markets and corporations, and the absence of planning and
        control in markets is one of its distinctive features.

240   "We need to give up": Tom Peters, Conference Board Review, 1991.

243   At the time of publication: Pinchot, Gifford. *Intrapreneuring : Why You Don't
        Have to Leave the Corporation to Become an Entrepreneur.* New York:
        Harper & Row, 1985.

245   When decision makers are: Bernstein, 1996.

247   Because of this: CCI Interviews.

248   The world little knows: Simonton, 1998.

250   Thermo Electron was founded: Baldwin, William. "Serendipity," *Forbes,* Nov.
        16, 1987.

251   "Then all hell broke loose": *New England Business,* Dec. 1989.

252   "There's no better way": Wilke, John R. "Innovative Ways: Thermo Electron
        Uses An Unusual Strategy To Create Products—It 'Spins Out' New
        Companies To the Public but Retains A Majority of the Stocks—For Sale:
        Core Technologies," *The Wall Street Journal,* Aug. 5, 1993.

252   "There's a physical limit": *The Wall Street Journal,* 8/5/93, p. A1.

253   "the risk is": Bulkeley, William M. "Thermo Electron to Take Pretax
        Charge, Reacquire Stakes in Four Subsidiaries," *The Wall Street Journal,*
        May 25, 1999.

259   "We became uncompetitive": Sellers, Patricia. "So You Fail. Now Bounce
        Back!" *Fortune,* May 1, 1995.

259   "Failure is only an opportunity": Ford, Cameron, M., and Dennis A. Giola.
        Creative Actions in Organizations: Ivory Tower Visions & Real World Voices.
        Thousand Oaks: Sage Publications, 1995.

CHAPTER 11
Setting the Pace and Scale of Change

262 Johnson & Johnson has typically grown: Source: 1972 Johnson and Johnson Annual Report, Chairman's Letter to Shareholders.

265 "We need to think about": All quotes from private meetings and correspondence unless otherwise noted.

271 "We are thrilled": Jones, Gladys Montgomery, "Framing the future: How Johnson & Johnson executives keep in touch with the changing marketplace—and one another," *Continental Airlines* magazine, March 1999.

272 Some of the savings: August 18, 1993, *Chemical Week* reports that J&J announced the elimination of 3,000 jobs and a related $200 million write-off.

280 Restructuring major manufacturing: Barrett, Amy. "J&J Stops Babying Itself," *Business Week,* Sept. 13, 1999.

282 What saved FrameworkS: Subsequently Russell Deyo took over responsibility for the program in 1998 from Roger Fine.

283 Even more important: Daretta and Gelbman played key leadership roles in later FrameworkS sessions.

287 "Is FrameworkS a single, simple approach": Ralph S. Larsen, "FrameworkS: Turning the Challenges of Change into Opportunities for Growth," 05/01/1999 *Chief Executive* (U.S.).

APPENDIX C
Dynamic Performance Analysis (DPA)

319 The mathematics of S-curves: Fisher, J.C., and R.H. Pry. "A Simple Substitution Model for Technological Change." *Technological Forecasting and Social Change* 3: pp. 75–88, 1971.

327 This approach has: Kahnemann, Daniel, Paul Slovic and Amos Tversky, eds. *Judgment Under Uncertainty: Heuristics and Biases.* Cambridge: Cambridge University Press, 1982.

329 Remedy is the error: Kerr, Richard A. "The Little Ice Age—Only the Latest Big Chill," *Science,* June 25, 1999.

336 "George Washington's winter": *Science,* June 1999.

Selected Sources

Overall we have drawn on more than five hundred references to inform our work. We have chosen not to publish that full list here, but rather to focus on the works that have been the most influential in our thinking

Amabile, Teresa M., et al., eds. *Creativity in Context: Update to the Social Psychology of Creativity.* Boulder, CO: Westview Press/Perseus Books, 1996.

Argyris, Chris. *Reasoning, Learning and Action: Individual and Organizational.* Jossey-Bass Series in Social and Behavioral Science and Jossey-Bass Series in Management. San Francisco: Jossey-Bass, Inc., 1982.

———. *Overcoming Organizational Defenses: Facilitating Organizational Learning.* Boston: Allyn & Bacon, 1990.

Arthur, W. Brian. *Increasing Returns and Path Dependence in the Economy.* Ann Arbor: University of Michigan Press, 1994.

Baker, George P., and George David Smith. *The New Financial Capitalists: Kohlberg Kravis Roberts and the Creation of Corporate Value.* Cambridge: Cambridge University Press, 1998.

Bernstein, Peter L. *Against the Gods: The Remarkable Story of Risk.* New York: John Wiley & Sons, Inc., 1996.

Christensen, Clayton M. *The Innovator's Dilemma: When New Technologies Cause Great Firms to Fail.* Boston: Harvard Business School Press, 1997.

Csikszentmihalyi, Mihaly. *Creativity : Flow and the Psychology of Discovery and Invention.* New York: HarperCollins, 1997.

———. *Flow: The Psychology of Optimal Experience.* New York: HarperCollins, 1991.

———, and Keith Sawyer. "Creative Insight: The Social Dimension of a Solitary

Moment." *Nature of Insight.* Ed. Robert J. Sternberg and Janet E. Davidson. Cambridge, MA: MIT Press, 1995.

Drucker, Peter F. *The Age of Discontinuity: Guidelines to Our Changing Society.* (1969) New Brunswick: Transaction Publishers, 1992.

———. *Concept of the Corporation.* (1946) New Brunswick: Transaction Publishers, 1993.

Dunbar, Kevin. "How Scientists Really Reason: Scientific Reasoning in Real-World Laboratories." *Nature of Insight.* Ed. Robert J. Sternberg and Janet E. Davidson. Cambridge, MA: MIT Press, 1995.

Epstein, Robert. *Cognition, Creativity and Behavior.* Westport, CT: Praeger, 1996.

Everdell, William R. *The End of Kings: A History of Republics and Republicans.* New York: The Free Press, 1983.

———. *The First Moderns: Profiles in the Origins of Twentieth-Century Thought.* Chicago: University of Chicago Press, 1997.

Ford, Cameron M., and Dennis A. Giola. *Creative Actions in Organizations: Ivory Tower Visions and Real World Voices.* Thousand Oaks: Sage Publications, 1995.

Forrester, Jay W. *World Dynamics.* Cambridge, MA: Wright-Allen Press, Inc., 1971.

Foster, Richard N. *Innovation: The Attacker's Advantage.* New York: Summit Books/Simon & Schuster, 1986.

Heifetz, Ronald A. *Leadership Without Easy Answers.* Cambridge: Belknap Press/Harvard University Press, 1994.

Ippolito, Maria F., and Ryan D. Tweney. "The Inception of Insight." *Nature of Insight.* Eds. Robert J. Sternberg and Janet E. Davidson. Cambridge, MA: MIT Press, 1995.

Isaak, M. I., and M. M. Just. "Constraints on Thinking in Insight and Invention." *Nature of Insight.* Eds. Robert J. Sternberg and Janet E. Davidson. Cambridge, MA: MIT Press, 1995.

Johnson-Laird, Philip N. *Mental Models.* Cambridge, MA: Harvard University Press, 1983.

Kahnemann, Daniel, Paul Slovic, and Amos Tversky, eds. *Judgment Under Uncertainty: Heuristics and Biases.* Cambridge: Cambridge University Press, 1982.

Kübler-Ross, Elizabeth. *On Death and Dying.* New York: Collier Books/Macmillan, 1969.

Lerner, Josh. *Venture Capital and Private Equity: A Casebook.* New York: John Wiley, 2000.

March, James G. *A Primer on Decision Making: How Decisions Happen.* New York: The Free Press—Macmillan, 1994.

Merchant, Kenneth A. *Control in Business Organizations.* Boston: Pittman, 1985.

Pinchot, Gifford. *Intrapreneuring: Why You Don't Have to Leave the Corporation to Become an Entrepreneur.* New York: Harper & Row, 1985.

Reston, James. *The Last Apocalypse: Europe at the Year 1000 A.D.* New York: Doubleday, 1998.

Schumpeter, Joseph A. *Business Cycles: A Theoretical, Historical and Statistical Analysis of the Capitalist Process.* 2 vols. New York and London: McGraw-Hill Book Co., Inc., 1939. Revised edition published in 1964.

————. *Capitalism, Socialism and Democracy.* (1942) New York: Harper & Row, 1976.

Senge, Peter M. *The Fifth Discipline: The Art and Practice of the Learning Organization.* New York: Currency/Doubleday, 1990.

————, et al., eds. *The Fifth Discipline Fieldbook: Strategies and Tools for Building a Learning Organization.* New York: Currency/Doubleday, 1994.

Simons, Robert. *Levers of Control: How Managers Use Innovative Control Systems to Drive Strategic Renewal.* Boston: Harvard Business School Press, 1995.

Simonton, Dean Keith. *Genius, Creativity, and Leadership.* Cambridge, MA: Harvard University Press, 1984.

————. *Scientific Genius: A Psychology of Science.* Cambridge: Cambridge University Press, 1988.

————. "Foresight in Insight? A Darwinian Answer." *Nature of Insight.* Ed. Robert J. Sternberg and Janet E. Davidson. Cambridge, MA: MIT Press, 1995.

Smith, Steven. "Getting Into and Out of Mental Ruts: A Theory of Fixation, Incubation, and Insight." *Nature of Insight.* Ed. Robert J. Sternberg and Janet E. Davidson. Cambridge, MA: MIT Press, 1995.

Sterman, John D. *Business Dynamics: Systems Thinking and Modeling for a Complex World.* New York: Irwin/McGraw-Hill, 2000.

Sternberg, Robert J., and Janet E. Davidson, eds. *Nature of Insight.* Cambridge, MA: MIT Press, 1995.

Tushman, Michael L., and Philip Anderson. "Technological Discontinuities and Organization Environments." *Administrative Science Quarterly,* September 1986, pp. 439–468.

Vail, Priscilla L. *Emotion: The On/Off Switch for Learning.* Rosemont, NJ: Modern Learning Press, 1994.

Winsemius, Peter. *The Emotional Revolution.* Amsterdam: McKinsey & Company, 1999.

Index

Page numbers of illustrations appear in italics.

Abbott Laboratories, 19, 34
Abernathy, Steve, 77, 80
Ackerman, Roger, 146–48
Acquisitions. *See* Mergers and acquistions.
Action (execution), 75, 76, 100–103, 162, 163, 166
Aerospace industry, 212
Age of Discontinuity, The (Drucker), 11
Agilent, 164
Air Products and Chemicals, 33
Airline industry, 3, 33, 44–45, *45*, 63, 216
Akers, John, 61–62, 63, 64, 67, 69, 78–79, 84, 263
Amabile, Teresa M., 120, 122, 222
Amazon.com, 82–83, 167, 290
Amdahl, 38, 92
Amdahl, Eugene, 92
America Online, 167
American Airlines, 33
American Home Products, 33, 154
American Locomotive, 128
American Research and Development, 169
Amgen, 9, 86
AMR, 33, 75
Anaconda Copper, 7, 128, 139
Anderson, Edward, 199

Apple Computer, 36, 39, 43
AOL, 83
AOL-Time Warner, 214
Argyris, Chris, 71, 186
Ariba, 81, 83
Arthur, Brian, 67
Arthur Rock & Co., 122
AT&T, 51, 53, 106, 146, 183, 214
Attackers (new entrants), 47–48, *47*
  Amazon.com, 82–83
  cannibalization of products, 85
  competing with customers, 85–86
  dominant company's response to, 83–84
  Enron, 216, 217
  failure of, 80, 83
  medical supplies, 49–50, *49, 50*
  MIDAS of, 76
  New Company Index, 48–52, *49, 50, 51, 52*
  oil industry, 50, *50, 51*
  returns, above-industry-average, 55–58, 60
  S-curve performance, 55–58, *56, 57, 58,* 80
  stage 1, foundation, and, 79–80
  telecommunications, 51–52, *51, 52*
  Transecure vs. General Motors, 77–78
  why "newness" works, 52–55

Aurelius, Marcus, 25
Aweida, Jesse, 90–91, 93, 94, 107, 109

Baker, George, 170, 171
Bakunin, Mikhail, 138
Banking industry, 36
    East River Savings Bank, 25–27, *26*, 36
Bankruptcy, 3
    American laws and, 140–41
    Anaconda, 7
    Storage Technology, 46
Barnes & Noble, 82–83
Baxter International, 33
Bayer AG, 153
Bayer aspirin, 16
Becton-Dickinson, 32–33, *33*
Berkshire Hathaway, 18
Bernstein, Richard, 245
Bessemer, 169
Bettencourt, Liliane, 202
Biotech industry, 217
Black, James, 119
BMC Industries, 94
Bonds, 12
Bristol-Myers Squibb, 33
Broadcom, 81–82
Brown, John Seely, 261
Buffet, Warren, 18, 67
Burke, James, 73–74, 232, 263, 277
Business Week, 71
Byers, Brook, 165

Cambridge Technology Partners, 198
Case, Dan, 214
"Cashing out," 144
Caulfield, Frank, 165
Cellular telephony, 106
Chambers, John, 86, 204
Champion International, 5, 34, *34*
Change (or innovation). *See also* Creativity;
    Discontinuity.
    adaptive challenges, 185–88
    below-average performance and inability
        to adapt, 21–22, 78
    clipper ship example, 110–13, *110, 111,
        112*
    convergent thinking and, 18–19
    corporate performance at average or above
        levels and, 60
    creativity and, 23, 102, 115–23

cultural lock-in and, 16–19, 24, 83–87,
    132–36, 162
defensive routines and, 18, 71, 84, 132
demise of companies, inability to adapt, 14
designing a process for increasing adaptive
    work, 192–93
divergent thinking, 19, 22, 102, 116–20,
    222–24
Enron and, 148–51
European economics and, 293
fears inhibiting, 84–87
GE, 151
government bailouts and, 20
inability to develop innovative strategies,
    101–2
incremental innovation, 107, 108,
    109–13, *110, 111, 112*
incrementalism, failure of, 291–92
industries vs. companies, 106
managing, 102, 183, 187–88, 254–60
markets and, 20, 21–22
1920s, 11
pace, accelerating, 12–13, 28, 58, 187,
    203, 205
perceived barriers to innovation, *247*
positive returns, 108
requirements, innovating organization,
    105–14
Richter Scale of Innovation, *108*
specific industries and, 30
substantial innovation, 106–7, 108,
    113–14, 201
transformational, 19, 106–9, *108*, 113,
    144, 158–59, 201
types of innovation, 106–14
value of, 246–47
waves, first, post-World War II, 11
waves, second, 1960s, 11–12
Charles, Bertie, 7
Chekhov, Anton, 64
Chemicals, commodity, 32
Chemicals, specialty, 3, 31–32, *32*
    R&D spending and TRS, 212
Chesterton, G. K., 53
Chevron, 2
Cheyenne Software, 125–27, 139, 140, 142
    acquisition by CAI, 127
    acquisition effort, McAfee, 127
    "cashing out," 144
    stock prices, 126

Christensen, Clayton, 85
Churchill, Winston, 1
Cisco, 2, 9, 58, 81, 85–86, 204, 214, 215, 216, 219, 231
Clark, Tom, 259
Clipper ships, 110–13, *110, 111, 112*
Coca-Cola, 259
Colgate-Palmolive, 59
Comcast, 195
Commerce One, 81, 83
Commodities, R&D spending and TRS, 212
Commodore, 39
Communications technology, 14
Compaq, 39, 85, 165, 167, 169
CompuCom (Machine Vision), 198, 199
Computer Associates International (CAI), 127
Computer hardware industry, 5, 6, 30, 34, *35*, 36–37, *37*, 53, 157
    boom in pace and scale, 94
    evolution of, 38–39
    R&D spending and TRS, 213
    S-curve pattern of performance, 57, *58*
    Sequent Computer Systems, 154–59
Con Edison, 76
Concept of the Corporation, The (Drucker), 10, 236
Continuity
    assumption of, 9–10, 18, 71, 78, 79, 87, 103, 106, 295
    decision-making systems and, 103
    extinction of, 14
    incremental change and, 113
    information systems, 104–5
    measurement and control systems, 104, 254–60
    need to abandon assumption of, 15–16, 87, 106
    portraits of, 30–36, *32, 33, 34, 35*
Control, 238
    balancing with permission, 236–48, 254–60
    culture and, 240
    decentralized, 170–71, 236–37
    determining what to measure and control at five levels, 254–56
    informal, 238
    making changes work, 254–60
    measure and control what you must, not what you can, 256–57

permission vs., at Enron, 248–50
    setting the balance with permission, 244–48
    systems, 4, 15, 18, 23, 75–76, 77, 78, 80, 104, 162, 163, 199
    systems inhibiting performance, 239–40
Convergent thinking, 18–19, 120
    control systems and, 238–39
    zoom-in, 120, 228
Cooper Industries, 128
COR skills, 19, 211
    conversational, 122
    observational, 122–23
    reflective, 123
Corning, 16, 144–48
    Ackerman, CEO, and fiber optics, 146–47
    acquisitions and alliances, 146–47
    assumption of discontinuity, 147, 178, 219
    founding and growth, 145–46
    Houghton, CEO, and change, 146
    sell-offs, 147
Corporations
    "act like the market" goal, 161–62, 215
    adaptive to technical work, changing ratio of, 205–7
    assumption of continuity, 9–10, 14, 15–16, 18, 71, 78, 87, 103–5, 151, 215
    balancing control and permission, 236–48, 254–60
    capital costs, decline in, 13, 14
    central purpose, 99
    change, ability to implement, 14, 15, 16–19, 60, 101–3, 162
    change, fears inhibiting, 84–87
    cognitive superstructure, 4
    control, decentralized, 170–71, 236–37
    control systems, 4, 15, 18, 23, 75–76, 77, 78, 80, 104, 162, 163, 199, 256–57
    convergent thinking, 18–19
    core concepts of, 18
    create, operate, trade model, 162–80, 201, 236
    creation vs. operations, 163
    creative destruction, increasing rate of, 15, 22, 23, 289
    creativity, fostering, 23, 102, 115–23, 163
    cultural lock-in, 16–19, 24, 79–87, 132–36, 162
    culture of, and mental models, 65, 73

Corporations *(continued)*
  decision making, 16, 17, 66, 75, 76, 77,
    78, 103–4, 162, 163
  defensive routines and failure to
    implement change, 18, 71, 84, 132, 219
  defined, 4
  destruction, levels of, incremental,
    substantial, and transformational,
    141–42, 148–54
  discontinuity embraced, 15, 151
  divergent thinking, 19, 21, 22, 294–95
  divergent thinking, replicating, 222–24
  escaping from old ideas and, 136–37
  execution, 75, 76, 100–103, 162, 163, 166
  leadership of, 23–24, 123
  life phases of, 17, 78
  long-term performance and
    discontinuities, 1, 23
  market vs., 87–89
  mental models in, 18, 65, 71, 73, 74–76,
    184
  MIDAS (corporate architecture), 76–84,
    99
  new companies vs. mature, 76–80
  1970s, 11
  operational excellence, 48, 60, 89, 91, 92,
    92–93, 94, 95, 97, 98, 99–100, 123
  planning or strategic planning, 4, 23, 64,
    211–15
  planning, improving, 215–21
  private equity firms vs., 173–80
  R&D, failure of internal, 212–14
  R&D, improving, 215–21
  redesigning based on discontinuity,
    20–21, 22
  risk (or surprise), 4, 23
  rules changed for, 16
  venture capital, 214–21, 232, 233–35
  taxes, 14
Craik, Kenneth, 63–64, 65
Create, operate, trade model, 162
  balancing control and permission,
    236–48, 254–60
  control in, 163, 164, 175–76
  creation vs. operations, 163
  decentralization, 176–77
  decision making in, 163
  GE and, 178–80
  limited-life investments, 173–74
  minimal "corporate" staff, 174

  private equity firms and, 172–78
  Safeguard Scientifics, 201
  trading vs. operating, 164
Creative destruction, 9–10, 137–41. *See also*
    Destruction; Discontinuity.
  American system and, 292–93
  balancing destruction and creation,
    143–44, 151–52, 154–59, 160
  capital markets and, 89
  Corning's commitment to, 147–48
  corporations and, 15
  discontinuity and, 48–52, *49, 50, 51, 52*
  Duracell, 168–69
  East River Savings Bank, 25–27, *26,* 36
  Enron and, 148–51
  "gales of," 138, 162, 164, 172, 200, 216
  gales of, and Intel, 129–36, *130, 135*
  GE and, 151
  importance of fostering, 59–60
  increasing rate of, 15, 289
  J&J and, 269–83
  Kleiner, Perkins, Caulfield, and Byers,
    164–67, 171
  Kohlberg, Kravis, and Roberts, 164,
    167–69
  as management philosophy, 201–5
  Monsanto, 152–54
  new companies, accelerating rate of,
    and, 30
  periphery and, 216–21
  private equity firms and venture
    capitalists, 21, 164–80
  operational excellence and, 48, 60, 89,
    91, 92, 92–93, 94, 95, 97, 98,
    100–103, 123, 183–85
  Sequent Computer and, 154–59
  simultaneous substantial creation and
    destruction, 144–52, 205
  simultaneous transformational creation
    and destruction, 152–54
  specific industries, 30–37, *32, 33, 34, 35,
    37,* 40–42, *40, 41, 42,* 44–45, *44, 45*
  Storage Technology and, 91, 92, 92–93,
    94, 95, 97, 98
  symbols in Buddhism, Greek mythology,
    Hinduism, and Chinese culture, 137
  trading and, 164
  ubiquity of, 294–95
Creative people, 122, 209–10, 222–23,
    228–29

Creativity, 115–16
 act of creation, 121, *121*
 changing the context, 227–28
 convergent thinking and, 120
 COR skills, 122–23
 corporations and, 120–22
 dialogue for, 227–29
 divergent thinking and, 116–20, 210–11, 222–24
 escaping from old ideas and, 136–37
 fostering, 23, 102
 incubation, 218, 223
 operations vs., 163
 perceived barriers to improving innovativeness, *247*
 process of discovery, 116
 slowing things down, 229
 using a muse, 228–29
 visualization, 228
Csikszentmihalyi, Mihalyi, 22, 115–16, 117, 119, 122, 222–23, 227–28
Cultural lock-in, 16–17. *See also* Mental models.
 avoiding, 22–24
 causes of, 18–19, 79
 emotional price of destruction, 129, 136–37, 140
 Intel and, 132–36
 leveraged buyouts and, 168
 mental models and, 18, 162
 stage 4 of corporate architecture: the emergence of the three fears, 83–87
Curry, Michael, 166
Customer, competing with, 85–86

Darretta, Bob, 283
Data compression, 65
DEC (Digital Equipment Corp.), 36, 38, 155, 156, 157, 169, 263
Defense industry, 3, 33, 41, 44, *44*, 63
 R&D spending and TRS, 212
Defensive routines, 18, 71, 84, 132, 219
Delphi Systems, 164
Destruction
 acts of, various, 139
 American Locomotive (AL), 128
 Anaconda Copper, 128, 139
 balance with creation, 143–44, 151–52, 159
 Cheyenne Software, 125–27, 139, 140

concept of, 137–41
 emotional difficulty of, 129, 136–37, 140
 Intel, 129–36, *130, 135*
 levels, incremental, substantial, and transformational, 141–42, 158–54
 simultaneous substantial creation and destruction, 144–52
 Studebaker, 127–28, 139
 trading, 164
Dell, 2, 14, 39, 58, 85, 215
Dell, Michael, 39
Delta Air Lines, 33
Deutsche Telekom, 214
Deyo, Russ, 282, 283
Discontinuity(ies), 1, 2, 295. *See also* Change; Creative destruction.
 adaptive challenges, 185–88, 200
 Age of, 13
 America and assumption of, 292–93
 attackers (new entrants) and, 47–48, *47*
 in companies, 46–48, *46, 47*, 106
 costs of, 294
 creative destruction and, 48–52, *49, 50, 51, 52*, 145–48
 dangers facing companies and, 264
 divergent thinking and, 19
 economic forces contributing to, 13–15
 Enron and, 149–51, 219
 forecasting difficulty and, 55–58, *56, 57, 58*
 in industries, 36–45, *37, 40, 41, 42, 44, 45*
 markets and, 10–15, *12, 13*, 20, 53–55
 mental models and inability to recognize, 61–62
 pace of change and, 11–13
 private equity firms and, 172
 redesigning the corporation based on, 20–21
 sources of, 45
 Sterman's findings on management performance and, 54–55
Divergent thinking, 19, 116–20, 210–11, 294–95
 adequate preparation time, 223–24
 collision phase, 119–20
 control systems and, 238
 COR skills of, 19, 122–23, 211
 five requirements, 222–24
 incubation phase, 118–19, 223

Divergent thinking *(continued)*
  picking the right people, 222–23
  as prelude to creativity, 22
  private equity firms and venture capital, 21
  provide resources, flexibility, deadlines,
    224
  provide senior coverage, 224
  search phase, 117–18
  set high aspirations, 224
  "a sunny pessimism" and, 22, 122, 222–23
  wide categorizers, 116
  zoom-out thinking, 116, 228
Doerr, L. John, 166–67
Dolkart, Andrew, 27
Doriot, George, 169
Dow Chemical, 33
Dow Jones Industrial Average, performance
    compared to long-term survivors, 9
Drucker, Peter, 10, 11, 236–37
Dunbar, Kevin, 122
Dunlop, Al "Chainsaw," 138
DuPont, 7, 59, 75
Duracell, 167–69, 177
Dynabook Technologies, 166

Earnings dilution, 86
East River Savings Bank, 25–27, *26*, 36, 54
  acquisitions, 27
  sale of, 27
Eastman Kodak. *See* Kodak.
Economist, 61
Edison, Thomas, 115
EDS, 218
Egan, Dick, 96
Einstein, Albert, 61, 64, 115, 228–29
Electric utilities, 3, 30, 32, 216
Electronic Data Systems, 42
EMC, 96, 97, 107
Employees
  aging companies and, 139
  costs of creative destruction, 294
  divergent thinking and, 23
  Enron and, 149–50, 248–50
  Monsanto downsizing, 153
  incentives, 175–76, 258–60
  strategies for facing destruction and
    job loss, 140
Enrico, Roger, 259–60
Enron, 16, 148–51, 224
  as attacking company, 216, 217, 219
    change in product, 148–50
    creative destruction and, 178
    Lay CEO, 148–49
    North American, 149
    organizational structure, 149–50
    permission vs. control at, 248–50
    Skilling and, 148–50, 248
Ericsson, 106
Ethyl Corporation, 33
eVolution Partners, 167
Exabite, 47
Excellence. *See* Operational excellence.
Excite, 167
Exxon, 2

Faraday, Michael, 248
Federal Reserve
  effectiveness, 14
  inflation and, 12
  market behavior and, 5
FedEx, 110
Fifth Discipline, The (Senge), 72
Fine, Roger, 181, 190–91, 263, 264, 282,
    283
Fitzgerald, F. Scott, 22–23
Floating Point Systems, 38
Flow (Cziskzentmihalyi), 22
Forbes
  100 list, Long-Term Survivors,
    1917–1987, 7–8, *8*
  richest list, 202
Ford, Henry, 259
Forrester, Jay, 72
Foster, Richard, 1, 47, 70, 85
Frazza, George, 267

Gap, 75
Gates, Bill, 67, 204
Gates Learjet, 34
GDP: global, 14
  Great Depression and, 288
Gelbman, Ron, 284
Geneen, Harold, 170, 171
General Atlantic Partners, 171
General Dynamics, 33
General Electric (GE), 3, 7, 8, *8*, 9, 16, 59,
    151
  acquisitions, 178–79
  create, operate, and trade model, 178–79
  divestments, 151

General Motors, 7, 77–79, 164, 236–37, 260

Genentech, 165

Gerstner, Lou, 79, 85, 161, 263

Gibson, Scott, 131, 157

Gillette, 168

Gödel, Kurt, 68

Goizueta, Roberto, 259

Gore, Al, 166

Government bailouts, 20

Gregg, Robert, 155

Grove, Andy, 129–34

Gupta, Arun, 209–10, 216, 217–18, 222, 223, 224

Hambrecht & Quist, 214

Hatsopoulos, George, 250–52, 253

Hatsopoulos, John, 251–53

Heifetz, Ron, 19, 23–24, 185–86, 188–89

Hewlett-Packard, 34, *35*, 59, 151, 164

Holding companies, 20, 180

Hongkong and Shanghai Banking Corporation, 27

Houghton, Amory, 145

Houghton, James, 146

Huai, ReiJane, 125–27

IBM, 36, 38–39, 42, 46, 85

acquisition of Sequent, 159

Akers, mental models, and demise of, 1980s, 61–62, 63, 64, 67, 69, 78–79, 84, 263

anti-trust case, 95

competitors, 156, 157

Gerstner, Lou, and, 79, 85, 161, 263

leadership mistakes, 191

price reductions, 93

production delays, 93

Storage Technology and, 90–91, 95, 97

Imation, 164

INC. magazine, 243–44

Incubator company, 179–80

current firms, 180

Industries

innovation in, 106

R&D spending and TRS, 212–13

Infineon Technologies, 164, 234

Inflation

1970s, 11, 12, 170

stagflation, 170

Information technology, 14

Enron and, 150–51

Innovation. *See* Change; Creative destruction.

Innovation: The Attacker's Advantage (Foster), 1, 47, 85

Innovator's Dilemma, The (Christensen), 85

Intel, 9, 75, 129–36

Black Monday, 131, 155

cultural lock-in, 132–36

DRAM destruction at, 129–36, 142

Internet and, 134

microprocessor innovation, 134, 158, 159

Sequent Computer Systems and, 131, 155

TRS (total return to shareholders), *130, 135*

venture capital spending, 214, 215

Interest rates, 1970s, 11

Intergraph, 38

International Flavors and Fragrances, 5, 33

International Paper, 34

International Rectifier, 47

Internet, 289–90

business proposals, 14

companies in growth stage, 80–81

discontinuity and, 53

as distribution channel, 86

dot.com companies, 24, 58

IPOs, 199–200

leadership decisions and, 71

start-up costs, 14

stock volatility, 290

telecommunications and, 39

Transecure, 77–79

venture capital and, 166–67

Intrapreneuring (Pinchot), 243

Inventions, 109

Invisible hand, 88

IPOs

Cambridge Technology Partners, 198

Internet-related start-ups, 199–200

number of, 1999, 170

stagflation and 1970s, 170

venture capital and, 167

James, Darwin R., 26

James, William, 115

Janssen, Paul, 277

Japan

entrance to DRAM market, 129–30

failure of incrementalism, 291

J. H. Whitney, 169, 171
Johnson & Johnson (J&J), 3, 16, 59, 151,
    178
  approach to strategic planning, 231–33
  balancing operational excellence with
    change, 262
  bringing entire organization into
    FrameworkS, 283–84
  control vs. permission at, 242
  corporate venture capital group, JJDC,
    232
  COSAT, 232
  Credo, 73–74, 190, 262
  design meeting, 266–68
  evaluation process, 282
  executive comments, 285–85
  executive committee, leadership role in
    FrameworkS, 263–82
  first steps in transformation: launching
    businesses and cutting costs, 271–72
  FrameworkS, inception of, 263–69
  FrameworkS I, 270–72
  general accomplishments of FrameworkS,
    284–85
  going to the source decision, 283
  Health Care Systems, Inc., and, 271
  improving operations, 280
  leadership, 181, 190–91, 263–83
  Los Angeles meeting, 1997, 277–78
  McKinsey assessment, FrameworkS,
    286–87
  mental models changed, 273–74
  pace of change, 281
  reflecting on the process, 280–84
  resistance to FrameworkS process, 282
  as self-transforming company, 269–83
  stimulating innovation, 275–80, 287
  sustained performance, sources of,
    261–63
  Tylenol crisis, 73–74, 261
  What's New project, 277–80
Johnson, Robert Wood, 73, 287
Johnson-Laird, Philip N., 64, 66, 73

Kahneman, Daniel, 88, 245–46
Keynes, John Maynard, 136, 288, 295
Khaishgi, Ahmed, 77, 80
Kidder, Bob, 168
Kimberly-Clark, 34–35, *35*, 59
Kinder, Richard, 149

Kleiner, Eugene, 165
Kleiner, Perkins, Caulfield, and Byers,
    164–67, 171
Knight, Phil, 226, 259
Kodak, 7, 8, *8*, 183
  acquisition of Sterling Drug, 16
Koestler, Arthur, 136
Kohlberg, Kravis, and Roberts (KKR), 164,
    167–69
Korea, 291–92
Kraft foods, 167, 169
Kübler-Ross, Elisabeth, 84, 136–37
Kuhn, 118

Larsen, Ralph S., 242
  asking the question, 263
  communications with employees, 283–84
  discontinuity, embracing, 272
  divergent thinking of, 263
  FrameworkS proponent, 274, 282
  leadership of, 287
  mental model change of, 267
  setting the inquiry in motion, 264
Larson, Bill, 127
Last Apocalypse, The (Reston), 15
Lay, Kenneth, 148–49, 248
Leadership, 181–208
  adaptive challenges, 185–88, 200, 224
  adaptive to technical work, changing ratio
    of, 205–7
  creative skills needed by, 123
  decision makers, common errors, 104–5
  deflecting the issues, 188–90
  designing a process for increasing adaptive
    work, 192–93
  designing the strategic planning process,
    224–30
  discontinuity and, 23–24
  events to encourage external mental
    models, 225
  IBM and, 191
  J&J and, 190–91
  loyalty to a flawed model and failure of, 70
  management committees, agendas, 254–55
  management committees, failure of,
    181–83, 191
  management committees, meetings as
    tool for change, 206–7
  managing the conflict between adaptive
    work and technical work, 191–92

private equity firms, 193–94
process for ongoing senior support, with a
  focus on its impact on divergence and
  creation, 259–60
setting the balance between control and
  permission, 246–47
standards for management effectiveness,
  207
suppression and cultural lock-in, 19
technical work vs. adaptive work, 185–88,
  190–91
Lee, H. K., 291–92
Lenehan, Jim, 283
Leveraged buyouts, 167–69
  LBO Association, 170–71
Lewellyn, Gary, 196
Ling, Jimmy, 170, 171
Long-term survivors, 5
  average level of performance, 34
  below-average return of, 8, 21, 34, 161
  change, inability to keep pace with, 21–22
  Forbes 100 list, 7–8, *8*
  future of, 14
  investor expectations and, 9
  performance in industry, 32
  S&P 500 index, 8
  superior performance, 34–35
  total return to shareholders, vs. S& P
    Median, 28, *28*
L'Oréal, 16, 201–5
  acquisitions, 202, 205
  innovation, obsession with, 203–4
  internationalization, 203
  management philosophy of creative
    destruction, 201–2, 203, 204, 205
  Nestlé and, 202
  Owens-Jones, CEO, and strong
    performance, 202–5
Lotus Development, 165
Lucent, 214

Machiavelli, 87
Magnuson Computer, 92
Mahoney, Dick, 152
Management, 9. *See also* Leadership.
  adaptive challenges, 185–88, 200
  committees, 181–83, 187–88, 191,
    205–8, 254–55
  conflict between adaptive work and
    technical work, 191–92

control process, 75, 76, 77, 78, 80, 81,
  104, 162
creative process and, 120–21
cultural lock-in and Intel, 131–36
decision-making process, 75, 76, 77, 78,
  80, 81, 103–4, 162
defensive routines, 18, 71, 84, 132
designing a process for increasing adaptive
  work, 192–93
designing the strategic planning process,
  224–30
for discontinuity and creative destruction,
  162–80
for divergent thinking, 23
domination of industry and, 81–83
employees, control of, 23, 149–50,
  258–60
Enron, 149–50
Enron, permission vs. control at, 248–50
executional capability, 75, 76
growth stage of company and, 80–81
implications of accelerated change for, 59
information systems and, 74, 76, 77, 78,
  81, 104–5, 257–58
innovation, problems with execution,
  100–103
issue avoidance, 71, 188–90
making changes work, 254–60
mental models and inability to recognize
  discontinuity, 61–63, 67–71
operation excellence and, 99–100, 123
perceived barriers to improving
  innovativeness, *247*
presentation and response meetings,
  182, 264
stalemate of, 183–85
standards for management effectiveness,
  207
Sterman findings on performance, 54–55
stimulation of creative destruction and,
  22
strategies for facing destruction and job
  loss, 140
types of innovation, need to recognize, 114
Management philosophy
  assumption of continuity, 9, 71, 78, 79,
    87, 103–5, 106
  assumption of discontinuity, 147, 151,
    172, 201–5
  origins of modern, 10

March, James, 67, 70, 72
Marine Midland Bank, 27
Market. *See also* Stock market
  adaptability of, 88
  capital markets, 4, 5, 9, 13, 294
  companies which outperform, 47–48
  control in, 5
  corporation vs., 87–89
  defined, 4
  destruction in, 127, 136, 138, 160
  discontinuity and, 10–15, *12, 13,* 20,
    53–55
  efficiency of, 9
  fears, lack of in, 87
  Federal Reserve and, 5
  forecasting discontinuity, 55–58, *56,*
    57, 58
  investors and why "newness" works, 52–55
  social process and, 88
  surprise in, 5
  valuation of new entrants, 47–48, *47*
  volatility, 59
Market index funds
  outperformance of, 87–89
  performance compared to long-term
    survivors, 8
McAfee Associates, 127
McDonald's, 71
McGowen, William, 228
MCI, 149, 151, 228, 242
McKinsey
  J&J FrameworkS management approach
    and, 263–83
  tool kit of questions, 227–29
McKinsey Corporate Performance Database,
  The, 2–3, 5–6, 29
  acceleration of new entrants, 30
  companies excluded, 3
  departures, 3, *29*
  long-term survivors, 5, *29,* 30
  New Company Index, 48–52, *49, 50,*
    51, 52
  new entrants, 3, *29,* 30, 47
  number of companies included, 3, 30
  performance charts, 31, *32, 33, 34, 35,*
    37, 40, 41, 42, 44, 45
  sales and market cap of companies, 3
  S-curve pattern, 55–58, *56, 57, 58*
  stock market decline or crash, 1974 and
    1975 in, 5, 6

total return to shareholders compared to
  S&P 500, *6*
Mead, 33
Medical products and supplies, 30, 32–33,
  33, 44, 49–50, 53
  Net Rate of New Company Entry, *49*
  R&D spending and TRS, 213
  TRS vs. Net Rate of New Company
    Entry, *50*
Medtronic, 34
Mental models, 18, 63–65
  assessment of, 69
  assumption of continuity and, 71, 78,
    79, 87
  barrier to change, 71, 184–85
  conversation or dialogue and changing,
    72–74, 221
  correct and timely information needed,
    69
  China and AIDS, 70
  create, operate, trade model, 162–80
  creating and changing, 72–74, 225
  defensive routines and, 18, 71, 84, 132
  improperly used, 68–69
  information systems and, 74, 76, 77, 78,
    104–5, 257–58
  issue avoidance and, 71
  J&J example, 263–83
  leadership failure and, 70
  limits of, 67–71
  loyalty to a flawed model, 70
  negative effects of, 18
  power of, 65–67
  start-ups and, 79–80
  visions as, 72
  wrong models, 68
Mental Models (Johnson-Laird), 66
Merchant, Kenneth, 238
Merck, 34, 248
Mergers and acquisitions (M&A), 288–89,
  289
  Cisco, 231
  earnings dilution fears and, 86
  number of 1999, 171
  private equity market vs., 171
Microsoft, 14, 36, 58, 83, 204
  Windows, 43, 113, 114
  Word, 43
MIDAS, 76, 162. *See also* Create, operate,
  trade model

breaking the pattern, 143–44
cultural lock-in and, 79, 132–36
limitations of the operating organization,
    103–5
natural evolution of, 76–79
stage 1, foundation (attack), 79–80,
    90–91
stage 2, growth, 80–81, 92
stage 3, dominate, 81–85, 93–94
stage 4, cultural lock-in: the emergence of
    the three fears, 83–87, 86, 96, 132–36
Transecure and General Motors, 77–79
Monsanto, 152–54
    down-sizing, 153
    merger, 154
    sell-offs, 152–53
Moore, Gordon, 131, 132
Mostek, 68–69, 71
Motorola, 106
Munger, Charlie, 18, 64, 65, 67
Musser, Warren "Pete," 194–201

NASA, 70
Nasdaq, 14, 194, 201
Netscape, 167
Network Systems, 97
NeuVis, 209–10, 216, 217, 222, 223
New Company Index or Newness Index,
    48–52, 49, 50, 51, 52
New Economy, 289–90
New York Times, 27, 84
Nike, 226–27, 259
NL Industries, 34
Nokia, 106
Novell, 125, 126, 157, 158, 197

Oil industry, 3, 5, 6, 41, 41, 50, 53
    Net Rate of New Company Entry, 50
    R&D spending and TRS, 212
    TRS vs. Net Rate of New Company
        Entry, 51
"One-decision" stocks, 12
Operational excellence, 48, 60, 89, 99–100
    creative destruction and, 91, 92, 92–93,
        94, 95, 97, 98, 100–3, 123
    imitators of products and, 109
    managerial stalemate and, 183–85
Oracle, 156, 158
Organization, 21
Other People's Money (film), 160

Owens-Corning, 11, 145
Oxenhorn, Eli, 125, 126

Pacific Bell, 183
Packard Motor Car Co., 128
Pai, Lou L., 151
Paper industry, 3, 32, 33, 34, 34, 35
    R&D spending and TRS, 212
Parkinson, C. Jay, 7, 128
Pasteur, Louis, 117
Pepsi, 259–60
Performance charts, 31, 32, 33, 34, 35, 37,
    40, 41, 42, 44, 45
Periphery
    defining, 216, 220
    implications of evolution, 218–19
    importance of, 219–21
    NikeTown stores, 226
    understanding, 217, 226
    understanding evolution of, 217–18
Perkins, David, 121
Perkins, Thomas, 165
Permission, 240–41
    control vs., at Enron, 248–50
    conundrum, 242
    experimentation and, 258
    failure of balance, Thermo Electron,
        250–54
    failure to grant, collapse of
        intrapreneuring, 243–44
    managers seeking, 241–42
    setting the balance with control, 244–48
Peters, Tom, 240
Pharmaceutical industry, 3, 33, 41, 42, 45,
    53, 154
    collapse, mid-1970s, 63
    Medicare and Medicaid and, 41, 53
    periphery and seeing the cutting edge, 217
    R&D spending and TRS, 212
Piaget, Jean, 72
Pinchot, Gifford, 243–44
Poppa, Ryal R., 94–97, 107, 109
Powell, Karl "Casey," 131, 155, 157, 159
Price cutting, 83, 93
Price-to-earnings ratios, new entrants and,
    57–58, 58
Principal investing firms (leveraged-buyout
    firms), 172–73
    differences and similarities with venture
        capitalists, 172–73

Principal investing firms *(continued)*
　　Kohlberg, Kravis, and Roberts (KKR),
　　　164, 167–69
　　S-curve and private equity, *173*
Private equity firms, 20–21, 172–73, 218
　　adaptive work in, 193–94
　　creative destruction and, 169–72
　　decentralization, 176–77
　　established names in, 169, 171
　　fixed fee, 174
　　growth of, 171
　　Investment Company Act of 1940,
　　　169–70, 177, 197
　　Kleiner, Perkins, Caulfield, and Byers,
　　　164–67, 171
　　Kohlberg, Kravis, and Roberts (KKR),
　　　164, 167–69
　　limited life investments, 173–74
　　M&As, 171
　　methods of control: contracts and
　　　incentives, 175–76
　　minimal "corporate" staff, 174
　　origins, 169
　　research activities, 21
　　restrictive covenant, 175
　　returns by asset category, *171*
　　S-curve and private equity, *173*
　　"take-out" strategy, 21
Procter & Gamble, 7, 35
Product cannibalization, 16, 17, 85,
　　204, 295

Quantum, 39
Quinlan, Mike, 71
QVC, 198

R&D (Research & Development)
　　failure of internal, 214
　　improving, 230
　　private equity firms, 21
　　TRS and specific industries, 212–13
　　venture capital spending vs., 220–21
Raytheon, 33
Recession 1990s, 12
Reston, James, 15
Risk (or surprise), 4, 23
　　failure and, 258–59
　　fear of (aversion), 247–48, *247*
　　nature of, 244
　　Nike and, 259

　　permission to take, 241
　　-taking behavior and goals, 244–46
Risk (Bernstein), 245
Rock, Arthur, 122
Rockwell, 33
Rohm and Haas, 33
Rolm, 5
Rubenstein, Barry, 125
Rubin, Vera, 228

Safeguard Scientifics, 125, 194–201
　　adaptive leadership, 200–201
　　Cambridge Technology Partners, 198
　　control and accountability, 199
　　create, operate, and trade model, 201
　　history, 194–96
　　Infotron, 198
　　Internet Capital Group, 199–200
　　Lewellyn stock disaster, 196
　　Machine Vision/CompuCom, 198, 199
　　Novell, Inc., stock purchase, 197
　　Radnor Venture Partners formed, 198
　　QVC equity, 198
　　rights offering, 197
　　stock, 200–201
Saks Fifth Avenue, 75
Salk, Jonas, 228
SAP, 218
Schmidt, Sr., Benno, 169
Schumpeter, Joseph Alois, 9–10, 15, 21, 30,
　　36, 59, 106, 127, 137–39, 162, 216,
　　288, 289, 294, 295
Scott Paper, 138
S-curve pattern, 55–58, *56, 57, 58,* 80
Seagate, 39
Seagram, 11
Semiconductor industry, 3, 37, *37,* 40, 53,
　　63, 68–69
　　DRAM decline and Intel, 129–36
　　R&D spending and TRS, 213
　　Return on Invested Capital vs. Economy,
　　　130, 135
Senge, Peter, 72
Sequent Computer Systems, 131, 154–59
　　acquisition by IBM, 159
　　transformational innovation and, 158–59
Shapiro, Robert, 152–54
Sherwin-Williams, 34, 36, 59
Skilling, Jeff, 148–50, 248
Siecor and Siecor GMBH, 146, 147

Siemens AG, 146, 147, 156, 164, 214, 263
Simons, Robert, 4, 20, 79–80, 82, 104, 238, 256–57
Simonton, Dean Keith, 66, 70–71, 117, 186
Sims, James, 199
Sloan, Alfred, 77, 236
Smith, Adam, 10, 88, 99
Smith, Arvin, 353
Smith, Fred, 110
Soaps and detergents, R&D spending and TRS, 213
Software industry, 3, 14, 40, *40*, 53
  decision support, 209–10, 216, 218
  discontinuity in, 216
  evolution, 42–43
  R&D spending and TRS, 213
Soros, George, 67
Sperry Rand, 263
Stafford, Jack, 154
Standard & Poor's, first index (90), 11
  average time on list, 11
  turnover rate, 11
Standard & Poor's 500 (S&P 500)
  accelerating pace of changes in, 28–30, *29*
  average time on list, 11, *13*, 161, 288
  change in, 7-year moving average, *12*
  change, predictions, 2020, 14, 161
  long-term survivors, 8
  substitutions, 12
  total return to shareholders compared to McKinsey Database, *6*
  total return to shareholders, long-term survivors vs. Median, 28, *28*
  turnover rate, 11
Start-ups, 79–80
Steel industry, 216
Steiger, George, 122
Sterling Drug, 16–17
Sterman, John, 54–55, 68, 73
Stock market
  bubble burst 1968, 12
  Cheyenne, 126
  collapse, 1980s, 12
  Corning, 144
  decline or crash, 1974 and 1975, 5, 6, 11
  Enron, 144, 149
  forecasting errors and decline in stockholder returns, 58–59
  Genentech, 165

ICG, 200
Internet stocks, 290
L'Oréal, 205
Machine Vision/CompuCom, 198
Monsanto, 153–54
mutual funds, 194
Nasdaq collapse, 194, 201
Novell, Inc., 197
"one-decision" stocks, 12
Safeguard Scientifics and, 195–201
Storage Technologies, 91, 94, 96
Thermo Electron, 252, 253, 254
Storage Technologies, 38, 46, *46*
  Aweida as CEO, 90–91, 93, 94, 107, 109
  acquisitions, 92
  bankruptcy, 93, 94, 140–41
  creative destruction and operational excellence, 91, 92, 92–93, 94, 95, 97, 98, 101
  founding of, 90
  IBM and, 90–91, 95, 97
  innovation, problems of, 107
  merger with Network Systems, 97
  NCR and, 97
  Poppa as CEO, 94–97, 107, 109
  production problems and faulty products, 93
  RAID system and Iceberg, 95–97, 107
  sales, 1982, 90
  sales growth vs. industry, *91, 98*
  share sell-off, 96
  Stage 4 denial, 96–97
  Stage 3 problems, 93–94
  stock market response, 91, 94, 96
  strategy, initial, of minimal innovation, 90–92
  Sun Microsystems and, 97
  total return to shareholders vs. industry, *92, 98*
  transition from Stage 1 to Stage 2 company, 92
  vision shift, 92
  Weiss as CEO, 97
Strategic planning, 4, 23, 64, 211–12
  business plan contests, 233
  corporate venture capital, 233
  designing the process, 224–30
  diagnostic questions to evaluate quality of, 235

Strategic planning *(continued)*
  design and conduct the first conversation, 227–29
  failure of, 211–15
  improving, 215–21
  Infineon Technologies, 234
  Johnson & Johnson, 230, 231–33
  overall process design, 225–26
  periphery and, 216–21
  post-dialogue reflection and decision making, 230
  preparing for the first dialogue, 226–27
  R&D, failure of internal, 212–14
  R&D, improving, 230–31
  rethinking as extended dialogue, 221–24
  venture capital, reconceptualizing corporate, 233–35
  venture capital spending, 214–15
Stratus, 38
Studebaker, 127–28, 139
Sun Microsystems, 97, 165
Swanson, Robert, 165
Swiss American, 196–97
Symantec, 209, 218
Syron, Richard F., 253

"Take-out" strategy, 21
Tandem Computers, 165, 167
Tandy, 39
Telecommunications industry, 30, 51–52, 53, 290
  Net Rate of New Company Entry, *51*
  R&D spending and TRS, 213
  TRS vs. Net Rate of New Company Entry, *52*
Texas Instruments, 75
Textron, 11
Thermo Electron, 250–54
  change in leadership, 253
  reward mechanism, 251–52
  share prices, 252, 253, 254
  simplifying company, opting for control, 253–54
  spin-offs, 251–52

Tecogen, 252
3M, 164
Time Warner, 83
Toiletries, 32
Transecure, 77–79
Trucking industry, 3, 32
Tversky, Amos, 88, 245–46

Unisys, 42, 156–57, 166, 263
Unitrode, 47
Utaski, Jim, 232

Vagelos, Roy, 248
Vail, Priscilla, 84
Valéry, Paul, 229
Value creation, 21
Value investors, 57
Venrock, 169, 171
Venture capitalists, 20–21, 288–89
  AddVenture! Program, 234
  corporate, 214–21, 232, 233–35
  differences and similarities with principal investing firms, 172–73
  growth of, 171
  Kleiner, Perkins, Caulfield, and Byers, 164–67, 171
  periphery and, 218, 219
  S-curve and private equity, *173*
Volcker, Paul, 12

Walker & Gillette, 26
Wall Street Journal, 178
Wang Laboratories, 38
Warner Lambert, 34
Wealth of Nations, The (Smith), 88
WebLaw, 77, 80
Welch, Jack, 16, 151, 178–89
Western Digital, 39
Westvaco, 33
Wilson, E. O., 116
Wilson, Robert, 266–67, 272, 274, 282, 283
Winsemius, Peter, 136
Woolf, Virginia, 65
Workplace environment, 150–51

RICHARD FOSTER is a Senior Partner and Director at McKinsey & Company, a leading global management consulting firm. He joined the Firm in 1973, was elected Partner in 1977 and Senior Partner in 1982. In his primary client service role within McKinsey & Company, he has worked in more than fifty industry segments, but primarily in the medical products, pharmaceuticals, imaging, electronics, chemicals, consumer products, retail, and asset-management industries. He has focused special attention over the past twenty-five years on improving the growth and innovative performance of large organizations.

Mr. Foster has written articles on innovation and business performance for *Business Week, The Wall Street Journal,* and *The Harvard Business Review.* His 1986 book, *Innovation: The Attacker's Advantage,* was voted one of the five best business books of the year in a *Wall Street Journal* CEO poll.

A Trustee of the Santa Fe Institute, he is also a board member of the Keck Foundation and serves on the Advisory Board of the Whitehead Institute. He received his B.S., M.S., and Ph.D. from Yale University in Engineering, and Applied Science. He lives in New York City with his wife and has three sons.

SARAH KAPLAN was an Innovation Specialist at McKinsey & Company consulting for more than a decade with firms around the world in industries as diverse as pharmaceuticals, medical devices, airlines and consumer products on issues of growth and renewal. She received her B.A. from UCLA and M.A. from Johns Hopkins School for Advanced International Studies. She is currently pursuing a Ph.D. in Management of Technology, Innovation and Entrepreneurship at the MIT Sloan School of Management and resides in Cambridge, MA.